Evaluation Strategies for Communicating and Reporting 2nd Edition

Evaluation Strategies for Communicating and Reporting

2nd Edition

ENHANCING LEARNING IN ORGANIZATIONS

ROSALIE T. TORRES
Torres Consulting Group

HALLIE PRESKILL
University of New Mexico

MARY E. PIONTEK
University of Michigan

SAGE Publications
Thousand Oaks ■ London ■ New Delhi

For information:

Sage Publications, Inc.
2455 Teller Road
Thousand Oaks, California 91320
E-mail: order@sagepub.com

Sage Publications Ltd.
1 Oliver's Yard
55 City Road
London EC1Y 1SP
United Kingdom

Sage Publications India Pvt. Ltd.
B-42, Panchsheel Enclave
Post Box 4109
New Delhi 110 017 India

Printed in the United States of America

Library of Congress Cataloging-in-Publication Data

Torres, Rosalie T.
Evaluation strategies for communicating and reporting: Enhancing learning in organizations / Rosalie T. Torres, Hallie Preskill, Mary E. Piontek.—2nd ed.
    p. cm.
Includes bibliographical references and index.
ISBN 0-7619-2754-9 (pbk.)
    1. Communication in organizations—Evaluation. 2. Organizational learning—Evaluation. I. Preskill, Hallie S. II. Piontek, Mary E. III. Title.
HD30.3.T674 2005
302.3'5—dc22   2004016441

04   05   06   07   10   9   8   7   6   5   4   3   2   1

Acquisitions Editor:	Lisa Cuevas Shaw
Editorial Assistant:	Margo Beth Crouppen
Production Editor:	Melanie Birdsall
Copy Editor:	Bill Bowers
Typesetter:	C&M Digitals (P) Ltd.
Proofreader:	Teresa Herlinger
Cover Designer:	Glenn Vogel

Contents

List of Figures, Tables, and Case Examples

Figures

Tables

Case Examples

Preface

The first edition of this book emerged out of our longtime interest in evaluation use. In that edition, we presented our evaluation approach, as well as 27 communicating and reporting strategies, within the context of organizational learning. Since then, our research, writing, teaching, and evaluation practice has continued to focus on evaluation use by positioning evaluation as a catalyst for learning. In the second edition we have retained and refined this framework by (1) increasing the number of strategies to 34; and (2) addressing how the strategies specifically facilitate individual, group, and organizational learning through the level of interaction afforded with evaluation audiences. In Chapter 1 we have placed each of the communicating and reporting formats along a continuum of least interactive, potentially interactive, and most interactive.

This second edition represents other developments over the last eight years. Technological advances have significantly increased evaluators' options for communicating and reporting. We have addressed how synchronous electronic communications (i.e., chat rooms, teleconferences, videoconferences, Web conferences), e-mail, and Web site communications can help evaluators keep in touch with primary stakeholders, as well as communicate with a broad set of audiences.

Another important addition to this edition is the inclusion of creative formats for communicating and reporting. Evaluators have recently begun to use several innovative strategies for communicating and reporting—poetry, cartoons, and drama. They offer exciting options for increasing the accessibility of findings to a wide variety of audiences.

Another new section provides guidance on communicating and reporting with evaluation's increasingly diverse audiences. We have also included more information on using visuals for communicating and reporting (e.g., photography, PowerPoint presentations, tables and figures, flip charts, posters), and on the design and layout of communications and reports. Throughout the book, readers are referred to the Sage Publications Web site to view many of the examples and illustrations in color.

For each of the 34 different strategies we again have provided explanatory material, implementation tips and cautions, as well as case examples and illustrations. However, we have included more implementation tips and decreased the number of cautions. We did this by expanding the implementation tips to explain what to do under a variety of challenging circumstances. Thus, the cautions primarily address issues for which there may be no solution.

Finally, we have expanded the first edition's communicating and reporting plan. The new version is designed to help you think through and plan for communicating an evaluation's process and findings while taking into account each different audience's needs and characteristics.

This book addresses many, but not all, aspects of evaluation. Therefore it is not appropriate as a basic text for evaluation. The book's particular approach to evaluation is not tied to either quantitative or qualitative methods. Strategies for communicating findings based on both types of data are presented.

The book will be of interest to potentially all practicing evaluators—but particularly those who are dissatisfied with the effectiveness of conventional communicating and reporting methods in today's complex and changing organizations, are interested in developing collaborative relationships, are seeking information on alternative formats, and/or are seeking to make their evaluation practice more effective.

Acknowledgments

Numerous individuals have contributed to our interest and ability to write this book. Among these are other practicing evaluators: Robert Stake, whose insightful, graceful work continues to fuel our abiding interest in the field of program evaluation; Larry Braskamp, Michael Patton, and Marvin Alkin, whose early work on evaluation use provided the foundation for our original work in this area; and Jennifer Greene and Jean King, whose approaches to evaluation practice resonate with our own. We would also like to acknowledge the early work of Nick Smith, who compiled the very first book in the field on communicating and reporting (Smith, 1982).

We are especially grateful to colleagues who listened to our ideas, provided further insights, and helped in compiling case examples:

Kim Alaburda	New Mexico Coalition of Sexual Assault Programs, Inc.
Ahna Ballanhoff	Youth in Focus
Zoe Barley	Mid-Continent Research for Education and Learning
David Berliner	Education Policy Studies Laboratory
Shannon Cahill	North Central Regional Educational Laboratory
Jill Casey	Development Studies Center
Merrill Chandler	University of Illinois at Urbana–Champaign
Chin Mei Chin	Curriculum Development Centre, Ministry of Education, Malaysia
Mary Cofer	Education Enterprises, Inc.
Tracie Constantino	University of Illinois at Urbana–Champaign
William Dudeck	Corporate Education, Development and Training Department, Sandia National Laboratories
Peter Dahler-Larsen	University of Southern Denmark
Jane Davidson	Davidson Consulting Ltd., New Zealand
Jacqueline Dugery	Pew Partnership for Civic Change
Patty Emord	University of New Mexico
David Fetterman	Stanford University

Leslie Goodyear	Education Development Center, Inc.
Jennifer Greene	University of Illinois at Urbana–Champaign
Arlen Gullickson	The Evaluation Center, Western Michigan University
Maura Harrington	Lodestar Management/Research, Inc.
Linda Helstowski	Consultant
Belinda Holley	Corporate Education, Development and Training Department, Sandia National Laboratories
Rodney Hopson	Duquesne University
Liz Humphrey	Boys & Girls Clubs of Greater Milwaukee
Jennifer Iriti	University of Pittsburgh, Learning Research and Development Center
Mark Jenness	Western Michigan University
Kiran Katira	University of New Mexico
Robert Linn	National Center for Research on Evaluation Standards and Student Testing
Jonathan London	Youth in Focus
Cheryl MacNeil	MacNeil Consulting
Donna Mertens	Gallaudet University
Stacey Miller	Harvard Family Research Project, Harvard University
Gary Miron	The Evaluation Center, Western Michigan University
Daniel Neumayer	Consultant
John Owen	Centre for Program Evaluation, The University of Melbourne
Michael Q. Patton	Utilization-Focused Evaluation
Linda Peacock	City of Charlottesville
Stephen Preskill	University of New Mexico
Stacy Rafter	University of New Mexico
Craig Russon	W. K. Kellogg Foundation
Dawn Satterfield	Centers for Disease Control and Prevention, Division of Diabetes Translation, National Diabetes Prevention Center
Eric Schaps	Development Studies Center
John Seeley	FERA, Inc.
Jeffrey Steiger	Center for Research on Learning and Teaching, University of Michigan
Dave Stolzenbach	ParkerBach Pages

Mary Tang	Corporate Education, Development and Training Department, Sandia National Laboratories
Mercedes Thompkins	Dorchester Community Roundtable
Kate Walker	University of Illinois at Urbana–Champaign
Fred Wall	Woodland Park School District, Colorado
Cheryl "Li" Walter	CalSTAT/California Institute on Human Services
Barbara Wauchope	RMC Research Corporation
Nazar Yousif	Developmental Studies Center
Kathy Zantal-Wiener	ZW Associates

The constructive criticism and suggestions for improvement provided by Susan Frankel, Saumitra Sengupta, Jennifer Martineau, and Donna Mertens, who reviewed various parts of the second edition's manuscript, helped us tremendously. We are especially appreciative of the thoughtful consideration they gave our work and the timely manner in which they responded to Sage.

Special thanks are due to Elisabeth Eliassen, who compiled, edited, and organized many elements of this book. We are especially grateful to Lisa Cuevas Shaw and Margo Beth Crouppen at Sage Publications for their abiding encouragement, support, and patience as we completed this work.

And finally, thanks to our close friends and loved ones who never seemed to tire of listening to our frequent chatter about the contents and process of writing this book: Daniel Neumayer, Jill Casey, Gary Hazard, Rosalie Torres (Sr.), Stephen and Benjamin Preskill, Karen and Ed Piontek, John Carson, Sheila Arens, and Tricia McElroy.

1

Introduction

Topics Discussed

- Individual, Group, and Organizational Learning
- Learning Approach to Evaluation
- Least to Most Interactive Communicating and Reporting Formats
- Organization of the Book

Questions to Ponder

- ☐ What is the relationship between learning and evaluation?
- ☐ What roles do communicating and reporting play in evaluation?
- ☐ What do we know about effective communicating and reporting?
- ☐ How can evaluation communicating and reporting support individual, group, and organizational learning?

The proper function of evaluation is to speed up the learning process by communicating what might otherwise be overlooked or wrongly perceived. . . . Success is to be judged by . . . success in communication. . . . Payoff comes from the insight that the evaluator's work generates in others.

—Cronbach, 1982, p. 8

Some 35 years ago, Lee J. Cronbach, one of the profession's most influential figures, wrote that, inherently, evaluation is about learning, and that the focal point for learning to occur is communication of the knowledge generated by an evaluation. For most practicing evaluators as well as theorists, evaluation is concerned with using systematic inquiry to yield some form of knowledge about a program, project, product, issue or concern, organization, or policy. Evaluation is also concerned with that knowledge being useful in some way. "The common denominator in all evaluation . . . is that it is intended to be both useful and used, either directly and immediately or as an incremental contribution to a cumulative body of practical knowledge" (Rossi, Lipsey, & Freeman, 2004, p. 21). In Patton's utilization-focused evaluation, "use concerns how real people in the real world apply evaluation findings and experience the evaluation process" (1997, p. 20). Describing responsive evaluation, Stake (2004) suggests that understanding is a determinant of use. "Users may go on to alleviate or remediate or develop or aspire, but the purpose of this evaluation is mainly to understand" (p. 89).

The goal of this book is to help evaluators facilitate understanding and learning among individuals, groups, and organizations by communicating and reporting more effectively. It will help full-time evaluators and others with evaluation responsibilities to successfully plan, conduct, communicate about, and report the findings of evaluations. It is a comprehensive book about communicating throughout the phases of an evaluation, from early planning stages through final reporting and follow-up; and it is grounded in an evaluation approach designed to help individuals and organizations grow and improve.

Effective communicating and reporting facilitates learning among stakeholders and other audiences. In our study of evaluators' communicating and reporting practices, we asked members of the American Evaluation Association to describe their most successful experiences (Torres, Preskill, & Piontek, 1997). They told us about using a variety of formats, including short reports and summaries tailored to audience needs. The reports and summaries they described were written in clear, jargon-free language, and the contents included graphs and charts; positive and negative findings; qualitative, contextual data as well as quantitative data; and specific recommendations. During and following the evaluation itself, they used ongoing, collaborative communication processes, involving stakeholders in the conduct of the evaluation as a whole, but especially in interpreting findings. In short, they spoke of techniques and strategies that helped audiences assimilate and use information from the evaluation.

Other research about evaluators' communicating and reporting practices produced similar findings (Piontek, 1994). During in-depth interviews, 19 veteran members of the American Evaluation Association stressed the importance of (1) meetings and informal conversations that create a context for dialogue, and (2) the use of interim memos and draft reports that focus on the perspective and language of the readers.

These findings about actual communicating and reporting practices echo what both the early literature on evaluation use (Alkin, 1985; Braskamp, 1982; Braskamp & Brown, 1980; Patton, 1986) and many of today's popular evaluation texts (Fitzpatrick, Sanders, & Worthen, 2003; Joint Committee, 1994; Mertens, 2004; Patton, 1997; Posavac & Carey, 2003; Rossi, Lipsey, & Freeman, 2004; Stake, 2004; Russ-Eft & Preskill, 2001) say about effective evaluation. That is, evaluators should

- Take into account the specific context of an evaluation.
- Identify the evaluation audiences, and involve them (the primary stake-holders, in particular) in designing the evaluation.
- Maintain frequent, close contact and report interim results throughout the evaluation.
- Tailor reports to audience needs, using a variety of formats that include short reports and summaries, verbal presentations, and opportunities for interaction.
- Present vivid, concrete illustrations of findings.
- Report results in a timely manner to a variety of audiences.
- Use clear, simple language.

Successfully implementing these strategies means overcoming constraints imposed by evaluation timelines and budgets, as well as the politics and complexities of organizational life. Not surprisingly, many evaluators report being dissatisfied with the outcomes of their communicating and reporting efforts (Piontek, 1994; Torres et al., 1997). We found, too, that experienced evaluators were somewhat more satisfied with their communicating and reporting efforts than those with less experience. This book is intended to support what evaluators learn from their own experiences by explicitly addressing the learning processes that mediate much of how users experience and benefit from an evaluation. Kushner (2000) reminds us that "to understand how to effect change we need to understand how people learn . . . evaluation is more or less, the study of people" (p. 201).

Individual Learning

How individuals receive, remember, and react to evaluation communications determines the effectiveness of those communications. The need for presenting information in a variety of modalities is clear. Adult learning theory maintains that individuals learn via their primary perceptual modalities: print, visual, aural, interactive, tactile, kinesthetic, or olfactory (Gardner, 1983; Pettersson, 1989). These theories suggest that some learn best through reading and writing; others through viewing videos, graphs, and charts; and yet others through listening or interacting. From a somewhat different perspective, and drawing on the work of Kurt Lewin, John Dewey, and Jean Piaget, Kolb's (1984) adult learning model describes four learning modes:

1. Those who learn best through *concrete experiences* do so by considering how successful they were at a task, and benefit most from hands-on activities, field work, observations, and role-plays.

2. *Reflective observers* learn best by stepping back from a task and thinking about what has been done and experienced. Instructionally, they benefit from demonstrations, videos, role-plays, keeping logs or journals, and brainstorming.

3. Those who learn best through *abstract conceptualization* look at events and attempt to understand the relationships among them. They like learning facts and enjoy creative theories to explain observations. They benefit from lectures, articles, videos, audiotapes, and the use of analogies.

4. *Active experimenters* process information primarily through their active engagement in an activity. They like using theories to solve problems and make decisions. They benefit from simulations, case studies, and handouts that can be used at a later time.

Consideration of adult learning theory poses an interesting question: How well do typical strategies for communicating and reporting accommodate different learning styles and modes? Many evaluators have had little time to expand the range of strategies they use beyond the traditional ones: comprehensive written reports, verbal presentations, and executive summaries. While these are not, in and of themselves, poor strategies, they can be more effective: first, when (as we describe in Chapter 3) they are developed in a way that makes their contents more appealing and easy to assimilate; and second, when combined with other, more interactive and creative approaches (see Chapters 4 and 5).

Group Learning

"Dissemination does not equate with use." This assertion is no less pertinent now than when Patton made it in 1986 (p. 278). One reason is that, as we have just mentioned, dissemination can often mean delivery of a final report or some other text-based evaluation product. Yet, participatory approaches to evaluation (see Cousins & Whitmore, 1998; Greene, 1988, 2001; Greene, Lincoln, Mathison, Mertens, & Ryan, 1998; King, 1998) are popular today precisely because they are based on significant degrees of interaction and opportunities for learning that pass between the evaluator(s) and the evaluation user(s). "It's the users, not the report that play . . . a critical role in the evaluation process" (King, 2004, p. 333). Constructivist learning theory proposes that learning is primarily about meaning making and suggests that individuals and groups learn by interpreting, understanding, and making sense of their experiences, often within a social context (Brookfield, 1991; Brooks & Brooks, 1993; Cranton, 1994; Dirkx, 1998; Jarvis, 1992; Mezirow, 1991).

Providing a social context for the interpretation of evaluation findings is one example of how group learning can support evaluation use. According to Wolcott (2001), "interpretation, by contrast [to analysis], is not derived from rigourous, agreed-upon, carefully specified procedures, but from our efforts at sense making, a human activity that includes intuition, past experience, emotion—personal attributes of human researchers that can be argued endlessly but neither proved nor disproved to the satisfaction of all. Interpretation invites the examination, the 'pondering' of data in terms of what people make of it" (p. 33). In Chapters 4 and 5 we describe how evaluators can provide users with opportunities for understanding, learning, and collaboration through working sessions and other creative forms of interactive communication.

Organizational Learning

Excepting some types of policy-oriented evaluation studies, most evaluations occur within some organizational context. This larger context is important because it typically exerts a significant influence on an evaluation, and because evaluation has the potential for impacting learning at an organizational rather than just a programmatic level. In our study of evaluators' communicating and reporting practices we found that evaluators were challenged by the following aspects of conducting their work within organizations: (1) lack of clarity among stakeholders about communicating and reporting needs; (2) unresponsiveness to communicating and reporting efforts; (3) client and audience turnover; (4) politically charged situations; (5) resistance to negative findings; (6) characteristics of particular individuals; and (7) misinterpretation of findings. Echoing the discussion of interactive learning above, some evaluators dealt with these challenges by taking a collaborative approach. Collaboration in evaluation is powerful: it enhances use by different audiences, it values individuals' experiences and opinions, it contributes to a sense of ownership, it produces better understanding and depiction of the context, it leads to more useful recommendations, it educates audiences about the program and evaluation, and it helps identify and resolve conflicts before the end of an evaluation. In essence, it embraces different perspectives and lets many voices be heard.

A collaborative learning approach to evaluation can support learning across the boundaries of a particular evaluand, thus invoking organizational learning. We define *organizational learning* as a continuous process of growth and improvement (1) that uses information or feedback about both processes and outcomes (i.e., evaluation findings) to make changes; (2) is integrated with work activities, and with the organization's infrastructure (e.g., its culture, systems and structures, leadership, and communication mechanisms); and (3) invokes the alignment of values, attitudes, and perceptions among organizational members. Organizational learning involves:

- Developing frameworks for relating findings about particular programs and initiatives to broader organizational goals.
- Sustaining a spirit of ongoing inquiry that calls for learning incrementally and iteratively over time.
- Providing time for reflection; examination of underlying assumptions; and dialogue among evaluators, program staff, and organizational leaders, and
- Reconsidering traditional evaluator roles and the skills evaluators need (Torres & Preskill, 2001).

Learning Approach to Evaluation

Success comes through communication and collaboration throughout the evaluation process and from the presentation of information in such a way that it is easily assimilated. Communicating and reporting are part and parcel of the entire evaluation endeavor—not something to be undertaken as final steps. We believe that successful communicating and reporting is most likely when undertaken as part of an overall evaluation approach that recognizes the role of individual, group, and organizational learning (Preskill & Torres, 1999). Figure 1.1 summarizes the phases of evaluative inquiry for facilitating individual, group, and organizational learning: focusing the inquiry, carrying it out, and applying learning.

Throughout these phases evaluators can use a variety of communicating and reporting strategies designed to facilitate individual, group, and ultimately organizational learning. Figure 1.2 shows the communicating and reporting formats presented in Chapters 3, 4, and 5, arranged according to

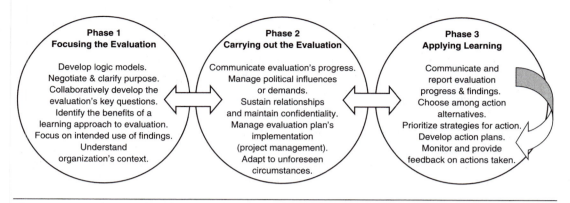

Figure 1.1   Phases of Evaluative Inquiry for Facilitating Learning.

the extent of audience interaction they afford. Chapter 3 covers the text-based formats shown under "Least Interactive" in Figure 1.2. All these formats involve written evaluation products that can be delivered to audiences without interaction with the evaluator(s). That is, they can be delivered via mail (postal or intraorganizational system), e-mail, overnight delivery, the news media, or the Internet, without there ever being any verbal or face-to-face interaction with the evaluator(s) or other stakeholders. In these cases, what recipients glean from the evaluation document is based upon its

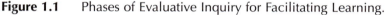

Least **Interactive**	**Potentially** **Interactive**	**Most** **Interactive**

➢ Short Written Communications
  – Memos and E-mail
  – Postcards
➢ Interim Reports
➢ Final Reports
➢ Executive Summaries
➢ Newsletters, Bulletins, Briefs, Brochures
➢ News Media Communications
➢ Web Site Communications
	➢ Verbal Presentations
	  – PowerPoint Presentations and Transparencies
	  – Flip Charts
	➢ Video Presentations
	➢ Posters
	
	➢ Photography
	➢ Cartoons
	➢ Poetry
	➢ Drama
		➢ Working Sessions
		➢ Synchronous Electronic Communications
		  – Chat Rooms
		  – Teleconferences
		  – Videoconferences
		  – Webconferences
		➢ Personal Discussions

Figure 1.2   Communicating and Reporting Formats by Degree of Interaction With Audience

contents, how much attention they give it, and how well the document itself helps them assimilate and understand the information it contains. Chapter 3 also provides information on how to enhance the design and layout of text-based evaluation products, how to use tables and figures, and how to write with clarity.

Many evaluation formats are potentially interactive, as described in the first half of Chapter 4. These are shown in the middle section of Figure 1.2. Verbal presentations, video presentations, and posters can all be delivered with or without interacting with audiences. This is also true of photographs and cartoons that might be included in the text of an evaluation report. On the other hand, a poster containing either could be part of a poster session facilitated by the evaluator to explain the illustrations and solicit reactions from the audience. Similarly, poetry and drama can be used to depict the evaluand, its context, or the evaluation findings. A poem constructed to represent the essence of participants' experiences in a program could be included in a report delivered to stakeholders. It could also be part of a presentation and discussion where participants themselves read the poem, and the audience is invited to respond. A dramatic performance about evaluation findings can be performed in the same way that most theatrical performances are held for entertainment. The audience attends and witnesses the play, but there is no prearranged interaction between audience members, or between audience members and actors, about the contents of the play, specifically. Dramatic performances about evaluation findings can also include significant opportunities for interaction between actors and audience members. Chapter 5 provides detail on all four creative formats: photography, cartoons, poetry, and drama.

Fully interactive formats, shown on the far right of Figure 1.2, include working sessions that are specifically designed for participants to collaborate, discuss, and quite often make decisions about any given aspect of a program or its evaluation. Synchronous electronic communications (chat rooms, teleconferences, videoconferences, Web conferences) occur in real time and provide the opportunity for participants to interact across different geographical locations—whether it is across the building, within the same city or country, or across the world. Finally, discussions between two individuals are inherently interactive, whether they occur over the telephone, via an Internet chat room, or in person. Over time, use of these interactive strategies to facilitate dialogue and reflection within a particular organizational context can contribute to a cumulative body of knowledge that informs issues and decisions related to broader organizational goals.

Organization of the Book

In the foregoing discussion we have outlined the contents of Chapters 3, 4, and 5, which present approximately 29 different strategies for facilitating learning for individuals and groups. Chapter 2 provides the background for understanding and planning for effective communicating and reporting. It covers the purposes, timing, audiences, and learning processes involved in successful communicating and reporting, as well as detailed guidance for creating a communicating and reporting plan. Chapter 6 addresses various issues and challenges that evaluators face: communicating and reporting for diverse audiences, communicating negative findings, integrating quantitative and qualitative findings, developing recommendations, and communicating and reporting for multisite evaluations. Chapter 7 addresses a number of persistent issues. We look at topics such as evaluator roles, organizational readiness for learning from evaluation, and time for collaboration.

The book can be useful to readers in a variety of ways. Reading Chapters 1 through 7 in sequence provides an integrated approach to working more effectively in organizations. Those who want immediate help in using different communicating and reporting formats can begin with any of Chapters 3, 4, 5, or 6, each of which provides implementation tips, cautions, and examples for each strategy. The homepage for this book on the Sage Web site (http://www.sagepub.com/escr) provides color versions of many of the examples.

Finally, readers should be aware that our views are primarily informed by local program evaluation experience as opposed to large-scale, federal-policy-oriented evaluations. Some readers may find some aspects of the collaborative learning approach to evaluation we describe here more applicable for evaluations conducted within organizations than for those conducted to inform policy at a broad level. We trust, however, that the perspectives and strategies discussed in this book will stimulate reflection, conversation, and growth for evaluators practicing in a variety of settings.

Understanding and Planning for Effective Communicating and Reporting

Topics Discussed

- Purposes, Timing, and Audiences for Communicating and Reporting
- Individual, Group, and Organizational Learning Processes
- Overview of Communicating and Reporting Formats
- Developing a Communicating and Reporting Plan

Questions to Ponder

- ☐ *Why communicate and report an evaluation's processes and findings?*
- ☐ *When should evaluators communicate and report on an evaluation's progress and results?*
- ☐ *How do evaluation audiences' characteristics influence the choice of communicating and reporting formats and strategies?*
- ☐ *How do the concepts of individual, group, and organizational learning relate to choosing communicating and reporting formats and strategies?*
- ☐ *What choices do evaluators have for communicating and reporting formats and strategies?*
- ☐ *How can evaluators develop a communicating and reporting plan?*

U nderstanding and planning for effective communicating and reporting involves careful consideration of (1) the various purposes for communicating and reporting; (2) the timing of communications and reports; (3) the audiences who are to receive them; and (4) the learning processes that are involved when audiences hear, read, view, understand, relate to, ask questions about, and make decisions on the basis of evaluation information. This chapter covers each of these topics in detail, and then presents a strategy for developing a communicating and reporting plan that accounts for each factor. The chapter concludes with the details of a completed plan based on a case example.

Purposes of Communicating and Reporting _____

Consistent with a learning approach to evaluation, there are three basic and interrelated *general* purposes for evaluation communicating and reporting, each building upon the next (see Figure 2.1). They are: to convey information about the evaluation process and its findings; to facilitate understanding and create meaning among audiences; and to support decision making.

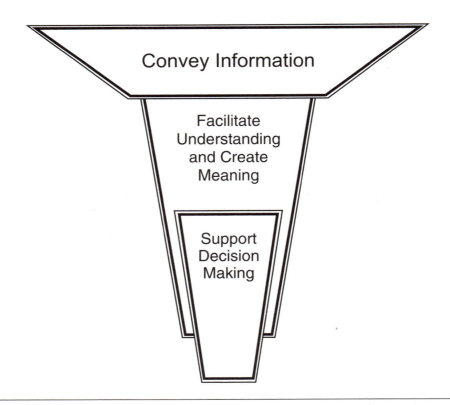

Figure 2.1   General Purposes of Evaluation Communicating and Reporting

Successively smaller proportions of the audiences are served by each of these purposes. First, conveying information involves crafting and delivering messages about any aspect of the evaluation (e.g., its design, activities, and/or findings) to intended audiences. Second, for some of these audience members or groups (but not all), the content, format, and delivery method of the information will facilitate their understanding about the evaluation in a meaningful way. Third, for yet a smaller proportion of the audience(s), the communication will support their decision making about something related to the program and/or the evaluation. This could be for teachers to decide to participate in an evaluation by allowing their classrooms to be observed; it could be for program staff to take action(s) that will make the program better; it could be for parents to decide not to enroll their child in a program; it could be to request more information; it could be for a foundation to discontinue funding for a program. It could be any decision related to the program or the evaluation that any stakeholder might make.

It is important to point out that while the ultimate goal of any attempt to convey evaluation information is to have it understood in a meaningful way, the ultimate goal of communicating and reporting is *not necessarily* to have decisions made at any given point in time. In our view, facilitating understanding is as important a goal as supporting decision making, if not more so. Nor do we wish to emphasize the understanding and decision making of program managers, staff, and funders over any other stakeholders. We do believe, though, that decisions—whatever they are, whenever they are made, and whoever makes them—are best made on the basis of meaningful understanding.

Particular reasons for communicating and reporting are to (1) build awareness and/or support, and provide the basis for asking questions, (2) facilitate growth and improvement, and (3) demonstrate results and be accountable.

Build Awareness, Support

Evaluation information is often provided to build awareness (and in some cases, support) for the program, the evaluation, or both among stakeholders (e.g., program staff, community members, parents, prospective clients, and those involved with similar programs and organizations). Communications and reports to build awareness can aid in decision making about participation and involvement in the evaluation and/or the program. For example, communications that describe a program, how it works, and to what effect, are sometimes used to let audiences know about the existence of a program and its uses and benefits. Or a communication might primarily be intended to build awareness about and solicit participation in the evaluation. In either case, the information provided is often the basis for audiences to ask questions and make decisions about engaging with the program, the evaluation, or both.

Facilitate Growth and Improvement

Communications and reports about process, implementation, or formative evaluations inform decision making about possible changes to improve the evaluand. In addition, program staff and/or those responsible for a department or organizational function learn from their experiences participating in the evaluation.

Demonstrate Results, Accountability

Communications and reports about outcome or summative evaluations are frequently designed to demonstrate results and/or be accountable to funders, board members, senior managers, legislatures, and the general public. Findings from evaluations of particular kinds of programs and services are also of interest to other professionals in the field. For instance, studies showing program effectiveness and lessons learned about school reform initiatives can be useful to a broad spectrum of educators. Evaluation communications and reports demonstrating results and accountability aid stakeholders and audiences in decision making about continued funding, prospective funding, and replication (or implementation of similar programs at other sites).

Timing

Communicating and reporting for various purposes takes place both during and after an evaluation, as shown in Table 2.1. Each is equally important.

Table 2.1   Timing and Specific Purposes of Evaluation Communicating and Reporting

During the Evaluation	After the Evaluation
• Include stakeholders in decision making about evaluation design and implementation.	• Build general awareness of and/or support for the program and the evaluation.
• Inform stakeholders and other audiences about specific upcoming evaluation activities.	• Communicate final findings to support change and improvement.
• Keep informed about the overall progress of the evaluation.	• Communicate final findings to show results, demonstrate accountability.
• Communicate interim findings.	

During the Evaluation

During the evaluation, evaluators write memos, facilitate meetings, exchange e-mails, and have one-on-one conversations with stakeholders about the design and implementation of the evaluation. The more collaborative and participatory the evaluation approach, the more frequent and inclusive this communication will be. Sometimes the communications are about decisions on how to design and conduct the evaluation; at other times they are to inform or remind, or thank stakeholders for their participation in data collection and other evaluation activities. Still other communications may be to update stakeholders and other audiences on the overall progress of the evaluation (i.e., what has taken place so far, and what events and activities are to come). Finally, some of the most important communicating and reporting during an evaluation will be to relay and support the use of interim findings through written summaries and reports, presentations, and working sessions.

After the Evaluation

After the evaluation, the same strategies just mentioned for interim findings (written summaries and reports, presentations, and working sessions) are frequently used to disseminate and support the use of final evaluation findings—either for understanding issues, making improvements, or demonstrating results. Documents like newsletter articles, brochures, and news releases are also sometimes created and disseminated to build general awareness among particular audiences about the program and its evaluation.

Audiences

One characteristic that distinguishes evaluation from research is the responsibility that evaluators have to provide useful information to stakeholders and other audiences who have an interest in the planning, implementation, and findings of the evaluation study. *Stakeholders* are those individuals, groups, or organizations who may be affected by the planning, activities, and/or findings of the evaluation. For example, those who request or sponsor an evaluation, as well as program staff are stakeholders. Stakeholders might also include groups such as parents of students in a particular school program. They may not directly participate in a program but do have a vested interest in it. *Audiences* are those who receive information about the evaluation and its findings. Audiences include, but are not limited to, stakeholders—for example, staff from other programs who would benefit from information about a particular program.

Identification

Most evaluations will have several stakeholders and stakeholder groups, as well as other audiences, including those who

- Sponsor or commission the evaluation.
- Will make decisions based on the results.
- Are in the target group from whom evaluation information is being requested.
- Are involved in planning or creating the program being evaluated.
- Are involved in running the program being evaluated.
- Are interested in the program (advocates and critics).
- Have a right to the information (e.g., legislators, taxpayers, parents).
- Might be affected by the evaluation results.

It is helpful to think of these individuals and groups in terms of primary, secondary, and tertiary audiences. Various factors determine which category an individual or group falls under, including degree of involvement with the program being evaluated, commitment and ability to use evaluation information, the requirements made by key decision makers or sponsors that evaluation results be used, and interest in the findings.

Primary audiences usually request the evaluation, are the major decision makers associated with the program being evaluated, and/or have funded the program. Sometimes, these groups include the program's staff, supervisors, managers, or external constituents. *Secondary audiences* are involved with the program in some way. They may have little or no daily contact with the program but may have a strong interest in the results of the evaluation. Secondary audiences will use the evaluation findings in some aspect of their work and decision-making processes. These groups might include some program participants, their supervisors or managers, and individuals whose work will be affected by decisions based on the evaluation results. *Tertiary audiences* are more distanced from the inner workings of the program but may want to stay informed about the program and would be interested in receiving the evaluation's results. These groups might include future program participants, the general public who has a "right to know," and special interest groups.

The *Program Evaluation Standards* (Joint Committee, 1994) highlight the importance of identifying the evaluation's audiences to ensure that findings are both valid and useful. How the results are disseminated to the various audiences is an act of negotiation between the primary stakeholders and the evaluator. Questions addressed in an evaluation will have different meanings for people who are not directly involved with the program but still have a vested interest in its future.

One way to identify the evaluation's audiences is to locate persons in leadership roles and ask them to identify other stakeholders. Throughout the evaluation, evaluators should be (1) alert to identifying additional audiences who will be interested in and affected by the results of the evaluation and (2) especially careful to ensure that the identified audiences are representative (e.g., gender, ethnicity, language background) of all possible audiences.

Characteristics

Different audiences will often want different information from the same evaluation. For this reason, different forms of communication should be considered for different audiences. Audiences vary along numerous dimensions that mediate how best to communicate with them about an evaluation, including their

- Accessibility
- Reading ability
- Familiarity with the program or evaluand
- Attitude toward and interest level in the program
- Role in decision making
- Familiarity with research and evaluation methods in general
- Attitude toward and interest level in the evaluation
- Experience using evaluation findings

Audiences vary in how *accessible* they are to you in terms of receiving evaluation communications and reports. If you are an internal evaluator, your primary audiences (program staff, for example) may be quite accessible on a daily basis for face-to-face communication. Or they could be located in another building or geographic location, but be highly accessible through telephone and e-mail. The president or CEO of your organization may be less accessible to you because his or her time is limited, or because of your relative status in the organization.

Maybe you are an external evaluator for a school-based program. The teachers and principal of the school will tend to be more accessible to you than parents, but probably less so than the curriculum coordinator who is responsible for the program and has an office at the school. It is important to consider the level of effort that will be needed to access each audience member or group.

Audiences for any one evaluation may vary in their *reading ability,* or ability to comprehend written material. For example, you may be communicating and reporting to audiences who are nonreaders, or with those who have a lower or higher ability to read. In reporting the results of an educational program evaluation, for example, school administrators and teachers would have little problem understanding evaluation reports and executive summaries. On the other hand, students and/or some community members who might be less comfortable with text-based information would be better served through verbal presentations using visuals, or other more creative forms of presentation.

Audience *familiarity with the program or evaluand* can influence how much background information is necessary to include in evaluation communications and reports. Evaluation products prepared by internal evaluators for in-house audiences may not include a description of the program at all. External audiences for the same evaluation would warrant a complete program description.

Audience *attitude toward and interest level in the program* is another factor that can influence the content, format, and delivery method of your communications and reports. For example, special efforts may or may not be needed to maximize parent attendance at a school meeting where findings about an unpopular program will be discussed. Highly vested stakeholders can usually be counted upon to readily open and read e-mails pertaining to an evaluation. For other stakeholders, a telephone call may be a better way to get their attention, or should be used to alert them to a particular e-mail you have sent. A brochure containing evaluation findings about a program that is unfamiliar to a particular target audience would most likely contain information on the front panel designed to spark their interest in the program, and entice them to open the brochure.

Audience *role in decision making* is often closely aligned with their interest level. The greater an audience's role in decision making, the more detailed information about an evaluation they are likely to want. Audiences can vary from having no role at all with respect to a particular program to having a significant role in decision making about a *similar type* of program. Yet, these two audiences might both want access to a detailed evaluation report.

Audience *familiarity with research and evaluation methods* typically influences how much information they will need to make sense of evaluation findings. A report written for audiences unfamiliar with statistics might include a glossary of terms or call-outs defining mean and standard deviation. A verbal presentation to the same audience would devote additional time to explaining these terms. The same amount of time on these topics would be of little interest to most academic audiences.

Attitude toward and interest level in the program and *in the evaluation* are similar, but not necessarily the same when it comes to decisions about your communicating and reporting efforts. An audience could be highly positive about and interested in a program, but also highly negative about its evaluation. Consider, for example, an evaluation of a program well liked by those who implement it and benefit from its services. It has been in operation for several years, but now the funders are requiring an external evaluation by a firm they have contracted. In communicating this information to the staff, the program manager has conveyed dismay and anxiety. An evaluator facing this situation will want to craft her initial communications with these stakeholders in a way that will help allay their concerns and solicit their cooperation.

Finally, prior *experience using evaluation findings* plays a role in the success of your communicating and reporting efforts with various audiences. Your efforts to explain how evaluation findings can be useful to them would be quite different for (1) internal evaluation audiences who routinely attend working sessions to interpret findings and develop action plans, and (2) audiences who have never had occasion to read about or use evaluation findings, much less spend time in a meeting devoted to this purpose.

Individual, Group, and Organizational Learning

In the previous discussion we have tried to show how audience characteristics influence their reactions to different communicating and reporting approaches you might use for any given evaluation. When the goal is to have stakeholders and other audiences assimilate and use evaluation information, it is also important to consider how individuals, groups, and organizations learn.

Individual Learning

"Learning has traditionally been defined as a process by which individuals gain new knowledge and insights that result in a change of behavior and actions. It comprises the cognitive (intellectual), affective (emotional), and psychomotor (physical) domains" (Marquardt, 1996, p. 30). Another way to think about individual learning is to specifically consider *how* individuals come to know something. For example, they may learn through

1. Direct experience (the receipt of sensory data such as color, sound, and pain)

2. Verbal transmission of information (ideas voiced by others, reports, books, formulas)

3. The reorganizing of what they already know into a new configuration (Dixon, 1994, p. 12)

Over the past 25 years we have become much more knowledgeable about how adults learn and process information. For example, research has shown that individuals learn more from experiences where they are (1) engaged with the learning material; (2) see, hear, and do something with its content; and (3) integrate new knowledge with what they already know. The adult learning research also tells us that

- Individuals can consciously think about only one thing at a time.
- Information groups of no more than seven points at a time are more likely to be retained.
- Information overload can lead to anxiety and diminished information processing effectiveness.
- Learners need to establish a mental set (an understanding of what will be addressed) so that they can naturally pay attention.
- Learners are goal-directed and often seek information to achieve a goal or satisfy a need (learning is a means to an end).
- Learning that is applied immediately is retained longer and is subject to more frequent use.

As mentioned in Chapter 1, still another way to view how learning takes place is in terms of individuals' primary perceptual modalities that may be print, visual, aural, interactive, tactile, kinesthetic, or olfactory (Gardner, 1983; Pettersson, 1989). Dunn and Dunn (1993) explain that there are four perceptual styles reflecting individuals' learning preferences—learning new material by listening (auditory); by reading or viewing (visual); by touching (tactile); or by doing (kinesthetic). In general, visual learners learn through seeing and learn best when information is presented visually and verbally. During a presentation, visual learners prefer to take detailed notes, make lists, organize information, and like illustrations, tables, charts, and pictures. Visual learners often prefer to learn on their own. About 65% of the population prefers to learn through visual means.

Auditory learners, who make up about 30% of the population, tend to learn most effectively through listening. These learners learn best through lectures, discussions, talking things through, and hearing what others have to say. They interpret the underlying meanings of conversations by listening to one's tone of voice, pitch, speed, and other nuances. These learners benefit from group discussion because they learn more easily from listening and speaking opportunities. Auditory learners tend to remember more of what they hear than what they see.

Kinesthetic and tactile learners learn through moving, doing, and touching, and learn best through hands-on activities or approaches. They tend to assimilate skills through practice, and learn information when they can manipulate materials. Kinesthetic learners learn best through performance-oriented activities, such as role-playing and dramatic exercises. They make up about 5% of the population.

When choosing from among communicating and reporting strategies to facilitate individual learning, evaluators may consider various techniques as described in Table 2.2. Given the fact that any group of stakeholders is likely to represent more than one learning style, modality, or preference, it is important to consider using a variety of communicating and reporting strategies to enhance individuals' learning throughout an evaluation.

Group Learning

Much of what we have just reviewed about individual learning strongly suggests that individuals learn best through interaction with others.

> Learning, ultimately, is a social phenomenon—our ability to learn and what we can know is determined by the quality and openness of our relationships. Our mental models of the world and of ourselves grow out of our relationships with others. Dialogue with others, which involves continuous critical reappraisal of our views, increases the possibilities for learning. (Marquardt, 1996, p. 31)

This "reappraisal of our views" through interaction with others results in the development of new meaning and understanding. The roles of community, social interactions, dialogue, reflection, and relationships are central to understanding how adults learn. These notions reflect a social constructivist theory of learning (Bruner, 1986, 1990). Lev Vygotsky, a Russian psychologist and philosopher in the 1930s, was one of the first persons to articulate this theory. His work focused on the influences of cultural and social contexts in learning and supported a discovery model of learning. "The central premise of social constructivism is that knowledge is constructed between individuals. The traditional view that the world exists 'out there,' and that we use our brains, logic, and language to discover the truth of the world, is being supplanted by the idea that the realities we observe are created by mutual influence with other people" (Campbell, 2000, p. 11).

Fundamental to team or group learning, then, is the ability for participants to engage in interactive learning processes. These include dialogue, reflection, asking questions, and identifying and challenging values, beliefs, and assumptions (Preskill & Torres, 1999). Through dialogue, individuals may reflect both privately and publicly about what they are hearing and learning. Dialogue helps achieve a level of understanding that is both personal and interrelational. By asking individuals to make their reflections public, they may be able to articulate their assumptions and beliefs about what they are hearing, seeing, and learning; and thus help create shared understanding within the group.

Table 2.2   Strategies to Facilitate Learning According to Individuals' Primary Perceptual Modalities

Auditory Learners	Visual Learners	Tactile Learners	Kinesthetic Learners
• Provide a brief explanation of what is coming. Conclude with a summary of what has been covered.	• Use visuals to capture and sustain attention: – Pictures – Diagrams – Flow charts – Timelines – Video – Demonstrations – Photographs – Cartoons – Concept maps – Tables and charts – Use of color – Computer displays and overheads – Outlines – Agendas – Handouts with space to take notes	• Use materials that help translate learning into something that can be touched such as – Worksheets – Index cards – Creative art (e.g., models, representations) – Concrete objects (e.g., artifacts from an evaluation site) – Categorizing adhesive notes from a brainstorming session • Provide opportunities for participants to skim material prior to their hearing about it in a verbal presentation. This gives them an opportunity for tactile engagement and orients them to what they will be hearing.	• Use strategies that ask participants to move around. • During lengthy meetings, provide frequent stretch breaks to clear the brain. • Provide toys such as Koosh balls, Slinkys, or other manipulatives to give participants something to do with their hands. This will help them stay focused on the presentation or activity. • Provide highlighters, colored pens and/or pencils so that participants can engage in movement for note-taking, drawing, and highlighting important ideas.
• Provide opportunities for questions and answers.			
• Consider using auditory activities, such as brainstorming or small-group work.			
• Provide sufficient time to debrief. This allows learners to make connections between what they heard and how they may use what they learned.			
• Discuss presented information in small groups.			
• Use verbal analogies and storytelling to communicate key points.			

In a facilitated dialogue, participants are encouraged to consider questions that can lead to greater understanding. For example, when using a *working session* to communicate evaluation findings and plan next steps, the evaluator could provide participants with an agenda and some guiding questions for discussion. The role of the evaluator would be to facilitate group members' understandings and interpretations of the findings through a dialogue that incorporates reflection and asking questions. She might ask the group to consider alternative interpretations; implications for certain findings; things participants found surprising; findings they thought would be represented but were not; and so on. The evaluator would make significant efforts to engage all participants, and would periodically ask group members to explain the assumptions they have underlying certain statements they make or points of view they offer. If the climate of the meeting became tense because of competing interpretations or other issues the evaluation raised, the evaluator might ask the group to take a minute or two for private reflection—to consider what has been discussed and what needs to happen to move the group forward. She would then ask each participant to share his or her reflections—without interruption from other members. Facilitating a working session in this manner helps participants understand not only the evaluation findings from a variety of perspectives, but it helps them understand their own and others' ways of thinking. These processes can be especially useful for reaching consensus on action plans to implement an evaluation's recommendations.

When using a communicating and reporting format that may be only moderately interactive, such as when giving *verbal presentations,* or presenting findings during a *poster session,* the evaluator can encourage dialogue, reflection, asking questions, and identifying underlying assumptions among audience members. In these cases, the evaluator should be prepared with discussion questions, handouts, and an agenda so that information regarding the presentation can be referred to and used to enhance the quality of the dialogue.

Engaging stakeholders through interactive forms of communicating and reporting, and using dialogue to facilitate learning, can reap many benefits:

- Individual and hidden agendas can be made more visible.
- Multiple points of view that need to be addressed and negotiated can be brought out into the open.
- A sense of community and connection can be established.
- There is an increased likelihood that learning at the team or group level will lead to learning throughout the organization.
- The organization's culture, policies, and procedures can be illuminated.
- Collectively made interpretations can lead to more relevant and useful recommendations.

- Stakeholders may be more likely to find the results credible because they understand how and why the evaluation was conducted and what the findings mean.
- A greater appreciation and support for future evaluations can be established.

Individuals learn in a number of ways and under many different conditions. When bringing people together for evaluation communicating and reporting purposes, the following conditions will support not only individual learning, but team or group learning as well:

- A sense of trust among participants
- Previous experience with what is being evaluated
- Respect for each other
- A need to know
- Interest in solving the problem or addressing the issue that gave rise to the evaluation
- Active commitment to and involvement in dialogue, reflection, asking questions, and identifying and challenging values, beliefs, and assumptions

Organizational Learning

To enhance the evaluation process and its findings, it is not enough that individuals, teams, or groups learn from communicating and reporting efforts. If an organization is to fully benefit from an evaluation, then it is important that the learning of teams or groups is translated into learning on an organizational level. When teams or groups collectively discuss, interpret, and act on evaluation processes and findings, they are able to develop new insights and new meanings that, when shared with others, have the potential for creating organizational learning.

We view organizational learning as a continuous process of growth and improvement (1) that uses information or feedback about both processes and outcomes (i.e., evaluation findings) to make changes; (2) is integrated with work activities, and with the organization's infrastructure (e.g., its culture, systems and structures, leadership, and communication mechanisms); and (3) invokes the alignment of values, attitudes, and perceptions among organizational members (Torres & Preskill, 2001). When operative, organizational learning transcends individual, group, program, department, and functional areas to a level of learning and decision making that could not happen at the individual or group level of learning alone. Thus, organizational learning occurs over time and within organizations that foster it.

The culture of a learning organization supports continuous learning for individuals and groups. Establishing this culture is part of the organization's overall strategy for achieving its desired results—better standardized test scores, more jobless people placed in decent-paying jobs, or improved profit margins for a particular product or service. Learning organizations are committed to the following:

- The use of their findings from systematic inquiry
- Establishing and using feedback loops so that organization members learn from past practices and avoid repeating the same mistakes
- Reframing problems into opportunities and testing out new approaches
- Encouraging collaboration, and individual and team learning
- Understanding that conflict is part of the change process
- Making sure that the reward structure is not based exclusively on measures of productivity but also on how new learnings are applied to the job
- Structuring themselves to speed the flow and accessibility of internal communications
- Making information easy to store and retrieve
- Using technology to facilitate information transfer
- Routinely reexamining individual, team, and organizational assumptions, values, practices, and policies

Learning organizations also (1) have frameworks for relating learning about particular programs, initiatives, and issues to broader organizational goals; and (2) are able to incorporate systematically derived findings (i.e., from evaluative inquiry) with other forms of information into their decision-making processes.

Evaluator Role in Organizational Learning

Evaluators are typically well positioned to facilitate individual and group, program area, or department-level learning. External evaluators contracted to support work at these levels may have little opportunity to influence organizational learning, if the organization does not already have a culture that supports it. On the other hand, external evaluators who work with the same organizations over time, or within organizations that support a learning culture specifically, are more likely to see the impact of their work on a broader scale. Internal evaluators face the same constraints and opportunities, although they may have more opportunity to promote the role of evaluation in organizational learning over time.

Like most professionals, evaluators seek to maximize the influence of their work in the best way possible, given the circumstances presented by their client organizations (whether internal or external). The more effective evaluators can be at facilitating individual and group learning, the more likely—over time—their work may effect organizational learning. Evaluators sometimes facilitate organizational learning indirectly when they have worked with a particular department or project in such a way that stakeholders understand the impact of their work (that is, through the evaluation findings) in terms of the broader organizational context. These individuals are then able to contribute that learning and perspective as input to a higher level of organizational learning and decision making—a level at which the evaluator may not be invited to participate, as is the case in many organizations. In those instances where evaluators' expertise is sought to support organizational learning directly, one example of how they might do so is to conduct a working session involving several departments or functional areas within an organization, which is designed to draw out common challenges and issues related to accomplishing the organization's mission.

Overview of Communicating and Reporting Formats and Options

To summarize, our major premise is that for evaluations to be fully effective they must result in individual, group, and ultimately, organizational learning. How communicating and reporting takes place during and after an evaluation is a significant mediator of this learning. Evaluation communications and reports designed with easily assimilated contents, and presented in conjunction with opportunities for interaction between the evaluator(s) and the stakeholders and other audiences are the most likely to facilitate learning.

Table 2.3 presents a matrix that crosses (1) the different communicating and reporting formats with (2) the different purposes that they can serve during and after an evaluation. You will notice that there is a wide application of the formats throughout an evaluation. In fact, the table reveals the most about when not to use particular formats. For example, the creative formats listed at the bottom of the first column (cartoons, poetry, and drama; see Chapter 5) are generally more suitable for communicating final evaluation findings than interim findings. These formats can create a significant impression upon audiences—a circumstance not usually desirable with the provisional nature of interim findings.

To learn more about each communicating and reporting format, you may wish to consult Table 2.4 for a summary of the formats, or proceed directly to the material in Chapters 3, 4, and 5, where each is thoroughly described.

Table 2.3 Overview of Communicating and Reporting Formats Used for Various Purposes

Communicating and Reporting Format	Communicating and Reporting Need or Purpose						
	During the Evaluation				After the Evaluation		
	Include Stakeholders in Decision Making About Evaluation Design and Implementation	Inform Stakeholders (and other audiences) About Specific Upcoming Evaluation Activities	Keep Informed About Overall Progress of the Evaluation	Communicate Interim Findings	Build Awareness, Support for Program or Evaluation	Communicate Final Findings to Support Change and Improvement	Communicate Final Findings to Show Results, Demonstrate Accountability
Facilitates Individual Learning							
Short Communications: Memos and E-mail, Postcards	◆	◆	◆	◆	◆	◆	◆
Interim Reports				◆			
Final Reports				◆		◆	◆
Executive Summaries				◆		◆	◆
Newsletters, Bulletins, Briefs, Brochures		◆	◆	◆	◆	◆	◆
News Media Communications				◆	◆	◆	◆
Web Site Communications		◆	◆	◆	◆	◆	◆
Facilitates Interactive Learning							
Verbal Presentations	◆	◆	◆	◆	◆	◆	◆
Video Presentations			◆	◆	◆	◆	◆
Posters and Poster Sessions		◆			◆	◆	◆
Working Sessions	◆		◆	◆	◆	◆	◆
Synchronous Electronic Communications: Chat Rooms, Teleconferencing, Web- and Videoconferencing	◆	◆	◆	◆	◆	◆	◆
Personal Discussions	◆	◆	◆	◆	◆	◆	◆
Photography*					◆	◆	◆
Cartoons*					◆	◆	◆
Poetry*					◆	◆	◆
Drama*					◆	◆	◆

*These creative formats might be included in or used in conjunction with some of the other formats listed.

Table 2.4   Overview of Communicating and Reporting Formats

Facilitate Individual Learning	
1. *Short Communications: Memos, E-mail, and Postcards*	• Can update audiences about ongoing evaluation activities and disseminate findings and recommendations in a timely manner. • Can convey a limited amount of information in a confined length and format. • Can be used to recap or follow up on decisions or points made during a telephone or face-to-face meeting. • Can be a cost-effective means for communicating and reporting with a broad range of audiences and stakeholders. • May not be a confidential means of communication.
2. *Interim Reports*	• Are used to present partial evaluation findings. • Are typically short reports but can be of considerable size in the case of multiyear, multisite, and/or very comprehensive evaluations. • Are usually produced prior to a more comprehensive report. • Should emphasize that conclusions based on interim findings are provisional.
3. *Final Reports*	• Are the most commonly used form of reporting. • Often use a social science research format that includes the study's rationale, guiding questions, methodology, results, and recommendations. • Provide an opportunity to portray the program in a more holistic and comprehensive manner. • Should be designed using text, graphics, layout, and clear writing to increase accessibility and readability. • Provide important archival documentation, often for accountability purposes.
4. *Executive Summaries*	• Are written to make vital information more accessible. • Are typically 1–5 pages in length, but can be longer in the case of large evaluations. • Briefly describe the evaluation's purpose, key questions, design, and data collection and analysis methods. • Emphasize the evaluation's findings and recommendations. • Can be used separately from the final report.
5. *Newsletters, Bulletins, Briefs, Brochures*	• Can be disseminated to publicize program information, upcoming evaluation activities, evaluation findings. • Can be distributed after evaluation activities to publicize evaluation findings or actions taken based on the findings. • Provide opportunities to reach broad groups of people. • Allow for presentation of text and graphics. • Are typically 1–4 pages in length, except briefs, which can be considerably longer. • Provide contact information.
6. *News Media*	• Includes mass media (newspapers, TV, radio) or specialized media (trade or interest group newsletters, journals, magazines). • Can disseminate evaluation information to a broad range of stakeholders and audiences. • Can facilitate conversations among outside groups affected by or interested in the evaluation results. • Requires careful thought and planning.

7. *Web Site Communications*	• Make evaluation information available to a broad national and international audience at minimal cost. • Provide an opportunity to stage the presentation of information into sections, accessible through links that the user selects. • Reduce the possibility of viruses being transmitted as may occur with e-mail attachments. • Provide easily accessible information to evaluators who may be conducting evaluations on a similar topic or program.
	Facilitate Interactive Learning
8. *Verbal Presentations*	• Are particularly useful for conveying information on complex, specialized topics. • Should be focused on a few selected topics. • Are most effective when audience members have an opportunity to interact with the information being presented. • Should be accompanied with visuals such as overhead transparencies, PowerPoint slides, handouts, and flip charts.
9. *Video Presentations*	• Are useful for conveying information about new or innovative programs. • Are useful for disseminating findings to broader audiences than those directly involved with a program. • Are effective for providing evaluation findings to groups whose time is limited and/or who might not be accustomed to reading evaluation reports. • Can be used in multisite evaluations to depict events and activities at different sites. • Are useful for documenting evaluation processes.
10. *Posters and Poster Sessions*	• Provide quick, visually oriented, easy-to-read information. • Typically include photographs, diagrams, graphs, tables, charts, drawings, and text on poster-size boards. • Provide a focused message with a clear purpose. • Can stand alone as a visual display or be used as part of a facilitated session.
11. *Working Sessions*	• Identify concerns about the evaluation; establish buy-in. • Are useful for making decisions regarding the evaluation's implementation and/or use of the findings. • Can be used to obtain input about evaluation design, procedures. • Are particularly effective for engaging stakeholders in interpreting findings and developing recommendations/action plans.
12. *Synchronous Electronic Communications: Chat rooms, Teleconferencing, Video, and Web Conferencing*	• Allow participants to exchange messages in real time through an electronically networked environment without being in each other's physical presence. • Are useful when face-to-face meetings are impractical or impossible. • Can lead to more timely dissemination of findings and subsequent decision making. • Provide opportunities to include stakeholders who might not otherwise be able or available to travel to a meeting. • Provide opportunities for planned or impromptu interaction and collaboration.

(Continued)

29

Table 2.4 (Continued)

13.	*Personal Discussions*	• May be either planned or impromptu, and may be initiated by the evaluator or by someone else. • Occur face to face, over the telephone, or via a chat room exchange. • Are one of the most powerful forms of communication; can facilitate insight, understanding, and new knowledge.
14.	*Photography*	• Can represent the realities of program participants; conveys various perspectives. • Can illustrate the activities of a single participant in a program. • Can be used to count, measure, compare, qualify, or track artifacts or information that can be captured visually. • Is particularly useful when language or cultural barriers may inhibit participants' ability to verbally express their opinions, and/or easily assimilate information in written reports. • May stimulate audiences' participation in interpreting important events and experiences, and enables them to use the findings.
15.	*Cartoons*	• Can illustrate simple or symbolically complex issues in an accessible and concise format. • May be used to convey information to children and those with low reading levels. • Can provide audiences with an informal, visually oriented understanding of program impact. • May be useful when language or cultural barriers inhibit participants' ability to assimilate information from written reports.
16.	*Poetry*	• Can illuminate the emotions, contradictions, and complexities of evaluation contexts. • Can be used to integrate the experiences and perspectives of multiple stakeholders into a collective voice. • Can be effective in communicating the tacit and the implicit. • Helps articulate contradictions, sensitive topics, emotional reactions, and challenges in the setting. • Can make evaluation results more accessible by using participants' language and avoiding evaluation or other academic jargon.
17.	*Drama*	• Recreates lived experience—combines realism, fiction, and poetic genres. • Helps create a balanced representation of the perspective of multiple stakeholders. • Can increase the accessibility of evaluation information for particular audiences. • May be used to convey findings based on qualitative data collection methods. • Is particularly powerful when used as a basis for interaction with program participants and stakeholders.

_____ Developing a Communicating and Reporting Plan

As a background to discussing the development of a communicating and reporting plan, we will first review the major elements of an evaluation plan—of which the communicating and reporting plan is a part. An overall evaluation plan is an essential tool, not only for planning and organizing an evaluation study, but also for determining the evaluation's role in meeting the information needs of its various audiences. Most practicing evaluators develop evaluation plans to guide their inquiry. The format may vary, but most plans typically address the following components:

- Background/organizational context
- Purpose of the evaluation
- Audiences
- Evaluation questions
- Evaluation approach and data collection procedures
- Data analysis procedures
- Evaluation products (including reports to be provided)
- Project management plan (schedule of activities)
- Evaluation constraints
- Budget/costs for the evaluation

Specific detail of activities related to communicating and reporting may not be included in the evaluation plan beyond mention of the formal reporting to be done. Most evaluation clients will not expect to see a detailed communicating and reporting plan. Yet, some level of planning for communicating and reporting evaluation findings begins at the first meeting with clients and stakeholders, where the rationale for the evaluation is addressed. Developing the study's rationale typically involves a lengthy discussion with primary stakeholders about the background of the program and the reason(s) for the evaluation. The motivation for conducting the evaluation may be specific to a program, for instance, concerns about effectiveness, general concerns about accountability, an external mandate to evaluate, and/or the desire to demonstrate a program's effectiveness to internal or external audiences. Evaluations are also undertaken to address broader issues when things do not appear to be going well with the program or organization; when unexpected outcomes arise; or when external changes occur in regulations, procedures, or customer demands.

During initial meetings with clients and stakeholders, most evaluators ask a series of questions that might include the following:

- What kinds of decisions would you like to be able to make about this program?

- What activities are being implemented as part of this program?
- Who are the target groups for each of these activities?
- What do you think is happening and why?
- How might the evaluation results be used?
- What would you do if the results indicate a major need for change?
- Who is likely to be affected by the evaluation results?

As we will address in more detail later, the information that results from these early discussions is useful for identifying the evaluation audiences and beginning ideas about the content and format of communications and reports.

It is important to develop a reporting plan that includes how and when evaluation findings are to be disseminated to all audiences. Lack of planning is one of the biggest factors contributing to evaluators submitting reports to stakeholders that are either not in a format that facilitates use, and/or are too late to be of much value. Evaluators can significantly increase the usefulness of the evaluation and its impact on the organization by working with primary audiences at the beginning of the evaluation to plan for dissemination of the study's results.

The communicating and reporting plan serves as a guide to ensure that all audiences receive timely information relative to their information needs. The plan can be amended as additional audiences are identified and new methods are found to be effective, or as information needs change during the course of the evaluation. The development of this plan also helps potential users focus on what information they need from the study. Evaluation stakeholders are not always clear about what they need or hope to learn from the evaluation. Helping them reflect on what they will do with the information is an essential step toward effective use.

On the following pages you will find two worksheets for creating a communicating and reporting plan, which take into account the factors critical to understanding and planning for effective communicating and reporting

- Identification of the evaluation's stakeholders and other audiences
- The characteristics of each audience
- The various purposes for communicating with each audience during and after the evaluation
- Prioritizing the evaluation's communicating and reporting tasks
- Implications of audience characteristics for communicating and reporting content
- Possible formats for each communicating and reporting task
- Timing and resources that might be needed

Worksheet 1 Identify Audiences

Step 1: Use the following set of guiding questions to generate a list of audiences for your evaluation. List each audience in the space below. (If not obvious, it may be helpful to make a note about what role each plays with respect to the evaluand*.)	Step 2: From the list generated in Step 1, identify which individuals and groups belong in each category below. Account for all individuals and groups listed in Step 1.
a. Which individuals or groups were mentioned when the rationale for the evaluation was established? b. Which individuals or groups will be asked to provide data for the evaluation? c. Which individuals or groups should be involved in planning or carrying out the evaluation? d. Which individuals or groups might use the findings for program development or improvement? e. Which individuals or groups might use the findings for making funding or resource decisions? f. Which individuals or groups might be interested in the findings but are not in a decision-making position relative to the evaluand*? g. What groups (if any) within the public at large should know about the evaluation's findings?	Primary audiences may have requested the evaluation, may have funded the evaluation, usually include those responsible for implementing the evaluand* (e.g., program staff, supervisors, managers), and can include external constituents.
	Secondary audiences may have a strong interest in the evaluation findings, but may have little direct involvement with the evaluand; could use the evaluation findings in some aspect of their work and decision making (e.g., parents, some program participants, their supervisors or managers, and individuals whose work will be affected by decisions based on the evaluation results).
	Tertiary audiences are more distanced from the inner workings of the evaluand but may want to stay informed about it and would be interested in receiving the evaluation's results (e.g., future program participants, the general public, special interest groups).

*Evaluand refers to the program, project, organization, concern, issue, or policy that is the subject of the evaluation.

33

Worksheet 2 Create Communicating and Reporting Plan for Each Audience

② Audience Characteristics

Step 1: List a single audience below: (individual or group) ①	How accessible?	Reading ability?	Familiarity with program or evaluand?	Attitude toward/ interest level in program?	Role in decision making about program or evaluation?	Familiarity with research and evaluation in general?	Attitude toward/ interest level in this evaluation?	Experience using evaluation findings
	Easily	High Level	Very Familiar	Positive/High	Crucial	Very Familiar	Positive/High	Substantial
	With some effort	Mid Level	Somewhat Familiar	Neutral	Important	Somewhat Familiar	Neutral	Some
	With substantial effort	Low Level	Not Familiar	Negative/Low	Minor	Not Familiar	Negative/Low	None
Step 2: *For each characteristic to the right, mark the response that best describes this audience.*	Don't Know	Non-Reader	Don't Know	Don't Know	No Role	Don't Know	Don't Know	Don't Know
		Don't Know			Don't Know			

	③ Communicating/ Reporting Purpose	④ Priority	⑤ Implications for Content	⑥ Format(s) to Use	⑦ Dates	⑧ Resources Needed
During the Evaluation	☐ Include in Decision Making about Evaluation Design and Implementation	HI MED LO				
	☐ Inform About Specific Upcoming Evaluation Activities	HI MED LO				
	☐ Keep Informed About Overall Progress of the Evaluation	HI MED LO				
	☐ Communicate Interim Findings	HI MED LO				
After the Evaluation	☐ Inform About Program and Evaluation to Build Awareness and/or Support	HI MED LO				
	☐ Communicate Final Findings to Support Change and Improvement	HI MED LO				
	☐ Communicate Final Findings to Show Results, Demonstrate Accountability	HI MED LO				
	☐ Other	HI MED LO				

Step 3: *Check the purposes for communicating with this audience.*

Step 4: *Considering the audience and the purpose, prioritize each communicating and reporting task.*

Step 5: *Note implications that the characteristics of this audience may have for the contents of communications and reports.*

Step 6: *Indicate appropriate formats to use.*

Step 7: *Indicate date for communication/report.*

Step 8: *Indicate resources needed.*

Each stage of the process for creating a detailed communicating and reporting plan is described below, integrated with tips for using the worksheets.

Identify Stakeholders and Other Audiences

The first step in developing any communicating and reporting plan is to identify the stakeholders and other audiences for the evaluation. Stakeholders are those individuals, groups, or organizations who may be affected by the planning, activities, and/or findings of the evaluation (e.g., clients, program staff, parents, community members, managers, funders). Audiences are those who receive information about the evaluation and its findings (e.g., staff from other programs who would benefit from findings about a particular program). Audiences include, but are not limited to stakeholders. Questions that can help you identify stakeholders and other audiences are:

- Which individuals or groups were mentioned when the rationale for the evaluation was established, and what role do they play?
- Which individuals or groups will be asked to provide data for the evaluation?
- Which individuals or groups should be involved in planning or carrying out the evaluation?
- Which individuals or groups might use the findings for making funding or resource decisions?
- Which individuals or groups might use the findings for program development or improvement?
- Which individuals or groups might be interested in the findings but are not in a decision-making position relative to the evaluand?

Tips for Worksheet 1

- Complete *Step 1* by addressing the questions shown left in a working session with the evaluation's key stakeholders, or use them as a guide to gathering this information in other ways (e.g., by reviewing documents or proposals that describe the evaluand, by conducting individual interviews).
- Complete *Step 2* to further describe the audiences identified.

- What groups (if any) within the public at large should know about the evaluation's findings?

Answers to several of these questions will become apparent as soon as the possibility of conducting an evaluation is considered. Note that the questions are not mutually exclusive; that is, responses to more than one question may identify the same individuals or groups. Once all audiences have been identified, it is helpful to categorize them as primary, secondary, or tertiary audiences (see the Audiences section earlier in this chapter, pages 15–19). This designation may or may not indicate the relative importance of the audience in terms of your efforts to communicate and report.

Identify the Characteristics of Each Audience

Tips for Worksheet 2

- Complete one copy of Worksheet 2 for each different audience identified. You may wish to concentrate on audiences with whom you currently have an obligation to communicate and report.
- In *Step 1* indicate the audience to whom each copy of Worksheet 2 applies.
- *Steps 3–8* can be completed by yourself or done in collaboration with key stakeholders.
- If you complete the steps by yourself, you may wish to review all or parts of the worksheet with stakeholders for feedback.

Refer to the earlier discussion on audience characteristics. Think about each audience member or group you have identified in terms of their

- Accessibility
- Reading ability
- Familiarity with the program or evaluand
- Attitude toward and interest level in the program or evaluand
- Role in decision making about the evaluand or the evaluation
- Familiarity with research and evaluation, in general
- Attitude toward and interest level in this evaluation
- Experience with using evaluation findings

For any of these characteristics that you do not know about an audience, seek to find out.

For Each Audience, Determine the Purposes for Communicating and Reporting During and After the Evaluation

Once the stakeholders and other audiences for your evaluation have been identified, you should determine the different purposes that communicating with them during and after the evaluation will serve, that is, to

- Include them in decision making about the evaluation design and implementation.
- Inform them about specific upcoming evaluation activities.
- Keep them informed about the overall progress of the evaluation.
- Communicate interim findings.
- Inform them about the program and its evaluation to build awareness and/or support.

- Communicate final findings to support change and improvement.
- Communicate final findings to show results and/or demonstrate accountability.

Refer to the earlier discussion under the heading Purposes for Communicating and Reporting at the beginning of this chapter (pages 12–14), and to Table 2.1.

Prioritize the Evaluation's Communicating and Reporting Tasks

Given numerous stakeholders and other audiences, and the various reasons you might communicate with them during and after the evaluation, there may be more to do than time and financial resources will permit. It is important to prioritize your communicating and reporting tasks. A communicating and reporting task consists of one audience and one purpose combination. For example, informing program staff about upcoming evaluation activities is a single communicating and reporting task. Communicating interim evaluation findings to the same audience is another, separate task. You will have as many communicating and reporting tasks as you have audience and purpose combinations.

Typically, your very highest priorities will be communicating with key stakeholders to

- Include them in decision making about the evaluation itself.
- Inform them about specific upcoming evaluation activities.
- Communicate interim findings.
- Communicate final findings.

Consider Implications of Audience Characteristics for Communicating and Reporting Content

At this stage of creating a communicating and reporting plan, it is useful to think about the implications each audience's characteristics may have for the content of your communications and reports. For instance, audiences not familiar with research and evaluation may require explanation of basic statistical terms. And, audiences with little prior experience using evaluation findings who are invited to a working session to interpret findings would need an explanation of the rationale for the session and why their participation is important. Refer to the discussion of audience characteristics on pages 17–19.

Select Formats for Each Communicating and Reporting Task

With knowledge about (1) the audience, (2) the purposes for communicating and reporting to them, (3) your thoughts about at least some aspects of the contents of your communications and reports, and (4) your understanding of the benefits and challenges of using different formats, you are well equipped to select format(s) for each communicating and reporting task. (See Figure 1.2 and Tables 2.3 and 2.4 for an overview of the communicating and reporting formats presented in Chapters 3, 4, and 5.)

Consider Dates and Resources Needed for Each Communicating and Reporting Task

The final stage of creating your communicating and reporting plan for each audience involves identifying dates when various communications and reports will be needed, as well as the resources that will be required to produce and disseminate them. Timing for the delivery of interim and final reports is often roughly, if not directly, tied to the life cycle of the program, department, organization, or issue that is the subject of the evaluation. Often there will be an impending decision that the evaluation is meant to inform. If so, it establishes the deadline for delivery of interim and/or final findings. Within any general time frame that you establish for the evaluation, there may be considerable discretion about when different communications take place. If you are conducting a collaborative evaluation, you will be in regular communication with many of those individuals and groups with the most need to know about any particular evaluation activity or finding. Note that specific dates for delivering many of the communications and reports will not necessarily have to be explicitly established for the evaluation team at the out-set. These dates will fall into place as a matter of course in your ongoing work with the team.

Specific dates and sufficient lead time will need to be established for communicating with and reporting, as needed, to wider audiences. Generally, lead time is necessary not only for (1) planning and scheduling, but also for (2) preparing the communication or report, and (3) involving others in reviewing, if not helping to develop it.

Resources needed for creating and disseminating communications and reports can include anything from stakeholders' e-mail addresses, to graphic design support for producing professional-looking, easy-to-read executive summaries, to videoconferencing support for conducting a working session for a multisite evaluation, to locating a venue for performing a drama piece based on evaluation findings.

Example Communicating and Reporting Plan

In this final section we present and discuss parts of a communicating and reporting plan based on the following evaluation scenario:

Morningside Charter School (grades 6–12) was founded to create a unique educational experience that embraced the best qualities of traditional education while introducing a progressive approach to learning. Morningside prides itself on being highly diverse in terms of socioeconomic status, race, ethnicity, religion, and cultural backgrounds. Most students enter Morningside in the 6th grade (middle school), while some are admitted in later grades based on the number of openings available.

Morningside loses the highest percentage of its students during the transition from 8th (middle) to 9th grade (upper school). Some of the students choose to attend other schools, while others move out of the area. Very few, if any, drop out of school completely. The principals of the middle and upper schools have been working hard to develop a stronger school transition program. Over the last year, several activities have been implemented to support the students' transition from 8th to 9th grade:

- A parent day for students to sign up for upper school classes
- A buddy day where 9th-graders guide 8th-graders through a typical high school day
- A meeting for 8th-graders with upper school administrators, who explain the differences and similarities between the upper and middle school
- A meeting of parents and several 8th- and 9th-grade teachers to address any questions parents might have about the transition
- A survey of parents whose children left the school to determine their reasons for leaving

The school's administration and leadership team (consisting of teacher representatives from each grade) have decided to conduct a more formal formative evaluation, and engage the services of an evaluation consultant. An evaluation team is established to conduct the evaluation. Its members are

- Two 8th-grade teachers
- Two 9th-ninth grade teachers
- Two school counselors, one from the upper school and one from the middle school
- The evaluation consultant

The evaluation team developed an evaluation plan that included the following data collection methods:

- Observations of and interviews with participants attending, and photographs of the transition program activities shown above
- Focus groups with 8th- and 9th-grade students
- Survey of 6th- through 12th-grade teachers

Using Worksheet 1, the evaluation team identified the evaluation's audiences, and determined whether they were primary, secondary, or tertiary audiences. See Figure 2.2.

To create a detailed communicating and reporting plan, they completed Worksheet 2 for each of the audiences identified on Worksheet 1. Figures 2.3 and 2.4 show their completed plans for two of these audiences: the principals

Worksheet 1 Identify Audiences

Step 1: Use the following set of guiding questions to generate a list of audiences for your evaluation. List each audience in the space below. (If not obvious, it may be helpful to make a note about what role each audience plays with respect to the evaluand*.)	Step 2: From the list generated in Step 1, identify which individuals and groups belong in each category below. Account for all individuals and groups listed in Step 1.
a. Which individuals or groups were mentioned when the rationale for the evaluation was established?	*Primary audiences* may have requested the evaluation, may have funded the evaluation, usually include those responsible for implementing the evaluand* (e.g., program staff, supervisors, managers), and can include external constituents.
b. Which individuals or groups will be asked to provide data for the evaluation?	• Principals of upper and middle Schools • Director of Admissions • School counselors • 8th- and 9th-grade teachers • 8th- and 9th-grade students • Morningside Governing Board
c. Which individuals or groups should be involved in planning or carrying out the evaluation?	
d. Which individuals or groups might use the findings for program development or improvement?	*Secondary audiences* may have a strong interest in the evaluation findings, but may have little direct involvement with the evaluand; could use the evaluation findings in some aspect of their work and decision-making (e.g., parents, some program participants, their supervisors or managers, and individuals whose work will be affected by decisions based on the evaluation results).
e. Which individuals or groups might use the findings for making funding or resource decisions?	• Parents of students in the school • 6th- and 7th-grade teachers • Current 6th-, 7th-, 10th-, 11th- 12th-grade students
f. Which individuals or groups might be interested in the findings but are not in a decision-making position relative to the evaluand*?	
g. What groups (if any) within the public at large should know about the evaluation's findings?	*Tertiary audiences* are more distanced from the inner workings of the evaluand but may want to stay informed about it and would be interested in receiving the evaluation's results (e.g., future program participants, the general public, special interest groups).
• Principals of upper and middle Schools • Director of Admissions • Students • Middle school teachers • Upper school teachers • School counselors • Parents of students in the school • Parents of students who have left the school • Morningside Governing Board • Prospective students and their parents • Students • Administrators of other private schools	• Parents of students who have left the school • Administrators of other private schools • Prospective students and their parents

Figure 2.2   Example of Worksheet 1 Completed

Evaluand refers to the program, project, organization, concern, issue, or policy that is the subject of the evaluation.

Worksheet 2 Create Communicating and Reporting Plan for Each Audience

② Audience Characteristics

Step 1: List a single audience below: (individual or group)

① Principals of middle and upper schools

Step 2: For each characteristic to the right, mark the response that best describes this audience.

How accessible?	Reading ability?	Familiarity with program or evaluand?	Attitude toward/ interest level in program?	Role in decision making about program or evaluation?	Familiarity with research and evaluation in general?	Attitude toward/ interest level in this evaluation?	Experience using evaluation findings
Easily	(High Level)	(Very Familiar)	(Positive/High)	(Crucial)	Very Familiar	(Positive/High)	Substantial
(With some effort)	Mid Level	Somewhat Familiar	Neutral	Important	(Somewhat Familiar)	Neutral	(Some)
With substantial effort	Low Level	Not Familiar	Negative/Low	Minor	Not Familiar	Negative/Low	None
Don't Know	Non-Reader	Don't Know	Don't Know	No Role	Don't Know	Don't Know	Don't Know
	Don't Know			Don't Know			

(Circled responses: With some effort; High Level; Very Familiar; Positive/High [program]; Crucial; Somewhat Familiar; Positive/High [evaluation]; Some)

During the Evaluation

③ Communicating/ Reporting Purpose	④ Priority	⑤ Implications for Content	⑥ Format(s) to Use	⑦ Dates	⑧ Resources Needed
☑ Include in Decision Making About Evaluation Design and Implementation	HI✓ MED LO	– Recognize what they already know about research methods	– Working session	– Sept-Oct	– Meeting room – Flip charts
☑ Inform About Specific Upcoming Evaluation Activities	HI✓ MED LO	– May need to follow up to be sure e-mail has been read	– E-mail or memo	– Nov-Apr	– N/A
☑ Keep Informed About Overall Progress of the Evaluation	HI MED LO	– See above	– E-mail or memo	– Sept-Jun	– N/A
☐ Communicate Interim Findings	HI MED LO				

After the Evaluation

③ Communicating/ Reporting Purpose	④ Priority	⑤ Implications for Content	⑥ Format(s) to Use	⑦ Dates	⑧ Resources Needed
☐ Inform About Program and Evaluation to Build Awareness and/or Support	HI MED LO				
☑ Communicate Final Findings to Support Change and Improvement	HI MED✓ LO	Explain reasons for collaborative interpretation of findings	– Verbal presentation – Working session to interpret findings – Final report	– Next Aug – Next Aug – Next Sept	– Projector for PPT presentation, mtg. room, flip charts – Binding, etc.
☐ Communicate Final Findings to Show Results, Demonstrate Accountability					

Step 3: Check the purposes for communicating with this audience.

Step 4: Considering the audience and the purpose, prioritize each communicating and reporting task.

Step 5: Note implications that the characteristics of this audience may have for the contents of communications and reports.

Step 6: Indicate appropriate formats to use.

Step 7: Indicate date for communication/report.

Step 8: Indicate resources needed.

Figure 2.3 Example A of Worksheet 2 Completed

41

Worksheet 2 Create Communicating and Reporting Plan for Each Audience

② Audience Characteristics

Step 1: List a single audience below: (individual or group) ① 8th- and 9th-grade students Step 2: For each characteristic to the right, mark the response that best describes this audience.	How accessible?	Reading ability?	Familiarity with program or evaluand?	Attitude toward/ interest level in program?	Role in decision making about program or evaluation?	Familiarity with research and evaluation in general?	Attitude toward/ interest level in this evaluation?	Experience using evaluation findings
	(Easily)	High Level	Very Familiar	Positive/High	Crucial	Very Familiar	Positive/High	Substantial
	With some effort	(Mid Level)	(Somewhat Familiar)	(Neutral)	Important	Somewhat Familiar	(Neutral)	Some
	With substantial effort	Low Level	Not Familiar	Negative/Low	(Minor)	(Not Familiar)	Negative/Low	(None)
	Don't Know	Non-Reader	Don't Know	Don't Know	No Role	Don't Know	Don't Know	Don't Know
		Don't Know			Don't Know			

	③ Communicating/ Reporting Purpose	④ Priority	⑤ Implications for Content	⑥ Format(s) to Use	⑦ Dates	⑧ Resources Needed
During the Evaluation	☐ Include in Decision Making About Evaluation Design and Implementation	HI MED LO				
	☑ Inform About Specific Upcoming Evaluation Activities	HI *MED* LO	Explain rationale for evaluation & why their input is important	– Flyers around school – A.M. announcements – Presentation at assembly	– Sep – Nov-Apr – May	– Card stock – N/A – Reserve gym?
	☐ Keep Informed about Overall Progress of the Evaluation	HI MED LO				
	☐ Communicate Interim Findings	HI MED LO				
After the Evaluation	☐ Inform about Program and Evaluation to Build Awareness and/or Support	HI MED LO				
	☑ Communicate Final Findings to Support Change and Improvement	HI *MED* LO	Explain analysis methods in simple language; pilot content	– Posters w/photos of activities – Verbal presentation at 8th/9th gr. parents' night	– Next Sep – Next Nov	– Poster board, photo paper – Projector for PPT Presentat'n
	☐ Communicate Final Findings to Show Results, Demonstrate Accountability	HI MED LO				

Step 3: Check the purposes for communicating with this audience.

Step 4: Considering the audience and the purpose, prioritize each communicating and reporting task.

Step 5: Note implications that the characteristics of this audience may have for the contents of communications and reports.

Step 6: Indicate appropriate formats to use.

Step 7: Indicate date for communication/report.

Step 8: Indicate resources needed.

Figure 2.4   Example B of Worksheet 2 Completed

of the middle and upper schools, and the currently enrolled 8th- and 9th-grade students.

As noted on Worksheet 1 (see Figure 2.2), the evaluation team designated the principals of the middle and upper schools as primary stakeholders in this evaluation since they are responsible for the operation of the school and make funding decisions. They will give approval for any changes made to the middle-to-upper school transition program.

Figure 2.3 shows the evaluation team's assessment of the principals' characteristics. That is, they believe that the principals: (1) are accessible with some effort (since they are highly busy throughout the day and often are in meetings with parents); (2) have a high reading ability; (3) are very familiar with the transition program and have a positive attitude toward it (they were most responsible for creating it); (4) have a crucial role in making decisions about the program; (5) are somewhat familiar with research and evaluation practices (through their graduate degrees and reading of professional journals); (6) have a positive attitude about this program's evaluation; and (7) have some experience using evaluation findings (they were the primary stakeholders for previously conducted evaluations of the 6th-grade curriculum, and the use of technology in their schools).

Given the principals' role in the school, the evaluation team decides that it is important to include them in discussions concerning the evaluation's design and implementation, and rates this task as a high priority. Based on the principals' characteristics, the evaluation team discusses the importance of recognizing what the principals already know about research methods, and plans to include them in a working session to decide on the details of implementing the evaluation's data collection methods (see Figure 2.3). They plan on conducting this phase of the evaluation in the September–October time frame, after school has gotten underway and things are settling down. All they will need is a meeting room that will accommodate the evaluation team and the principals, and two flip charts.

The evaluation team wants to make sure to inform the principals about upcoming evaluation activities, as well as keep them informed about the evaluation's progress. They think that sending them periodic memos via e-mail will be sufficient. And one of the evaluation team members agrees to follow up with the principals, to make sure they have received and read the e-mail messages. They expect to be sending e-mail updates during the course of the evaluation, which is planned for November through April.

When the evaluation has been completed, the evaluation team knows that it is extremely important to work with the principals to interpret findings, and to help them make decisions about the future of the transition program. Thus, they plan to propose to the principals that they write a formal evaluation report, and that it be done on the basis of a collaborative interpretation of the findings. For this activity they plan to conduct a working session with the principals, at which time they will also develop recommendations. Both the interpretations and the recommendations will be included in the final report. For these communicating and reporting tasks, the evaluation team will need to secure a meeting room for the working session where they can deliver a PowerPoint presentation, and they will need resources for reproducing and binding the evaluation report.

Another communicating and reporting plan was developed for the 8th- and 9th-grade students, who are also designated as primary stakeholders (see Figure 2.4). They are participants in some activities of the current transition program, will be affected by whatever changes may result from implementing the evaluation's findings, and will provide data for the evaluation. When considering the characteristics of these students, the evaluation team determined that (1) the students are easily accessible; (2) generally have a mid-level reading ability; (3) are somewhat familiar with the transition program (based on their participation in it as 8th-graders and what they may have heard from parents, teachers, and other students); and (4) are thought to be more or less neutral about the program (the team is not aware of any particularly positive or negative perspectives that they may have). The team is uncertain about (5) the extent of the students' role in decision making about the future of the transition program. They would like to have the students involved in some of the planning that will occur once the evaluation is complete. The team is fairly certain that (6) the students as a whole have little to no familiarity with research or evaluation practices, (7) are likely to be neutral about the evaluation, and (8) have no experience using evaluation findings.

Based on these students' characteristics, the evaluation team decided that they would want to inform these students about specific upcoming evaluation activities, and as part of this communication would need to explain the rationale for the evaluation study and why their input is important. The team decided on informing students and soliciting their participation in the data collection activities by putting flyers around the school, by making periodic updates about the evaluation during the school's morning announcements, and by briefly describing the next steps for the evaluation during the closing assemblies for the current school year. The team will need card stock for the flyers and will need to schedule the gym far in advance for the end-of-year assembly (or they may plan on making this presentation as part of another school assembly; in this case, they will have to make sure to get on that program's agenda).

Soon after the new school year begins, the evaluation team will communicate and report the evaluation's findings by placing posters around the school that highlight key findings and recommendations. The posters will include photographs that were taken of the various transition events during the previous school year. The team anticipates that the photographs will attract students' interest in the posters. In November, the evaluation team will make a verbal presentation of the findings and recommendations to the 8th- and 9th-grade students and their parents during the "parents' night" for each of these two grade levels (which are held separately). To present the findings, the team will make a PowerPoint presentation and provide handouts. The evaluation team will pay particular attention to make sure that the methods of data collection and analysis are explained clearly and simply, and to use as little research and evaluation jargon as possible. They will pilot drafts of the presentation and handouts with both students and parents who are on the school improvement committee. They have determined that they will need poster board for the posters and will need to make sure they are added to the agenda for the parents' meeting.

Creating this communicating and reporting plan helped the evaluation team focus their work over the coming months, in particular because they detailed exactly what the evaluation products were going to be, and when and how they would be delivered. They made adjustments to the plan as the evaluation proceeded. For example, it turned out that rather than use e-mail for keeping the principals abreast of the evaluation, it was more beneficial for the evaluation consultant to attend one of the principals' meetings each month, to give them an update and resolve any issues that had surfaced regarding the evaluation. Also, the working session with the principals to interpret findings was expanded to include two student representatives.

S U M M A R Y

In this chapter we have described the importance of planning for effective communicating and reporting during an evaluation's design and implementation, as well as after an evaluation has been completed. We have explained the purposes for communicating and reporting: to convey information, to facilitate understanding and create meaning, and to support decision making by various kinds of stakeholders. Throughout the chapter we have emphasized the importance of understanding the characteristics of audiences who will use the communications and reports. Different audiences' accessibility; reading ability; familiarity with the program or evaluand; attitude toward and interest level in the program; role in decision making; familiarity with research and evaluation methods; attitude toward and interest in the evaluation; and experience using evaluation findings all influence the formats and strategies used for communicating and reporting purposes. In this chapter we have also discussed the value of bearing in mind how individuals and groups learn, since your choice of communicating and reporting strategies can directly influence learning in a variety of ways. To this end, we have outlined a variety of communicating and reporting formats and have organized them according to the level of interaction they potentially have with audiences. Finally, we have provided a format and guidance for developing a communicating and reporting plan based on identifying the evaluation audiences; their characteristics; the purposes for communicating with and reporting to them; the formats to use; and the timing and resources needed for each communicating and reporting task.

3

Communicating and Reporting Strategies to Facilitate Learning

Questions to Ponder

- ☐ *How can evaluators make the contents of their communications and reports more appealing and easy for readers to assimilate?*
- ☐ *How can different communicating and reporting formats best be used to facilitate individual learning?*
- ☐ *Which text-based formats are the most appropriate for the different phases of an evaluation?*

I n this chapter we first describe how the contents of evaluation communications and reports can be designed to enhance individual learning (using
design and layout, tables and figures, and writing). We then present seven
text-based formats that facilitate individual learning (short written communications; interim reports; final reports; executive summaries; newsletters,
bulletins, briefs, and brochures; news media communications; and Web site
communications). Our goal is for you to consider this information relative to
how individuals learn most effectively. The guidance we provide in each of
these areas has one central theme—making the contents of different text-
based formats easy for individual readers to understand and use.

Making Contents Easy to Assimilate

Evaluators can make the contents of their text-based documents more
readable, appealing, and instructive by paying attention to their design and
layout, using tables and figures to condense information and represent findings, and writing clearly and concisely. We address these three topics below
with further explanation of their importance, implementation tips and cautions, and concrete examples.

Design and Layout

Traditional social science research reports, including many evaluation reports,
typically follow the formatting requirements of the American Psychological
Association's (2001) *Publication Manual*. It calls for headings in a prescribed
format, a single font size, no use of color, and limited graphics and illustrations
(to keep production costs down). This approach serves its purpose well:
submission of formal research reports for publication in academic journals.

Increasingly, reports and communications written for more practical purposes include design elements to enhance readability and appeal to intended
audiences (varied type size and style, generous spacing, and incorporation of
tables, figures, illustrations, and photographs).

Advances in computer hardware and software have made production of
appealing documents significantly easier and less expensive. Word-processing
programs support a variety of styles and formats:

- Variation and differentiation in headings with the use of different type
  styles
- Integration of boxed text, charts, graphs, tables, figures, and graphic
  images within the main text of the report
- Variation in print color, from multiple shades of gray to a full spectrum
  of colors

Use of design elements to enhance readability need not detract from the credibility of evaluation work. "Sharing what you have learned draws from both your systematic and creative sides. You want to engage your audience and, at the same time, convince them that what you are giving them is real" (Rossman & Rallis, 2003, p. 332). The main considerations for the style and format of an evaluation report or communication should be the extent to which it (1) compels people to read it and (2) facilitates the assimilation of its contents. This means avoiding overly academic reporting styles and formats. Figure 3.1 shows a single-page "snapshot" of evaluation findings created in Microsoft Word. It features boxed text, color graphics, and variation in type size. It was created as a companion piece to a final evaluation report and was used for wider distribution among secondary and tertiary audiences. (To view this figure in color, go to http://www.sagepub.com/escr.)

Good visual appearance is increasingly the standard in scientific and technical works. In terms of evaluation use and impact, evaluation communications and reports should be designed to grab and hold readers' attention. Using the tools on desk- or laptop computers, many evaluators or staff within their organizations have the skills to produce reports and communications in these kinds of easily understood and engaging formats. And, some evaluation budgets can support the services of graphic designers and document production companies for a variety of products—reports, executive summaries, and brochures. The following implementation tips for effective design and layout are generally applicable to most types of evaluation documents—complete reports, summaries, memos, brochures, postcards, and Web sites.

Implementation Tips for Design and Layout of Evaluation Communications and Reports

■ **Plan for the resources you will need to create your evaluation communications and reports.**

Resources can include anything from additional time needed to format documents, to learning the features of graphics software and computer hardware, to procuring outside services. Planning for document production is especially important if you are using new and/or more creative approaches for the first time.

■ **When creating evaluation documents, use design principles that maximize readability.**

The basic design principles for maximizing readability are proximity, alignment, repetition, and contrast (see Williams, 2004). *Proximity* helps organize information and reduce complexity by grouping related items close together. *Alignment* means that every element on a page has some visual

A Snapshot of Home Visitation in LA County

Findings

Indication of service need: Over 137,000 families with children under 5 years old live in poverty in Los Angeles County. (2000 Census)

Home Visitation Agency Survey Results:

✓ *Just over a third of the home visitation programs in LA County use a standard curriculum or program model. The most common are Family Preservation, Early Head Start, and Black Infant Health.*

✓ *Most agencies have developed their own programs to serve their client population.*

✓ *The most common services provided in the home are case management/assessment, child abuse prevention, parenting education, growth/development and home safety. Surveyed agencies provide an average of 12 different services in the home to their clients.*

✓ *The average number of home visitors employed by the agencies surveyed is nine, each having an average caseload of 21 clients.*

✓ *Home visitors in LA County serve an estimate 67,383 children each year.*

Note: 28 First 5 LA and 65 other home visitation programs in LA County responded to the survey

Primary Outcome Areas Targeted by Los Angeles County Home Visitation Programs (N = 95)

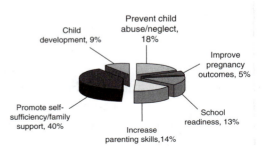

Number of Sources Funding Local Home Visitation Programs (N = 95)

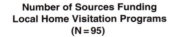
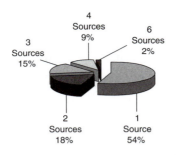

Experiences

"Our program acts as a bridge for newly immigrated families, allowing them to cross safely into American society and the school system."

– Home Visitor

"I value the satisfaction I get from watching the families' self-esteem and skills improve, and the bond I form with the families."

– Home Visitor

"Even the services which may seem small to us are big for the family. If a client hasn't seen her mother in a long time and I can facilitate them getting together, that's a big deal for the family."

– Program Administrator

"Home visitation allows for a relationship to start so that families can be introduced to more services."

– Service Provider

Serving and Connecting Families and Communities

➢ *Home visitation works best as a system of services, linking clients to other resources.*

➢ *Home visitation is the preferred service delivery strategy for situations where a parent is unwilling to seek services outside the home.*

Figure 3.1   Example of Single-Page Snapshot of Evaluation Findings

SOURCE: Produced by Lodestar Management/Research, Inc. for the First 5 Los Angeles Home Visitation Research & Evaluation Project, April 2003. Report can be found at: http://www.first5.org/ourprojects/homevisitation2.php4.

connection with another element on a page. *Repetition* of colors, shapes, spatial relationships, line thicknesses, fonts, sizes, and graphic concepts develops the organization of a written piece and strengthens its unity. *Contrast* adds visual interest and attracts readers. A well-designed page layout uses these principles to enhance and arrange information on a page. Design elements include spacing, type size and style, headings, headers and footers, columns, color, and tables and graphics.

Figure 3.2 shows a newsletter page from the National Center for Research on Standards and Student Testing (http://cresst96.cse.ucla.edu). It illustrates the design principles of alignment (fuchsia-colored bar in left margin and fuchsia-colored box with page number are aligned vertically); repetition (fuchsia color is used for boxes in left margin and headings, as well as text of call-outs; call-out text is enclosed in a box with light fuchsia shading); and contrast (between deep fuchsia color and white background). (To see this figure in color, go to http://www.sagepub.com/escr.)

In the remaining implementation tips we describe how various design elements can make text-based documents easier for evaluation audiences and users to assimilate.

■ **Break up long stretches of text with lists, boxed text, and tables and graphics.**

Use indented *lists* to improve the readability of a long series of items, and/or to emphasize the contents of the list. *Boxed text* and call-outs provide visual relief and highlight important information. *Tables and graphics* include charts and graphs, illustrations, and photographs (see the next section for more detail on these items). Tables are more efficient than text for presenting large amounts of data. As shown in Figure 3.1, graphics create interest and are more memorable than text.

■ **Choose a typeface consistent with the length and formality of the evaluation document.**

Serif typefaces are the best choice for the large amounts of text typically found in evaluation reports. They are defined by their stylistic finishing lines, and are highly readable. More plainly styled sans serif typefaces are better suited for headings (see main heading of Figure 3.1). Figure 3.3 shows examples of serif and sans serif typefaces.

■ **Design reports in easily understood and engaging formats to enhance their readability.**

The main considerations for the style and format of a final report should be the extent to which it (1) compels people to read it and (2) facilitates the

Di Weddell of the Australia Commonwealth Department of Education and Peter Titmanis of the Western Australia Education Department described how a sampling procedure has been used to equate the tests from the different jurisdictions. Expert judges, using an item pool from all of the tests, developed a common scale based on level of difficulty and a cut score on the scale. This allows each jurisdiction to calculate the proportion of their students who had a score at or above the benchmark on their own scale. The sample approach won over state officials, according to Titmanis.

CHILE

A new assessment in Chile measures higher order thinking skills, using both multiple-choice and extended response formats. Given for the first time to fourth graders in

> The first year's data revealed that student performance in public schools and in subsidized private schools was not significantly different.

1999, it will expand to eighth grade soon and is intended to assess school performance, according to Claudia Matus of the Chile Ministry of Education. The first year's data revealed that student performance in public schools and in subsidized private schools was not significantly different. Officials are dealing with issues of reliable scoring on open-ended questions, generating appropriate items for higher order skills, and informing the public.

KOREA

Korea is now implementing its seventh revision of a national curriculum since 1948, according to Sung-Sook Kim and Hye-Sook Kim of the Korea Institute of Curriculum and Evaluation. Through Grade 10, the curriculum is differentiated based on ability. In Grades 11-12, the curriculum is different for students based on their interests and career choices. The revised curriculum reduces content coverage by 30%.

Korea has three types of assessments: school activity records that evaluate students; a National Assessment of Educational Achievement, which controls the quality of the system by providing information on overall educational achievement; and a college scholastic ability test administered nationally. The reforms advocate replacing a norm-referenced system with a criterion-referenced system and using student records for diagnostic purposes as well as a cumulative evaluation.

SINGAPORE

Unlike Korea's homogeneous population, Singapore is multi-cultural with four official languages; English is the primary language of administration. Singapore has gone through several education reforms with the latest reform characterized by five features: bilingual-

> Assessment data are used to determine promotion to the next grade, and streaming (placement), and as feedback to pupils on their readiness for the national exams.

ism (English and a mother tongue); streaming, the placement of students in different levels at primary, secondary and pre-university points); special curriculum for each stream; curriculum and assessment in two languages plus math up to Grade 10; and compulsory but nontested moral, physical and national education through Grade 12. According to Quek Choon Lang and Toh Hoon Sin of the Singapore Ministry of Education, the assessment system consists of school-based assessment by teachers and national exams at Grades 6, 10, and 12. Assessment data are used to determine promotion to the next grade and streaming (placement), and as feedback to pupils on their readiness for the national exams.

THAILAND

Based on 1999 reforms, Thailand's new assessment framework will be instituted in 2002. The reforms decentralize authority and shift assessment responsibility to schools,

6

The CRESST *Line*

Figure 3.2　　Example of Page Layout Illustrating the Design Principles of Alignment, Repetition, and Contrast

Serif Typefaces	Sans Serif Typefaces
Times New Roman	Arial
Lucida Bright	Lucida Sans
Century Schoolbook	Century Gothic
Palatino	
Garamond	

Figure 3.3 Examples of Serif and Sans Serif Typefaces

assimilation of its contents. This means avoiding overly academic reporting styles and formats, and too much print per page. Figure 3.4 shows an example of a summarized version of an evaluation report that is formatted for easy reading. The headings for different report sections are placed on the left side of the page, and the main points of the text are arranged in bullets down the right side of the page, leaving plenty of white space on each page.

■ **Use columns to make text more inviting.**

Columns give evaluation documents a more professional look. They are commonly used in newspapers and other commercial publications because a shorter line of text is read faster than a full line of text. Columns can be justified or flush left. Left-justified text with a right jagged edge is friendlier, less formal, and adds more white space to the page. Design your evaluation reports, summaries, and newsletters with no more than two or three columns of text.

■ **Use signposts, headers, and/or footers to help readers find their way around, especially in longer reports.**

Organizing elements are essential to help reduce the complexity of and enhance readers' ability to assimilate long evaluation reports. In addition to headers or footers identifying report sections, graphics and creative use of headings can guide the reader through a report. Figure 3.5 shows a one-page excerpt from a lengthy evaluation report. The vertical side headings, different colors for different levels of headings, and bullets were repeated throughout the report to enhance its visual appeal and guide the reader. (To see this figure in color, go to http://www.sagepub.com/escr.)

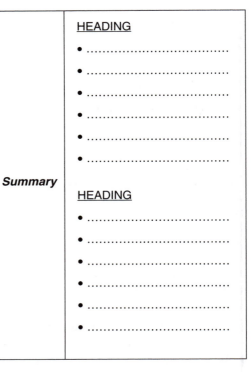

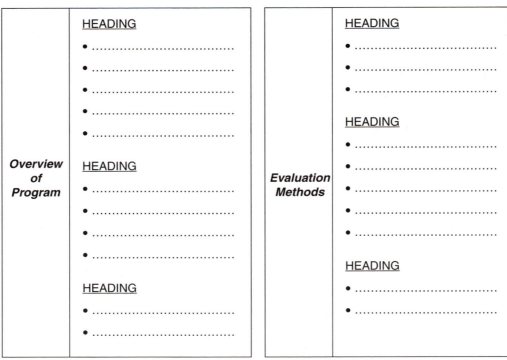

Figure 3.4   Example of Half-Page Report Format

Key Outcomes

Outcomes for Participants (the strongest result of FCL):

The major finding from the 1993 evaluation is that the program appeared to be succeeding in its goals of increasing participants' understanding of leadership and policy issues and methods useful in their resolution, as well as increasing participation in public and family affairs.

In addition to increasing their knowledge and involvement, most participants felt the program was worthwhile and, if given the choice, most would participate in FCL again.

Homemakers experienced the most benefits from participation in FCL. The most meaningful outcomes from participation were increased confidence and improved leadership skills.

Leadership Outcomes:
- Overall, participants indicated moderate to substantial increases in all aspects of leadership skills.

Self-Confidence:
- At least 85 percent of participants reported moderate to substantial increases in self-awareness and personal growth (particularly homemakers), and over 20 percent increased their education since completing FCL (typically CES staff).

Public Affairs Interest and Skills:
- The majority of participants felt their public affairs interests and skills, and their confidence in public affairs abilities improved at least moderately. However, the extent of change in these areas was somewhat less dramatic than the growth in leadership skills.

Participation in Public and Community Affairs:
- Participants in the FCL program tended to be very active in their communities prior to FCL training, and their involvement appears to have increased even further following the program.

The Multiplier Effect:
The evaluation examined the multiplier effect and found that it worked well. The program demonstrates an effective degree of dissemination or "multiplier" effect with apparent ability to produce results at the second and even third level of people trained in the model.

Outcomes for Organizations:
Although not specifically stated, a goal of FCL was to strengthen the partnership organizations in FCL and the relationships between them. The very structure of FCL, the teaming of CES agents and volunteers in training and payback teams brought about a parity in the relationship that hardly existed before.

Figure 3.5   One-Page Excerpt From Lengthy Final Report Showing Creative Use of Headers to Orient Readers

SOURCE: Used with permission of W. K. Kellogg Foundation.

■ **Use clip art or other graphic images to improve the overall look of evaluation documents, convey meaning, and/or reduce complexity.**

Figure 3.6 shows a one-page newsletter article about a regional collaborative in Minnesota that supports youth programs. The article describes the work of the collaborative, evaluation efforts to document attitude changes, and interpretation of findings and action planning with stakeholders. The two photographs depict young people actively involved in two of the programs—one, a summer arts program; and the other, an arts and drug-prevention program themed "Don't Mess Around With Horses." These photographs are both appealing and meaningful—two primary considerations for clip art or graphic images used in evaluation communications. Make sure the images you use specifically relate to the document content and are meaningful for intended audiences. Avoid gratuitous use of readily available clip art or unrelated photographs. (See Chapter 4 for in-depth information on using photography in evaluations.)

■ **Avoid overdesign.**

The easy-to-use features of word-processing programs can at once be an advantage and a liability. It can be tempting to go overboard! Too many design elements can detract, rather than add to, an evaluation document's appeal and readability. Begin with the basic guidance for enhancing your design and layout provided in this section. Add features with an eye to their cumulative effect, and get feedback on the overall look of your piece.

■ **Use a consistent page layout and format for various evaluation documents seen by the same audience.**

If several reports or other written pieces will be produced from your evaluation, format them in the same way. Consistency improves reader comfort, and helps readers find and assimilate information more easily. Carry overall design and color elements from one piece to another. The format might even contain a particular logo, creating an identity for the evaluation project and/or a program or organization.

Tables and Figures

Visual forms of information, such as tables and figures, are commonly used as effective tools for communicating and reporting evaluation findings. They condense information and can leave the audience with a lasting image. If you are making a short presentation or constructing a visual display, the use of tables and figures will allow audiences to quickly absorb a large quantity of data while still imparting the essence of the evaluation findings. Not only can these methods provide a framework or referent for discussing key findings, but visual representations of data can reveal patterns, trends, and relationships that are not apparent in the text, thus allowing for easier comparisons

Several churches have banded together to hold summer arts programs. At left, young people "wear" their masks, the products of one recent handicraft seminar.

REGIONAL NETWORK HELPS YOUTH IN RURAL MINNESOTA FIND HEALTHY FUN

Fighting years of tradition and practice, a region of Minnesota is undergoing a powerful change. Underage drinking and tobacco use, once regarded as a "rite of passage," is gradually being seen instead as a threat to its youth.

This shift has been the work of hundreds of volunteers and every institution from school, church, police, government, even a widows' book club.

Providing the backbone is the Region Nine Prevention and Healthy Communities Network, led by Executive Director Anne Ganey. The Region Nine PHC Network binds together 13 coalitions toward a common goal: decreasing drug, alcohol and tobacco abuse by young people. The staff helps the coalitions with activities that span the gamut from mentoring to garage band concerts to community service stints and provides support and valuable resources.

Picture the region: 72 cities and 147 townships, 45 of which have populations under 1,000, 18 more with populations under 2,500. The area has undergone rapid change since the 1980s farm crisis, which resulted in rapid depopulation, school consolidations and centralization of jobs, services and recreational opportunities.

"We are working on systems change," Ganey said. "A large part of our mission is to help each community partnership tailor programs that will work for them, for their size, their particular population mix and develop new leaders to carry on the work."

Ganey stresses that "this work is not about finding a program that works in one town and then replicating it." Part of the challenge is helping funders understand this.

From its inception 10 years ago, Ganey says Region Nine has always been a science-based program using local data and the community-organizing model." This made being designated as a *Wanted: Solutions for America* site a perfect fit.

"*Wanted* came along when we were beginning to investigate the possibility of working with an evaluator, Laura Bloomberg," Ganey said. "We have great interest in proving scientifically that what we do works. *Wanted* made this possible."

Bloomberg, who has her own consulting firm, has focused her work with the Region Nine PHC Network toward documenting the attitude changes and tying them back to the work being done in the communities.

"There is clearly evidence that youth are making healthier decisions and communities are increasingly aware of the challenges youth face making these decisions," Bloomberg said. "We can definitely chart tremendous progress."

In 12 months, one survey showed 5 percent *more* people believe alcohol abuse among young adults is a moderate to big problem, and 37 percent *more* believed their community partnership efforts were very likely to result in a decrease in alcohol use.

In meetings with the coalitions to discuss survey results, Bloomberg leads members to interpret the data and decide how to use it.

Another result of Region Nine's work is on the enforcement side. The region now has a region-wide drug policy, making enforcement consistent.

For more information go to www.rndc.org

Maple River Community Network held an arts and prevention program involving horses as a medium and a message and called it "Don't Horse Around With Drugs." Here a young participant gets some help with her drawing from one of the program instructors.

Figure 3.6   Example of Newsletter Article With Appealing and Meaningful Photographs

SOURCE: Used with permission of Pew Partnership for Civic Change.

among the data. Audiences are more likely to discuss findings represented in tables and graphics or other visual displays, because this information is quite often more easily assimilated. In this section, we provide an overview of tables and figures (which include graphs, charts, and illustrations), and provide guidance for their development and use.

Tables

Tables present numbers or text in rows and columns to show identifiable relationships and trends. They are convenient for presenting a large quantity of data. Because they emphasize discrete rather than continuous data, tables are not well suited for showing trends or directions in the data. In some ways, then, tables are not predominantly visual—the reader must translate one number into a relationship with every other number. Therefore, tables are most useful when it is important to provide a significant amount of information with great precision in a very small space, as shown in Figure 3.7. This table presents data on several variables: school, grade-level grouping, recommended days of implementation, mean number of days teachers implemented, and percentage of recommended days teachers implemented.

Table 8
Average Number of Days per Week Teachers
Provided Instruction in Reading Curriculum
by School and Grade-Level Group

	Year-End Findings											
	Grade K				Grades 1–2				Grades 3–6			
School	Recommended: 2 days				Recommended: 3 days				Recommended: 4 days			
	N	Mean	SD	%*	N	Mean	SD	%*	N	Mean	SD	%*
A	4	1.88	.25	94%	9	2.44	.53	81%	10	3.35	.67	84%
B	5	2.00	.00	100%	6	2.17	.75	72%	13	3.69	.48	92%
C	2	2.00	.00	100%	8	2.25	.71	75%	9	3.00	1.00	75%
D	3	2.00	.00	100%	5	2.10	.22	70%	4	2.50	1.00	63%
E	5	2.00	.00	100%	9	2.78	.44	93%	9	3.33	.87	83%
F	3	2.00	.00	100%	6	2.50	.55	83%	9	3.11	.78	78%
G	N/A				N/A				3	3.00	.00	75%
	3	1.33	.58	63%	7	2.29	.76	73%	8	2.56	1.05	64%
All Schools	25	1.90	.29	95%	50	2.39	.60	80%	65	3.17	.84	79%

*Percentage of recommended days

Figure 3.7   Example of Table Used to Present Quantitative Data

Tables can also be effective for organizing and displaying text—for example, to provide an overview of program and/or evaluation activities. Follow these guidelines when constructing tables:

Guidelines for Constructing Tables

- Assign each table an Arabic number if you are using several tables.
- Present tables sequentially within the text.
- Always place the title immediately above the table.
- Make each quantitative table self-explanatory by providing titles, keys, labels, and footnotes so that readers can accurately understand and interpret them without reference to the text.
- When a table must be divided so it can be continued on another page, repeat the row and column headings and give the table number at the top/bottom of each new page.

Figures

We use the term "figure" here to denote any chart, graph, or illustration used to convey quantitative or qualitative data in a visual form. Charts and graphs can present statistical and complex data fairly quickly and easily. Illustrations include diagrams, maps, or drawings. Consider the different purposes that each type of figure serves, as shown in Table 3.1.

A *pie chart* is a very simple chart depicting 100% of a variable divided into parts, or "slices," to show relationships of each part to the whole and to the others parts. As shown in Figure 3.8, an extended pie chart can be used to present the findings of a survey question as well as its follow-up question (see Brown, Marks, & Straw, 1997). (To see this figure in color, go to http://www.sagepub.com/escr.)

Table 3.1   Purposes of Different Types of Figures

Figure Type	Purpose
Charts	Depicting processes, elements, roles, or other parts of some larger entity, and its organization or interdependencies
Graphs	Presenting data and relationships that show trends, movements, distributions, and cycles
Illustrations	Conveying a visual representation of ideas that are difficult to express in words in a short period of time or space

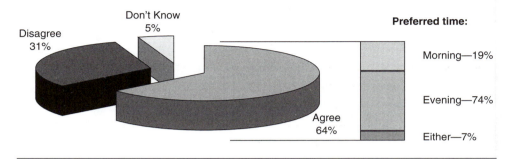

**Parent Opinion About Need for
Additional Parent-Teacher Conference**

Figure 3.8   Example of Extended Pie Chart Showing Responses to Survey
Question and Follow-Up Question

When constructing pie charts, follow these guidelines:

Guidelines for Constructing Pie Charts

- Use six or fewer slices to illustrate information.
- Arrange the slices with the largest or the most important data starting at the 12 o'clock position, and the remaining slices positioned in a clockwise fashion.
- Increase the readability of pie charts by using bright, contrasting colors to emphasize a certain piece of data or by moving a slice out from the circle. (Most computer graphing programs allow you to do this.)
- Label the pie slices on the slices themselves or right next to them.
- If you use three-dimensional pie charts, be aware that distortions of the data are possible because the slices that seem closest to the viewer will be deemed the most important ones.

Bar charts can be quickly constructed and are also easy to understand. They are particularly effective for showing (1) quantities associated with one variable at different times; (2) quantities of different variables for the same period; or (3) quantities of the different parts of a variable that make up the whole (Lannon, 1991). Figure 3.9 illustrates a clustered bar chart to show a three-way comparison (see Bonnet, 1997). (To see this figure in color, go to http://www.sagepub.com/escr.)

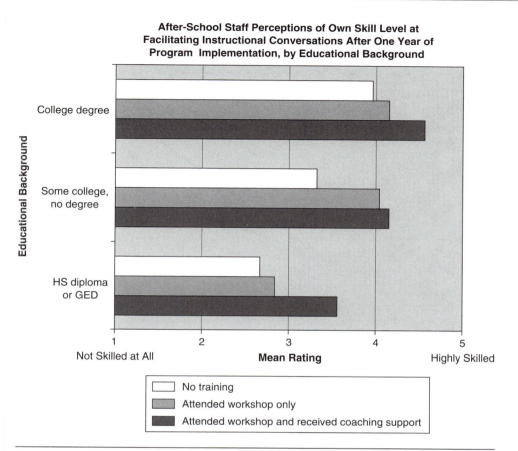

Figure 3.9   Example of Clustered Bar Chart to Show a Three-Way Comparison

When constructing bar charts, follow these guidelines:

Guidelines for Constructing Bar Charts

- Use as few bars as possible. Six is typically considered the maximum unless you are showing data over a 12-month period.
- Emphasize one aspect of the data by changing a bar's color or texture.
- To make the data in the chart easier to comprehend, (a) place the numbers showing each bar's value at the top of the bar or inside it in a contrasting color, or (b) draw horizontal lines across the chart, beginning at each interval of the vertical axis.
- Use patterns of icons or blocks of color to make the image more attractive to the eye. For example, use apples or figures for students to show an increase in student achievement. Most programs allow you to modify the size and shape of the selected images to fit the size of the chart.

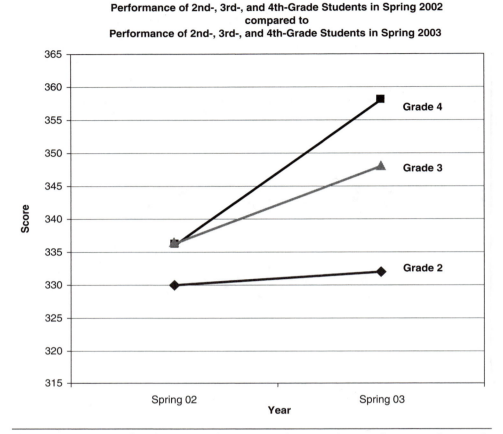

Figure 3.10   Example of Line Graph Distinguishing Student Performance by Grade Level

The *line graph* is an effective tool for conveying two types of information when there are several points that must be plotted or where there are small changes between the points. Data are plotted on the graph to form one or more continuous lines that enable complex quantitative data to become visually understandable. Figure 3.10 shows a line graph distinguishing student performance by grade level. (To see this figure in color, go to http://www.sagepub.com/escr.)

When constructing line graphs, follow these guidelines:

Guidelines for Constructing Line Graphs

- Label the lines rather than using a legend.
- Three lines are the recommended maximum, and each should be a different color if possible, with the most important line being the brightest color.

- If printing in black and white, each line should be a different shape or texture.
- Always title the graph clearly and concisely at the center of the page, above or below the graph.

Figure 3.11 is a form of a line graph that shows change in quantitative data. Both the color and the movement of the lines are used to show mean differences over time (pre-test to post-test, for example) in a group's knowledge about five different skill sets. Each vertical bar depicting one of the five levels of knowledge (from "not yet familiar with concepts" to "fully able to apply") is a different color. Each of the five arrowheads representing the post-test finding for each skill set is shown in a shade of the vertical bar color to which it is closest. (To see this figure in color, go to http://www.sagepub.com/escr.)

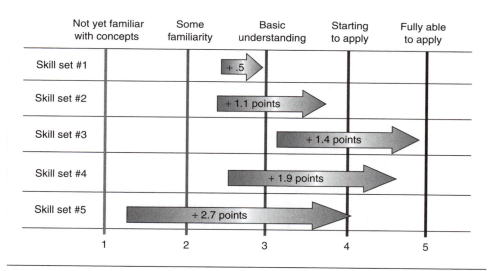

Figure 3.11 Example of Figure to Represent Change in Quantitative Data

SOURCE: Used with permission of Jane Davidson.

Up to this point we have discussed visual forms of representation most useful for presenting quantitative data. Evaluators who wish to visually describe aspects of qualitative data, however, should consider using *illustrations* such as diagrams, flow charts, maps, cartoons, or drawings. Case Example 3.1 describes how the use of illustrations positively affected an audience's understanding and appreciation of a complex and difficult issue.

CASE EXAMPLE 3.1

When Words Alone Can't Get the Job Done

An evaluator was asked to assess the effects of change on individuals within a university department where job descriptions and responsibilities were shifting as a result of the university's reorganization. The evaluator realized that the staff might be hesitant to verbally communicate their reactions and thoughts about the change process through the usual interview process. Therefore, as one of her evaluation methods she asked program staff to draw their images of the "old" organization and what they hoped for in the "new" organization. After participants illustrated their thoughts, she asked them to explain what they had drawn. One year later, near the end of the evaluation study, she went back to each of the participants and showed them their drawings. During this session she asked them to add anything they thought would further the evaluator's understanding of how they experienced the changes that were occurring. For the most part, the drawings depicted people who were confused and concerned, not only about their future but also about the university's.

The evaluator then analyzed the drawings in light of the other data she had collected. When she presented the evaluation findings in a verbal presentation to the university's administration, she showed selected drawings on an overhead projector to help explain what she had found. The reaction of the administrators was one of surprise and realization. They admitted they had not thought out all the implications of the change effort for the people who worked in the unit. Several mentioned that the illustrations confirmed that the changes had indeed had a demoralizing effect on some of the employees. The evaluator believes that, without the drawings, the administrators would not have gained as deep an understanding of the human side of change so quickly. It is unlikely that her words alone, even supported by verbatim quotes from the employees, would have had such an impact.

Figure 3.12 presents an illustration used to depict various stakeholders and their relationship to each other for an after-school enrichment program. Illustrations like this can be created in PowerPoint (see section on verbal presentations in Chapter 4) and shown in a staged presentation to audiences, allowing them to build understanding as each component is added to the figure. The result in this case is a comprehensive view of the program's stakeholders, which in particular, meets the needs of visual learners.

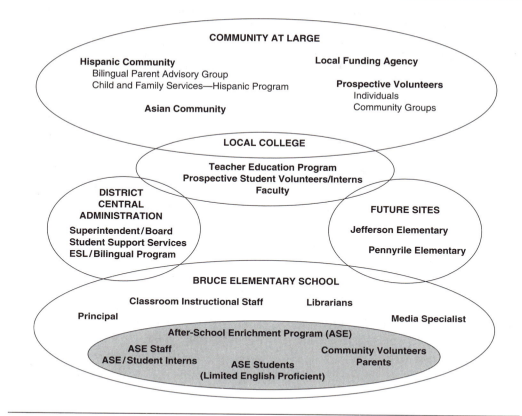

Figure 3.12 Example of an Illustration to Show Comprehensive View of Stakeholders for After-School Program

When creating illustrations, follow these guidelines:

Guidelines for Creating Illustrations

- Keep the illustration as simple as possible—if it needs a lot of explanation, it is probably too complicated.
- Be careful not to over-illustrate within any one communication. Save the use of illustrations for instances where they make a significant contribution to communicating your message.
- Include a key that identifies or defines all the symbols used.
- Depending on its dimensions, present the illustration in a horizontal position for easy reading.
- Provide enough white space around and within the illustration.
- Make sure that the illustration's meaning is clearly described in the text.

⇨ *Implementation Tips for Using Tables and Figures*

- **Think about the essence of the message and the type of presentation that will describe it most accurately and effectively.**

When deciding to use tables and figures, evaluators need to ask themselves, "What am I trying to say with this visual?" The message and the type of data you have determine the type of representation that describes the data most accurately and effectively.

Remember that your evaluation questions can provide a guide for thinking about the information that will be useful to represent in tables and figures. Because these are the major questions you are seeking to answer and those that the stakeholders will be most interested in, it is likely that presenting data in terms of the evaluation questions will be especially effective.

- **Compile all available summarized data.**

To most effectively and efficiently develop tables and figures, it is important to have summarized data readily available. That is, begin organizing descriptions of the program, data summary sheets from surveys and interviews, computer analyses, and so forth as soon as possible after data are collected.

- **Keep your tables and figures simple.**

Wanting to provide as much information as possible in tables and figures often leads evaluators to overload the table or figure. This is especially true with figures that try to describe program theories, models of implementation, linkages between various program components, and complex quantitative findings. Evaluators need to carefully consider the primary audiences for each table or figure, weighing the effects of creating a complex table or figure, which may inhibit rather than enhance understanding. When several layers of information are required to illustrate a finding or circumstance accurately, consider presenting the information in stages (using a PowerPoint presentation, for example) building in complexity with each piece that is shown.

- **Include headings and titles for all tables and figures.**

If you are using several tables and figures, assign a number to each one throughout the text. Each table or figure should have a title and clear headings describing the type of data it reports. Generally, tables and figures should be as self-explanatory as possible. Some readers will focus primarily on the tables and figures in a report.

■ **If including tables and figures in the text, describe the information to be found in each.**

When you insert a table or figure into the text, also include an explanation and/or interpretation of its meaning. Make sure that the visual is as close as possible to the text explaining it. Never assume that a reader will fully understand the visual and its implications. Given people's different learning styles, some readers will skip the visuals. If no written explanation is presented, they may miss an important finding.

■ **Construct the tables and figures first, then write the text.**

Producing effective tables and figures results in your thoroughly understanding the trends and relationships among the variables in question. When these are clearly understood, it is easier to write the supporting interpretations and explanations of the findings.

■ **Make tables and figures accessible within a report.**

Because the purpose of using visuals is to make findings more understandable, tables and figures should be easily accessible within a formal report. The reader who wants to think more about a visual or share it with someone should be able to quickly locate it within the report. If there are more than five tables or figures, they should be listed in a table of figures by title, along with the page number where each can be found. This list immediately follows the table of contents for the text.

■ **Do not overuse color.**

The use of color in visuals is an area where evaluators should be cautious. In the desire to make visuals eye-catching and appealing it is tempting to use a variety of colors. A few carefully chosen colors are much more effective. Strong primary colors used consistently throughout a series of visuals best command an audience's attention (Parker, 1992). However, more than three colors in a visual can be confusing to readers.

■ **Allow sufficient time for developing tables and figures.**

For most types of evaluation data, a table or figure is essential for effectively communicating findings. Remember that several drafts typically are necessary to produce high-quality tables and figures. Evaluators need to plan for the cost and time it takes to develop tables and figures—particularly if expert in-house designers or software are not readily available.

■ **Always present tables and figures to outside audiences with a verbal or written explanation.**

If disseminated without a written or verbal explanation, tables and figures can be misused and misinterpreted. Outside audiences may not understand the statistics, scaling methods used, or relationships among sets of data. The result may be oversimplification of the data, leading to interpretations and conclusions that could adversely affect program participants and other stakeholders.

Writing

Almost nothing is more important to written communication than clarity and readability. Writing in a clear, jargon-free, reader-focused style is essential to help assure that audiences understand and use the information conveyed in evaluation products. Without clear and effective communication, even the most well-designed and implemented evaluation's impact will be weakened (Kingsbury & Hedrick, 1994).

When producing evaluation products, most evaluators draw on whatever training in writing they have received in undergraduate and graduate courses. This may or may not be sufficient to make them good writers of evaluation communications and reports. The U.S. Department of Health and Human Services Office of Inspector General believes that the overall success of an audit or evaluation depends on the evaluator's ability to communicate the results in a clear and concise manner. Toward this end they provide training for their auditors, inspectors, and evaluators in communications courses that cover report writing and editing, and writing to the point (Office of Inspector General, 2004). The following implementation tips provide ideas that you can use immediately to improve your writing (but should not be considered a substitute for courses or workshops that you might also take). Remember that clarifying your writing has a major benefit: in the process you have the opportunity to clarify your thinking. Writing and thinking processes are inextricably linked.

Implementation Tips for Writing

■ **Avoid jargon and technical terms that your audience may not understand.**

One respondent to our survey on evaluators' communicating and reporting practices (Torres et al., 1997) put it this way:

> I do not speak in tongues but provide basic information which is not dressed in the cloak of sophisticated statistical language. What is reported must be almost instantly comprehended.

Not surprisingly, terminology that is unfamiliar to audiences will interfere with their understanding. Complex terminology can appear in evaluation reports in two ways. Evaluators sometimes use it to describe qualitative or quantitative methodologies, or they may use it to describe unique aspects of a particular program.

Madison (2000) describes the successful evolution of language in evaluations: "The language used in evaluating social programs encompasses the language of social policy, which is interpreted into the technical language of evaluation, which is then translated into language to meet the informational needs of multiple audiences" (p. 17). Evaluators must take care that these translations occur and should carefully scrutinize each written communication to reduce its complexity while bearing in mind its intended audience. Terminology specific to a program is appropriate for a detailed final report read primarily by program participants, whereas a summary of the same evaluation findings presented in a bulletin and distributed to other audiences should be written in simpler terms. The choice of language can directly affect audiences' perceptions of a program, and ultimately, decisions they make on the basis of the evaluation results.

Choosing the appropriate style of writing requires that evaluators know their different audiences. The Program Evaluation Standard on Human Interactions (P4) provides guidance to "make every effort to understand the culture, social values, and language differences of participants" (Joint Committee on Standards for Educational Evaluation, 1994). As stated earlier, we typically identify audiences at the outset of an evaluation. Subsequent experiences with audiences who are also stakeholders can help us know how to best communicate with them in writing. One option is to work with stakeholders and other audiences to derive clear, understandable language that is both true to sophisticated concepts and comprehensible to various groups. Another possibility is to provide a highly visible section that defines key terms (e.g., inside the front cover of a report). (Chapter 6 presents more information on communicating and reporting for diverse audiences.)

■ **Adopt a direct, conversational style.**

Except for evaluation reports published in scholarly journals, a conversational style is more appropriate than an academic style for most of our audiences. Some evaluators write in both venues and should take care that they do not slip back into an academic style when writing for stakeholders and other audiences.

Try to write in the language you would use in a serious conversation (Scott, 1989). This typically means using only as many words as necessary to make your point. For instance, limiting consecutive prepositional phrases can usually make your writing more concise. The next two tips on long sentences and passive voice describe other ways to keep written communications to the point.

■ **Check the clarity of long sentences.**

Long sentences are more difficult for readers to comprehend. Even when evaluators know exactly what they are trying to say, their writing can be confusing to readers if their sentences contain too many ideas. One helpful technique is to read aloud what you have written. Convoluted writing is sometimes more evident to the ear than to the eye.

You will find that some 25- or 30-word sentences are understandable. They should, however, be interspersed with shorter sentences. Variety in sentence length creates a rhythm and makes your writing more interesting to read. A document replete with short sentences sounds choppy; one containing only long sentences is difficult to follow. Finally, consider using bullets or other conventions to break up long sentences, e.g., using (1), (2), (3), and so on to number common elements within the sentence.

■ **Limit the use of passive voice.**

Writing in the active voice makes information clear, direct, and accessible to the reader. It helps keep writing more concise because it generally requires fewer words. There are, however, some instances where the use of passive voice is appropriate, such as when the subject of a sentence is clearly implied or unimportant. You should limit your use of passive voice to those instances. The following guidelines are designed to help you express active voice in your writing.

Guidelines for Writing in Active Voice

- Place the subject matter of the sentence at the beginning of the sentence.
- Place the verb close to the subject.
- Avoid making the subject matter the object of some action.
- Avoid "-ion" words (Scott, 1989; Williams, 1989).

■ **Use word-processing tools for spelling, grammar, and writing style.**

Word-processing programs feature writing tools such as a spelling and grammar editor and a thesaurus. Spelling editors check documents for misspelled words, duplicate words, and irregular capitalization. Although these programs will catch most errors, you must still proofread documents to find instances where a misspelled word in one context is a correctly spelled one in another (e.g., from/form, word/work).

Grammar checkers scan documents for grammar and style errors by looking for certain word patterns. Typically, they flag long sentences, passive voice, consecutive prepositional phrases, split infinitives, and consecutive nouns. For some errors, these programs suggest revisions. Most programs also allow for customizing the editing style the program uses (e.g., scientific writing, fiction, or informal memos).

A word-processing thesaurus provides synonyms and antonyms for words within your document. This program is especially useful for finding words to simplify the language of your document and to combat repetitiveness.

■ To improve your writing, write and rewrite.

Almost nothing is more time consuming than writing and rewriting. Yet nothing is more effective to make you a better writer. Rewriting should be done based on constructive feedback. One method is to have someone else review part of your writing so that you can get ideas about how to improve it. Ideally, the reviewer will give you specific suggestions for how convoluted sentences, passive voice, or unappealing tone can be rewritten. A reviewer might also provide advice about choice of vocabulary for specific audiences (avoiding jargon and defining acronyms) and organizing content for maximum clarity and impact. Stay open and try not to be too sensitive about the feedback you receive; the focus should be on producing the best written communication for its intended audiences.

Another way to revise a document is to use a grammar editor included in word-processing programs, as noted above. Most feature an interactive mode that allows you to make changes in your document while you consider the revisions suggested by the program.

Most writers will see an improvement in their work as soon as they spend some time on revisions. At this point, they begin to realize the biggest time-saver: an improvement in the quality of first drafts.

■ Use collaborative writing to stimulate creativity and reduce individual workloads.

Many evaluations are conducted by teams of evaluators whose members can help produce written communication about the evaluation. Collaborative writing can result in a better product. Discussion and feedback among team members can stimulate thinking, and a team member may have a particular expertise that especially enhances the written document, for example, extensive knowledge of the preferred language and structure of communications to particular audiences (e.g., policy makers, program managers, media representatives, different ethnic groups). Dividing the writing task among several persons can make it easier.

However, collaborative writing can result in a disjointed, incoherent document if the team does not undertake a specific strategy for working together effectively. At least three approaches are possible (Berger, 1993). First, an evaluation team can produce a team draft in work sessions where group dynamics stimulate creativity. Second, as suggested above, the team can assign parts of the document to different members. One person or a smaller team then edits and revises the document. Third, one team member writes the first draft and the others critique it, submitting changes, additions, and deletions as they see fit. With any of these approaches, the team must take care to ensure that the final product has a consistent style, is logically presented, and does not have repetitions or omissions of important information. (See Figure 3.22 for a report checklist that can be used to delegate, coordinate, and monitor the progress of multiple authors to a report.)

- **Allow sufficient time for writing several drafts, getting feedback, and proofreading.**

   Once individual evaluators or evaluation teams have given their best effort to producing a written communication, it should still be considered a draft. Evaluators must allocate time for obtaining feedback, making changes to the document, and proofreading the final copy. Stakeholders should be asked to review the document for two reasons: First, to make the document more relevant to its intended audiences (i.e., by examining it for clarity, style, and choice of words); and second, to inform them of its contents and give them an opportunity to request revisions, particularly when evaluation findings will also be presented in verbal presentations or working sessions to these and other audiences.

Short Written Communications

Short communications like memos, e-mail, and postcards are vital tools for establishing and maintaining ongoing contact among evaluators, clients, and other stakeholders. Brief, sometimes frequent communications about the evaluation are useful for reaching a wide range of individuals and groups. They can elicit responses to evaluation activities and findings, and help establish rapport. Further, they provide a record of events, activities, and decisions about a program, its evaluation, or both. This record can also be the basis for more formal reports later on. Short written pieces can be used

- At the beginning, to communicate with stakeholders about an evaluation's purpose and activities.
- Throughout the evaluation process, to elicit feedback and discussion and to inform stakeholders of continuing activities and/or interim findings.
- At the end, to disseminate key findings, information on important issues, and/or next steps.

The focused content of short communications makes for easy reading and assimilation of information. Flexible formats can heighten visual attraction and attention through the use of color and interesting layouts with varied headings and graphics. Information clearly and succinctly presented in these ways is more likely to be remembered. Further, short communications can be sequenced so that they present limited, simplified information early in the evaluation and then build to longer, more complex communications (Macy, 1982). Combined with frequent phone contacts and discussions about their contents, memos, e-mail, and postcards can facilitate timely interaction with clients and stakeholders. The following sections discuss how each type of short written communication can be used during various stages of an evaluation.

Memos and E-mail

The most common short form of written communication is a memorandum, or memo for short. A memo conveys a select amount of information addressed to one or more readers in a consistent format. It tends to be crisp and brisk in tone, lacking the social conventions of a letter. Because of its brevity (from a paragraph or two to three or four pages), it is often used for frequent, ongoing communication among individuals, teams, programs, or organizations.

The format of a memo can vary according to individual needs or organizational style, but typically a memo has these components:

- Date it is written
- Names of the addressees
- Name of the sender(s)
- A "cc:" notation indicating the memo's carbon copy distribution to persons other than the addressees—often, colleagues of the sender, program staff or directors, funders, or other stakeholders in the evaluation process
- Subject line with a short phrase about the topic or purpose of the memo
- Text or contents
- An "encl:" notation indicating any enclosures or attachments

Also, tables and figures can be incorporated into the text of a memo to further facilitate audience comprehension and use of the evaluation information.

The familiarity of this format and its condensed length make memos easy to reproduce and distribute. Most memos are now sent via e-mail, either in the text of the e-mail or as an e-mail attachment, but can also be faxed or mailed. By using communication mediums like memos and e-mail, you can capitalize on routine communication channels and facilitate integration of the evaluation with the ongoing work of the organization. You can use short written communications to

- Update audiences about the progress of the evaluation, and/or invite them to participate in upcoming evaluation activities.
- Inform about and request support for various evaluation activities. (See Figure 3.13, e-mail flyer; to view this figure in color, go to http://www .sagepub.com/escr.)
- Recap or follow up on decisions or points made during a telephone or face-to-face meeting.
- Solicit feedback on the evaluation plan, data collection instruments, particular findings, or a draft of the evaluation report.
- Communicate a summary of the evaluation's findings and recommendations.
- Communicate about how the evaluation's recommendations will be used and/or how an evaluation's recommendations are being implemented.
- Orient recipients on how to use, interpret, and/or work with an evaluation document that is sent with the memo or e-mail (see Figure 3.14).

Guidelines for Using E-mail

- Make sure you have recipients' current e-mail addresses. Consider setting up a group contact list, and keep it updated.
- Try to keep what you say to one computer screen page—approximately 25 lines of text. Consider sending lengthier documents as attachments.
- Use fairly terse prose—but don't be too blunt. Use constructive and respectful language and avoid any semblance of blaming or hostility.
- Review your e-mails before sending them. Read the e-mail from the perspective of the recipient.
- If you want to emphasize certain words or phrases, use HTML formatting (color, bold, italics, etc.), or use various forms of punctuation with regular type. Use all capital letters sparingly, as they connote that you are shouting.
- Add a subject line that pertains to the e-mail body to get people in the right frame of mind to open and read your message.
- Carefully consider which stakeholders should be copied on the e-mail message.
- Keep a log of the e-mails you send to remind you of what communication has taken place.

- If the message is particularly urgent or is time-sensitive, consider labeling it as a "high priority" (if that option is available with your e-mail software). Be careful not to overuse this feature, though.
- Request a return receipt to be notified when the recipient has received your message. (Note that recipients' software must support this feature and the recipient has to have enabled it.)
- Consider including a disclaimer at the bottom of all e-mail messages to provide some protection against misuse of your e-mails.
- Install and frequently update the latest virus protection software on your computer.

In addition, e-mail communications are particularly well suited for

- Asking primary stakeholders questions as they arise during the evaluation.
- Informing stakeholders that the evaluation has been completed.
- Transmitting draft and final versions of evaluation documents or information about where they may find the evaluation's results (see Figure 3.15).

Figure 3.13 Example of E-mail in Flyer Format to Announce/Remind About Focus Group

Memo

Research, Evaluation, and
Organizational Learning

To: Coaches, John, Christine

From: Research, Evaluation, & Organizational Learning (Cindy, Ann, Jason)

CC: George, Jerry, Kim

Date: 9/17/04

Re: 03–04 Evaluation Findings

Here are two versions of the 03-04 evaluation findings to be read in preparation for the coaches' meeting on 9/19/04.

For each school there is a separate narrative report.

The 11 × 17 sheets summarize findings across all of the schools, and present an initial set of questions to consider in terms of implications.

Please read the report for your school, and then review the large sheets to see the findings on the other schools.

As a final step in preparation for the meeting, review the implication questions that are presented. These are not necessarily exhaustive. What other questions come to mind?

Don't hesitate to call or e-mail us if you have questions in the meantime.

Figure 3.14   *Cover Memo Accompanying Evaluation Findings and Instructing Recipients How to Prepare for Meeting to Discuss Implications*

Using e-mail to communicate and report an evaluation's activities, progress, and/or findings has the following advantages:

- By saving paper and distribution expenses, e-mail is an inexpensive way to get information out to a large number of people in a timely way.
- E-mails are short, take little time to write, and can keep stakeholders well informed and involved in the evaluation.
- The body of an e-mail can be formatted as a memo; it can also contain pictures and be formatted using color and graphics (see Figure 3.13).
- Recipients can read e-mail at their own convenience.
- E-mails can be printed out and/or stored electronically for future reference.

From: Department Director
Sent: Tuesday, November 4, 2004 8:52 AM
Subject: Final Evaluation Report

To all the fine folks in the Corporate Education, Development, and Training Department and others who participated in our evaluation effort:

A major part of the evaluation process is sharing the results with those who participated so that you know your efforts were of value and useful. The final report from our evaluation is now available for your viewing at the following URLs:

Final Report (full text): http://abc.abc

Executive Summary: http://def.def

The entire report is interesting and noteworthy. You will want to pay particular attention to the recommendations and suggestions for future actions.

A note of interest: Our evaluation consultant made it a point to mention that we are truly pioneers with respect to our work in this area. She emphasized that very few organizations have attempted to build a comprehensive evaluation system that integrates how they do their work with the organization's larger mission and goals. The consultant further commended our efforts to develop action plans for each of the recommendations. I think her comments highlight our dedication to taking risks, being innovative, and becoming a learning organization.

Because this effort is not a one-time event, nor is there an "evaluation finish line," stay tuned, as there will be several initiatives stemming from this assessment and initial work.

The Evaluation Team would like to extend our sincere thanks to everyone involved for their feedback, participation, and dedication to this effort.

Thank you again,

The Evaluation Team

Figure 3.15   Example of E-mail Used to Communicate Appreciation, Location of Final Report, and Next Steps After an Evaluation Has Been Completed

Implementation Tips for Memos and E-mail

■ **Before deciding to use e-mail, determine stakeholders' and clients' e-mail access.**

Some organizations may not have e-mail; people in various positions within an organization often do not have access to computers; and in many parts of the world, e-mail is either unavailable or expensive. And even if evaluation stakeholders have e-mail access, it does not necessarily mean that they use it. Many people, especially those who are not accessing e-mail in a work environment, do not read e-mail every day and therefore might not see your message in time for it to be useful. Consider the audience to whom you are sending e-mail messages and determine the frequency with which they are likely to check their e-mail. During first contacts with evaluation stakeholders, ask about their use of e-mail and its suitability as a means of communication. If necessary, use alternative methods such as telephone or fax.

■ **Determine whether to send a memo within the text of an e-mail, as an e-mail attachment, or on hard copy.**

As mentioned earlier, the text of an e-mail can be formatted to look like a typical memo. Alternatively you can create a memo, save it in a file, and then attach it to an e-mail. You can also fax a memo, and send it via the postal service or an organization's internal mail system. Although there are no absolutely clear guidelines about which method to use, there are some things to consider. The more formal or significant (in content) a memo is, the more likely you may choose to send it as an e-mail attachment or in a hard copy form. Routine communications about evaluation processes and activities are typically communicated in the text of e-mails.

E-mail attachments require a little more effort from recipients, who must open them up and print them out. This, however, yields a hard copy of the memo and a traditional, formal record of it. The memo can be saved on recipients' computers for future reference; but this also means that it can easily be altered. For highly sensitive information or in politically charged situations, you may choose to send your memo via fax or mail.

Sometimes you will write memos to accompany evaluation documents, and both can be sent via e-mail if the documents can easily be opened and printed by the recipients, although some documents are best transmitted via mail (e.g., those that are bound, have special formatting that may be lost, are formatted on paper larger than 8.5 × 11 inches, or are color coded).

■ **Beware of how easy it is to use memos and e-mail.**

When using memos and e-mail to communicate and report an evaluation's process and findings, be sure to give your reader at least a brief context. A challenge with using short communications for evaluation purposes is that messages can lack information about the context in which to interpret the message. In a conversation, there is at least some minimum of shared context. For example, you might be in the same physical location. Even on the phone there is the commonality of time.

Carefully consider which stakeholders should be copied on your memos and e-mails. Think about which stakeholders should be aware of the information you are communicating, and any implications or consequences. It is easy to inadvertently copy someone you did not intend to, and it is also easy to forget to copy those you did.

When writing memos and e-mail messages, remember to think about how your message will be heard. Since memos and e-mails are less formal than a letter, it is especially important to write with a professional tone. These are one-way communications, and as a result, there is a greater chance for misunderstandings and misinterpretations.

Remember that e-mails and files attached to them constitute legal documents, and can be used in a court of law. Do not say anything in e-mail that you would not want retrieved. Every word may be scrutinized as if it were a formal written document. Though messages may appear to have been deleted from a computer, they can remain in the system's backup files. Therefore, try not to use e-mail to communicate sensitive or emotional topics if you are concerned with how a message might be received and used.

▥ To the extent possible, follow up on memos and e-mail you send.

The popularity of memos and e-mail can be a disadvantage. Either can get little attention if they are among many that stakeholders receive. And, without some further contact, you may never know if recipients received them. Although the postal system tends to be reliable and you can know if a fax was transmitted successfully, within large organizations these communications may not ultimately make it to the intended recipient. The service of most e-mail systems is interrupted at one time or another. Although dependent on the e-mail software both you and your recipients are using, requesting a "return receipt" for e-mails sent can be helpful. You can also request in the text of your e-mail that the recipients let you know they have received it successfully.

▥ Consider including a disclaimer at the bottom of all e-mail messages.

It is possible for e-mail messages to be modified by receivers who might then send them on to others. If you are concerned about a highly political or controversial evaluation, you may want to consider communicating and reporting using methods that protect the content from being altered. Another option for some level of protection is to include a disclaimer at the bottom of all your e-mail messages. As shown in Figure 3.16, disclaimers can warn recipients about receiving the e-mail in error, use of the e-mail, transmission of viruses, and/or liability for errors and omissions.

If you received this e-mail in error, please notify the sender by e-mail at the above e-mail address immediately. This e-mail transmission may contain confidential information for the exclusive use of the individual(s) or entity to whom it is intended, even if addressed incorrectly. Please delete it from your files if you are not the intended recipient. Thank you for your cooperation.

The information, materials, or attachments embodied in this e-mail are considered confidential. Recipients understand that this correspondence is privileged and its contents should be protected. Aside from the intended recipients, it is strictly forbidden to copy, print, discuss, reproduce, forward, or distribute the contents of this e-mail without permission.

If you have received this e-mail in error, please immediately delete it, notify the sender, and understand you are bound to keep the contents confidential.

This message contains confidential information and is intended only for the individual named. If you are not the named addressee you should not disseminate, distribute, or copy this e-mail. Please notify the sender immediately by e-mail if you have received this e-mail by mistake and delete this e-mail from your system. If you are not the intended recipient, you are notified that disclosing, copying, distributing, or taking any action in reliance on the contents of this information is strictly prohibited.

E-mail transmission cannot be guaranteed to be secure or error-free, as information could be intercepted, corrupted, lost, destroyed, arrive late or incomplete, or contain viruses. The sender therefore does not accept liability for any errors or omissions in the contents of this message that arise as a result of e-mail transmission. If verification is required please request a hard-copy version.

Figure 3.16   Examples of E-mail Disclaimer Statements

CAUTIONS FOR MEMOS AND E-MAIL

■ **Despite your best efforts, short communications can be misinterpreted.**

As with any other written communication that does not include audio or visual contact, there is still the possibility that e-mail messages can be misinterpreted, leading to misunderstandings, as well as a lack of response or follow-up.

■ **Recipients of your e-mail might not read messages from those they do not know, or whose e-mail addresses they do not recognize.**

Given the proliferation of junk e-mails, also known as "spam," and e-mail viruses, this is a legitimate concern for evaluators wishing to use e-mail as a communicating and reporting strategy. If your address or name is not familiar, recipients may delete your e-mail message without reading it. Also, in fear of viruses, some e-mail users decline to open attachments, regardless of who has sent them.

Postcards

A postcard is a quarter-page to half-page document on heavy paper most often sent through traditional mail channels, but may also be attached to an e-mail. As with a memo, it conveys a limited amount of information in a confined length. Dentists, doctors, and other health practitioners routinely use postcards to remind clients of upcoming appointments. Retailers use postcards to inform the public of sales events. Invitations to events hosted by all types of organizations are frequently sent on postcards. They are a convenient, inexpensive, and sometimes catchy way of soliciting participation and maintaining contact. The novelty of receiving a postcard related to an evaluation may catch stakeholders' attention and make the information it conveys more memorable. A color postcard, possibly including graphics, can be inviting to read—especially in the midst of the multitude of e-mails that many audiences receive daily. Also, audiences may associate the format of the postcard with quick, concise communication, requiring little effort for a response (Parker, 1992). The following implementation tips describe three uses of postcards for evaluation communications.

Implementation Tips for Postcards

■ **Use postcards to maintain contact with stakeholders and build interest in the evaluation.**

Figure 3.17 shows a series of six postcards used by an evaluation team over six months. These monthly postcard alerts were designed to keep stakeholders engaged, build anticipation for the full report, and encourage evaluative thinking.

January: Postcard sent after initial evaluation workshop involving key stakeholders:

> *The standards for the profession call for evaluations to be judged by **their utility, feasibility, propriety**, and **accuracy**.*

February: Postcard describing the "evaluation version of the Genesis story":

> *In the beginning God created the heaven and the earth.*
>
> *And God saw everything that he made. "Behold," God said, "it is very good." And the evening and the morning were the sixth day.*
>
> *And on the seventh day God rested from all His work. His archangel came then unto Him asking, "God, how do you know that what you have created is 'very good'? What are your criteria? On what data do you base your judgment? Just exactly what results were you expecting to attain? And aren't you a little close to the situation to make a fair and unbiased evaluation?"*
>
> *God thought about these questions all that day and His rest was greatly disturbed. On the eighth day God said, "Lucifer, go to hell."*
>
> *Thus was evaluation born in a blaze of glory . . . . (Utilization-Focused Evaluation, Patton)*

March: Postcard providing excerpts from interview data collection:

> *Striving for balance.*
>
> *Interviews are underway; perspectives vary. Here are two examples:*
>
> *"I look forward to attending the program. The sessions are always interesting and I get so much out of it every time."*
>
> *"One word—boring. It's just so boring."*

April: Postcard providing update on survey data collection:

> *The survey is now completed—with a 79% response rate.*
>
> - *39% rated the program very helpful*
> - *42% somewhat helpful*
> - *11% not too helpful*
> - *8% not at all helpful*
>
> *The full analysis will show what categories of participants found the program more or less helpful—and why they rated it as they did.*

May: Postcard reporting on themes emerging from the data analysis:

> *A major theme in the analysis is **responsiveness**.*
>
> *Sample quotes:*
>
> - *"From the beginning the staff have been very open to feedback about how to improve things and relate to our concerns."*
> - *"Our questions are taken seriously. The staff keep telling us to let them know what we want and they really do respond."*
> - *"I think the staff get off track by always trying to do what people say they want. They're staff. They should know what we need to learn."*
>
> *The full report will present eight major themes from the interviews and relate those results to the survey data.*

Figure 3.17   Series of Monthly Postcard Updates

SOURCE: Used with permission of Michael Patton.

June: Postcard alerting clients about upcoming evaluation meeting and draft report dissemination:

> *In two weeks you'll get a draft copy of the report in preparation for our meeting together to review results on June 28.*
>
> *As you read, keep in mind the evaluation's utility standard:*
>
> *An evaluation should serve the practical information needs of intended users.*
>
> *You are the primary intended users. We'll need your help in interpreting the findings and generating useful recommendations.*

Figure 3.17 *(Continued)*

■ **Use postcards to invite stakeholders to evaluation meetings or events, and/or remind them of data collection or other upcoming activities.**

Figure 3.18 shows the front and back of a postcard used to remind evaluation participants to return a survey. It contains graphics to add interest and could be printed in color or on colored paper to attract attention. Note that the e-mail shown in Figure 3.13 could also be sent as a postcard.

■ **Use postcards to solicit reactions to preliminary findings.**

Requests for reactions to preliminary data or findings can be communicated using a postcard during the evaluation's data collection and/or analysis phases. Doing so can (1) establish stakeholder involvement in drawing conclusions and making recommendations and (2) help detect information that might be controversial, incomplete, or inconsistent.

One strategy is to communicate a key finding, direct quote, or result from preliminary analyses using a postcard like the one shown in Figure 3.19. Here stakeholders are asked to record their reactions on the postcard and then return it using the address label provided. Using this method, you can (1) gain a better understanding of various stakeholders' perspectives, including the meaning and importance they associate with the issue or finding; and (2) facilitate their involvement by providing data or information that is palatable because of its clarity and brevity.

Be aware, though, that a postcard will be viewed (intentionally or unintentionally) by a number of persons other than its recipient, if it is distributed through the regular mail or an organization's internal mail system. For soliciting feedback on controversial or confidential information, distributing the postcards in an envelope or in an e-mail text is a better choice.

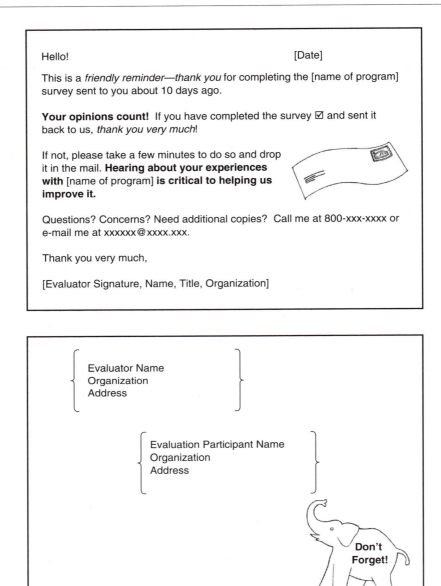

Figure 3.18 Back and Front of Example Postcard Reminder to Return Survey

Interim Reports

Interim reports present partial evaluation findings. They are typically short reports, but can be of considerable size in the case of multiyear, multisite, and/or very comprehensive evaluations. They are almost always produced in

[Date]

Dear [Stakeholder/Evaluation Participant Name]:

Progress on the evaluation is going well! As you are aware, currently we are interviewing staff in _____ about _____.

One of the themes that is emerging from the interviews is the notion that

_____

One person put it this way: "_____

_____."

Any thoughts, reactions, or comments on this? Please write in the space below. Slip this postcard into an envelope, and use the label attached below to send it back to me. Your reaction:

_____

_____

_____

Thanks for your continued interest and cooperation!

[*Evaluator Signature*]

[Evaluator Name]
[Evaluation Title]

[Removable Return Label With Evaluator Name/Address]

P.S. To maintain the anonymity of your response, peel the address label off the back of this postcard.

Figure 3.19   Example of Postcard for Soliciting Stakeholder Feedback on Emerging Findings

anticipation of a more comprehensive report to be made available later. Further, they are typically planned at the outset of the evaluation. The scheduling of interim reports is usually dictated by

- The life cycle of the program
- When certain data collection activities can and will be completed
- Specific decision-making needs of clients and stakeholders

Although interim findings, conclusions, interpretations, and/or recommendations can be presented in short communication formats, some clients and stakeholders will expect a more formal report at this time. In these cases, an interim report can look much like a comprehensive final report, fully addressing the program's context and the evaluation's background and methodology.

Much of the information in the section that follows on final reports is relevant to formal, lengthy interim reports.

Regardless of their format, interim reports are important because they help integrate evaluation activities and findings with key stages in the life of a program or organization. Interim reports often provide findings on program implementation, and can alert clients and stakeholders to important issues requiring their attention. Without successful implementation, it is unreasonable to expect many of an intervention's intended outcomes to occur. And increasingly, funders who typically focused primarily on outcomes are recognizing the importance of understanding implementation issues and progress early in a program's life cycle.

⇨ *Implementation Tips for Interim Reports*

■ **Begin planning for interim reports at the outset of the evaluation to meet early reporting deadlines.**

Every effort should be made to deliver interim reports on time. The life cycle of a program is likely to be such that, for evaluation findings to be most useful, they must be available at a particular time. Typically, these factors are taken into consideration when schedules for interim reports are established. Nonetheless, the scheduled date for an evaluation's first interim report may be relatively soon after the evaluation has begun. Without advance planning, you could easily miss this date.

■ **Consider an informal presentation of findings rather than a formal interim report.**

Producing formal written reports can take more time than is available, if your evaluation is going to meet client and stakeholder needs for interim findings. Consider presenting quantitative findings in tables and graphs and qualitative findings in a bulleted format, rather than taking the time to develop a formal report. This can be especially appropriate for internal evaluations, and/or when there is little risk of misinterpretation. Presenting these findings in a working session to help clients and stakeholders understand and interpret the findings can be especially effective. Case Example 3.2 describes an internal evaluation where implementation findings were presented via a working session as soon as they had been summarized into tables and bulleted lists.

CASE EXAMPLE 3.2

"Just-in-Time" Reporting of Interim Findings

The internal evaluation group of a nonprofit educational agency was conducting an implementation and outcome evaluation of an educational reform initiative in six urban elementary schools. Data collection included principal interviews conducted in November and April, mid- and year-end teacher surveys, and ongoing staff developer reports of teacher progress with classroom implementation. Outcome findings would be based on spring-to-spring comparisons of student achievement using a time series design. These data would not be available until the early fall of the subsequent school year.

Among other responsibilities, three evaluation staff members were assigned to this project. It was crucial for program staff to get a sense of implementation progress during the year so that adjustments and/or additional support could be provided to the schools. On the other hand, the evaluation staff would not have been able to produce a formal, comprehensive interim report in time for the findings to meet this need. Alternatively, in late January they produced tables summarizing the responses to the midyear teacher implementation survey, an outline of staff development provided to date, and bulleted lists summarizing principals' and staff developers' assessments of implementation progress.

Program staff and grade-level teacher representatives had been involved in the design and some of the data collection, and did not require much explanation of the instruments or presentation of the data. The summary documents were delivered via an e-mail attachment approximately one week before the working session to discuss them was to occur. During that week the evaluators reviewed the findings and developed a tentative list of conclusions. At the working session, the findings were briefly reviewed to check for understanding within the group. Then, the evaluators presented their tentative list of conclusions, invited discussion, and asked the group to revise the list as appropriate. Once consensus was reached around conclusions for each aspect of implementation, the group discussed implications of the findings and developed a set of actions to be taken. The result was an action plan with its contents prioritized in terms of need for immediate, short-term, or longer-term attention.

■ **Use a style and format for the interim report that make its contents easy to assimilate.**

The Joint Committee's (1994) *The Program Evaluation Standards* offers this guideline in support of the standard on report clarity: "Keep the presentation of reports as brief as possible, simple and direct, and focused upon addressing the evaluation questions" (p. 49). We feel this guideline is particularly applicable to interim reports. They should be presented in a style and format that maximize the likelihood that clients and stakeholders will read and assimilate their contents. Figure 3.20 shows a five-page interim report from the U.S. Department of Education. It is formatted with wide margins and two levels of headings to guide readers. Color is used to set off the title and subtitle of the report, as well as the first letter of each major heading. The text includes bulleted lists. Notice that the first page presents a summary of findings. The next several pages present more detail. The final page fully describes the evaluation and refers the reader to additional reports. (To see this figure in color, go to http://www.sagepub.com/escr.)

The National Evaluation of Upward Bound:

Summary of First-year Impacts and Program Operations (1997)

The Upward Bound program is intended to fill an important need: helping disadvantaged high school students realize the dream of a college education. An ongoing evaluation of the Upward Bound program, the largest of the federally funded TRIO programs, is yielding important new information about the program's effectiveness, showing that it affects students early on, and in positive ways.

The federal government spent $172 million on Upward Bound in 1996. Most students enter Upward Bound when they are in the ninth or tenth grade of high school. Once enrolled, students participate in a multiyear program of weekly activities during the school year and an intensive summer program that simulates college. In 1996, 45,000 students across the U.S. participated in the program, through projects offered by 601 grantees. The average federal cost per student was $3,800.

The U.S. Department of Education asked Mathematica Policy Research to evaluate Upward Bound's effectiveness. Mathematica was assisted by its subcontractors, Educational Testing Service, Westat, and Decision Information Resources. This publication summarizes Mathematica's findings on the program's short-term impacts on students and the academic content of its services. All impacts reported are statistically significant. In October 1997, information about longer-term impacts on students will be available.

Findings in Brief

- Two impacts emerge early on from Upward Bound. First, students who participate in the program expect to complete more schooling than similar students who do not. Second, the program has a positive impact on the number of academic courses participants take during high school.

- The students who benefit most initially are those with lower academic expectations.

- When impacts are examined by racial/ethnic groups, Hispanic students benefit the most from Upward Bound.

- The program shows no impact in the first year on participants' high school grades.

Figure 3.20   Example of Interim Report

- Many students leave the program in the first year.

- Most Upward Bound projects focus on providing a rich and challenging academic program.

A Closer Look at Specific Findings

Expectations About Continuing in School

During the first year that students participate, Upward Bound bolsters the expectations for continued schooling that they and their parents hold.

- Participants expected to complete almost 0.25 more years of school on average than nonparticipants. Both groups of students typically experienced some decline in educational expectations between the time of application to the program and the follow-up survey. The decline, however, was much larger for the control group.

- According to participants, their parents expected them to complete about 0.3 more years of schooling than did parents of children in the control group. The expectations of participants' parents changed little; however, the expectations of control group parents declined substantially.

Credits Earned

Upward Bound increases the number of high school academic credits students earn during the first year of participation.

- Participants earned about one credit (Carnegie unit) more than nonparticipants. This impact is quite large when compared with the experiences of a typical high school student, who each year is expected to complete about five academic and/or elective credits.

- Participants earned substantially more credits in science, math, English, foreign languages, and social studies than nonparticipants.

- Participants also earned more credits than nonparticipants in vocational education and remedial math courses.

Students Who Benefit Most

Before participating in Upward Bound, almost three-quarters of applicants who are eligible for the program expect to complete at least a four-year college degree. But those who benefit most from Upward Bound are those who do not expect to complete a four-year college degree.

- Parents' educational expectations for their children increased when their children started Upward Bound with lower expectations. For example, Upward Bound increased fathers' expectations by 1.2 years for these participants.

- In contrast, parents of children with higher initial expectations for continued schooling neither increased nor decreased their expectations.

In terms of academic preparation, Upward Bound has a large positive impact on the high school credits that students with lower expectations earn in math, English, and social studies.

Figure 3.20 *(Continued)*

- Participants with lower educational expectations gained almost 0.6 more math credits than their counterparts in the control group; the corresponding figure for students with higher expectations was 0.1 credit.

- Participation in Upward Bound also led to an increase of about 0.8 credits in English and social studies for students with lower expectations and less than 0.1 credit for those with higher expectations.

- Across all academic subjects, Upward Bound increased the number of credits earned by 3.1 for participants with lower expectations and by 0.5 credits for those with higher expectations.

Course taking for the three largest racial/ethnic groups in Upward Bound follows a consistent pattern: Hispanic students routinely experience larger gains from participation than either African American or white students.

- Hispanic students gained more than two credits; African American and white students gained less than 0.5 credits.

- Larger gains for Hispanics are apparent in several subjects: math, English, foreign languages, social studies, and vocational education.

First-Year Program Dropouts

Although Upward Bound has a substantial effect on educational expectations and course taking, the effect could be even larger if more students stayed in the program. Even in the first year, participants who leave Upward Bound early, for example, do not earn as many credits in high school as those who remain. Despite the value that comes from staying, many students do choose to leave Upward Bound in the first year. Furthermore, attrition from Upward Bound may be quite substantial by the time a group of entering students finishes high school.

- About 32% of those who entered Upward Bound before summer 1993 left by the end of the 1993–1994 academic year.

- Projections based on the experience of all students in the study suggest that 37% of those who participate will leave within the first 12 months.

- The program's dropout rate is very likely to increase at the end of the junior year, when project staff have reported that students are most likely to leave Upward Bound for summer and after-school jobs.

The Academic Challenge of Upward Bound

Most Upward Bound projects offer programs that emphasize academic preparation for college. Although an evaluation conducted in the 1970s by Research Triangle Institute prompted concern that Upward Bound projects did not devote enough time to academic instruction, recent evidence counters this view. The academic intensity of projects is evident from three perspectives:

- Number of Courses Offered. Fifty percent of the Upward Bound projects offer more than 17 academic courses in the summer and more than 10 academic courses during

Figure 3.20 (Continued)

the regular school year. These courses are in addition to the tutoring, academic counseling, study skills, and SAT/ACT test preparation courses that almost all projects provide.

- Nature and Content of Courses. More than two-thirds of the projects focus on instruction that is not remedial. These projects either support the curricular content in the college preparatory program of the high school, or they adopt an enrichment focus that teaches content the schools are unlikely to teach. Most projects offer courses that reflect a traditional precollege preparatory curriculum and a wide range of subjects.

- Course Requirements. Eighty percent of the projects require students to complete at least six courses in the Upward Bound program. The majority prescribe the set of courses that must be taken. Projects that specify courses fall into two groups. The first, which represents one-third of all projects, emphasizes completing a "foundational" curriculum comprising reading, writing, algebra I and II, and geometry. The second, which represents a slightly larger fraction of projects, has a math/science orientation with requirements for precalculus, calculus, and science courses in addition to the foundational requirements.

- Intensity of Contact With Students. Among first-year participants, the typical number of academic sessions attended was 179, and the typical number of non-academic (counseling, SAT prep, skill development, etc.) sessions attended was 95. Two-thirds of these sessions took place during the summer and the rest took place during the academic year.

Summing Up

The short-term impacts of Upward Bound, even though they are not evident for every kind of outcome, are both impressive and important. For just one year of involvement, Upward Bound offers real benefits to students. It exposes them to academically challenging courses in addition to those they take in high school. It results in participants and their parents holding higher expectations about future education. It leads to participants' earning more academic credits in high school. Moreover, Upward Bound is particularly beneficial for students who initially expect to complete fewer years of education and who come from Hispanic origins.

While these results are promising, they give only a partial view of how well Upward Bound works. Will the initial results endure and become larger as participants graduate from high school and face the challenge of college? Will the grades of participants and other outcomes that have yet to show impacts change as a result of students' involvement in the program? Answers to these questions will come as future reports about long-term program impacts are produced by the national evaluation.

About The Study

The national evaluation of Upward Bound is a six-year, longitudinal study commissioned by the Planning and Evaluation Service of the U.S. Department of Education. The evaluation incorporates data from many sources, including nationally representative samples of regular Upward Bound grantees and their target schools, and a nationally representative sample of students who applied to the program between 1992 and 1994 and were randomly

Figure 3.20 *(Continued)*

assigned either to Upward Bound or to a control group. Additional data were collected through field visits to a representative sample of 20 Upward Bound projects in the spring and the summer of 1993.

Because of the study design, findings on the impact of Upward Bound are generalizable to all Upward Bound projects hosted by two- and four-year colleges. The design uses a nationally representative sample of 67 Upward Bound grantees at two- and four-year colleges. Of students who were eligible applicants to these 67 projects, the evaluation randomly assigned 1,524 to Upward Bound and 1,320 to a control group. Short-term impacts are based on comparing students in the two groups across a range of measures, including high school grades and course taking, attitudes and educational expectations, misbehavior in school, and parental involvement. All students completed an initial survey form before they were randomly assigned to Upward Bound or the control group; more than 97% responded to a follow-up survey in 1994. Students' high school transcripts also were collected in 1994.

The survey of Upward Bound grantees collected detailed information about project operations and staffing for the 1992–1993 year. Questionnaires were mailed to a nationally representative sample of 244 projects, and 92% of the questionnaires were returned. The survey of target schools collected information from principals and Upward Bound liaisons in the schools (generally school guidance counselors) on a variety of topics, including the educational climate, availability of precollege programs in the school, contacts with Upward Bound, and perceptions of program effectiveness. Target school questionnaires went to a sample of 754 middle schools and high schools; 96% of these schools responded.

Reports From the National Evaluation of Upward Bound

Two major reports describing the Upward Bound program and its short-term impacts are available:

- Moore, Mary T. *A 1990's View of Upward Bound: Programs Offered, Students Served, and Operational Issues.* Washington, DC: U.S. Department of Education, Planning and Evaluation Service, 1996.

- Myers, David E. and Allen Schirm. *The Short-Term Impacts of Upward Bound: An Interim Report.* Washington, DC: U.S. Department of Education, Planning and Evaluation Service, 1996.

Figure 3.20 *(Continued)*

■ **Emphasize the provisional nature of interim findings to stakeholders and other audiences.**

Although formal interim reports can be critical to the usefulness of an evaluation, they can also effect great damage if interpreted inappropriately. The danger is that incomplete findings will be taken as being conclusive. It is a good idea to fully describe at the beginning of the report: (1) which data collection activities are being reported on; (2) the other data collection activities that are part of the evaluation; (3) when the final evaluation results will be available; and (4) any cautions that readers should heed in interpreting the findings.

■ **Provide drafts of formal interim reports for review by stakeholders and other audiences.**

Time should be allocated for clients and stakeholders to review the drafts of formal interim reports for the same reasons that drafts of final reports are typically reviewed. Interim reports can carry considerable weight in clients' decision making and can influence stakeholders. Primary stakeholders should be given the opportunity to respond to them before they are released. The reactions of clients and stakeholders to drafts contribute to interim reports' relevance and usefulness.

CAUTION FOR INTERIM REPORTS

■ **Despite your best efforts, information in interim reports can be interpreted inappropriately.**

Even if you have gone to great lengths to make sure that clients and stakeholders understand the preliminary nature of interim reports, danger of misuse still exists—particularly in the case of formal, written reports delivered without an opportunity for discussion with stakeholders. Once conclusions, interpretations, and/or recommendations have been made and "put in print," it is possible for readers to interpret them as conclusive. These readers may not be part of a client or primary stakeholder group who has been in communication with those more familiar with the evaluation—the evaluator or other stakeholders. While it is critical that readers understand the bases for interim reports, they may skip over or disregard the information that explains any limitations.

Final Reports

Comprehensive final reports are the most commonly used form of reporting by evaluators (Torres et al, 1997). The framework for these reports is found in the reporting traditions of basic social science research. This approach mandates formal, thorough treatments of a study's rationale, design, methodology, results, and implications. The objective is to provide sufficient documentation for readers to draw alternative conclusions and/or replicate the research. (See Figure 3.21 for the typical sections and contents of comprehensive written evaluation reports.)

The need for comprehensiveness in evaluation reporting is reflected in the Joint Committee's (1994) fifth Utility Standard, which calls for evaluation reports to "clearly describe the program being evaluated, including its context, and the purposes, procedures, and findings of the evaluation so that essential information is provided and easily understood" (p. 49). The intent here is not so much for others to be able to replicate the evaluation study but rather for them to use its findings—something best done when clients understand how the evaluation was conducted. Yet, recognizing our roots in social science research traditions, the Joint Committee cautions against "overemphasizing methodology at the expense of findings" (p. 50). Evaluators' most long-standing concern about the lack of use of their work has to do with the dust-gathering qualities of unread final reports.

Indeed, typical expectations dictate that evaluators provide lengthy, comprehensive evaluation reports that are time consuming to produce. Not surprisingly, the most frequently cited impediment to success in communicating and reporting is insufficient time (Torres et al., 1997). Further, it is unclear that such reports provide the most cost-effective means for communicating evaluation findings in ways most useful to stakeholders (Alkin, 1990). Written reports serve important archival purposes, including accountability needs, but they are quite impotent if change and improvement are the expectation. Well-informed talk is a more powerful means by which to report good and bad findings and to actively engage stakeholders in the shared commitment to better programs (Mathison, 1994, p. 303).

Despite these concerns, there are times when formal, comprehensive evaluation reports are required and appropriate. Program funders and/or policy makers most often expect such documentation. Case Example 3.3 describes one federal grant program's work with grantees to improve the content of their reports.

Introduction

- Purpose of the evaluation, including evaluation approach
- Brief description of the program
- Evaluation stakeholders/audiences
- Relationship between/among organizations involved and those serving in evaluator roles
- Overview of contents of the report

Program Description

- Program history, background, development
- Program goals/objectives
- Program participants and activities

Evaluation Design and Methods

- Evaluation questions
- Data collection methods (including participants and schedule) used to address each question
- Analysis methods for each type of data collected

Findings/Results

- Description of how the findings are organized (e.g., by evaluation questions, logic model components, themes/issues, etc.)
- Results of analyses of quantitative and/or qualitative data collected (usually represented in tables, charts, graphs, illustrations, and text)

Conclusions and Recommendations

- Conclusions drawn about the evaluation results
- Recommendations for action based on these conclusions
- Suggestions for further study, if applicable

Figure 3.21 Typical Sections and Contents of Comprehensive Written Evaluation Reports

SOURCE: Adapted from Torres (2001).

CASE EXAMPLE 3.3

Communicating Evaluation Findings in Federal Government Annual Reports

Most federally funded grant programs require grantees to submit annual reports. The general purpose of the reports is to provide the program director assigned to monitor the grant an overview of what has occurred during the previous year. Federal agencies have limited control over the format or content of the report, although many provide suggested guidelines. The reports submitted vary, but most provide descriptions of the year's activities, demographic data about the population served, and statistics about key aspects of the project. Primary authors of the reports tend to be grant or project staff, not the evaluator(s) for the project.

With the Government Performance and Results Act of 1993 (GPRA), the primary audience for these annual reports has moved beyond the federal program director. GPRA requires federal agencies to report annual outcome data to Congress for each major program within their agency. Agencywide GPRA reports demonstrate accountability for federal expenditures and highlight each agency's annual performance. Key sources of GPRA data are large-scale evaluations of federal programs and the grantees' annual reports. Federal program officers increasingly use annual report data to justify the existence of a specific initiative, create GPRA nuggets or vignettes, develop a future research agenda, and propose budget authorizations.

The grant program staff of one federal education agency sought technical support to help grantees in writing annual reports that would highlight the grants' accomplishments and outcomes. The grant program staff had found that the grantees' annual reports often did not

- Summarize major accomplishments or outcomes.
- State the intended outcomes in measurable terms.
- Present data to support goals for the reporting year.
- Incorporate evaluation data, relying only on accountability measures used by the school district.
- Explain how activities facilitated intended outcomes.
- Provide formative data that focused on project implementation.
- Describe how the data are being (or will be used) to make decisions about program activities.
- Identify challenges encountered in the past year and what was being done to overcome them.
- Present data in a uniform, consistent display.

Technical support was provided to the grantees through a series of presentations at periodic conferences attended by grantee teams, which include staff, data managers, and evaluators. The presentations ranged from 45 to 90 minutes and began with definitions and examples of messages, outcomes, activities, and evidence. Next, the grantees responded to four questions about their projects—questions that should be answered prior to writing the report:

1. What overarching messages do you want your reader to walk away with?

2. What outcomes will support your messages?

3. What activities led to those outcomes?

4. What evidence demonstrates outcome achievement?

In addition, the presentation showed that, in writing the report, the authors should:

- Use the active voice.
- Present the context (e.g., background information) about the setting of the grant and the participants.
- Offer compelling explanations of goals, activities, and progress.
- Write concise, data-based summaries of outcomes, as well as an executive summary.
- Present data (balancing text and graphics, choosing and displaying data)
- Prepare a visually pleasing report by creating summary boxes, labeling data exhibits, inserting page numbers and footers, using subheadings, and including a table of contents.

As a follow-up to the presentation, grantees voluntarily sent the support team their draft annual report for review. After reviewing the draft report, the support team conducted a 60- to 90-minute conference call with the grant team. Grantees were encouraged to include data managers and evaluators in the call. Throughout the call, the support team assisted the grantees in developing key messages and identifying data to support those messages (e.g., classroom observations, classroom walk-throughs, SAT/ACT scores, college admission statistics, end-of-course or grade data, and high-stakes assessment data across all grade levels and subgroups of students).

Federal program directors reported that the technical support improved how the grantees' reports (1) highlight key information related to accomplishing the program's goals; (2) align the data displays and the narrative; and (3) organize the data and narrative in a useful and usable manner.

SOURCE: Case described with permission of Kathy Zantal-Wiener.

External evaluators are more likely than internal evaluators to write a final/technical report (Torres et al., 1997). This practice serves both as a means of accountability for their work and as a basis from which stakeholders can work with the findings, with or without the involvement of the external evaluator. Also, comprehensive final reports can help orient new personnel. They can be given copies of recent evaluation reports for a concise, often incisive orientation to a program or issue.

Figure 3.22 shows a report checklist that details characteristics of a comprehensive report, from the title page through references and appendices. It also includes specific standards from *The Program Evaluation Standards* (Joint Committee, 1994) relevant to evaluation reporting. As the instructions indicate, this checklist can be used as a tool to guide a discussion between evaluators and their clients about the contents of evaluation reports (see also Figure 3.23) and also as a means of providing formative feedback to report writers. When several persons are working on the same report, the checklist can help to delegate, coordinate, and monitor progress among contributors.

Evaluation Report Checklist

Gary Miron
April 2004

The Evaluation Report Checklist has two intended applications:

1. A tool to guide a discussion between evaluators and their clients regarding the preferred contents of evaluation report(s)
2. A tool to provide formative feedback to report writers. Evaluators can self-rate their own progress during the writing phase. They can also use the checklist to identify weaknesses or areas that need to be addressed in their evaluation report(s). When there are two or more persons working on the same report, the checklist can help to delegate, coordinate, and monitor progress among the contributors.

Evaluation reports differ greatly in terms of purpose, budget, and a whole host of other factors. If one uses this checklist to evaluate actual reports or draw comparisons across reports, one would need to consider or weigh these factors.

This checklist draws upon and reflects the Program Evaluation Standards (Joint Committee on Standards for Educational Evaluation, 1994).

Instructions: Rate each section of the report using the following rubrics. Place a numeric character or check in the cell that corresponds to your rating on each checkpoint. If the item or checkpoint is not applicable to the report, indicate the "NA" cell to the far right. The formula for the overall score reflects the mean rating for each section. This will calculate automatically in the spreadsheet version of the checklist. Additional checkpoints may be added as agreed upon by those using the checklist.

Figure 3.22   Evaluation Report Checklist

SOURCE: Used with permission of The Evaluation Center, Western Michigan University.

**0 = Not addressed,   1 = Poor/inadequately addressed,   2 = Fair/partially addressed,
3 = Good/mostly addressed,   4 = Excellent/fully addressed   NA = Not applicable**

	0	1	2	3	4	NA
1. Title Page Overall Score: **0.0**						
A. Title identifies what was evaluated, including target population, if applicable						
B. Title is sufficiently clear and concise to facilitate indexing						
C. Authors' names and affiliations are identified						
D. Date of preparation is included						
E. Text and material on title page are clearly and properly arranged						
F.						

Comments:

	0	1	2	3	4	NA
2. Executive Summary Overall Score: **0.0**						
A. Description of program/project						
B. Evaluation questions and purpose of the evaluation						
C. Concise summary of main findings						
D. Implications of findings						
E. Recommendations, if appropriate						
F.						

Comments:

Figure 3.22 *(Continued)*

0 = Not addressed,   1 = Poor/inadequately addressed,   2 = Fair/partially addressed,   3 = Good/mostly addressed,   4 = Excellent/fully addressed   NA = Not applicable

	0	1	2	3	4		NA
3. Table of Contents and Other Sections That Preface the Report Overall Score: **0.0**							
A. Table of contents contains at least all first- and second-level headers in the reports							
B. Titles and page numbers are accurate							
C. Lists of tables, figures, and appendices are included, if appropriate							
D. List of acronyms or abbreviations is included, if appropriate							
E. Acknowledgments section with reference to sponsors, data collectors, informants, contributors to the report, research assistants, reviewers of the report, etc., is included							
F.							

Comments:

	0	1	2	3	4		NA
4. Introduction and Background Overall Score: **0.0**							
A. Purpose of evaluation and evaluation questions, if not covered in the methodology section							
B. Description of the program/project or phenomenon being evaluated (including historical context, if appropriate)							
C. Identification of target population for program, and relevant audiences and stakeholders for the evaluation							
D. Review of related research							
E. Overview and description of structure of report							
F.							

Comments:

Figure 3.22 (Continued)

0 = Not addressed,   1 = Poor/inadequately addressed,   2 = Fair/partially addressed,
3 = Good/mostly addressed,   4 = Excellent/fully addressed   NA = Not applicable

	0	1	2	3	4		NA
5. Methodology Overall Score: **0.0**							
A. Purpose of evaluation and evaluation questions, if not covered in the introduction							
B. Evaluation approach or model being used, as well as rationale for the approach or model							
C. Methods of data collection							
D. Design of the evaluation including timing of data collection and use of specific data collection methods							
E. Sources of information and data							
F. Limitations of the evaluation							
G.							
Comments:							

	0	1	2	3	4		NA
6. Results Chapters Overall Score: **0.0**							
A. Details of the evaluation findings are clearly and logically described							
B. Charts, tables, and graphs are appropriately labeled and understandable							
C. Discussion of evaluation findings is objective and includes both negative and positive findings							
D. All evaluation questions are addressed or an explanation is included for questions that could not be answered							
E. Findings are adequately justified							
F.							
Comments:							

Figure 3.22 *(Continued)*

0 = Not addressed,   1 = Poor/inadequately addressed,   2 = Fair/partially addressed,
3 = Good/mostly addressed,   4 = Excellent/fully addressed   NA = Not applicable

	0	1	2	3	4	NA
7. Summary, Conclusion, and Recommendations Overall Score: **0.0**						
A. Summaries of findings are included in each chapter or all together in a summary chapter						
B. Discussion and interpretation of findings are included						
C. Summary and conclusion fairly reflect the findings						
D. Judgments about the program that cover merit and worth are included						
E. If appropriate, recommendations are included and they are based on findings in the report						
F.						

Comments:

	0	1	2	3	4	NA
8. References and Appendices Overall Score: **0.0**						
A. A suitable style or format (e.g., APA) is used consistently for all references						
B. References are free of errors						
C. References cover all in-text citations						
D. All appendices referenced in the text are included in the appendices section, and vice versa						
E. Data and information in the appendices are clearly presented and explained						
F.						

Comments:

Figure 3.22 *(Continued)*

⇨ *Implementation Tips for Final Reports*

- **Carefully consider the need for a formal, comprehensive final report with stakeholders at the time the evaluation is being designed. Budget adequate time and funds to produce a final report.**

A major consideration in the decision to produce a comprehensive final report is cost. From beginning to end, the production of a final report can be the most expensive aspect of the evaluation endeavor. First, the primary authors of the report must (1) compile and organize the presentation of data; (2) make interpretations and draw conclusions; and (3) develop recommendations. Then, considerable time is required to (1) format and paginate the report; (2) make revisions in wording, format, spelling, and grammar; and (3) complete final editing. The production of charts, tables, and graphics is also time consuming. In particular, sufficient time must be allocated for catching typographical and formatting errors in the final version. Invariably, reports that leave the author's hands too quickly for duplication end up containing errors. Further complicating this process, completion of the report usually must be timed to coincide with organizational (decision-making) events involving use of the evaluation's findings. Case Example 3.4 illustrates a situation where a decision was made not to produce a traditional, comprehensive final report. The evaluation was designed to collect no more data than could be successfully analyzed, interpreted, and reported for the time and money available.

- **Recognize that developing the final report plays a key role in the analysis and integration of findings.**

The biggest advantage to the comprehensive report is that it provides the opportunity to take the most integrative approach to interpreting data and making recommendations. In the analysis stage of either quantitative or qualitative data, findings are not necessarily integrated, but rather, distinctly represented in quantitative tables and/or separate piles of coded and sorted interview transcripts or observation notes. Forgoing a final report can leave the analysis and integration process at this beginning level. Conversely, development of a comprehensive report forces the evaluator to consider how various findings are interrelated. Some of the most compelling and useful reports integrate all sources of data on particular aspects or issues. Reports fashioned in this way can tell a story about the program.

This integration provides a view of the program that in many instances would not otherwise be seen. Nor are clients likely to know that such a view is missing if they agree to a situation where a comprehensive report is not produced. This fuller synthesis is something clients often appreciate once they have seen it.

CASE EXAMPLE 3.4

Deciding Not to Produce a Comprehensive Final Report

The Woodland Park School District is a small rural district in Woodland Park, Colorado. Over a 2-year period, the district had been experiencing the frequent use of overtime by its support staff in the high school office. The superintendent and director of business services were concerned about this expense and had been searching unsuccessfully for an external consultant who could conduct an efficiency study. Finally, the superintendent contacted a local evaluator (one of this book's authors) about the possibility of investigating this issue.

After several site visits to the district, the evaluator and district administrators established that the purpose of the desired study would be to develop a thorough understanding of how the high school office operates, including (1) how the job responsibilities of staff are carried out; (2) how school administrators and students are involved in the work of the office; (3) the extent to which the work is accurate; (4) the nature and amount of work conducted beyond normal working hours; and (5) the internal and external factors that contribute to how the office operates. Data collection methods would be primarily qualitative—observations and interviews with school personnel. The superintendent intended to use the study's findings in collaboration with school personnel to determine how the efficiency of the office could be improved while at the same time maintaining the district's commitment to excellence in the education of its students. Staffing implications of any recommended changes would be considered in time for the following school year. This schedule meant that the study would have to be completed in three months—by April of the previous school year.

It was decided at the outset that the evaluator's work would not include the production of a comprehensive final report. The superintendent's intent was to resolve the issues surrounding overtime accrual in the most cost-effective manner possible. There was no plan to make a formal presentation of the study's findings to the board but, rather, to use them as quickly and effectively as possible to make improvements.

Findings from the interviews and observations would be integrated and illustrated in a graphic representation of how the high school office operates, including influencing factors. This illustration was to be presented in draft form to high school and district personnel. Their input concerning its accuracy and completeness would be solicited in a working session. The outcomes of this session would then be used to modify the illustration. In the second phase of the same session or in a subsequent session, implications of the study's findings would also be developed in collaboration with school and district staff.

The reporting plan (included in the evaluation plan) specified that the evaluator would provide a brief report about one week after these working sessions. It was to contain (1) the revised illustration of the high school office operations; (2) a concise explanation of the illustration; and (3) a summary of the recommendations developed by school and district personnel. The appropriate staff would be asked to review a draft version of this report before the final version was submitted.

SOURCE: Case described with permission from Woodland Park School District, Woodland Park, Colorado.

■ **Involve stakeholders in the preparation and review of final reports.**

From our standpoint, the best evaluation practice is a collaborative one, where participants and other stakeholders are involved in the evaluation from beginning to end. This means, of course, that their major involvement with the evaluation would not be merely as recipients of the final report. Figure 3.23 shows a form used by FERA, Inc., a Michigan-based evaluation consulting group, to get input from their clients about the audiences, length, and characteristics of the final report FERA will deliver. Notice Item 4, which asks for an opportunity for dialogue about the evaluation findings.

At a minimum, program participants should always be given the opportunity to review a draft version of a final report. (Hopefully, prior to this time, stakeholders have been involved with the development of a reporting plan that includes the timing and format of reports, and they have seen interim results, if called for.) A major aspect of evaluation use begins with the participants' review of the draft version of the report. (In some cases, this review may constitute their only reading of the final report, as they may find little time among competing priorities to do so again once the revised version comes out.)

Yet, obtaining and incorporating feedback about a final report from a large number of program participants can be cumbersome. Figure 3.24 shows instructions given to a program staff of approximately 50. They are asked for their input on (1) the report's clarity, accuracy, and format and (2) the appropriateness of its conclusions and recommendations. They are also reminded about a meeting to discuss revisions to be made on the basis of their input. Evaluation use invariably begins during this kind of working session. Using the evaluation's description of the program as the basis for discussion, staff members have the opportunity to clarify any misunderstandings about the program that may exist among themselves. Consideration of the report's conclusions and recommendations almost always leads to discussion about how to implement recommendations. (See the sections on working sessions in Chapter 4 and on developing recommendations in Chapter 6 for further information on these topics.)

■ **Select an organizing framework for the findings that maximizes the report's relevance and use for evaluation audiences.**

The findings section of the final report can be organized according to any of several frameworks:

- The evaluation questions
- The program's logic model or theory of action
- Decision-making processes within the life cycle of the program
- Emergent themes or categories that tell the program's story

We believe the main criteria for your choice among these should be maximizing the audiences' learning from and use of the report. Given that the *evaluation questions* reflect stakeholders' leading concerns about the evaluand,

FERA *Formative Evaluation Research Associates*

REPORTING RECOMMENDATIONS

1. What individuals or groups do you see as the primary audience(s) for the report? Please circle the **most** important group.

    a.

    b.

    c.

2. What length report, given the demands on people's time, do you think is appropriate?

Audience (from above)	Abstract (1–2 pp)	Executive Summary (5–10 pp)	Medium Length (11–25 pp)	Lengthy (26+ pp)
a.	_____	_____	_____	_____
b.	_____	_____	_____	_____
c.	_____	_____	_____	_____

3. How important are the following reporting characteristics?

Characteristics	Very	Quite	Somewhat	Not Too	Not At All
a. Quantitative presentation (e.g., tables, graphs)	_____	_____	_____	_____	_____
b. Narrative description	_____	_____	_____	_____	_____
c. Discussion of the implications	_____	_____	_____	_____	_____
d. Presentation of recommendations	_____	_____	_____	_____	_____
e. Extensive documentation of the research methods	_____	_____	_____	_____	_____

4. How important is an oral presentation of the report by the research team which would allow for clarification, elaboration, and brainstorming on the implications of the evaluation?

    _____ Very   _____ Quite   _____ Somewhat   _____ Not Too   _____ Not At All

5. What one piece of advice would you offer regarding our final reporting?

Figure 3.23   Example of Form for Soliciting Client Input to Style and Length of Final Report

SOURCE: Used with permission of FERA, Inc.

Staff Feedback Form for Final Draft of the Evaluation Report

INSTRUCTIONS

1. Please provide feedback about the final report, considering each of the following:
   a. areas/sections you feel don't make sense

   b. areas which you feel may be inaccurate and require further explanation (keeping in mind differences across program sites)

   c. any conclusions or recommendations you feel should be added or revised

   d. any other questions or comments you have about the report

2. Complete page 2 as appropriate. In giving feedback, be sure to identify the page and line number you are referring to, and then explain your concern. For example, *p. 6, lines 10–15 — The point of the paragraph is not clear to me. What is meant by . . .?*

3. Alternatively, you can make comments in the margins of the report pages, but don't forget to complete the last page of this attachment.

4. As you review this report, please consider being part of a Focus Group meeting on September 7th at 3:45 P.M. to discuss feedback to the report and revisions that will be made.

5. Return your feedback to the Program Office on or before Monday, August 29th.

6. If you have any questions or concerns, don't hesitate to call [the evaluator] at xxx-xxxx.

Figure 3.24   Form for Obtaining Feedback on Draft Version of Final Report

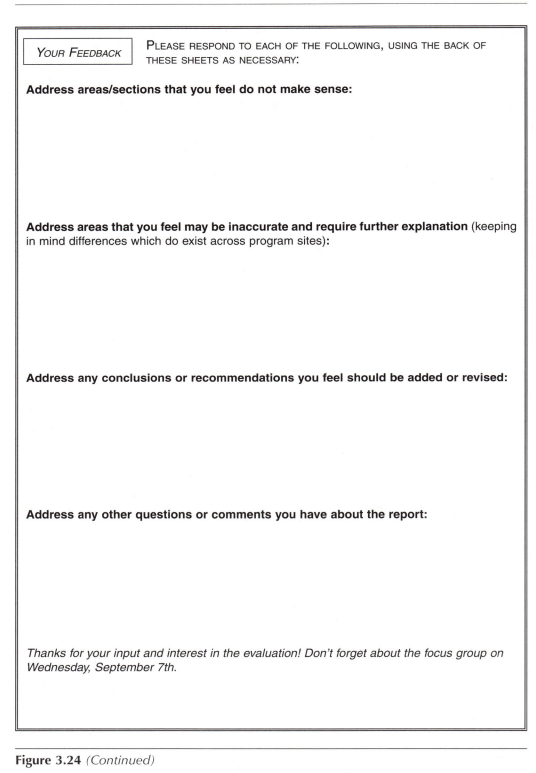

| Your Feedback | PLEASE RESPOND TO EACH OF THE FOLLOWING, USING THE BACK OF THESE SHEETS AS NECESSARY: |

Address areas/sections that you feel do not make sense:

Address areas that you feel may be inaccurate and require further explanation (keeping in mind differences which do exist across program sites)**:**

Address any conclusions or recommendations you feel should be added or revised:

Address any other questions or comments you have about the report:

Thanks for your input and interest in the evaluation! Don't forget about the focus group on Wednesday, September 7th.

Figure 3.24 *(Continued)*

this may be the obvious choice for organizing the report. It's important to consider, though, that another framework may better represent the evaluand in terms of how the audience relates to it at the time findings are available. For example, following the program's *logic model* or *theory of action* (see Torres, 2005, p. 240) may help audiences better understand the crucial linkages between program activities and outcomes. Figure 3.25 shows the theory of action for KidzLit, an after-school enrichment program developed and disseminated by the Developmental Studies Center (DSC) in Oakland, CA. Organizing formative evaluation findings according to the components of this theory of action helped DSC program staff reflect on the program holistically, taking into account key linkages between program activities and outcomes.

Another strategy is to identify an approach to the report that relates the findings to stakeholders' *decision-making processes,* that is, the ongoing planning and improvement processes within the life of the program (Morris et al., 1987). For instance, many programs in school districts have committees composed of staff members who are charged with planning and improvement activities for specific aspects of the program. The evaluation report can be organized to present findings according to the charges of the different committees. Case Example 3.5 illustrates how this approach was used with a companywide task force charged with developing a compressed workweek program.

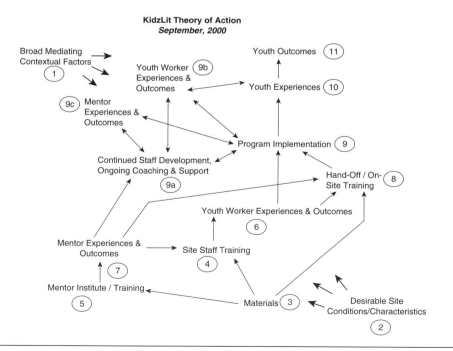

Figure 3.25   Theory of Action for After-School Enrichment Program

SOURCE: Used with permission of Developmental Studies Center.

CASE EXAMPLE 3.5

Aligning the Format of a Final Report
With Decision-Making Processes

An internal companywide task force of a large training organization was charged with developing a compressed workweek program for employees. After several months' work, the task force produced an employee handbook explaining the program and all aspects of its implementation, including work schedule options; use of the program during holiday weeks and in conjunction with vacation; how to record overtime; core hours when employees must be present; and so forth. The task force also had worked with an external evaluator to document the outcomes of the program and to identify ways in which it could be improved. Specific issues investigated by the evaluation included those articulated by senior management about costs of the program and those identified through interviews with employees about their experiences with the program. Based on the evaluation findings, the task force intended to modify the program and produce a new version of the employee handbook.

During a meeting with the evaluator, when initial evaluation findings were being presented and discussed, members of the task force expressed their desire that the evaluation report be structured along the lines of the original employee handbook. They reasoned that this approach would simplify the process of modifying the handbook based on the evaluation findings. The evaluator developed the report accordingly, matching evaluation findings with the appropriate sections of the handbook. To further facilitate the work of the task force, key sections of the handbook were reproduced within the report in shaded boxes.

The final report will also be used by the organization's senior managers, who are interested in results on specific issues for each of their departments. The report's 78 tables, which show survey results by department and position, are listed in an alternative table of contents under the main headings "Program Impacts" and "Program Implementation."

An executive summary that accompanies the final report presents the findings according to three main issues: impact of the program, employee support for the program, and program implementation. This organization paralleled a conceptualization of the program that had been developed by the evaluator based on interviews with program participants.

The trade-off with this strategy is that it may not allow for a perspective on the program that is very different from the way participants and other stakeholders saw it to begin with. That is, the framework for presenting the evaluation findings comes from within the program or organization itself. Yet, in some cases, primary stakeholders are particularly well informed by an alternative perspective on themselves—one afforded by a different set of eyes.

A solution to this trade-off, although time consuming, is to develop two reports: one that organizes findings according to the program's decision-making framework and the other that organizes findings according to an alternative framework. In Case Example 3.5, the evaluator produced both a report organized according to the contents of an existing employee handbook and an executive summary that described the relationship among three major elements as conceptualized by the evaluator (program impact, employee support for the program, and program implementation).

A fourth approach is to consider the *emergent themes or categories* that tell the program's story. For some evaluations the most compelling framework for presenting the findings may be unknown at the outset. That is, an inductive approach to the analysis of the evaluation data often reveals an organizing framework that in and of itself represents the evaluation findings, and does so in a way that describes the program from a new perspective. This approach was used in Case Example 3.4. (The section on integrating qualitative and quantitative findings in Chapter 6 provides more information about developing useful organizing frameworks for the presentation of findings.)

■ Consider alternative sequencing for the arrangement of report sections.

Rather than using the traditional format of a journal article (introduction, methodology, findings, conclusions, and recommendations), you can make the most interesting and useful contents of your evaluation reports more accessible by moving the findings and recommendations forward in the report. Consider these options:

- Describe the methodology briefly in an introductory section, and present it fully within an appendix.
- Organize the report by the evaluation questions (or other questions which guide the reader or main topic areas). Immediately after each question, describe the data that addresses the question, and then present a summary of the findings and recommendations. Detailed presentations of methods and findings can be included in appendices.
- Organize the report by the recommendations. For each recommendation, present conclusions and evidence (i.e., the evaluation findings) to support it.
- If you have numerous tables or graphs, put them in an appendix and reference the specific appendix pages throughout the section that describes the findings.

Whatever organizational structure your report has, another strategy to engage readers is to describe how the report is organized inside its front cover, as shown in Figure 3.26.

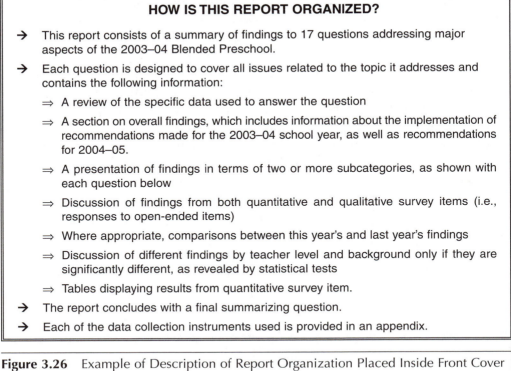

HOW IS THIS REPORT ORGANIZED?

→   This report consists of a summary of findings to 17 questions addressing major aspects of the 2003–04 Blended Preschool.

→   Each question is designed to cover all issues related to the topic it addresses and contains the following information:

⇒   A review of the specific data used to answer the question

⇒   A section on overall findings, which includes information about the implementation of recommendations made for the 2003–04 school year, as well as recommendations for 2004–05.

⇒   A presentation of findings in terms of two or more subcategories, as shown with each question below

⇒   Discussion of findings from both quantitative and qualitative survey items (i.e., responses to open-ended items)

⇒   Where appropriate, comparisons between this year's and last year's findings

⇒   Discussion of different findings by teacher level and background only if they are significantly different, as revealed by statistical tests

⇒   Tables displaying results from quantitative survey item.

→   The report concludes with a final summarizing question.

→   Each of the data collection instruments used is provided in an appendix.

Figure 3.26   Example of Description of Report Organization Placed Inside Front Cover of Evaluation Report

Executive Summaries

An executive summary or abstract is essentially a shortened version of a longer evaluation report. It enables readers to get vital information about the evalu-and without the time constraints of reading and assimilating an entire report. It typically is written to address the needs of busy decision makers and is especially useful for quick dissemination of findings. Evaluators write executive summaries for up to 75% of the evaluations they do (Torres et al., 1997).

Summaries are usually positioned at the front of the longer document. Their chief advantage is that they can be reproduced separately and disseminated as needed. Summaries can vary in length from one paragraph to several pages. When resources for reproduction and distribution are limited, an executive summary offers an alternative to the longer document (Joint Committee, 1994).

Comprehensive executive summaries usually contain condensed versions of all the major sections of a full report: background/program description, methodology, findings, conclusions, and recommendations. The intent is to communicate the essential messages of the original document accurately and concisely. Few people will read the entire document, some will skim parts of it, but most will read the executive summary. For this reason, it is especially important that executive summaries be well written.

Summaries can also be tailored to address the needs of particular audiences, emphasizing different program elements and findings. They can consist solely of significant or essential information required for a particular audience or dissemination situation (Lannon, 1991). Case 3.6 describes how an executive summary was adapted to meet a variety of audience information needs during and after an evaluation. Decisions about what to include in a summary depend largely on

- The audience's familiarity with the program or organization
- The audience's interests or expectations
- The audience's needs for particular kinds of information
- Both the author's and the audience's time constraints
- Dissemination plans/costs
- The type(s) of data collected and the analyses conducted during the evaluation
- The existence of multiple sites or multiple audiences within a site

CASE EXAMPLE 3.6

Meeting a Variety of Information Needs With an Executive Summary

After working on a yearlong curriculum review of a Master's degree program within a university department, the evaluator prepared an 80-page report outlining the findings from document reviews and interviews (individual and focus group) involving approximately 100 individuals from seven different stakeholder groups. The 80-page report covered the traditional areas of evaluation design and data collection, summary of evaluation findings, recommendations and next steps, and appendices of the data collection instruments. Within the report, the evaluator included a 15-page executive summary that provided a condensed version of the evaluation design and the overall findings, along with a list of the 21 recommendations and 68 subrecommendations for improving the Master's level program.

While the 80-page report was of great interest to the faculty and staff who served on the curriculum committee that worked with the evaluator throughout the project, the 15-page executive summary was a more appropriate document for distributing to the department's faculty and staff who had participated in the data collection. The executive summary was also appropriate for other audiences who were tangentially involved in the evaluation, including university administrators and professional organizations. The evaluator used the executive summary to create two additional documents for use at the department retreat the following month, at which she was serving as a facilitator: (1) a survey for the faculty and staff to rank the recommendations they considered most important for discussing at the department retreat; and (2) a two-page retreat worksheet used by small groups of faculty/staff to prioritize subrecommendations and create action steps for implementation in the subsequent academic year.

⇨ *Implementation Tips for Executive Summaries*

■ **Tailor the content of the executive summary to audience information needs and dissemination plans.**

Sometimes, an audience is unfamiliar with the evaluand or has been involved only peripherally with the evaluation. In this case, a greater proportion of the executive summary should contain descriptive information on the program or organization itself and on the purpose and procedures of the evaluation (including, but not limited to, the evaluation purpose, questions, and methodology). This more inclusive approach should also be considered if dissemination plans include reaching a wide range of audiences, multiple sites within a program or organization, or the news media. In many cases the executive summary will be distributed without the full evaluation report and is intended as an independent, self-contained message. Sufficient background information on the program, the purpose of the evaluation, and its methodology should be included. In addition, whatever the contents or format of a summary, remember to avoid jargon, abbreviations, acronyms, and colloquialisms or slang—or, clearly define them in simple, commonsense language.

If an audience is familiar with the program or organization, then a smaller proportion of the executive summary may include descriptive material. Sometimes, a summary may contain only findings and recommendations. It is not uncommon for an executive summary that exclusively focuses on findings and recommendations to be reformatted and disseminated as a bulletin, memo, postcard, or fax, or as a poster presentation in other settings or for other audiences. Figure 3.27 shows a summary containing interim findings across seven community-based, after-school programs within a school district. The evaluators organized this report in terms of "lessons we're learning" in an attempt to "keep it positive, appreciative, focused on what's working, and focused on how different sites can learn from the other sites about what is effective" (Preskill, S., 2004).

■ **Format the executive summary for easy assimilation of its contents.**

Multiple formats can be used that best elicit interest and response from particular audiences or that most efficiently present different types of information. The executive summary should be consistent in tone and intent with the original document but can be rearranged, reworded, and re-proportioned. Frequently, an executive summary will follow the format of the longer document—a full page of single-spaced text with headings and subheadings as appropriate. Alternatively, it can take on a question-and-answer format, using the evaluation questions and program outcomes to report findings and recommendations.

If findings and recommendations make up the bulk of the summary, statements set off by white space, boxes, lines, bullets, or other graphics make it easier to assimilate, as shown in Figure 3.27. Another way to make the summary easy to read is to format it into two columns. Similarly, colored print or paper and/or separate binding of the summary facilitate its dissemination as an alternative document (Worthen, Sanders, & Fitzpatrick, 1997). Figure 3.28 provides a four-page executive summary created by the Pew Partnership for Civic Change. Several features make it appealing and useful for readers: color, interesting graphics, text formatted in columns, boxed call-out, recommendations highlighted in a separate section, and information about where to get the full report. (To see this figure in color, go to http://www.sagepub.com/escr.)

■ **Use a summary process to ensure coherent, consistent content.**

One approach to creating an executive summary is simply to cut and paste portions of the original document into the summary, and to write appropriate transitions. Usually, though, producing an executive summary requires some kind of summarizing process that focuses your attention on the key ideas and significant information you want to communicate. One strategy that produces a concise summary consists of seven steps (adapted from Lannon, 1991, p. 143):

Guidelines for Writing a Summary

- *Read the original document from beginning to end.* It is important to fully understand all aspects of the original document before attempting to summarize it.
- *Reread and underline all key ideas, significant statements, and vital recommendations.* Focus on the main ideas and major supporting statements.
- *Edit the underlined information.* Eliminate all but key phrases; you will rework these into sentences later.
- *Rewrite the underlined information.* Do not worry about conciseness; you will edit later.
- *Edit the rewritten version.* Eliminate needless/repetitive words and phrases and combine related ideas.
- *Check the edited version against the original document.* Focus on verifying that you have captured the essential information/message of the original. Check to see if you have altered the meaning of any statements or added unrelated information; if so, delete.
- *Rewrite your edited work.* This final version should be written for clarity and conciseness, focusing on smooth transitions and clear connections of ideas.

Lessons We're Learning

What Works in After-School, Community-Based Programs
November 20, 2003

Strong Leadership

Site facilitators are good listeners, observers, and guides who develop and share powerful conceptions of a quality program; maintain ongoing communication with staff; support the staff and the program in continuing to improve; stay in close touch with parents; and continue to invite and increase parent participation.

Relationship Building

Time and space are found for adults and kids to develop relationships, to have "downtime" together. One of the most striking findings of the entire evaluation has to do with the rich and moving bonds that have brought youth and adults closer together. Clearly, these relationships are among the project's most attractive aspects for youth and adults alike. Relationship building also enhances learning, especially since it occurs in a racially and ethnically diverse group of people.

Visions of Literacy

Kids develop their reading and writing skills in a variety of settings to serve multiple purposes. Time and space are found to support and reinforce a love of reading and writing. The activities the youth engage in and the materials they use are themed to anti-racism, nonviolence, civic literacy, community appreciation, community information gathering, and empowerment.

Management and Organization

The sites establish simple organizational procedures for kids, rehearse them regularly, and then stick to them. Formal and informal dialogues are important parts of the curriculum where respect, listening, and turn-taking are observed. Attention is paid to taking positive, respectful, yet prompt action to maintain discipline and enhance cooperation. Space for homework is found, while leaving room for plenty of other creative activities.

Love of Learning

A mix of activities is used, including painting, cooking, building, role-playing, storytelling, and experimenting. Projects are occasionally introduced that allow the whole group to work on something for a sustained period. Staff members frequently bring their interests, passions, and academic studies into what they teach the youth. Staff members consistently model their own love of learning.

Planning

Regular planning sessions are built into the weekly schedule, and time is allowed for exploratory conversations among adults that focus on how to continue to improve the program.

Parental/Community Involvement

Regular parent and community meetings are held, as well as special sessions that are likely to attract more and new parents and community members. Feedback is invited from parents about what is happening in the programs. Parents and community members are encouraged to play a leadership role in continuing to improve the programs.

Figure 3.27   Executive Summary of Interim Findings

SOURCE: Used with permission of Stephen Preskill, University of New Mexico.

In It for the Long Haul: Community Partnerships Making a Difference

Executive Summary

America's tradition of working together is alive and well according to a survey of 600 of the top business, nonprofit, and local government leaders in the 200 largest cities. The survey, conducted in July 2001, by the Campaign Study Group for the Pew Partnership for Civic Change, probed leaders about the status of partnership in their communities, why partnerships are important, and the kinds of interactions across sectors that have become business as usual. The clear message from these cross-sectoral leaders was that working together is not only better but essential. Over ninety percent of the leaders across sectors and locales said loud and clear, "working with others to solve problems takes more time but works in the long run." Further, these relationships have worked over the long haul because each sector feels that it has an important niche to fill.

The importance of community partnerships has taken on a greater significance since the tragedy of September 11th. Even before September, every community in the country was feeling some effects of the recession. At the federal level, we have seen a significant decline in the budget surplus. Critical areas such as education, healthcare, and job training must get in the funding line—the portions are smaller.

While federal support is critical to the launch and sus-

tainability of many basic human services, we learned from the survey that community partnerships can be invaluable in assisting a community to tap the resources available and make them stretch further. They do this in three very tangible ways: first—community partnerships can raise visibility on local issues—it is hard for communities to solve problems they do not know about; second, partnerships can assist communities set priorities for the allocation of resources; and third, community partnerships can unleash new talents and resources to address old problems. This survey gives some clues about how and with whom this can be done and toward what end.

How do the sectors see the problems?

When polled about the issues of critical importance to their community, the leaders weighed them differently but ultimately there were several problems that appeared on all three sectors' lists. Nine issues—illegal drugs, affordable healthcare, the lack of affordable housing, the lack of living-wage jobs, teenage pregnancy, the lack of affordable childcare, insufficient public transportation, too many unsupervised children and teenagers, and the lack of affordable care for the elderly—rank among the top problems according to each sector's leaders. These priorities across sectors provide considerable room for discussion and coordinated efforts to solve identified problems.

An area where the three groups of leaders clearly diverged was on the severity of problems facing the community. Local government officials proved the least likely to believe their communities have serious problems. At the opposite extreme, nonprofit leaders were more often than not the most likely to describe the same range of issues as posing serious problems for their communities. The

---

There are clear signals that the sectors are reaching beyond their own organizations to address communitywide issues.

Promising Areas

The news is very good for cross-sectoral partnerships in the nation's largest cities. A majority of business, nonprofit, and local government leaders are working together to address major community issues. But there are places and situations where more could be done and where bridges could be built. There are opportunities for business to use its leadership to critically analyze the problems and provide needed expertise toward the solutions; there are opportunities for the nonprofit sector to be the information and brokering arm of the community—joining needs with resources;

and there are opportunities for local governments to take the lead in bringing the problem solvers together on a regular basis in order to make the community more aware of the issues facing it and their impact. Approximately half of all respondents reported that their community had no formal mechanism or organization to bring the sectors together around critical issues.

The survey data were rich with the documentation of the existence of strong partnerships in the largest metropolitan areas but there is still room to strengthen and develop local efforts. The following recommendations spotlight additional areas of exploration for all three sectors that can sustain existing efforts and open new vistas for partnership.

Specific Recommendations for Successful Partnerships

BUSINESSES

It's more than writing a check.

- Contribute expertise in management and marketing—not just financial resources.
- Conduct regular briefings with nonprofit and government leaders to ensure understanding of the problems facing your community and to prioritize the potential impact on employees and your region.
- Know the roles that nonprofits and specific government agencies play and what issues they are addressing.

NONPROFIT ORGANIZATIONS

It's more than just funding.

- Make marketing, media relations, and public awareness priorities to increase visibility and understanding of your issues.
- Communicate the impact of your program. Tell the stories of lives changed as a result of your work and resources.
- Solicit professional help—beyond fund-raising—from businesses in marketing and management strategies.

LOCAL GOVERNMENTS

It's going to take more than government.

- Recognize the contributions and resources that other community sectors can make in solving problems and solicit their opinions and assistance.
- Take advantage of your ability to convene or facilitate collaboration by assembling diverse leaders to address problems.
- Make information sharing among partners, potential partners, and the public a priority.

For a copy of the data highlights report, contact the Pew Partnership at (434) 971-2073 or visit www.pew-partnership.org

4

Figure 3.28 Four-Page Executive Summary

SOURCE: Used with permission of Pew Partnership for Civic Change.

opinions of business leaders tended to fall between the two other groups although they generally expressed attitudes closer to those held by government officials. This lack of agreement on the severity of the problems challenges the ability to agree on priorities—in fact, it almost guarantees disagreement and the need for deliberation—in times of economic scarcity. This finding provides a powerful opportunity for communities to assess their situations and to come to some consensus as a community on the longterm impact of social problems on the three sectors and the community at large.

One surprising finding from the survey dealt with the quality of life in the communities and the most likely of the three sectors to express a "go it alone" attitude toward problem solving. This disjuncture with other sectors suggests the need for an "honest broker" process in communities led by leaders from all sectors that gathers facts and figures about community issues. There should be a clear and agreed-upon assessment of the baseline data and information that relate to community issues.

How well do partnerships work?

Despite disagreements about the priority of issues, the ability of local partnerships to join interests with multiple resources has had overwhelming success according to those surveyed. Seventy-two percent of business leaders and approximately fifty percent of nonprofit leaders reported that the partnerships they have been involved with have been very successful. Only two percent or less indicated that their cooperative relationships had not been successful at all. This satisfaction with cooperative relationships begs the question, "What does it take to have a successful partnership?"

Respondents said that the two most important components of successful partnerships are: 1) a formal collaboration to which each sector contributes; and 2) long-term relationships and commitment. Other factors cited were dedicated people, commitment, ability to draw on multiple resources, ability to achieve objectives, and mutual trust.

What do partnerships do?

With all the talk about partnerships, we were very curious about the work of the partnerships: how each sector perceives partnership and its own role in collaborations. The respondents gave a clearer picture of both. The categories of partnership run from the particular to the general but generally rest in three areas: information sharing, financial and in-kind support, and tackling tough issues together.

Information Sharing

At the most basic level, these cooperative relationships began with the sharing of information. Nearly three-quarters of all nonprofit executives reported that their organizations currently send newsletters outlining their work or their resources to local business leaders and almost seventy percent correspond with local government.

Approximately two-thirds of the government officials interviewed also indicated that the city or county where they work distributes information about their programs and resources to the local business community and local charitable organizations.

Similarly, almost half of the business leaders interviewed said that their companies offer a community resource directory to all employees.

Validating the interaction between the sectors, half of all nonprofit leaders said that they had had an unsolicited offer from their local government in the last year to share information. The most frequently offered information was U.S. Census/demographic information, funding/financial information, and public health information. The nonprofits themselves count on the local government as an information source with two-thirds requesting data from local government over the last year.

Financial and In-Kind Support

Money and in-kind support were seen by all sectors as vehicles to join with community organizations to solve problems. Ninety-six percent of companies donate money to nonprofits according to the respondents. More than half of the business executives said that their companies match employee donations to charity. More than three-quarters of local government leaders reported that their local government provides funding to nonprofit groups. Seventy-nine percent of the business leaders surveyed said that their companies donated used or surplus equipment to local non-profit organizations. Further, sixty-nine percent of business leaders reported that their companies provide educational scholarships.

Approximately half of the nonprofit leaders said that their organizations had received public relations assistance, technology expertise, and strategic planning assistance from a local company. Local government was also a strong player in providing technical assistance to local nonprofit organizations with fifty-four percent providing such assistance.

Vast majorities of local government officials (89%) and nonprofit executives (82%) said they provide local community groups free access to their facilities for meetings or other activities. Slightly less than half of business leaders indicated that they make their corporate facilities available for the same purposes.

While financial support by the government and business sectors was strong, so was the attitude toward civic participation that was fostered in the workplace. Nearly nine out of ten business leaders and eight out of ten government officials indicated that their employers have organized programs to encourage employee charitable donations.

Tackling Tough Issues Together

There was a clear indication that the sectors are discussing the challenges and opportunities facing their communities—and acting on them. Almost three-quarters of the business and nonprofit leaders and ninety percent of the government leaders said that they work with other groups in the community to address important community issues. Although partnerships take different forms and directions, the survey found they clearly tend to be forged around key issues facing the community. When leaders were asked what they do specifically in the community to address problems several action strategies emerged.

• First and foremost, the leaders of the different sectors know each other and communicate on a regular basis. Nearly two-thirds of the government officials and slightly more than half of the business leaders surveyed said they meet regularly with local charitable and other nonprofit leaders.

• Second, they provide direct services to community organizations beyond giving and create a culture of caring within their organizations. More than half of all business lead-ers said their companies had organized employee participation in a formal mentoring program. This number reached seventy-five percent among those companies that indicated working closely with leaders from other sectors. About half of government leaders and nonprofit leaders said they do the same.

• Third, fifty-four percent of the business leaders surveyed said that their companies gave employees paid time off to volunteer.

Perhaps more surprising, forty percent of government officials said that their localities provide employees with paid time off to volunteer. As a way to recognize employee activities, three-quarters of the major employers have a formal recognition program.

• Fourth, eighty-six percent of the business leaders and eighty-one percent of local government leaders say their employers organize employee participation in community activities such as walk-a-thons, food drives, and neighborhood cleanups. Likewise, eighty-three percent of the nonprofit leaders surveyed said they actively enlist the support of suppliers and clients to volunteer or help solve a community problem.

Beyond these specific activities, leaders from business, local government, and nonprofit organizations serve on boards, commissions, and committees aimed at community problem solving. More than half of both the business and nonprofit executives indicated that either they or someone else within their organization had offered to serve on such a board in the last twelve months. More than half of the business and nonprofit leaders said that a county or city government had extended an invitation to serve to someone in their organization. Almost seventy percent of local government officials said that they had invited a local nonprofit leader to serve on a problem-solving commission and seventy-five percent had invited one or more business leaders to serve.

> Seventy-two percent of business leaders and approximately fifty percent of nonprofit leaders reported that the partnerships they had been involved with had been very successful.

Figure 3.28 (Continued)

■ **Allow sufficient time for creating summaries.**

Time constraints on both yourself and the audience may limit the content and format of the executive summary. Deciding which information is most vital in the full report, and rewriting and reformatting that information into an executive summary takes time. Condensing 50 pages of a final report into a two-page summary can be a challenge! As mentioned earlier, sometimes you can create an executive summary by cutting and pasting from the original report, but you must also allow time for reworking some of the content to create smooth transitions from one idea to the next. The longer the full report is, the more time it will take to summarize it.

■ **Once the final report has been developed, if possible, create and disseminate an executive summary while the full report is in final production.**

In many cases, the distribution of executive summaries need not be held until the final versions of full reports are ready. This approach gives one solution to the length of time it often takes to produce comprehensive reports. An executive summary can be developed and distributed immediately after the content of the final report has been finalized but before the report itself is ready for distribution. This strategy can reduce the time before stakeholders and other audiences receive findings.

■ **Include the executive summary at the front of the final report to reach those evaluation audiences who might not read the entire report.**

Many more persons intend to read final evaluation reports than actually do. A likely circumstance is that they begin to read the report but, because of its length and other competing priorities, do not get around to finishing it. These persons may be key audiences for the report who, as a result, are left with an incomplete sense of what the evaluation produced. Providing the executive summary with the final report gives the reader an opportunity to at least get through this shorter version. There is the risk, of course, that including the executive summary will entice some recipients to read only the summary, and not the full report. This strategy, however, gives readers a choice and provides them with the executive summary that they may wish to copy and share with others not on the original distribution list of either version of the report.

CAUTION FOR EXECUTIVE SUMMARIES

■ **Summaries can be misused or misinterpreted by audiences who have limited contact with the program and/or evaluation.**

The difficulties with creating a coherent and concise executive summary multiply when one considers the possible use and misuse of the information. At issue is the extent to which information in the summary has been oversimplified. If you have limited contact with the various audiences who receive the summary, clarity is key. In these situations, there may be few, if any, opportunities for questions, elaboration, or discussion. The danger here is that audiences can easily misuse a summary, especially in instances where it largely contains findings and recommendations or is distributed through the media or to diverse audiences. Because the summary cannot focus on all the key descriptive or contextual pieces of the longer document, some information that may be vital to a thorough understanding of the evaluation or the program or organization is left out. When audiences unfamiliar with, or perhaps even hostile to, the program or the organization receive a summary, they may misconstrue or misinterpret the information.

Newsletters, Bulletins, Briefs, and Brochures _____

Newsletter, bulletins, briefs, and brochures are convenient publication types for relaying evaluation information and findings to a broad group of stakeholders and audiences. These formats are particularly well suited for reporting news about an evaluation, and presenting both interim and final evaluation findings. They can help keep channels of communication open between the stakeholders and the evaluator(s) and promote conversation among program participants as evaluation findings emerge. Newsletters, bulletins, briefs, and brochures that contain evaluation information are typically created and disseminated by organizations that

- House the evaluand
- House the evaluator(s)
- Fund the evaluand or the evaluation
- Support the evaluand and/or
- Support the development of the evaluation profession.

For example, the Boys & Girls Clubs of Greater Milwaukee developed the brochure campaign described in Case Example 3.7 for their youth development program. This collection of printed materials combines information about the program's mission, current activities, clients, and volunteer and fund-raising information, in addition to program evaluation findings.

CASE EXAMPLE 3.7

Brochure to Report Program Information and Evaluation Findings to Diverse Audiences

The Boys & Girls Clubs of Greater Milwaukee (B&GCGM) is committed to learning what impact its programming has on the central-city youth it serves. A full-time staff member directs its evaluation program, which includes three longitudinal studies (two national, one local) and ongoing annual program evaluation activities.

The agency's staff and board of directors agree that in order to provide the best possible services for Club participants, the agency must understand its effects and then work to continually strengthen its programming. Equally important is sharing evaluation findings with its stakeholders—first, to raise community awareness of what the agency does; second, to appeal to past, present, and future agency supporters; and third, to recruit program participants. The challenge is to summarize findings in a succinct and interesting way for diverse audiences in a low-cost manner. Target audiences include the general public, donors, volunteers, and program participants.

To do this the Boys & Girls Clubs of Greater Milwaukee has developed a series of brochures and other printed materials (annual reports, fact sheets, envelopes, donation tags, posters, and table tents). The brochures use a common color scheme (blue, green, and white) with pictures of youth of a variety of ages and ethnicities, both male and female. The images used in all of the materials are actual clients (photos taken with permission), not stock photography. The graphics are crisp and clear, with one to three photos per brochure. Simple typeface draws attention to focused information. The primary brochure, a tri-fold format (8.5" tall and 3.75" wide), provides bulleted information in three content areas. "Who We Are" and "What We Do" describes the agency's programs, clients, and activities. "How We Change Lives" reports on program outcomes and evaluation findings, e.g., impact on school attendance/retention, academic achievement, and reducing involvement in high-risk behaviors. "How You Can Help" describes volunteer and donation opportunities. Two additional printed items are single-page, double-sided brochure inserts. These are formatted to be inserted into the primary brochure or accompany other program materials. The first of the two details "Club Results" such as the agency's impact on clients. Inserts provide a format to disseminate the most recent or targeted findings with a brochure. The second brochure insert provides "Club Facts" such as program history and client demographics.

(Continued)

CASE EXAMPLE 3.7 (Continued)

Ancillary printed materials (e.g., snowflake donation tags, posters, and table tents) used in a fund and awareness development campaign in 2003 were designed to coordinate with the primary brochure and insert materials. The organization's average individual financial supporter is 45 years of age or older. This campaign was specifically designed to appeal to adults between the ages of 25 and 45. Rather than hosting an event (at cost to the agency) that would appeal to this audience, the materials were designed for use in places where the target group socializes, thereby minimizing the costs of the campaign. These printed materials were designed in the style of point-of-purchase displays and were placed at local pubs and restaurants during the month of December. Patrons learned about the organization's mission, programs, and impact primarily through these table tents, posters, and brochures. Patrons had the option to purchase a snowflake that also explained program impacts. The purchased snowflakes were displayed on the wall of the establishment with the name of the donor.

SOURCE: Case described with permission of the Boys & Girls Clubs of Greater Milwaukee.

Many organizations that conduct evaluations disseminate newsletters with information about their evaluations activities, the resources they provide, their staff, and evaluation findings. For example, the Evaluation Center of Western Michigan University (www.wmich.edu/evalctr) produces a biannual newsletter. *Perspectives* is the newsletter of TCC Group (www.tccgrp.com), a consulting firm that develops strategies and programs to enhance the efficiency and effectiveness of nonprofit organizations, philanthropies, and corporate citizenship programs.

The newsletter excerpt shown in Figure 3.6 is from *Community Matters*, produced biannually by the Pew Partnership for Civic Change to update audiences on their programs and strategies. The Partnership funds both programs and evaluations.

Case Example 3.8 describes *The Evaluation Exchange*, a newsletter produced by the Harvard Family Research Project (www.hfrp.org). This newsletter disseminates information about evaluation practice to diverse audiences of evaluators, researchers, community-based organizations, policy makers, and other constituencies.

CASE EXAMPLE 3.8

Newsletter Used to Disseminate Information About Evaluation Practice to Diverse Audiences

Harvard Family Research Project (HFRP), founded in 1983 and affiliated with the Harvard University Graduate School of Education, promotes the educational and social success and well-being of children, families, and their communities. HFRP helps programs and policies working with these groups to be more effective through its research, evaluation, training, and technical assistance.

As part of its evaluation and accountability services, HFRP publishes a periodical, *The Evaluation Exchange*, which serves as a forum for the exchange of ideas, lessons, and practices about the evaluation of programs and policies affecting children, youth, families, and communities. *The Evaluation Exchange*'s accessible style and format, combined with content that highlights innovative methods and practical theory, make it a unique resource for diverse evaluation stakeholders who want to learn about and share complex information efficiently. Articles are written by both well-known and lesser-known authors who are selected for their varying perspectives and voices. Regular features include Theory & Practice, Promising Practices, Evaluations to Watch, Questions & Answers, and Ask the Expert. It is published four times per year and is distributed internationally to policy makers, program practitioners, educators, researchers, evaluators, funders, and other constituencies. The subscription is free, and subscribers can opt to receive it in the mail or receive an e-mail notifying them when it is available online on the HFRP Web site. Illustrations 1 and 2, on the following pages, show the cover page and an example of a regular feature from Volume 9, No. 2 of *The Evaluation Exchange*.

As these examples show, *newsletters* take many shapes and forms. A newsletter may be devoted solely to communicating evaluation findings from one study. Or, articles about the evaluation activities and/or findings may be included in existing internal or external newsletters, which have a broader purpose. A newsletter can be a single page containing key findings, or it can be several pages created in a newspaper format describing particular elements of the evaluation and its findings.

Generally, *bulletins* are brief news statements about some matter of concern. They may look similar to one-page newsletters but are typically characterized by their sole dedication to reporting research and evaluation findings, and the frequency of their publication during the evaluation. Once the study or project has been completed, bulletins are often discontinued, only to start up again when a new study begins.

the
evaluation
exchange

A PERIODICAL ON EMERGING STRATEGIES IN EVALUATING CHILD AND FAMILY SERVICES

HARVARD FAMILY RESEARCH PROJECT ■ HARVARD GRADUATE SCHOOL OF EDUCATION ■ VOLUME IX NUMBER 2 ■ SUMMER 2003

from the director's desk

Heather Weiss

Twenty years ago the release of *A Nation at Risk*[1] created a sense of urgency to address the mediocrity of the U.S. education system. It set off a wave of reforms that have become part of the educational landscape today—notably the drive toward high academic standards, the improvement of the teaching profession, and the extension of learning opportunities beyond traditional institutions. While there is disagreement about the strategies to reform a decentralized educational system, few would contest the need for long-term research and ongoing evaluation to determine which reforms are successful, for whom, and under what conditions.

In this issue of *The Evaluation Exchange* we consider multiple perspectives on current education reform efforts and their evaluation. The implementation of the No Child Left Behind Act drives many of the current themes in the practice and evaluation of education reform. The emphasis on scientifically based research (SBR) and experimental research as the gold standard of education scholarship is a watershed for evaluation. In the Special Report in this issue, expert researchers and evaluators comment on the opportunities and challenges that SBR presents.

The increased emphasis on using evidence to inform education practice also carries implications for schools of education to prepare future educators, researchers, and evaluators with solid research skills and a broad conception of what constitutes good educational scholarship. As several authors in this issue note, this conception includes training in and use of multiple and mixed methods because of

the richer understanding that they yield.

Yet education reform proceeds at different levels, and its complex demands call not just for the participation of universities and federal- and state-level education administrations. This issue highlights the role of youth, families, communities, and the broader public in education reform as they too have a vested interest in high-performing schools.

Parents, for example, are participating in new ways in school reform, networking with other parents, and developing leadership skills that allow them to influence critical education issues. Yet in order to effect change and hold schools accountable, parents and the broader public must be educated about the standards-based movement and other education reforms. Otherwise, the public actually may be part of the philosophical resistance to efforts such as standards, as Wendy Puriefoy of Public Education Network points out in Questions and Answers.

The placement of multiple stakeholders and research rigor in the center of conversations on education reform requires a rethinking of methods for evaluating such reform. This issue provides information about several evaluations in key areas of education reform, such as technology in education, comprehensive school-based reform, and reducing the achievement gap. Evaluators share insights on their experiences of participatory action research, formative evaluation, quasi-experimental designs, and large-scale impact studies.

The world of education reform is complex and evolving and certainly not possible to cover comprehensively in one issue. As always we welcome your thoughts and contributions.

Heather

Heather B. Weiss, Ed.D.
Founder & Director
Harvard Family Research Project

[1] The National Commission on Excellence in Education. (1983). *A nation at risk: The imperative for educational reform.* Washington, DC: U.S. Department of Education.

Illustration 1 Newsletter Cover Page Example

> evaluations to watch

Flexibility and Feedback in a Formative Evaluation

Marjorie Weschler of SRI and Jane David of the Bay Area Research Group describe the importance of flexibility and feedback in conducting formative evaluation.

How do you evaluate a reform agenda that is constantly adapting to changing circumstances and feedback? That is the challenge we face as formative evaluators for the Bay Area School Reform Collaborative (BASRC). Created in 1995 in response to the Hewlett-Annenberg Challenge,[1] BASRC is a San Francisco-based reform organization dedicated to improving student achievement and closing the achievement gap. Schools and districts receiving BASRC funds participate in regional networking opportunities and inquiry-focused activities around teacher practices, equity, assessment, and leadership. The cornerstone of BASRC is inquiry- and data-driven decision making—not just for its grantees, but for itself. Accordingly, BASRC contracted with the Bay Area Research Group and SRI International to conduct a formative evaluation to help increase its effectiveness.

Given BASRC's learning stance and the developmental nature of its work, the goal of our formative evaluation is to increase the efficiency and effectiveness of its organizational learning. Ironically, it is BASRC's learning stance that complicates our task, because as BASRC learns, it adopts new strategies for supporting reform. With the launch of its second five-year funding period in 2001, BASRC changed from focusing on individual schools to providing support for collaboratives of schools and their districts. In 2002 BASRC again shifted its emphasis, providing comprehensive support to five districts and lighter support for school collaboratives in other districts.

Asking the Right Questions

Our research questions not only get at the heart of our formative task, but also remain pertinent in a changing environment. The following overarching questions guide our work: To what extent are BASRC's strategies to promote and support reform effective? How might they become more effective, through either modifying or better implementing the current strategies? For each of BASRC's primary strategies, we gather data to answer three questions:

1. Is the intent of the strategy clear to BASRC staff and to the field?
2. Is the implementation of the strategy consistent with its intent?
3. Does the strategy contribute constructively to the progress of reform in schools and districts?

Each question includes an implied "why or why not," from which we draw inferences about how strategies might be better designed, targeted, or strengthened in practice. These questions are applicable to any new strategies implemented.

[1] In 1995, the Hewlett-Annenberg Challenge was established for public school renewal in the San Francisco Bay area's six counties. The five-year $100 million grant has been supported by William R. Hewlett, the William and Flora Hewlett Foundation, the Annenberg Foundation, and matching local funds.

Being Flexible and Responsive

Because BASRC's reform effort is complex and is coupled with a serious attempt to learn along the way and adjust accordingly, plans never roll out exactly as expected. As BASRC adjusts to feedback from the field directly and from us, its plans and strategies change. Our evaluation tasks must change accordingly. For example, when BASRC's focus on creating collaboratives of schools shifted to concentrating attention on both schools and central offices in fewer districts, our emphasis shifted as well.

Timely Feedback

BASRC develops its annual strategic plan for the following academic year while it is still implementing the plan for the current year. Our feedback must correspond with BASRC's planning and decision-making cycles. Therefore, an end-of-year report is not sufficient. BASRC also needs just-in-time feedback so it does not waste time or resources on failing strategies and builds on success.

Continual Feedback

We provide feedback in multiple ways throughout the year, including brief memos and occasional reports summarizing data collected from grantees, "real-time" feedback during events, and frequent email and conversations with staff in response to observations or questions. We meet regularly with planning groups and with management teams to present findings, hear reactions to our interpretations, discuss strategies, and solicit their questions to guide subsequent inquiries. Such an approach encourages staff to think about what their next steps will be. The key to making feedback useful is to ensure that there is a mechanism for translating the results into actions.

Our guiding questions and flexible stance have enabled us to provide constructive feedback to BASRC. Some of our influence is tangible. For example, our recommendations contributed to BASRC's decision to differentiate training for experienced and novice reform coaches who help schools implement inquiry-based practices. Often our influence is subtler. For example, we may steer thinking in a different direction by the questions we raise, or provide validation to support a decision. Either way, our task as formative evaluators is to focus on BASRC's strategies and actions that are amenable to feedback and improvement, and to direct our energies and BASRC's attention to the areas where changes will have the biggest impact on its grantees.

For more information visit SRI's website at: www.sri.com/policy/cep/edreform/BASRC.htm.

Marjorie E. Wechsler	Jane L. David
Education Policy Analyst	Director
SRI International	Bay Area Research Group
333 Ravenswood Ave.	3144 David Ave.
Menlo Park, CA 94025	Palo Alto, CA 94303
Tel: 650-859-4822	Tel: 650-493-4425
Email: marjorie.wechsler@sri.com	Email: jld@bayarearesearch.org

Harvard Family Research Project   21   *The Evaluation Exchange* IX 2

Illustration 2 Newsletter Feature Example

SOURCE: Case described and illustrations used with permission of the Harvard Family Research Project, Harvard University.

Although the distinction is not absolutely clear, *briefs* tend to be longer than bulletins. They are also typically dedicated to research and evaluation findings on a single topic, which is likely to be addressed from the perspective of multiple and/or longitudinal studies. Most often briefs address national and international policy issues. They can be of almost any length, but often tend to be from two to ten pages. They sometimes include photographs, and more than other publications, may be written in an academic style. A few examples from among the numerous organizations that produce periodic single-topic briefs are:

- The National Center for Research on Evaluation, Standards, and Student Testing (CRESST, www.cse.ucla.edu)
- Mid-Continent Research for Education and Learning (McREL, www.mcrel.org)
- Research Institute on Secondary Education Reform for Youth With Disabilities (RISER, www.wcer.wisc.edu/riser)
- United States Agency for International Development (USAID, www.usaid.gov)
- International Fund for Agricultural Development (IFAD, www.ifad.org)

Brochures typically are intended to generate interest and some follow-up on the part of readers. This might be to find out more about a program, an organization, and/or an evaluation. A typical brochure is printed on 8.5 by 11-inch paper and folded twice along the 8.5-inch side to create six panels (front and back). Often, as described in Case Example 3.7, organizations use brochures to stimulate interest or enrollment in a program and include evaluation findings to describe its benefits.

Brochures that focus solely on an evaluation can be used to invite audiences to a verbal presentation and strategic planning session, or to inform them of the study's findings. Brochures can focus solely on recommendations, lessons learned, or best practices that have been derived from evaluation studies.

Today's inexpensive desktop publishing software has dramatically increased the ease with which newsletters, bulletins, briefs, and brochures can be created. In general, newsletters and brochures are more likely to include photographs and other visuals—and require greater graphic design skill—than bulletins and briefs. You may choose to create any of these publication types yourself using word-processing or other software that contains design templates. You may also choose to engage professional services for creating newsletters and brochures, in particular. The following sets of guidelines for brochures and newsletters can be used to support your own work, or to review work you have commissioned.

Guidelines for Creating Newsletters and Brochures

- Select the data, graphics, and other information to be presented, keeping in mind that your goal is to make the content interesting for the intended audience(s) with attractive formatting and well-organized information.
- Collect brochures and newsletters from other organizations. Decide what you like or dislike about the formatting of these. Diagram a sample layout for your own newsletter or brochure.
- Make sure that each section, while concise, has a clear beginning, middle, and end.
- Use no more than two or three typefaces.
- Verify that all facts listed are accurate.
- Keep records that document the sources of all evaluation findings presented.
- Use colors, background, and text that are clear and easy to read.
- Make sure graphics are used consistently, contribute to the overall flow of information, and do not clutter or confuse the reader.
- Proofread the material carefully before going to press. (It is always best to have someone other than the author of the material proofread.)
- Select paper color that is not too bright or too dark. Matte finish reduces glare for the reader.
- Include contact information.
- Reference other published evaluation documents, including URLs if appropriate.
- If reprinting material from other publications, be sure to clear permissions from the sources.

Particular to Newsletters

- Decide on a name (or masthead), format, and frequency of distribution for your newsletter; retain the same format for each publication.
- Decide on an optimum size for the newsletter and word count per article. Brevity and clarity are always a winning combination.
- Make article titles descriptive of content; there should be a headline for every article.
- Be creative with your use of boldface, capitalization, and underlining with any text, particularly for time-sensitive information.
- Include a table of contents to help your readers find the information they need quickly.

(Continued)

(Continued)

Particular to Brochures

- Think about your primary audience(s) and design the front cover to grab their attention and get them to want to open the brochure.
- Consider spreading copy across all three inside panels rather than sticking to the three-column format.
- Avoid being too wordy; leave some white space. Use short sentences, short paragraphs, and clear visuals.
- Limit your use of boldface, capitalization, and underlining.

Implementation Tips for Newsletters, Bulletins, Briefs, and Brochures

■ **Determine the type of publication best suited for your purpose and audience(s).**

Consider the following factors when deciding whether to use a newsletter, bulletin, brief, or brochure

- Purpose of the publication
- Audience interest
- Access to audience
- Amount of information you wish to convey
- Other existing or planned publications
- Time and financial resources available
- Overall scope of the dissemination effort

If your purpose is to inform the evaluation audiences of the study's findings or create interest in the program or evaluation process, using a newsletter, bulletin, brief, or brochure will increase the scope of the dissemination effort. Note that evaluations which draw primarily on qualitative data (yielding rich descriptions and verbatim quotes, and where the evaluation context is critical to interpreting the results) may not be appropriate for communicating through newsletters, bulletins, and brochures because of their limited length.

■ **Maximize your use of space, while providing sufficient detail to support the publication's purpose.**

An important decision, and a difficult one, is deciding what to include in and leave out of the document. Questions you might ask yourself include the following:

- Is it important to provide information about the evaluation's design and implementation?
- Which findings should be reported?
- Should it include graphics (e.g. photos, tables, figures, etc.)?
- What about alternative viewpoints?
- Should recommendations be included?

With the limited space of newsletters and bulletins, and for briefs and brochures, in particular, the answers to these questions are essential. For additional information about content, refer to the guidelines earlier in this chapter on writing, and on the use of tables and graphs.

■ **Determine the resources required and frequency of publication.**

The major advantage of using newsletters and brochures in particular is their visual appeal. It is important to create attractive, eye-catching documents. Whether you use professional services or in-house personnel skilled at using desktop publishing programs, producing newsletters, bulletins, briefs, and brochures also requires (1) staff to coordinate the publication's development and (2) resources to print, copy, and distribute these documents to the intended audiences.

Whatever publication type you choose, you must also decide how often it should be published and disseminated. The purpose of the publication and resources available will influence this decision. The time period and nature of the evaluation—whether it is formative or summative—are other factors to consider.

■ **Develop a project management plan to ensure timely and efficient production.**

To ensure that the documents are produced when they are needed, it is a good idea to develop a management plan. The plan should specify the various tasks, timelines, and people involved in developing the publication and the dissemination strategy.

■ **Consider posting newsletters, bulletins, and briefs on the Web.**

You will find that most organizations post their newsletters, bulletins, and briefs on the Web, while at the same time disseminating paper copies. These documents can easily be converted to portable document format (.pdf), posted on the Web, and then downloaded by audiences. Since brochures are more difficult for Web users to reproduce in their original form, these tend not to get posted on Web sites. (For more information on Web communications, refer to the section at the end of this chapter.)

CAUTIONS FOR NEWSLETTERS, BULLETINS, BRIEFS, AND BROCHURES

■ **Once evaluation findings have become available, organizations may make decisions about including them in short publications without consulting the evaluator.**

Many programs and organizations will want to include evaluation findings in their promotional materials, particularly to the extent that the findings are favorable. Even if you have offered to provide consultation about how best to accurately represent the findings in a newsletter or brochure, you may not always be given the opportunity. Different personnel than those who worked with you on the evaluation often develop the organization's publications, and frequently this function is outsourced entirely.

■ **Audiences may overlook newsletters, bulletins, briefs, and brochures.**

The value different audiences place on newsletters, bulletins, briefs, and brochures affects their credibility and usefulness. Despite your best efforts to align these publications with audience interests, needs, and access, they may pay little attention to them, or overlook them entirely as junk mail.

News Media Communications

In many evaluations, the findings need to be disseminated beyond the primary stakeholders. In these cases, using the news media to communicate and report evaluation findings helps reach the general public as well as specific industry or professional groups. It also has the potential for facilitating discussion among outside groups affected by or interested in the evaluation results. Some of these groups may include influential opinion and policy makers.

The two kinds of broad-based media are *mass* and *specialized* media. The general public is the audience for *mass media*, namely print (newspapers) and electronic media (e.g., television, radio, the Internet). Examples are publications such as *The New York Times, Time* magazine, *The Wall Street Journal,* and local newspapers. In addition, community and ethnic media that publish local weeklies or biweeklies for particular neighborhoods, or targeted populations, can be an effective means for disseminating evaluation information and findings to various audiences.

Evaluation results may find their way into mass media through three established routes. First, newspaper writers may obtain copies of evaluation reports from one of the stakeholder groups and write an article based on the report. A second method involves the newspaper writer interviewing the evaluator and possibly the program staff and participants. From these interviews, the reporter writes an article.

The third method is the press or news release. An evaluator and/or primary stakeholders may contact a reporter by phone and provide evaluation information. On the more formal side, a written press release is produced. This is typically a one- to two-page summary of the evaluation's findings sent to both print and electronic media. If the press release is brief and written like a news story, it may be published as is, or it may be excerpted. If the release creates enough interest in the topic, a reporter may call the evaluator for an in-depth interview. Figure 3.29 shows a three-page press release used to report research findings.

Notice how the text of the press release in Figure 3.29 reflects several of the following guidelines for press releases:

Guidelines for Press Releases

- Use clear language the general public will understand—avoid jargon.
- Begin the press release with a statement that sparks the interest of reporters. This is called a "lead" and is intended to grab the reader's attention.
- Use the active voice.
- Use short paragraphs.
- Use quotations to make the content more interesting.
- Print it on letterhead or on a "news release" form.
- Indicate the date on which the press is free to use the information with the words, "FOR RELEASE." If the contents' use is not date specific, use the statement, "FOR IMMEDIATE RELEASE."
- Provide the name, institutional affiliation, and phone number of a contact person (typically the evaluator or the organization's public relations officer).
- Use "# # #" or "-30-" to indicate the end of the news release text.
- Target smaller newspapers, since they are more likely to print "community" news.
- Send the release to a particular person at the news agency so that it doesn't get lost in the organization.

EPSL   Education Policy Studies Laboratory
              Education Policy Research Unit

****NEWS RELEASE****
From the Education Policy Research Unit (EPRU) and the
Education Policy Studies Laboratory (EPSL)
at Arizona State University

FOR IMMEDIATE RELEASE

Saturday, December 28, 2002

CONTACT:
Audrey L. Amrein
ASU Research Professional
amrein@asu.edu

David C. Berliner
Regents' Professor, College of Education
(480) 965-3921
Berliner@asu.edu

Alex Molnar, Director
Education Policy Studies Laboratory
(480) 965-1886
epsl@asu.edu

Find the complete text of this report at:
http://www.asu.edu/educ/epsl/EPRU/epru_2002_Research_Writing.htm

New Research Casts Doubt on Value of High-Stakes Testing to Improve School Performance

TEMPE, Ariz.— The high-stakes testing policies adopted by many states and the new annual student testing required by the federal government in the 2001 No Child Left Behind legislation may be counterproductive, according to two studies conducted by the Education Policy Studies Laboratory at Arizona State University for the Great Lakes Center for Education Research and Practice, a Michigan-based think tank.

The two reports, "The Impact of High-Stakes Tests on Student Academic Performance: An Analysis of NAEP Results in States With High-Stakes Tests and ACT, SAT, and AP Test Results in States With High School Graduation Exams" and "An Analysis of Some Unintended and Negative Consequences of High-Stakes Testing," are the first in what will be a series of annual reports on the impact of high-stakes tests.

Arizona State University researchers Audrey L. Amrein and David C. Berliner conducted both studies.

"The impact high-stakes tests and high school graduation exams have on academic achievement is, at best, ambiguous," according to Amrein. She adds: "Contrary to popular thought, high-stakes tests do not increase academic achievement. Instead, after states implement high-stakes tests, academic achievement continues to look much like it did before

Figure 3.29   Three-Page Press Release to Report Research Findings

SOURCE: Used with permission of the Education Policy Research Unit and the Education Policy Studies Laboratory, College of Education, Arizona State University.

high-stakes tests were implemented. In addition, negative or unintended consequences emerge as students, teachers, and schools attempt to reconcile learning and the attachment of serious consequences to test performance."

According to co-author David Berliner, "The relative failure of high-stakes tests to achieve their intended purpose and their numerous negative consequences must be considered as America prepares to launch a massive testing program in the effort to improve our schools."

Impact on Student Academic Performance

"The Impact of High-Stakes Tests on Student Academic Performance" looked at data from 28 states where high-stakes testing programs are already in place. These programs include tests that students must pass in order to advance to the next grade, and graduation tests that students must pass in order to receive a high school diploma, regardless of their performance in the classroom.

Results from these states' high-stakes tests were compared with the performance of students from those states on other widely recognized measures of student achievement: the National Assessment of Educational Progress (NAEP), American College Test (ACT), Scholastic Aptitude Test (SAT), and Advanced Placement (AP) assessments. The study found that these measures showed no systemic evidence of improved achievement after states implemented high-stakes testing programs. States that implemented other high-stakes testing programs performed "much like the rest of the nation" on the ACT, SAT, AP, and NAEP tests, Amrein and Berliner found.

The Amrein-Berliner data also suggest that in states that implemented high-stakes graduation exams, academic achievement appeared to decline. According to Amrein and Berliner, ACT, SAT, and AP scores fell in states that implemented high-stakes graduation exams.

The Berliner-Amrein analyses suggest that, as indicated by student performance on independent measures of achievement, high-stakes tests may inhibit the academic achievement of students, not foster their academic growth.

The researchers found that when state high-stakes test scores rise, it is likely as a result of student training that focuses on taking the tests. They conclude "such training does not appear to have any meaningful carryover effect when assessment of student learning is made on the independent measures of achievement that we used."

Unintended and Negative Consequences

"An Analysis of Some Unintended and Negative Consequences of High-Stakes Testing" examined the unintended consequences of high-stakes tests in 16 states that have implemented high-stakes graduation exams. In those states, Amrein and Berliner found increased dropout rates, decreased graduation rates, and higher rates of younger people taking the GED equivalency exams.

Examining news reports and qualitative data, the pair also found associations between high-stakes testing and

☐ Higher rates of retention of low-performing students in years before high-stakes tests were administered, possibly to better prepare students to take high-stakes tests;

☐ Higher numbers of low-performing students being suspended before testing days, expelled from school before tests, or being reclassified as exempt from testing because they are determined to be either Special Education or Limited English Proficient (LEP)—"all strategies to prevent low-scoring students from taking high-stakes tests," the authors noted;

Figure 3.29 *(Continued)*

☐ Reduced offerings in art, music, science, social studies, and physical education—all subjects that are less often tested;

☐ Higher numbers of urban school teachers, in particular, "teaching to the test," limiting instruction to only those things that are sure to be tested, requiring students to spend hours memorizing facts, and drilling students on test-taking strategies;

☐ Increased flight from public schools by teachers who sought to escape state testing mandates, "because state rules make them feel compromised as professionals," according to Amrein and Berliner;

☐ Instances of cheating by teachers and other school employees under pressure by high-stakes testing programs.

Amrein and Berliner conclude that there are enough negative unintended consequences to call into question the value of high-stakes high school graduation exams. Their data indicate that it is quite possible that the adverse consequences of high-stakes tests outweigh the benefits that advocates claim for them.

The Education Policy Research Unit (EPRU) conducts original research, provides independent analyses of research and policy documents, and facilitates educational innovation. EPRU facilitates the work of leading academic experts in a variety of disciplines to help inform the public debate about education policy issues.

Visit the EPRU Web site at http://educationanalysis.org

The Education Policy Studies Laboratory (EPSL) at Arizona State University offers high-quality analyses of national education policy issues and provides an analytical resource for educators, journalists, and citizens. It includes the Commercialism in Education Research Unit (CERU), the Education Policy Analysis Archives (EPAA), the Education Policy Reports Project (EPRP), the Education Policy Research Unit (EPRU), and the Language Policy Research Unit (LPRU).

The EPSL is directed by ASU Professor Alex Molnar.

Visit the EPSL Web site at http://edpolicylab.org

Figure 3.29 *(Continued)*

There are several benefits to using the print media. First, people may tend to have more confidence in what they read than in what they hear. Second, this medium can act as a reference. If people miss details the first time they read the document, in many cases they can easily refer to the paper again to gain a better understanding. A newspaper can also repeat information in successive editions to make a point and provide additional details or new interpretations of previously reported news. Finally, a newspaper's ability to reach a large audience is often the major reason for using this method.

Television and radio are mass electronic media that include cable news, network television, and news radio. These media are also well suited to reaching large segments of the public. Like videotape presentations, they can

- Transmit evaluation findings using language, sight, and sound
- Feature program participants
- Use spoken and visual language to reinforce the message
- Inspire and motivate audience

The *specialized media*, which are more trade and interest group oriented, offer evaluators an effective means for communicating evaluation findings. Newsletters, journals, and magazines published by groups such as the American Hospital Association, American Evaluation Association, or American Association of Retired Persons report information that is of greatest interest to their constituents. (For more information on the use of newsletters, see the previous section in this chapter.) These kinds of organizations and associations often post their newsletters on the Internet, increasing their accessibility to stakeholders and other audiences.

Although the news media can contribute greatly to evaluators' efforts to disseminate evaluation findings, they can be unpredictable. There are no guarantees of what information will be disseminated on the page, screen, or air because much of what the evaluator conveys will be abbreviated due to space and time restrictions. Evaluators wishing to use the media should do so only after careful thought and planning.

Implementation Tips for News Media Communications

■ Involve primary stakeholders in the media strategy as much as possible, especially if they are taking action on the findings.

Become informed about primary stakeholders' past experiences with the media. It is a good idea to benefit from these experiences and use them to the evaluation's advantage. Together you may decide that a press conference is preferable to a news release, or that an interview on a local public broadcasting station is more effective than an interview with the local newspaper. The decision to involve the media should always be done collaboratively. Case Example 3.9 illustrates how two school districts and program evaluators worked with the local newspaper to disseminate their evaluation results, raising the awareness level of the community and increasing dialogue about the two districts' consolidation plans.

CASE EXAMPLE 3.9

Establishing Linkages With the Local Media

An evaluation team studying the consolidation of two school districts in central Illinois published the evaluation's executive summary as an addendum to the local newspaper. It included a note "To Our Readers," which read,

> The future prosperity of Central Illinois and the superior quality of life which we enjoy is, in large measure, directly related to the stability and the excellence of our school systems, particularly at the primary and secondary levels. For this reason and as a public service, we have reproduced the Executive Summary of the recently conducted study of these two systems. We hope you will find it informative, that you will read it carefully, and that you will retain it for future reference.

The newspaper, of traditional size and printed on typical newsprint, included a table of contents and was created using two columns per page. Interspersed with the text were various tables and charts describing the evaluation's results. The 30-page executive summary resulted in an 8-page newspaper. As a follow-up to the newsletter, several public forums with school board members, super-intendents, school personnel, community members, and the evaluators were held. At the meetings, questions and concerns about the findings were discussed. The evaluators believe that the newsletter and public meetings served to raise community members' awareness and increased discussion and exchange of ideas about the two districts' consolidation plans.

SOURCE: Case described with permission of North Central Regional Educational Laboratory, Oak Brook, Illinois.

■ **Contact the media only after primary stakeholders have had a chance to read and reflect on the evaluation findings.**

It is important that primary stakeholders have time to consider evaluation findings before responding to the media's questions. No one likes to be sur-prised by reading about his or her program or organization in the press. Decision makers need time to develop a thoughtful response to findings.

■ **Enlist the aid of a journalist or someone who has a media communica-tions background.**

Public relations firms and consultants are a resource evaluators can use when working with the media. Someone with a print media background can be particularly helpful in determining what information should be printed, and how it might be formatted so that the general readership of the paper can assimilate the information.

■ **Be available to the media. Cooperation will improve media access and fair treatment in the future.**

A sure way to lose the media's interest is to be difficult to reach. Although you do not need to say much if you are concerned about divulging too much information too soon, being accessible shows an interest and concern for disseminating the study's results. Provide reporters with phone numbers and addresses so they can reach the evaluator or other spokesperson. If the media believe you are interested in working with them, they are also more likely to be interested in learning about a study. As a result, they may provide more airtime or space in their reports.

■ **Have a good summary of the evaluation study prepared to provide to reporters.**

It is rare that media personnel have enough time (or perhaps interest) to wade through lengthy reports. Their interest is primarily in the "facts" and key findings of the evaluation study. If you provide them with too much information, they may choose to report less important findings, thus increasing the potential for the results to be misinterpreted or misused. Sometimes an executive summary provides the right balance between too much and too little information.

■ **Be selective in choosing reports to send to the media.**

The press does not print everything it receives. It is important to determine with the project's stakeholders what information should be made available to the public. If the evaluation team sends everything, the press may choose pieces that are not particularly representative of the key aspects of the study. Do not rely on reporters to know which studies, findings, or parts of the evaluation are most important to communicate.

■ **Learn the language of the media and what it means to be "on" or "off the record."**

Before talking with reporters, know what it means to go on the record, or to be cited in the article. Many evaluators have learned the hard way that what they thought was an "aside" ended up being a major headline. Some reporters may wish you to say more even if you do not have data or findings in hand. When working with the news media, you should consider what you are and are not willing to share. It is wise to assume that when speaking with a reporter, everything is on the record.

CASE EXAMPLE 3.10

Challenges of Using the Local Media

This case concerns the evaluation of a school's first year of educational reform. Three months after the evaluation began, the education writer of one of the local newspapers spent several hours at the school interviewing students, teachers, and the paraprofessional staff. She had also contacted two or three students' parents or guardians. In the early afternoon, while the evaluator was doing her usual observing, the reporter asked if it would be all right to interview her for about 30 minutes. Naive to the workings of the press, she pleasantly agreed to be interviewed. The reporter asked several questions, mostly focusing on how well the school was doing after the first three months (something like the United States president's first 100 days). The evaluator described some of the successes and challenges the school faced, but distinctly remembers being fairly upbeat about the school's progress. Although she did notice that the reporter took only a couple of notes in a small notepad, she had left the interview feeling good about the information she'd shared. That is, she didn't believe any of it was anything the teachers at the school didn't already know.

A few days later, on the front page of the local section of the newspaper was the article about the school. The headline read: "School rates a C+." The article was a negative portrayal of the school and its teachers. There was little of the positive information shared by the evaluator, and several things she had said were taken out of context. The information provided wasn't wrong, but it wasn't reported in the way the evaluator had presented it. The evaluator also strongly objected to the summative rating of the school, which she had not suggested. This, she was later told, was the copywriter's addition.

After this episode, the evaluator was invited to be interviewed several times over the course of the three years. She politely declined and recommended that the reporters read the formative evaluation reports when they were delivered. Later articles written by the same reporter were consistently negative about the school. The reporter most likely did read parts of the evaluation reports, but most in the school believed her agenda was singular in purpose. Comments from parents who withdrew their children from the school during the first two years of its implementation indicated that they had believed what the reporter had communicated about the school and therefore did not want to "risk their child's education to an experiment." Later, as these parents learned more about the school from other sources, some regretted having removed their children. They realized too late that they didn't have the whole story. In retrospect, the evaluator wishes she had not been so forthcoming in her remarks and that she had been more cautious in the words she used. At the same time, it is quite possible that the reporter would have written the same story even without the evaluator's interview.

- **Deal in facts, and avoid any temptation to lie to a reporter.**

Be honest and forthright, but do not feel you have to answer every question. For some questions, you may wish to confer with the primary stakeholders and get back to the reporter at a later time. For others, you may explain that the data have not been sufficiently analyzed to draw any conclusions. Avoid any temptation to lie to a reporter in an effort to deal with questions you would rather not answer.

- **Avoid reporters who appear to have a single agenda and may fail to represent the evaluation's findings accurately.**

Some reporters, for various reasons, are out to prove a hunch or theory. Be wary of reporters who are only interested in the evaluation findings to support their assertions. The results could be disastrous. If you find yourself in this position, it is wise to discuss a strategy with the primary stakeholders. If this is not possible, then be available to the reporters (don't hide), but plan what you will say, and say no more. Case Example 3.10 describes an evaluator who faced this challenge and unfortunately learned too late the need for carefully assessing a reporter's intent.

CAUTIONS FOR NEWS MEDIA COMMUNICATIONS

- **The news media may not be an appropriate medium for communicating formative evaluation findings.**

  As the school's evaluator discovered in Case Example 3.10, the formative report immediately became summative when it was provided to the press. Those reading the newspaper saw the article as a definitive assessment of the school instead of describing it as a work in progress. The news media may be a more suitable reporting format for summative evaluations where it is appropriate to communicate a conclusive result or decision.

- **Reports via news media usually must be kept short.**

  When using television, radio, and the press, you are forced to keep your format short due to severe space and time restrictions. Thus, the information conveyed must be limited to a few key findings. For evaluations where the program's context is critical to understanding the evaluation findings, these media may not be your first choice.

  Print media, television, and radio are one-way communication systems. That is, none allow audience members to ask questions, get more details, or engage in any discussion about the findings. The fact that people tend to listen to radio or television somewhat casually, tuning in and out of a broadcast, is a further limitation of this approach.

■ **The news media tend to focus on the negative or on failures, especially concerning government or other public agencies and organizations.**

Reporters do not always report evaluation findings in the tone or manner expressed by the interviewees. Their job is to sell papers or to increase their audience. Though hard to accept, bad news sells. Thus, if an evaluation report identifies several areas of concern or makes significant recommendations for improvement, it is likely that a newspaper article will focus on the program's problems, failures, or weaknesses, rather than on the things that are positive and are working well. In cases such as these, a different communicating and reporting method might be more useful and appropriate.

Web Site Communications

A Web site is a location on the World Wide Web with information about a topic, an organization, an individual, or products (www.ucla.edu/articles/comm_websites.htm). The possibilities for evaluation communicating and reporting via Web sites are numerous. Possible Web postings include

- Interim and final evaluation reports
- Video presentations
- PowerPoint presentations
- Newsletters and brochures
- Meeting schedules and agendas
- Press releases and other forms of media coverage, including video clips from news broadcasts

Figure 3.30 shows two pages from the Web site of The Evaluation Center at Western Michigan University (www.wmich.edu/evalctr). The first is their introductory page for "The Advanced Technological Education (ATE) Program Evaluation Project." Selecting the link for "Evaluation Products" (fourth item in left column) takes you to the second page, which shows the variety of items available—including reports, executive summaries, at-a-glance summaries, brochures, PowerPoint presentations, descriptions of the program; and the evaluation approach, evaluation staff, and advisory panel members. Finally, the page names a specific person to e-mail with questions and comments. (To see this figure in color, go to http://www.sagepub.com/escr.)

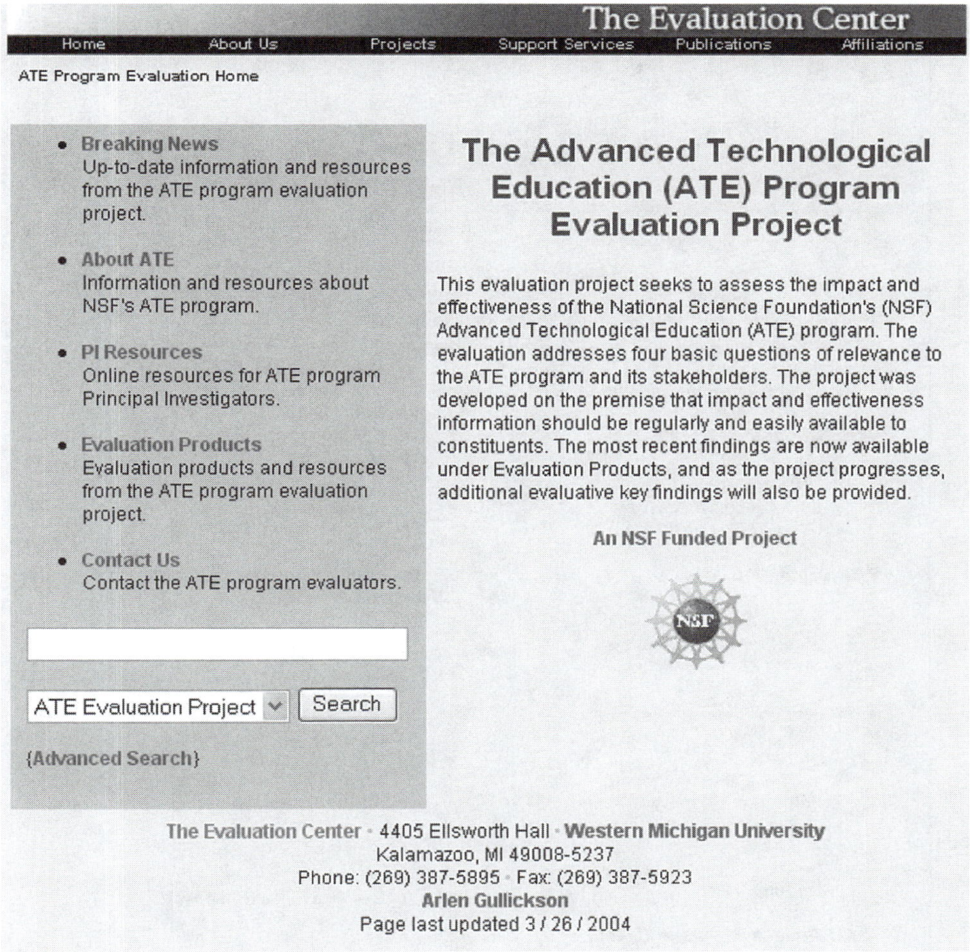

Figure 3.30   Example of Home Page and Evaluation Products Page for a Single Project

SOURCE: Used with permission of The Evaluation Center, Western Michigan University.

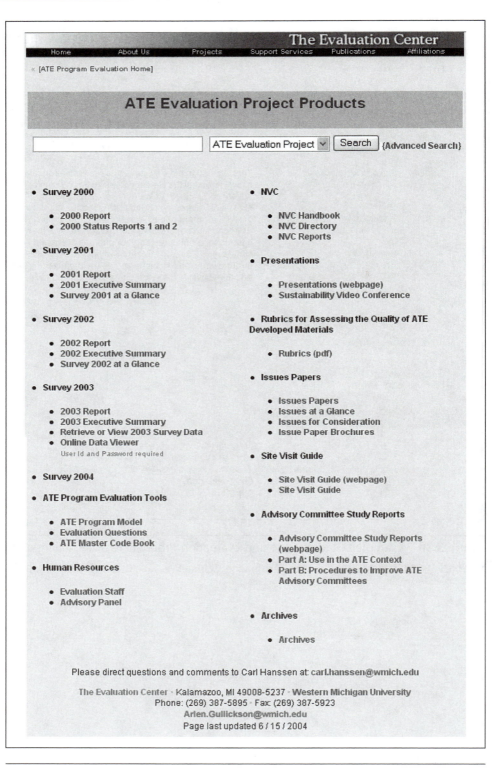

Figure 3.30 *(Continued)*

Web postings of evaluation products have several advantages:

- The evaluation information can be made easily accessible to a very broad national and international audience at minimal cost.
- Web sites allow you to stage the presentation of information into sections, accessible to users through links that the user selects. Links to related information and resources can also be included on the Web site, increasing users' access to knowledge, organizations, and contacts that may be especially useful to them.
- Dissemination through the Web allows large document files to be sectioned, and reduces the download times required when the document is transmitted in one piece via e-mail attachments.
- Because software to open the Web attachments is usually made available at the Web site (e.g., Adobe Acrobat), users do not face problems they sometimes have being unable to open e-mail attachments.
- Web dissemination also reduces the possibility of viruses being transmitted when documents are downloaded.

Implementation Tips for Web Communications

■ **Determine your audiences' Internet access and practices prior to establishing it as a mainstay for communicating and reporting.**

While Web use is commonplace to many, particular audiences may not have Internet access, and if they do, may not use it regularly. Also, the access they have may not support the technical features (e.g., connection speed, browser type) that your communications will require to work successfully. While most organizations and businesses have high-speed Internet connections, evaluation audiences accessing the Web from home may have a slower service, which can significantly increase access and download times.

■ **Before developing a Web site to facilitate evaluation communicating and reporting, determine if one already exists where a section could be used or created for your purposes.**

Developing and maintaining your own Web site requires both creative and financial resources. Existing Web sites of organizations or associations involved in your evaluation work may be good options for making evaluation information available. Many organizations with Web sites have in-house technical expertise to maintain and expand them. This expertise may be available to create Web pages and links to include your evaluation communications and reports.

Another option is to post evaluation documents on an FTP (file transfer protocol) site, which makes the documents available for downloading, but does not require the creation of Web pages. The site contains folders and files that are displayed to the user, similar to the way folders and files are displayed for the hard disk of your computer. In addition, FTP sites can be password-protected. Most Web hosting servers provide the means to create FTP sites without additional costs. You may find it convenient to post working documents on an FTP site for evaluation team members to access easily.

■ **If building a Web site specifically for the evaluation, determine if you will develop it yourself or seek outside expertise.**

Relatively simple Web authoring tools are available on the Web for free and through most Internet service providers, which will also host the Web site. In addition, Web pages can be created using most word-processing software. More sophisticated authoring software may also be an option, depending upon your time, technical expertise, and budget. General guidelines for developing a Web site and creating Web pages are presented here. (More in-depth treatments are readily available on the Web and in any number of books.)

Guidelines for Developing a Web site and Creating Web Pages

- Establish the purpose of your Web site, and assemble all of the information you wish to provide.
- Develop a logical flow between introductory information and the content of subsequent pages.
- Review existing Web sites for ideas about design and organization.
- Create the Web pages to fit the width of the lowest monitor resolution the majority of your audience is likely to use.
- Maintain the same basic design across all Web pages on your site.
- Use high contrast between background color and type.
- Choose typeface to maximize readability: Make sure text is not too small. Avoid using all caps, which slows reading time.
- Make sure you use commonly available text fonts (e.g., Arial, New York Times, Helvetica, or Times New Roman). Text fonts not supported by readers' computer systems will be translated into something similar, which could be visually unappealing.
- Position headings close to the related text.
- Choose graphics wisely: Make sure they are related to your topic and will be meaningful for readers. Do not allow too many different graphics to clutter the page. Avoid graphics that require a long download time.
- Make sure your page functions (links, downloads, etc.) properly.
- Test your Web site with different browsers to make sure it appears as you intend and functions properly.

Many organizations use commercial firms and consultants to design, create, and maintain Web sites. In the long run, this may be the better option if you anticipate significant use of and frequent revisions to your Web site.

■ **Consider making your Web site and postings accessible to people with disabilities.**

In 1998, the U.S. Congress amended the Rehabilitation Act to require federal agencies to make their electronic and information technology accessible to people with disabilities (see www.section508.gov). This requires that federal agencies' Web sites (and private sector Web sites provided under contract to a federal agency) must be accessible to individuals with disabilities such as blindness, low vision, and motor and hearing impairments. Web site features that increase accessibility include

- Text labels or verbal descriptors for graphics
- Electronic forms that allow people using assistive technology (e.g., input and output devices [voice, Braille], alternate access aids [headsticks, light pointers], modified keyboards, speech recognition software) to complete and submit them
- Text-only pages, with equivalent information or functionality as pages written in HTML
- Voice enabling

These features are worth considering whether or not some of your audience members are likely to be disabled. "Accessible sites offer significant advantages that go beyond access. For example, those with 'text-only' options provide a faster downloading alternative and can facilitate transmission of Web-based data to cell phones and personal digital assistants" (www.section508.gov). Voice enabling allows employees away from their desks to use the resources of the Internet via telephone.

■ **Provide various options for accessing and downloading large evaluation documents.**

Providing options increases the accessibility of your evaluation documents to audiences with various computer and Internet technologies. One option for posting large documents on a Web site, which has the advantage of reducing download time, is to divide the document into chapters or sections and post them individually. You probably have noticed that many documents available on the Web are presented in sections to be downloaded separately. This allows users to quickly access those areas they are most interested in, without waiting for the entire document to download, and then search it. You will probably also want to include the full report as a single posting for those who want to print it without accessing each chapter or section individually. Other options are to post documents in several formats: portable document format (.pdf), text-only format (.txt), Microsoft Word (.doc). Also, you can easily post large documents on FTP sites (see second implementation tip).

■ **Consider securing your posted documents so that they cannot be modified, and/or requiring password access.**

Unless they are created and posted as "read-only" files, it is possible for evaluation documents posted on the Web to be modified and redistributed. Parts of documents can be excerpted, and presented or used in ways you had not intended. Both Microsoft Word and Adobe Acrobat have features to prevent the modification of files posted in the formats that they support (.doc and .pdf, respectively). Doing so provides some protection. Remember, though, that anything that can be displayed via a Web site can be copied. Another option is to restrict access to the Web pages containing the documents to only those persons to whom you have provided a password.

■ **As with any means of dissemination, make sure evaluation documents, photographs, videos, and presentations posted on the Web have been fully vetted with your evaluation team, clients, and stakeholders.**

Dissemination through the World Wide Web makes many evaluation products accessible to a wider range and greater number of individuals than ever before. You will want to make your most stringent efforts to obtain feedback and assure accuracy before posting on the Internet. One particular concern is making negative evaluation findings publicly accessible. Evaluators may be reticent to fully address negative findings in reports they know are going to be made available on the Web. Stakeholders may not fully realize the implications of having negative findings widely available. Finally, consider getting formal, written permission to include in a Web posting the names, contact information, and/or visual images that are part of an evaluation document or video.

■ **Write summaries of evaluation information/findings for inclusion on Web pages, and post full versions of documents to be downloaded.**

Figure 3.31 provides an example of a Web page displaying evaluation findings with brief text, a link to the full study, and simple graphics. (To see this figure in color, go to http://www.sagepub.com/escr.) Web pages are well suited for presenting limited amounts of text rather than complete reports. Research on Web users' practices revealed that they tend to scan contents

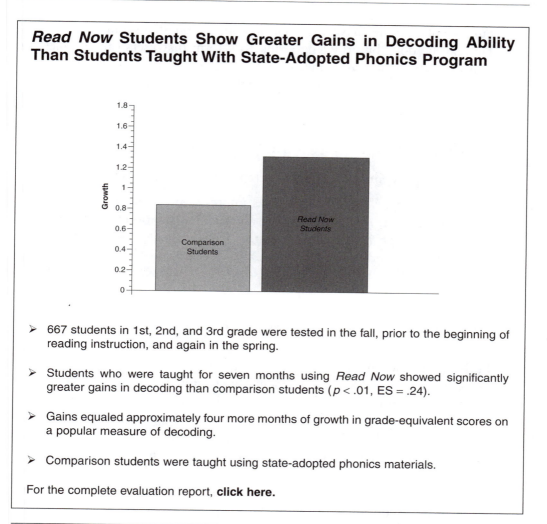

Figure 3.31   Example of Web Page Displaying Evaluation Findings With Brief Text, Link to Full Study, and Simple Graphics

of Web pages rather than read them word-for-word (www.useit.com/alertbos/97). Bulleted summaries of findings are a good choice for Web page content.

■ **Consider including a mechanism for evaluation audiences to ask questions, request further information, and/or provide feedback.**

While Web postings are primarily a one-way means of disseminating evaluation information, asynchronous interaction with audiences and stakeholders can take place if they have an opportunity to ask questions and give feedback. This can be done by providing a link to a form that users can complete, or providing contact information (e.g., e-mail address, phone). This feature should not be offered on your Web site, though, unless you have the resources to provide timely responses.

CAUTION FOR WEB COMMUNICATIONS

■ **Web site communications and reports are highly visible.**

The World Wide Web provides unprecedented means for disseminating information. Access to evaluation information made available on the Web is virtually unlimited. This makes it open to critique, feedback, and praise by anyone who sees it.

S U M M A R Y

In this chapter we have focused on evaluation strategies and formats that are primarily text based and are particularly effective for facilitating individual learning. The strategies we have described include: memos and e-mail, postcards, interim reports, final reports, executive summaries, newsletters, bulletins, briefs, and brochures, news media communications and Web site communications. Throughout the chapter we have emphasized the value of considering a communication's design and layout to enhance the accessibility of the information; the importance of using tables and figures effectively; and using clear, jargon-free language.

4 Communicating and Reporting Strategies to Maximize Learning

Topics Addressed

- Verbal Presentations
- Video Presentations
- Posters and Poster Sessions
- Working Sessions
- Synchronous Electronic Communications
- Personal Discussions

Questions to Ponder

- ☐ *Which communicating and reporting formats can be used with or without interacting with audiences?*
- ☐ *Which communicating and reporting formats are inherently interactive?*
- ☐ *How can audience interaction maximize learning?*
- ☐ *How can different communicating and reporting formats be used effectively when interaction with stakeholders and other audiences is not possible?*

In this chapter we provide information on a variety of communicating and reporting formats that rely on some level of team or group interaction. The formats covered in this chapter include: verbal presentations, video presentations, posters and poster sessions, working sessions, synchronous electronic communications (chat rooms, teleconferencing, video- and Web conferencing), and personal discussions. Our primary goal in this chapter is to present interactive and potentially interactive communicating and reporting strategies that facilitate individual, group, and organizational learning.

Potentially Interactive Formats

Verbal presentations, video presentations, and posters can be delivered with or without interacting with audiences. In what follows we emphasize the opportunities each provides for interaction and how it supports learning. We also point out how these communicating and reporting formats can be used to best advantage when time or other circumstances do not allow for interfacing with stakeholders and other audiences.

Verbal Presentations

Frequently, evaluators make verbal presentations concerning the progress of an evaluation and/or its findings to stakeholders and other audiences. Face-to-face communications are particularly useful for conveying information on complex, specialized topics. Making a verbal presentation usually allows audiences the opportunity to ask questions, and at the same time you may be able to facilitate further interaction on the evaluation.

After hearing a verbal presentation about an evaluation, members of an audience might

- Reflect on what the evaluation information and/or findings mean.
- Seek additional information.
- Contact someone else who should know about the evaluation's progress or findings.
- Hold a meeting with program participants to develop an action plan and implement recommendations.
- Provide additional program level support.
- Make changes in a program.
- Expand or reduce a program's resources and/or availability.
- Revise or develop a policy.

Case Example 4.1 describes the work of a youth-led evaluation team that culminated in their making a verbal presentation about the evaluation findings to a group of adult stakeholders. The dialogue between the evaluation team and stakeholders that occurred following the presentation was crucial to the action taken based on the study.

CASE EXAMPLE 4.1

Dialogue on Evaluation Findings Empowers Youth, Facilitates Change

Youth In Focus (YIF) is a nonprofit organization based in northern California that fosters the development of youth, organizations, and communities by supporting youth-led research, evaluation, and planning. YIF is committed to increasing the use of youth-led evaluations by organizations and institutions that serve youth. Its work is based on the belief that youth can effectively partner with adults to address social and institutional challenges, and that these partnerships are crucial to achieving just, democratic, and sustainable social change.

In youth-led research, evaluation, and planning projects (Youth REP), young people play lead roles in identifying information that could serve to change or initiate a program, organization, community initiative, organizing campaign, or policy that affects them and their peers. They then frame questions, design and use methods to collect data, analyze the information, make recommendations, and work with others to follow through to action. Often an initial project becomes the foundation of youth leadership in ongoing cycles of needs assessment, planning, action, and evaluation. YIF provides training and technical assistance through an eight-step process that covers planning the research through developing an action plan (Youth in Focus, 2003).

YIF requires the support and participation of executive leadership from the host organization. Arguably, the most crucial interaction comes when findings are presented by youth and discourse about their meaning and implications takes place. Although preparation and submission of a report would be a learning experience for the youth, and perhaps of some benefit to the organization, YIF goals could not be realized without significant engagement between youth and adults on the evaluation findings and action planning.

This case from YIF describes a youth-led study to investigate sexual harassment at a San Francisco middle school, and the actions that took place as a result of it. A group of seven students formed a student research team (SRT) that chose to study sexual harassment, as they felt it was one of the most obvious forms of violence at their school and that it greatly impacted their lives. The school's drug prevention and safety coordinator facilitated the work of the team, and YIF staff provided evaluation technical assistance.

The team's main form of data collection was a survey of 6th- and 7th-graders to find out their opinions about sexual harassment at the school, and specifically if they had ever observed, been a victim of, and/or a perpetrator of sexual harassment. Prior to administration of the survey, the team made a presentation to their peers on sexual harassment "to show how it happens a lot to the students at our school." In all, 77 students responded to the survey.

The SRT prepared a written report detailing the study's background, research team, purpose, methods, findings, and recommendations. They also developed a PowerPoint presentation of the study's highlights. A copy of the final report

(Continued)

CASE EXAMPLE 4.1 (Continued)

was handed out during a 50-minute class period when the team delivered their presentation to a group of approximately 22 adults including the school's principal, vice principal, counselors, faculty, YIF staff, and staff from a collaborating organization that provides services at the middle school. Among the team's key findings were the following:

- 72% of responding students thought sexual harassment was a problem.
- 94% wanted it stopped.
- Rude comments, spreading rumors, and inappropriate touching are the most common forms of sexual harassment.
- It happens most frequently to females.
- It happens (in descending order of frequency) in the schoolyard, classroom, hallway, and cafeteria.
- 75% of those who witnessed sexual harassment did not try to stop it.

Their recommendations were to (1) train teachers and administrators on how to deal with sexual harassment when they see it; and (2) have an assembly or 6th-, 7th-, and 8th-graders (with separate sessions for each grade level and for each gender) to train students on ways to stop sexual harassment when they see it.

The presentation was an overview, but as the adults reviewed the details of the full report they had received, they asked specific questions. The questions were addressed when the session was opened up for dialogue during the last 20–25 minutes. Among the points of the dialogue were the following:

- The middle schools counselors related that students do not come to them about sexual harassment. They acknowledged that the survey showed it was really a problem.
- The study showed that a high percentage of students reported seeing sexual harassment, but a much lower percentage reported experiencing it. The SRT explained to the audience that feedback from responding students indicated that some students did not want to disclose this on the survey. Also the team speculated that it may be easier to identify sexual harassment when you witness it than when you are the victim of it.
- The adults took note of the particular finding indicating that students felt adults in the school would not do anything about the sexual harassment if the students did report it. In particular, the teachers were very concerned that there was the perception that adults would not act.
- The principal had specific questions about the recommendations, e.g., "What would the training look like?" The team reported that their recommendations were based on their own brainstorming, but they had not done research on what would be the best intervention.
- Teachers and counselors were struck by student respondents' notion that sexual harassment was an act of violence. The SRT explained that they felt it was just as important to have some intervention for sexual harassment as it was for physical violence. The teachers expressed support for the

SRT's recommendation that there be some kind of awareness training with the faculty, so that they understand that sexual harassment is a problem, and that it is a source of violence.

- The SRT responded to questions about the study's methodology and acknowledged the limitation of their small sample size. They explained reasons for this and legitimately convinced the adults of the value of the study. The students were articulate about the details of the study, demonstrating that they understood the data.

This dialogue between the SRT and the adult stakeholders was crucial to the action taken based on the study. The findings themselves were important, but would have had much less impact if the dialogue with the student researchers had not taken place. As one YIF staff member explained

> The immediate steps taken, as well as those that will take place in the future, will happen as a result of things that happened in that meeting. . . . The discussion provided an opportunity for students to respond to questions and they gave a lot more information about the study. In all, they were advocates for the study. For them it is rare that they are asked something, and that something is actually done. . . . The students had a celebration afterwards. They felt a lot of pride in the work they had done."

One immediate outcome of the dialogue was a deeper commitment to youth-led research among the adults present who were impressed with the quality of the work. Another was reinstatement of the sexual harassment orientation for all the middle school students, which had been dropped two years earlier. The administration has also committed to developing similar sexual harassment orientations for teachers.

SOURCE: Case described with permission of Youth in Focus.

As evaluators, we find ourselves in the challenging position of presenting findings to a wide variety of audiences, ranging from colleagues at a professional conference, to parents of children in an inner-city school, to high-level policy makers. The primary objective of presenting information on an evaluation's progress or its findings is for audience members to understand the information being presented. Based on this understanding, they may consider it further, and/or act on what they have learned.

Further complicating the challenge of making an effective verbal presentation, evaluation findings vary widely in their technical complexity, depending on the data collection and analysis methods used. Quantitative methods always involve the use of statistics, ranging from simple frequencies to advanced statistics (e.g., multiple regression, factor analyses). Almost nothing is more agitating, and even insulting, to audience members than to be presented with statistical information they do not understand. Conversely, underestimating the level of audience sophistication with respect to quantitative methods can be equally problematic. Making a verbal presentation of qualitative results is challenging, too, because the evaluator often must choose from among more data than can be covered in any one presentation. The following implementation tips address various aspects of making effective verbal presentations.

⇨ Implementation Tips for Verbal Presentations

■ **Take the audience's perspective when planning your presentation.**

The success of any verbal presentation depends on its relevance to your audience. Sometimes, evaluators and audiences differ in their perceptions of what is important about an evaluation. For instance, because we as evaluators are most familiar with the evaluation's methodology, we tend to focus on it. When the presentation begins with too much time spent on the methodology, too little time is left for discussion of specific evaluation findings and reaction from the audience. To orient yourself to the perspective of audience members when planning the presentation, consider these questions:

- What is my audience's level of prior knowledge about the evaluation?
- What do I think the audience hopes to get from the presentation?
- What type of information is the audience likely to find most credible?

Another way to tailor your presentation to the needs of the audience is to introduce the general topic of the presentation and provide sufficient background information for members of the audience to relate it to their concerns about the evaluation. Next, you may ask them for specific questions or topics they would like answered or discussed. Alternatively, you can present a list of topics and ask the audience to prioritize them. You would then adjust the presentation accordingly, being sure to cover the topics considered most important.

■ **Focus the presentation on a few selected topics.**

We have all been members of audiences when the presenter was trying to cover too much information. For evaluation topics, it is much more likely that we have too much rather than too little information to present within any given time period. This is particularly the case if you are making a presentation based on the findings given in a final evaluation report. As with summarizing, the process of deciding what information to present typically involves several stages of reduction. Essential questions to consider are

- What are my objectives for this presentation?
- What key things do I want the audience members to understand once they have heard my presentation?

Try to think in terms of approximately five main points that you want to get across. You may have specific examples and evidence from the evaluation in mind, but these should be considered subpoints to your main ideas.

For those instances beyond your control, when you have been allocated insufficient time for your presentation, carefully consider what you will be able to communicate and report. If you have only a few minutes to speak, develop two to four key points and allow a few minutes for questions and answers.

There are also times when you might be asked, with only a few hours' or a day's notice, to present on some aspect of the evaluation; and you may not have time to prepare a formal presentation. In these cases, make an outline of things you want to say, and perhaps prepare a few flip chart pages that can support your key points.

■ Organize the presentation for yourself and the audience.

Remember that the best flow and sequencing of an evaluation report is not necessarily the best flow and sequencing for a presentation, even if it covers some of the same content. Organize the presentation so that it has an introduction, body, and conclusion. The body, which covers your main points and subpoints, should be developed first. What is in the body often determines what should be put in the introduction and the conclusion. Remember to develop clear transitions between the main points of your presentation. Audience members are entirely dependent on you to organize the content of the presentation for them.

Introductory information might include any or all of the following: purpose and objectives of the presentation; evaluator background; project and evaluation background; and agenda for the meeting. Finally, remember to develop a conclusion to the presentation. It should end on an upbeat, summarizing note, with reference back to the presentation's objective(s).

■ Plan ways to involve the audience.

Communication and learning are more effective when the audience is involved in the process. There is almost no reason to make a presentation without some form of interaction with the audience. Ideally, evaluation processes are part of a program's or organization's ongoing planning and improvement efforts. Every opportunity to communicate with clients and stakeholders should be maximized. Audience involvement should be planned for, even if your presentation is being made to people who have had little direct involvement with the program or organization in question. Consider the following suggestions for involving your audience:

Guidelines for Audience Involvement

- Use humor and stories.
- At the beginning of the presentation, solicit expectations and questions about the presentation topic.
- Use worksheets that solicit information from audience members and then ask them to share their ideas.
- Adjust your presentation according to audience reaction and nonverbal cues.
- Use variety in your body language and the pace of your speech to engage and retain the audience's attention.
- Allocate time at the end of the presentation for questions, answers, and discussion.
- Get audience members' reactions to the presentation and ask about additional information needs they have.

■ **Use handouts to support your presentation.**

Most presentations are more effective if they include handouts for the audience. A single-page handout outlining the presentation can help the audience follow the sequence of topics. Or, if you are using PowerPoint in your presentation, you might provide audience members with a paper copy of the slides. Handouts that supply supporting or more detailed information give audience members something to refer to (1) in the future; (2) during the presentation should their attention lapse; or (3) should they miss the meaning of something you are saying.

Sometimes, audiences are given a copy of the evaluation report at the same time they hear a verbal presentation of the findings. It is a good idea to think through how the audience will react to the handout. For example, if you provide a copy of the evaluation report at the beginning of the presentation, audience members may give their attention to the report rather than to you. You may want to hand out the report later, at which time you can review how it is organized for them and answer questions they may have about it.

■ **Practice your presentation and use effective presentation techniques.**

Regardless of how carefully you plan and organize a presentation, it can still be considered a failure if not delivered effectively. Follow these guidelines to ensure a successful presentation.

Guidelines for Giving a Verbal Presentation

- Direct the audience's attention appropriately throughout the presentation (e.g., turn off the overhead during discussions, use overlays to build an overhead illustration).
- Assume a relaxed, natural posture.
- Move about to enhance your involvement with the audience.
- If you are using visuals, focus on one idea per visual.
- Do not read every word on the visual—they are there to support what you have to say. Make short notes for yourself in large print to cue you about what you want to say. This approach helps establish a more personal, conversational style.
- If you want to point to certain words or phrases on a visual, either use a laser pointer directed to the screen or flip chart, or use a small stick or pen on the transparency itself.
- If you are using overhead transparencies, keep track of key slides that you are likely to refer to more than once. Set them aside so that you do not have to hunt for them among the other slides.
- Maintain eye contact with the audience.
- Maintain your attention on the audience, not on the visuals. Remember to face the group when discussing a visual; don't turn your back and read from the visual.
- If you are distributing handouts during the presentation, do so quickly. Alternatively, you can have them available at audience members' seats or to be picked up as they arrive.

■ **Consider the room arrangement for your presentation.**

How the room is arranged can also influence the effectiveness of your presentation and any activities you may use in conjunction with the presentation. Ideally, the room should be large enough to hold the expected number of participants. Consider the following seating arrangements, which are almost always preferable to orderly rows of chairs:

- Chairs positioned in a semicircle
- Chairs along the outside of long tables positioned to form a U
- Chairs positioned around several smaller tables (ideal for small-group discussions)

■ **Evaluate your presentations so that you continuously improve your communication of evaluation information.**

Making good verbal presentations is an art that few individuals feel they have completely mastered. Whenever possible, get feedback from audience members about your efforts. Asking them to complete a short evaluation form or give verbal feedback is essential to your knowing whether or not the presentation met audience needs, and if some follow-up is indicated. You will want audience members to tell you the extent to which the objectives of the presentation were met, what they liked and disliked about it, and what additional questions they have. If audience members have additional questions, then you may be able to follow up with a written communication about findings or other issues they raise. Finally, asking for their opinions is another way to involve stakeholders and maintain ongoing communication about the evaluation.

■ **Use visuals in your presentation.**

Incorporating visuals into a presentation makes information more understandable, piques interest, supports visual learners, and stimulates discussion. The most commonly used visuals for presentations are PowerPoint slides, overhead transparencies, and flip charts. Research conducted by Wharton Business School's Applied Research Center (cited by Meilach, 1994) found that presenters using visuals were rated significantly more persuasive, credible, and interesting than those who did not. Moreover, groups reached a consensus in almost 30% less time when visuals were used to present information about their topic of discussion. Conceptually clear and well-designed visuals can support audience understanding and help maintain their interest during the presentation.

It is important to consider what you want a visual to communicate and how participants will benefit from it. Visuals must provide a clear and consistent message with what is being verbally presented. If they contain too little information or are overly complex or crowded, they lose their effectiveness.

In choosing from among visual aids, consider both the resources you have and the size of the room and how it will be organized. To present visuals on a large screen you will need transparencies and an overhead projector, or a computer-generated presentation (i.e., using PowerPoint) and projection device. Flip charts require an easel and/or wall space for hanging them. In some cases you may want and be able to use both visuals projected onto a large screen and flip charts, during the course of the same presentation. Flip charts are only effective as a presentation tool when they are used with groups smaller than 25–30, since they are difficult to see from a distance. If presenting to a larger group, consider using a PowerPoint presentation or overhead transparencies. In larger groups, however, flip charts can still be used for small-group work.

The sections that follow discuss PowerPoint presentations and transparencies, and flip charts in detail.

PowerPoint Presentations and Transparencies

Evaluators frequently use PowerPoint or other computer software to create visuals for use during their verbal presentations. This enables the presentation to be projected from a computer without producing transparencies and using an overhead projector. If you are unfamiliar with PowerPoint, check out the many Web sites that provide tips for using it effectively.

Even though most presenters prefer to use a laptop computer connected to a projection system when using PowerPoint to facilitate their verbal presentations, this technology may not be available. In situations like these, it is still useful to have overhead slides that have been developed using PowerPoint or some other presentation software.

Implementation Tips for PowerPoint Presentations and Overhead Transparencies

■ **Design PowerPoint slides prudently.**

One of the main features of PowerPoint is the design options it has for format and layout, color, font size, use of animation, and inclusion of photographs and video clips. These options can be both a benefit and a challenge. They can help you create professional-looking, powerful visuals that support audience members' learning. On the other hand, too many design elements invoked at once can be distracting and even annoying. Consider the following design principles:

Design Principles for PowerPoint Slides and Overhead Transparencies

Format

- As you develop each slide, make sure that your font style and size, formatting, and grammar are the same for every slide.
- Choose a template (a design) that supports your message—you don't want the design to detract from your message. Use this same design for all your slides.
- Follow the "6 × 6" rule: no more than six lines of text and no more than six words per line per slide. If you start with writing sentences, fine, but go back through and edit down to some key words. Try to present the information in "bullets."

(Continued)

(Continued)

- Number your slides.
- When using PowerPoint animation, it is easier to read text when it drops down from above, or comes from the left. Don't change the direction of entering text for each slide—consistency is key. Do not overdo the special effects.

Color

- Make sure that the font color contrasts with the background color so that the text shows up well.
- Be careful how you use red—the eye goes there first, and some suggest that red is a difficult color for males to see.
- Use no more than five colors on charts and graphs.
- Highlight key points with a bold font or color.

Fonts

- Font size should be no smaller than 20-point (minimum ¼-inch high letters).
- Avoid ornate font styles that could be difficult to read.
- Vary the size of the font to illustrate the relative importance of information, but don't use more than two font styles in your presentation.
- Use upper- and lowercase letters (don't use only uppercase).

Content

- If using photographs, cartoons, or other art in the presentation, consider your audience and how they might react to certain clip art or other visuals embedded in the slides.
- Don't rely on spell check alone. Go through each slide and double-check for typos and misspelled words. Even better, ask someone else to proofread the slides.

■ **Budget adequate time for creating your PowerPoint slides or transparencies.**

To develop an effective PowerPoint presentation or set of overhead transparencies, care needs to be taken to ensure that each slide or transparency is formatted consistently; that just the right amount of information is presented; that the presentation flows from one point to another; and that the effects chosen are supportive of the content. As a result, it is easy to spend several hours developing a PowerPoint presentation. Though probably worth it, this needs to be considered when calculating the amount of time needed for communicating and reporting.

■ **Gauge the number of slides or transparencies you use according to the time available.**

When presentations include too many slides or transparencies, participants stop thinking about the content of the presentation and begin to wonder how many more slides they will have to sit through. Having too many slides can also cause the presenter to read the slides rather than using them as an outline of the presentation.

A general rule of thumb is to have no more than one visual per minute of presentation. For example, if you have 20 minutes to give the main body of your presentation, have no more than 20 slides. It's helpful to include a title slide that focuses the presentation, a slide that shows the presentation's agenda, and one that summarizes the presentation at the end.

■ **Be prepared to handle the mechanics of your presentation.**

Especially if you are making a PowerPoint presentation for the first time, you will want to make sure all the mechanics of doing so are in order. Using transparencies and an overhead projector requires attention to mechanical details as well. Follow these guidelines:

Guidelines for Handling the Mechanics of Projecting Visuals

PowerPoint Presentations

- Make sure that you have your presentation backed up on a disk, in case your computer fails and another one has to be brought in.
- Arrive at the room with plenty of time to set up the projection system, connect it to your computer, set up the screen, and make sure everything is in working order.
- Locate outlets and determine if an extension cord is needed. It is a good idea to bring one with you just in case.
- Bring an extra cable that attaches your computer to the projection system in case the one that is provided does not work.

Transparencies and Overhead Projector

- Before the presentation, make sure that there are two usable bulbs in the projector so that if one burns out, there will be another one easily accessible. It's also a good idea to bring an extra extension cord.

(Continued)

(Continued)

- Make sure that the projector is not blocking anyone's view of the screen. (Corners of a room are considered to be the best place for a screen and projector.)
- Focus the projector before you start your presentation.
- Position the transparency on the projector before turning it on so the bright light does not bother participants.
- Be careful not to stand in front of the screen.
- Position the transparency as high on the projector's screen as possible.
- Turn the projector off after the last slide.
- Since transparencies are prone to slide off the projector, use transparency frames to keep them in place. This will also keep them in better shape if they are to be used again.

Flip Charts

The use of flip charts can add visual focus and clarity to a verbal presentation. Sometimes called newsprint, flip chart paper is a cost-efficient and effective means for

- Communicating a meeting's agenda
- Communicating key points of a presentation and reinforcing your message
- Recording a meeting's progress and next steps

Using flip charts during a presentation has several advantages for evaluators: They require no electricity, are relatively inexpensive, can be used creatively, and allow for last-minute changes to be made. Using flip charts also has advantages for audience members, aiding in their understanding, reference, and participation. Specifically, flip charts can

- Remind participants what has been covered or what will soon be covered in the presentation.
- Encourage participation when audience members are asked for their input.
- Document their ideas, thoughts, and reactions about the evaluation information being presented.
- Help those who come late to see what has been covered.
- Create a warm and inviting atmosphere when a welcoming message or agenda is posted on a flip chart.

➡️ *Implementation Tips for Using Flip Charts*

■ **Prepare attractive and legible flip charts.**

A poorly prepared flip chart can be distracting and appear unprofessional. It's best if you can prepare flip charts used to present information prior to your presentation, and not on site just before the presentation. Follow these guidelines to create attractive and legible flip charts:

Guidelines for Creating Flip Charts to Present Information

- If possible, prepare flip charts ahead of time and store them carefully so that they do not get folded or torn.
- Write out the content on regular-sized paper before writing it on the flip chart paper.
- Use the largest size paper available to maximize visibility.
- Use markers that do not bleed through the paper, and that have a wide tip, so that the writing can be visible to participants who are farthest away.
- Avoid writing on the bottom quarter of the paper, since this part of the page is often blocked from view.
- Print or write legibly and in a large, bold style.
- Use multiple colored markers to heighten interest and aid retention. Avoid pale colors and red (except as a highlighter). Do not use more than three colors on a page.
- If you have multiple flip chart pages, consider attaching different colored tabs to cue you into where the presentation's topics shift or change.
- If you make an error on a prepared flip chart page, instead of starting all over, cover it with a paper patch and invisible tape.
- Whenever possible, use flip chart paper that has gridlines, allowing the writer to print on the lines.
- Consider lightly writing the content in pencil on the flip chart paper before you write it using the markers.
- Follow the "7 × 7" rule: No more than seven lines of text and no more than seven words per line on a flip chart page.
- Consider writing some notes in pencil on the flip chart page to remind yourself of key points you want to make.
- Consider having a blank sheet of paper between each flip chart page of information. This will prevent the written material from other sheets showing through.
- If you do not have access to an easel, put the flip chart paper up on a wall where the participants can see it.

■ **Gauge the number of flip charts you will need.**

As is true with overheads and slides, this method can actually detract from the presentation's message if too much time is spent moving from one flip chart page to another, or if the presenter ends up reading from the pages. Overuse of flip charts may be seen as wasting time, and can slow down the presentation.

■ **Determine how you will transport flip charts.**

Because of their size, flip charts can be difficult to transport. If you need to carry an easel and flip chart pads with you to another location, this can be very challenging. Instead of transporting this equipment, you might instead bring the prepared flip charts and blank pages with you, rolled up. You can then affix them to a wall in the room where you will be presenting.

For travel, consider purchasing PVC tubing or mail tubes to hold the rolled-up flip charts.

■ **Use flip charts to record participants' comments and questions during a presentation.**

Following presentation of the evaluation information, you may wish to use flip charts to record audience members' comments, reactions, or questions. This acknowledges their perspectives on the topic and invites participation. Follow these guidelines:

Guidelines for Using Flip Charts to Record Information

- Be sure that you are capturing the words of the participants as much as possible. If you are unsure, repeat what you have heard to verify the participants' comments.
- If some participants' responses are too lengthy or difficult to para-phrase, consider writing keywords or short phrases, emphasizing with multiple colors, arrows, circles, and underlining. Another approach would be to use check marks next to ideas that have already been offered.
- Consider having someone else mark the flip chart while you facilitate the discussion.
- Consider using two or more flip charts so that you can easily refer back to comments that have been made and charted.
- If you wish to hang the flip chart sheets on the wall, make sure that you have enough wall space on which to do this. Choose a room that can accommodate the activity. Tear off pieces of tape before the

---

meeting so that they are handy and will not slow down the pace of the conversation.

- If you are facilitating the presentation and writing on the flip chart, try to do both at the same time.
- Stand to the side of the flip chart as you write so that your writing is visible to the majority of participants.

Video Presentations

Video presentations can bring the combined power of visual imagery, motion, and sound to evaluation audiences and stakeholders. Traditionally, videotapes have been created and edited on specialized equipment by videographers. Now, video can be shot in digital format with relatively inexpensive cameras and edited on desk- and laptop computers. This allows the video to be saved and disseminated in both CD-ROM and digital videodisk (DVD) formats. Videos can also be presented on the World Wide Web, and inserted into PowerPoint or Word documents.

For communicating and reporting information, video presentations can be especially useful when you want to

- Present qualitative evaluation findings.
- Use an inviting medium to broadly disseminate and assure consistency in the presentation of evaluation findings.
- Present findings from multisite evaluations.
- Provide feedback to stimulate reflection among stakeholders.
- Document evaluation processes.
- Present evaluation findings about new, innovative programs.

Videos can be an especially useful means for presenting qualitative evaluation findings. Interview and observation excerpts and photographs are typically included in written reports to convey the experiences of program participants. Videos can capture the sound and motion of these experiences, capturing their subtlety and complexity. This feature of video is illustrated in Case Example 4.2. It describes how video was used to depict long-term outcomes for participants in a family community leadership program across several regions of the United States.

CASE EXAMPLE 4.2

The Need for Visual Images to Tell the Story

Family Community Leadership (FCL): The Ripples Spread . . . is a retrospective study conducted for the W. K. Kellogg Foundation (WKKF) by evaluation consultant Linda W. Helstowski. The study was designed to: (1) consolidate and summarize key information and results of FCL program projects supported within WKKF's Food Systems and Rural Development program area; (2) identify and highlight compelling examples of FCL program longitudinal impacts and spin-offs; and (3) assess and reflect on the strategies and approaches that were utilized, building on a 1993 national evaluation. A key purpose of the study was to revisit the cluster of FCL projects that had been supported in each state across the country, and to assess what (if anything) had been sustained over time since Kellogg's funding of the FCL program had officially ended about ten years earlier. The intended audiences for the study were internal sources, specifically the Kellogg Board and program staff.

WKKF went into this retrospective study quite uncertain about whether much of anything remained of the original FCL programming. Once the study got underway, it became apparent that people (particularly women) had experienced lasting impact from the program in various ways; and that some aspects of the program continued to exist in many states (and had been "morphed," as one project director described, into various follow-on activities). Helstowski felt that being able to most effectively capture these exciting and somewhat unexpected insights would entail photos and audio. She became convinced of this, based in part on a prior experience:

> When I conducted the Agriculture Leadership study [an earlier retrospective study for WKKF], I was particularly struck by a young Hispanic from a farming family who had become one of California's youngest Assemblymen. He was choked with emotion as he spoke about how the Kellogg programming (leadership training) had been the second largest influence on his life, next to his immigrant parents.
>
> My audio equipment was not high enough quality to transfer to any final piece (not to mention that it malfunctioned during the interview), nor did I have a digital camera on hand to capture his expressiveness as he spoke: "I cannot describe what the Program has meant to me—there are no words. The Program changed my life and made me what I am today. I represent the American Dream." That was the turning point for me—realizing through this lost opportunity how much more impactful these retrospective studies could be if we could actually capture participants' words and faces as "voices from the field."

WKKF staff overseeing the study agreed, and provided financial and developmental support in moving forward. The original evaluation plan and budget had enough flexibility (that is, allowing for some of the specific methodologies/approaches to be based on findings revealed along the way) to provide consultant training, and support the creation of a short digital production, viewable in both

CD and video format, to accompany the written report and serve as an important documentation and storytelling overview.

The piece is four minutes in length and consists of a series of still photographs narrated by Helstowski. The majority of photos are head shots of FCL participants, shown at the same time that audio clips of interviews with the participants are being played. This approach helps provide a firsthand sense of the breadth and diversity of FCL participants and impacts, ranging from: (1) a young mother in an urban Head Start program expressing newfound self-confidence ("If I can make a difference in one kid's life, I feel my life's been worth something."); to (2) a small business owner motivated to serve as a model for others ("I was the first Hispanic/Native American in the state of Nebraska to be on the city council, and that is probably the highlight of my life. I just wanted to be an example so that other minorities knew that if I can do it, they could also do that."); to (3) a Louisiana homemaker in her late 60s who had been searching for a way to heal from the loss of her son ("I know there are mountains out there yet to be climbed. . . . I'm not planning on sliding down to the valley. FCL has taught me I'm on the way up").

The video is not intended as a stand-alone piece, but rather to accompany the final report and/or be introduced with substantial background information about the retrospective study. It demonstrates that an effective piece (accessible and viewable in multiple formats) can indeed be developed at minimal cost for equipment and off-the-shelf software, and can be easily edited for electronic dissemination.

WKKF was pleased with the products of this study, which also included a well-designed comprehensive report, and considers it to be among the more creative retrospective studies they have commissioned. The Foundation plans to feature the study (including the video) prominently in the written publications and electronic book that are being prepared for its upcoming 75th anniversary recognition of significant work over the past several decades.

SOURCE: Case described with permission of the W. K. Kellogg Foundation.

Videos are an effective tool for broad dissemination of information about a program and its evaluation findings. They are useful for providing evaluation findings to groups whose time is limited and/or who might not be accustomed to reading evaluation reports—parent and community groups, for example. Case Example 4.3 describes the advantages of a short video in comparison to a written report in terms of audience impact.

CASE EXAMPLE 4.3

Advantages of a Videotaped Evaluation Report

The Fitness Is Fun Project is a fitness- and nutrition-based community develop-
ment initiative sponsored by General Mills, and administered by the Newton
County Community Partnership. Community partners include the Covington
YMCA, Washington Street Community Center, Newton Health Department,
Newton Board of Education, and Newton Juvenile Courts. The initiative's activ-
ities include

- Teaching children and their parents about the value of nutritious meals
  and snacks
- Providing nutritious snacks at each training session
- Providing physical fitness instruction
- Providing transportation for children to participate in water safety training
- Purchasing pedometers for use by children in kindergarten through
  5th grade
- Purchasing easy-to-use physical education equipment for two elementary
  schools

The purpose of its evaluation was to capture and document the return on
investment of the Fitness Is Fun project from a community and programmatic
perspective. In the original proposal, the evaluators indicated that in addition to
a more traditional evaluation report, they would also deliver a brief videotape.
They believed that videotape would be able to convey more effectively the
community atmosphere in which the program was taking place.

According to Mary Cofer, the lead evaluator, the written report was first distributed to the Executive Board of the Newton County Community Partnership
because they are the decision-making body of the organization and are responsible for the program's administration. This group then approved the video and
the report for wider distribution to all the participating Community Partners, as
well as to others in the community who may want to participate in future projects. These stakeholders, many of whom saw the video prior to their reading
the report, said they "loved the video reporting medium in part because they
can now show it to other community organizations in groups or individually
without relying on someone to read the written report, which they would likely
skip through and miss important points." Cofer reported that when the stakeholders and other audiences viewed the video, they came away surprised at
the breadth of the program as well as its depth. Audiences learned that elementary school children are not only capable of taking responsibility for their
own physical fitness, but that the children were excited and enthusiastic about
healthy physical fitness and nutrition. Cofer believes that the videotape worked

particularly well because the visual images serve as cues to remembering specific information. People tend to retain what they see much longer than what they hear. Therefore, an interesting ten-minute videotape report is more likely to be "read" and remembered than a written report that too often ends up on a shelf.

The funder, General Mills, was also pleased with the videotape because it not only showcased the results of the project, but also gave a positive view of General Mills as a corporate partner in the community. As a result, the Newton County Community Partnership was asked to submit a proposal to repeat the program the next year, adding four additional elementary schools to the project.

SOURCE: Described with permission of Evaluation Enterprises, Inc.

Although verbal presentations might also serve various audiences well and would have the advantage of allowing interaction between the presenter and the audience, videos can be an effective medium of presentation without the presence of the evaluator, whose time might be limited. For instance, copies of videos might be distributed to the parent and community groups for each school within a district, allowing them to receive evaluation findings on a program with districtwide implications. If the school district is large and the evaluation staff is small—a typical scenario—this means of presentation might make evaluation findings available to groups who otherwise would not get them. Delivery of the findings via video also assures consistency across audiences in how they are presented.

Another particularly good use for videos is in multisite evaluation, as described in Case Example 4.2 above. Videos depicting events and activities at different sites provide one means of comparing sites and understanding differences across sites. Another approach is to capture the main themes and issues occurring across sites, as described in Case Example 4.4.

CASE EXAMPLE 4.4

Video Documentary of the Community-Based Public Health Initiative

The W. K. Kellogg Foundation funded a community-based public health (CBPH) initiative at seven sites across the United States for four years. The intent of the initiative was to include each local community as a full partner in serving its public health needs. Each site established a consortium of members from public health agencies, schools of public health and other academic programs, and community-based organizations. Rather than follow a single model for public health services, the initiative's intent was to allow each community to develop unique means for addressing the different problems it faced.

Part of the funding allowed support for a cluster evaluation across the seven sites. The evaluation was coordinated by staff from the University of Minnesota's Center for Urban and Regional Affairs. The evaluation focused on these questions:

1. What kinds of collaborative, community-based, public health models are being developed by CBPH consortia?
2. Is participation in the CBPH affecting the communities' capacity to solve public health problems?
3. Is participation in the project affecting the capacity of member organizations to carry out their CBPH missions?
4. Is participation in the CBPH affecting the capacity of consortia members to influence policy?
5. For individuals and organizations involved, do the benefits of participation in the CBPH outweigh the costs?

During the program's second year, a video was produced for two reasons: to help develop the initiative by promoting communication within and between consortia, and to serve both formative and summative evaluation purposes. Formatively, the video would allow participants to collectively reflect on what they have done from an outsider's perspective. Summatively, it would document what was accomplished, including the quality of experience that resulted from program activities.

The agenda for the video was guided by the evaluation questions given above. To address these questions and the purposes just discussed, videographers at each site were asked to film the cluster evaluation team's annual site visit, special or distinctive consortium events occurring during the year, governance processes, and geographical contexts of consortium sites.

In keeping with the initiative's community-based approach, consortium members and citizens from local neighborhoods served as videographers. They were trained by the University of Minnesota's Media Resources Department, where they learned about such things as when and how to obtain informed consent, variations in quality with different types of equipment used, and techniques for protecting people's identity during filming.

Videotaping at each site occurred over a ten-month period. Approximately 200 hours of video were produced across the seven sites and sent to the cluster evaluation team. Evaluators then worked with Grey Lizard (a video production company) to find footage that represented ideas and responses relating to the five evaluation questions.

The resulting 90-minute video has two parts. Part 1 provides a background on the CBPH, introduces all the partners in the CBPH, and summarizes the Kellogg Foundation's intentions for the CBPH. It then tells about some of the experiences members went through in building their consortium. Part II offers views and activities "from the field." It begins with a brief segment on the problem of defining community and the importance of building community capacity. It then has sections on community organizations, public health practice, and academic programs.

Copies of the video were sent to each site along with information describing the video, its overall goal, how it could be used, tips for showing it, and evaluation forms. This material explained three basic points about the video:

- *It is a mirror—not an advertisement.* The video is a form of feedback. Like a survey or site visit, it attempts to reflect information (images, conversations) about the initiative back to those who are absorbed in making it happen. The film was made to promote learning and sharing across consortia members and the Kellogg Foundation. It was not meant to be a public relations tape to explain, show, or convince external audiences about the CBPH.
- *It is a scrapbook, a family album—not a movie.* The film was shot by local CBPH members and videographers and edited by video producers working with the cluster evaluation team. It was not filmed according to a script, therefore, it does not have a plot with a beginning, middle, and end. It is a collection of scenes and conversations, mostly from site visits, but inclusive of other events, organized around a loose framework, with very little narration. Because the CBPH is still evolving, we consider it an unfinished "scrapbook"; many more pictures could be added.
- *It is a group portrait—not seven separate profiles.* Those looking forward to this film telling each individual consortium's "story" will be disappointed. Early on, the producers and cluster evaluation team decided not to try to tell each consortium's story individually for several reasons: (1) It would take far too long, given the number of organizations and complexity of each consortium; (2) it would get boring and redundant because, despite the uniqueness of each consortium, all have similar issues, activities, and problems; and (3) it was not technically possible given the unequal amount and type of footage we received.

The 200 hours of tape were edited to capture the main themes, challenges, and issues occurring across the initiative, rather than contrast and compare individual consortia. The accompanying materials further explained the goal of the video documentary:

(Continued)

CASE EXAMPLE 4.4 (Continued)

We hope that viewers of this film will (a) learn something about the CBPH that they didn't know before; (b) see themselves as they were at a particular point in time and recognize how the consortium has grown or changed since the interviews were taped or recognize how enduring some challenges or issues are; (c) see themselves as others see them and assess whether they want to continue or strengthen some aspect of their work; (d) see themselves in context with the larger initiative and recognize some common challenges, opportunities, and goals that consortia members can work on together; and (e) see what was missing from the video that was important and should be better captured next time (in the fourth-year video).

SOURCE: Case described with permission of WKKF Community-Based Public Health Initiative.

Note that one of the specific purposes of the video described in Case Example 4.4 above was to stimulate participating communities to reflect on their work in the public health initiative. Similarly, Rosenstein (1997) used an approach called FAVOR (Feedback and Analysis via Video Observation and Reflection), in which videotaped observations facilitated stakeholder reflection and problem solving. "The process produces solutions to problems that are inherent in the program, its design, goals, strategies, or operation."

Videos are also useful for documenting evaluation processes, as described in Case Example 4.5. David Fetterman routinely makes videos of his empowerment evaluation work. The videos serve a variety of purposes: to provide a point of comparison when assessing the group's progress over time; to build commitment to the project; to document how evaluation processes relate to outcomes achieved; and to provide evidence to funders on the effectiveness of a group's functioning.

CASE EXAMPLE 4.5

Video Recordings of Empowerment Evaluations
for Documentation and Process Use

Videotaping of empowerment evaluation (see Fetterman, 2001) activities is a routine matter for David Fetterman, either handling the camera himself or having a colleague assist. On Fetterman's Web site (http://www.stanford.edu/~davidf) you can find several pieces of his work, viewable by clients, stakeholders, and other evaluators with a program called QuickTime (free and available for Mac and Windows users to download from the site). The following paragraphs overview how Fetterman makes and uses these presentations.

Content and Purpose. To ground viewers in the local context, the presentations open with shots of the community where the evaluation is taking place. Then key elements of the empowerment evaluation process are shown: dialogue about the mission, taking stock and rating activities critical to the mission, tabulating and recording responses, dialogue about the results of this self-assessment, and planning for the future. Fetterman narrates the presentations, using voice-over with summary statements about each of these elements. Program participants and staff members narrate with a voice-over as well. Footage of participants' comments, opinions, and dialogue gives further detail to each part.

This video documentation is useful for groups seeking additional funding by demonstrating how the group is capable of functioning effectively. The video can be included in CD format with a written proposal or inserted into the Word document as a QuickTime video. It can also be posted on the Web, and the URL can be noted in the text document or proposal. When the video is distributed on CDs or posted on their own Web site, clients have the opportunity to make the content and process of their work visible to their constituents in a short, appealing format.

This documentation of process is also helpful for clients and stakeholders to view at a later time, as their work has progressed. The presentation becomes part of the collective history of the group. It documents past achievements and is a reminder of past commitments, for example, the original energy and enthusiasm (even anger) the group had relative to a particular initiative. Viewing the video can rekindle that commitment. It can also give them a point of comparison as they review the current status of their work. It can help them see how the processes they used contributed to the outcomes achieved.

Finally, Fetterman taught himself how to produce these videos, and uses the process of creating them to show his clients both their value and how relatively easy they are to make. In addition to providing a creative outlet for clients, this process becomes another tool that helps them become immersed in the evaluation. The more they are involved in helping to conduct the evaluation, in this case using video documentation, the more likely they are going to be committed to the findings and the recommendations for change—because they are an integral part of the process. In addition, the power of video is enormous. For some people, according to Fetterman, "the process of video documentation and production etches the commitment into their consciousness." In other words, their learning is deeper and richer by putting the pictures together to compose the community's story.

(Continued)

CASE EXAMPLE 4.5 (Continued)

Music. In the beginning the presentations did not have background music unless they were a natural part of the background or environment. Now, almost all of them have music added to the video. Music provides another dimension to help depict the mood of the work and the culture of the participants. For the Baltimore site of a multisite empowerment evaluation, the accompanying music is a lively jazz piece. For the San Diego site involving 18 American Indian tribes, it is more serene and reflective of their culture. Fetterman makes selections from among royalty-free music pieces available on the Web.

Length. Most of the pieces are three to four minutes long, which Fetterman finds sufficient for conveying the essential elements of the empowerment evaluation work and its context. This short length also makes the pieces more widely accessible because they require very little viewer time or bandwidth. A further advantage is that for many aspects of production, shorter pieces take less time to create and can be made available more quickly.

Permission to video. At the beginning of his empowerment evaluation workshops, Fetterman distributes a form soliciting participants' permission to video the sessions. This process itself helps create buy-in for the audiovisual product, and because they are being filmed, participants tend to make their comments more focused and precise. Getting agreement is not usually a problem because the presentations capture the evaluation processes, not necessarily the specific outcomes. In addition, the videos are made primarily for the group. Sometimes obtaining permission is a more complex process, involving higher levels of leadership, such as the council of elders when working with American Indian tribes.

Selection of images to include. Using a digital camcorder and digital camera, Fetterman does not record the empowerment evaluation sessions in their entirety. Rather, with experience he has learned to focus on key aspects for each phase of the process. He also knows to get head shots of individuals talking and to take a limited number of whole-group shots (which are good to show the context, but boring if overused in the final product).

Afterward, Fetterman may compile a draft presentation himself, or involve stakeholders in the editing process. In either case, he gets feedback from clients, who give suggestions for adding and/or revising elements. Ultimately the pieces typically consist of an introduction, transitions, the main story, footage of key individuals, some sense of where the work is going or what has been found, and a conclusion. For Fetterman, an ethnographer and qualitative researcher, the production process is much like writing up a case study where you use selected representative pieces from among all the data collected.

Technical aspects of production. Fetterman uses iMovie, a product of Apple Computer, Inc. to create the presentations. (Premiere Pro by Adobe is the PC equivalent of this software product.) He creates a CD version that can be played on most people's computers, posted on the Web, and/or inserted into Word or WordPerfect documents. For the higher quality resolution needed for display to a large audience, he creates a DVD version.

Creation of the presentations takes two to three days in total, including the time needed for going "back and forth" with stakeholders. In some cases, for a mini-version, Fetterman can compile something in two to three hours—but this requires, from the outset, an especially strong sense of what the content will be.

Fetterman's clients typically are enthusiastic about the video documentation. They value the power of the video to tell their story. In addition, they appreciate the power of this tool to help secure additional funding. One client expressed her feeling poignantly: "The pictures capture who we are and what we are doing together. We have been able to use these films to tell our story and show the world what we can do."

SOURCE: Case described with permission of David Fetterman.

Finally, video can be useful for disseminating evaluation findings about new, innovative programs. The more unique a program is, the greater the challenge to precisely describe it through a text-based report. While still photography can be used to support audiences' understanding of an innovative program, the sound and motion of video might be necessary to fully convey the program's features and benefits to participants.

Implementation Tips for Video Presentations

■ **Carefully design the video's purpose and script.**

Sometimes, a video is made to supplement a written evaluation report. That is, its intent is to present the major contents of the report in a more vivid, succinct version. Following the content of the evaluation report may appear to be the simplest approach to developing the content of the video. As with developing the content of verbal presentations, however, this may not be the best approach. Typically, you must select from among more information than can be presented within a reasonable period of time. Important questions to consider and engage stakeholders in dialogue about are

- What is the objective of the video? Why is it being made?
- What do we want the audience to know, understand, and/or do about what they hear and see in the video?

■ **Establish the criteria for the selection of program events and activities to be included in the video.**

Depending on the video's purpose, possible selection criteria are the study's main evaluation questions; themes and issues identified in observations and interviews; and balanced representation of program events, activities, and sites. Various stakeholders may have different ideas about what to include. Professional videographers' criteria for selecting aspects of a program to be included may tend to focus more on technical and aesthetic criteria; your criteria will tend to focus more on selections that accurately represent the evaluation findings (Ingle, 1984). Program funders and participants might take the same perspective as video producers if they view the video primarily as a marketing device for the program. Input on and consensus about selection criteria typically are best solicited at the same time that the video's purpose is established.

■ **Determine if you will produce the video yourself or engage the services of a videographer.**

Evaluators producing videos often work with specialists who have expertise in video production. As mentioned above, however, technological advances have made video production much easier and less expensive, giving evaluators the option of creating videos themselves (see Case Examples 4.2 and 4.5). Video editing software is now a standard component of most computer operating systems. Evaluators who teach themselves about video production can supplement their learning with workshops and courses in videography.

■ **Anticipate the need for using video, and budget adequate time and financial resources.**

Whether you produce the video yourself or use professional services, developing a well-designed video can take considerable planning and development time. If the time and budget have not been allocated at the outset of your evaluation, it may be difficult to add them later.

■ **Obtain permission from program participants prior to filming.**

Obtaining permission to video program participants is an important element of the planning process for producing videos. Because exactly who will be included in any one film shooting cannot be predicted ahead of time, it is a good idea to request permission from all program participants. A permission or release form typically (1) includes information about the purpose of the video; (2) authorizes you to record the person's image and voice; (3) specifies that the recordings may be edited as deemed appropriate for the purpose of the video; (4) releases the sponsoring organization(s) from any liability; and (5) specifies the terms of compensation, if any. Parents of participants who are minors should be asked to sign the release. Naturally, any persons not wishing to be filmed should be respected in the same way you respect individuals' rights not to be photographed or interviewed. (See the section on photography in Chapter 5 for examples of release forms.)

■ **Make sure videos intended as stand-alone pieces contain sufficient background information about the program and its evaluation.**

Program personnel and/or evaluators are often not present when videos are shown. This is, of course, almost always true when videos are made available for viewing on Web pages. For this reason, it is especially important that the video contains sufficient (but not overbearing) information about the program and its evaluation. Because you are so familiar with the program, sometimes you and primary stakeholders can lose sight of the need for this information during production of the video. There are some important items to include:

- Name, purpose, and location(s) of the program
- Program sponsors and/or funders
- Evaluation's purpose
- Institutional affiliation of the evaluator(s) and relationship to the program (internal, external, etc.)
- Purpose of the video

In Case Example 4.4 the evaluators provided written material that accompanied the video and helped further set the context for how it could be used.

■ **Carefully consider the intended audience(s) when determining the length of the video.**

Videos are often distributed to broader audiences who, although they may have an interest in the program and its evaluation, are less interested than those more involved. The attention spans of these audiences will be shorter, so a brief video presentation is more appropriate for them. Videos require resources (time, money, expertise) not traditionally budgeted for in evaluations. You may be tempted to make a video serve too many purposes—a circumstance likely to increase its length. The shorter the video is (20 or 30 minutes rather than 60 or 90 minutes), the better chance it will have at being included in an organization's or community group's meeting agenda. Videos included within Word documents or disseminated through Web sites should be much shorter in length, lasting no more than four or five minutes.

CAUTION FOR VIDEO PRESENTATIONS

■ **Low credibility is sometimes associated with video.**

In our society, video is most commonly associated with television news reporting and commercials—both are sometimes assumed to have been developed with a particular agenda. Sometimes, organizations produce videos as marketing devices for programs, again with a specific agenda. In none of these situations is unbiased, comprehensive, fair reporting (see Joint Committee, 1994) assumed. If you produce videos, you must realize that some audiences will be skeptical about the credibility of the contents. Poor technical quality can also detract from a video's credibility.

Posters and Poster Sessions

A poster session provides quick, visually oriented, easily read information to an audience who may have little or no knowledge about a program or organization. It is an informative display that can be combined with a verbal presentation, working session, or videoconference. Displays typically include photographs, diagrams, graphs, tables, charts, drawings, and text on poster-size boards. The content of a poster session provides a focused message with a clear purpose. Concise titles, a well-organized flow of information, and intriguing visuals help to communicate methods, findings, recommendations, implications, or other significant aspects of an evaluation to the intended audiences (Russell, Gregory, & Gates, 1996).

Poster sessions are frequently used at large, multisession conferences or association meetings as a way to display condensed evaluation information on a program or organization in an easily accessible manner. At public meetings, school/community open houses, meetings within an organization, and other situations that call for a quick transfer of information, poster sessions can create a strong impression and communicate vital information. They are useful when evaluators do not have a captive audience or in situations when they must communicate main ideas and findings within a short span of time. As audience members pass by the display or stop for brief discussion, the evaluator can emphasize key ideas and issues and elicit questions.

Figure 4.1 shows a poster that was used at a Centers for Disease Control (CDC) conference to report on the evaluation of a local program that was one of ten grant-funded sites. (To see this figure in color, go to http://www.sagepub.com/escr.) The local program evaluator developed the poster using a variety of evaluation data sources, and the executive director of the program presented the poster at the 2003 CDC National Center for Injury Prevention and Control Conference. Poster sessions can also be set up to stand alone as visual displays after they have been used in a meeting or conference event, as described in Case Example 4.6. In this situation, the evaluation poster was subsequently displayed at the program site to remind participants of the evaluation process and encourage additional data gathering.

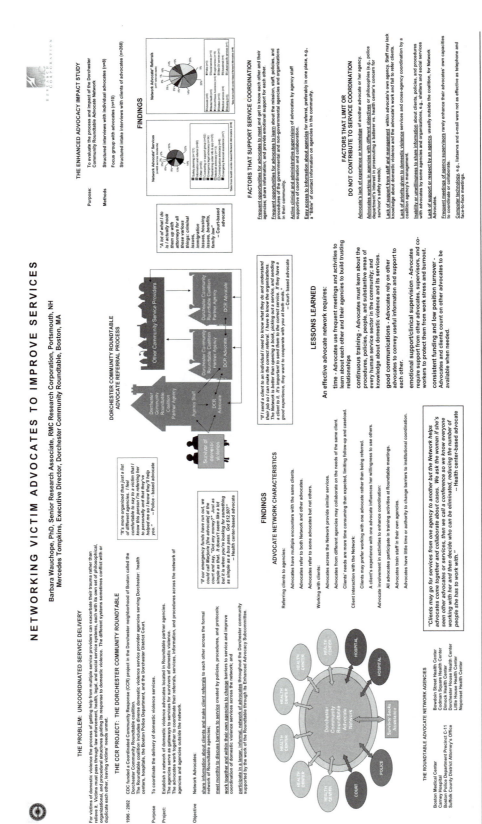

Figure 4.1 Example of Poster to Report Evaluation Findings

SOURCE: Used with permission of RMC Research Corporation and Dorchester Community Roundtable.

CASE EXAMPLE 4.6

Evaluation Reporting and Additional Data Gathering Using a Poster

An evaluation of a peer support center operated by successful recipients of mental health services (MacNeil, 2000) included a focus group interview with program staff during the evaluation design phase. The intent of the focus group was to elicit staff members' thoughts about the special gifts, skills, and talents that peer professionals have to offer. It was specifically designed to have the participants discuss and define their work using their own vocabulary, jargon, and descriptors (without feeling the need to use professional diagnostic languages); and was audio-recorded by the evaluation team. In reviewing the transcripts of the interview, a member of the evaluation team identified the descriptors that the interview participants had provided. She then used the descriptors to design a poster (standard size 24" × 30" with a yellow background), as part of the evaluation's communicating and reporting efforts.

Insider Knowledge and Heart Gladdening:

What Peers Have to Offer

Art
Music
Poetry
Writing
Journaling
Inspiration
Rejuvenation
Survivor Skills
Bringing Light
A Lot of Courage
Capacity Seeking
Important Purpose
Listening to Stories
Antidote to Urgency
Releases From Isolation
Knack for Interviewing
Honoring of Spirituality
Appreciation of Animals
Retriever of Better Times
Getting Off to a New Start
Willingness to Love Oneself
A Campground Atmosphere
Finding That Something Special
Bringing People in From the Cold
A Common Bond Beyond Mental Illness
A Different Way of Being in Conversation
Understanding What People Give Value To
Rescuing the Sparkling Tellings From the Told
Responding That Honors One's Lived Experience
Helping People Stand Back From Traumatic Memories

Illustration 1 Sample Poster

SOURCE: Copyright MacNeil, C. 2002. Printed with permission of Cheryl MacNeil.

(Continued)

CASE EXAMPLE 4.6 (Continued)

To report the findings from the design phase of the evaluation, the evaluation team offered the framed poster for display at the peer center. The evaluators explained how the poster, as a visual display, could help to remind the participants to continue thinking about the evaluation question, "What are the unique qualities a peer professional has to offer?" This was one of several evaluation questions to be addressed in the coming year. The poster became a tool for sustaining or enculturating attention to the evaluation process and key questions. It hangs in the main room where the peers conduct their community meetings. On occasion it is used as reference in orientation to the center, showing viewers that the center is a place that promotes a different way of thinking and talking about mental health and peer support.

The evaluation team also transposed a miniaturized version of the poster onto the cover of a thick sketchbook, and named it A Community Memory Book. The inside cover of the book reads

A Community Memory Book

This book is for anyone interested in recording thoughts about peer support, the journey of recovery and discovery, or whatever else you are moved to share. A collection of ideas, stories, poems, insights, drawings, reflections, questions, and learnings will help to create a portrait of what peer support and the peer center mean to everyone. This book is a public document open to anyone for reading or recording.

The book was placed in the living room area of the peer center. Individuals who had any thoughts to share about the new peer center could so do so in the sketch book, which served as an ongoing means of data gathering and reporting by participants. Over time, people have continued to write in the book, making it into a collective journal of sorts.

SOURCE: Case described with permission of Cheryl MacNeil.

Implementation Tips for Posters and Poster Sessions

■ **Determine how you will produce posters.**

Posters can be produced in a variety of ways. And, as with several of the communicating and reporting formats we present, you can create them yourself or use outside services. Many evaluators create their own posters using desktop publishing and word-processing programs, combined with poster printers. If you do not have access to a poster printer, they are usually available at document service firms, who can use files you have created. These firms also have poster-size enlargement devices that can be used to increase the size of a poster you have created. Another option is to produce the content of the poster on 8.5×11 sheets and then arrange them on one or more display boards. Design and production support is readily available at the document service firms just mentioned, or from advertising and graphic design firms.

The following items, available at art supply stores, can be used for posters and displays that you create:

- Lined, flip chart paper
- Extra-broad colored markers with 0.75-inch tips
- Stencils
- Construction paper
- Half-size flip charts attached to tabletop easels
- A three-ring binder with an easel to make a stand-up display

Velcro, magnet, or felt boards (where pieces can be easily removed and rearranged) are particularly useful for presenting phases of an idea or process. The pieces can be built up upon each other or rearranged to show changing relationships.

■ Keep the format of posters simple and easy to read from a distance.

The objective of the poster format is to convey main ideas clearly and concisely. A particularly useful way of presenting information on posters is to concentrate on the headings or main sections of your report. These can be converted into key words or phrases that draw the audiences' attention to the poster display. They should be understandable at a glance and large enough to be read from across the room. Use at least half-inch lettering for headings.

Below these headings, bulleted points presented in large, block-style print make the information easy to read, and white space increases visual appeal. Lettering for this text can vary from 0.25 to 0.75 inch. A simple presentation draws interest and highlights important information.

When using posters to accompany an oral presentation, lettering must be larger than for a stand-alone display. Make sure it is 1 to 2 inches high with 1 to 1.5 inches between lines. Scalable fonts available on most personal computers make lettering easy. When lettering by hand, use block-style print or purchase stencils to help you maintain uniformity.

■ Include visuals and color to help get your message across.

Photographs, tables, graphs, and charts provide visual attractiveness and draw others to a poster presentation. They also reinforce the message of the text and make the information more memorable. Abstract concepts can be transformed into more concrete illustrations. Visuals can compare and condense large amounts of data and show relationships among issues, program components, or sites. Always make sure, however, that the visuals you use relate to your message.

Color can also attract attention and make a presentation more memorable. A presenter can use it to add emphasis to certain points. Ink-jet color printers have made the use of color both easy and affordable. Construction paper can be used as a frame for information presented on white paper. Information can also be color-coded with markers or pencils. However, too much color can be distracting. (For additional guidance on creating posters, see Chapter 3 on tables and figures, and the section earlier in this chapter on using visuals in presentations.)

■ **Create a storyboard to provide an impression of the program or organization that was evaluated.**

Using storyboards is a technique garnered from film production that can be incorporated into a poster session (Anderson, 1991). In a two-column format, words and pictures are juxtaposed. For instance, pictures of program participants could be positioned next to direct quotations from interviews or surveys. The audience's ability to view the information as if it were a scene from a play, movie, or television production creates a deeper impression than if the information were only in text form. The text of the storyboard can even be converted into an audiotape accompaniment so that the audience hears the voices of the participants. The audience gets a sense of the action and spirit of the program or organization by viewing it and hearing it simultaneously.

■ **Avoid the use of posters alone for communicating and reporting to stakeholders for decision making.**

As with any communication that demands condensation of ideas and concepts, poster sessions can leave out important information for decision making and program development. Poster sessions may need to be included as part of a series of other written materials or verbal presentations and working sessions, if the intended audience is made up of program directors, funders, primary stakeholders, and/or decision makers. Working with these stakeholder groups to construct the poster session is one way to ensure that their information needs are met.

Fully Interactive Formats

The three formats presented next are, by definition, fully interactive. Working sessions are specifically designed for participants to collaborate and quite often make decisions about any given aspect of a program or its evaluation. Synchronous electronic communications (chat rooms, teleconferences, video-conferences, and Web conferences) occur in real time and provide the opportunity for participants to interact across different geographical locations—whether it is across the building, within the same city or country, or across the globe. Finally, discussions between two individuals are inherently interactive, whether they occur over the telephone, via an Internet chat room, or in person.

Working Sessions With Stakeholders

Working sessions with clients and stakeholders are the hallmark of collaborative, participatory evaluation. Evaluators and stakeholders can conduct them at any time throughout the evaluation. Working sessions are particularly useful

- As a very first step to identify stakeholders' concerns and conceptualize the evaluation problem.
- To develop and refine the program's theory of action or logic model.
- To make decisions about data collection methods and other evaluation activities.
- To engage stakeholders in interpreting data (see Figure 4.2).
- To solicit feedback about initial evaluation findings and/or interpretations developed by the evaluator.
- To develop recommendations based on evaluation findings.
- To develop action plans based on evaluation findings (and/or recommendations).

Our assumption is that evaluators cannot be effective without working collaboratively with stakeholders. Working sessions not only solicit needed information from stakeholders but also engage them in the very organizational learning processes the evaluation is designed to support. Organizational learning does not begin once evaluation findings have materialized. It begins with stakeholders taking ownership of the learning process, and being intentional about their learning throughout the evaluation (Preskill, Zuckerman, & Matthews, 2003). Involving organization members in decisions about what the evaluation should address and how its activities should be carried out is an activity they should expect, and is essential to their taking ownership. In short, a participatory approach empowers those the evaluation work is designed to help and improves its relevance, validity, and usefulness. At any stage of the evaluation, working sessions help build a collective sense of mission and purpose.

Steps for Working Session to Interpret Findings

1. Begin with a presentation of findings via posters, overheads, a PowerPoint presentation, or other form of visual display so that participants receive and process the findings together rather than individually.

2. Give sufficient opportunity for participants to ask questions about the evaluation procedures and data analysis.

3. Provide an interactive experience for participants to engage with the findings. For example, have participants work in small groups to develop conclusions based on the findings. The groups might each take a different section of the findings.

4. Have each group present its conclusions, and give the evaluator an opportunity to comment on or raise questions about conclusions which may have been missed or overstated.

5. Then, post findings and conclusions around the room and have groups of participants visit each poster, recording their thoughts about implications and actions to be considered.

6. Debrief in a large-group discussion on the implications and actions.

7. Conclude with a more detailed action-planning activity or definite next steps that will lead to action planning.

Figure 4.2   Example of Steps for Working Session to Interpret Evaluation Findings

SOURCE: Torres (2002).

As shown in Figure 4.2, a working session often begins with a verbal presentation on some aspect of the evaluation. Refer to the guidance on verbal presentations provided earlier in this chapter when developing working sessions that include a verbal presentation.

Many popular evaluation approaches use working sessions routinely. Patton's (1997) utilization-focused evaluation calls for ongoing interaction with client groups to assure "intended use by intended users" (p. 20). Each step of Fetterman's (2001) empowerment evaluation (developing a mission, taking stock, planning for the future) is accomplished through collaborative, evaluator-facilitator working sessions with program staff members and other participants. Our own evaluative inquiry approach (Preskill & Torres, 1999) is based upon constructivist, team-based learning that takes place throughout the evaluation, from focusing the inquiry, to carrying out the inquiry, to applying learning. In Cousins' (2003) approach to participatory evaluation, stakeholders are involved in "some or all of the shaping and/or technical activities required to produce evaluation knowledge" (p. 245; see also Cousins & Whitmore, 1998). O'Sullivan (2004) details how to work collaboratively throughout an evaluation, from responding to evaluation requests through reviewing findings. The following implementation tips will help you design and conduct successful working sessions during any phase of the evaluation.

Implementation Tips for Working Sessions

■ **Assess and refine your skills for facilitating working sessions.**

Evaluators' formal educational and professional experiences are quite varied—ranging from terminal degrees in evaluation design and methodology to one undergraduate course in research design; from extensive experience in multiple data collection and analysis strategies to a limited exposure to statistics and interviewing techniques; and from international, multicultural settings to internal, public school departments. Evaluators may or may not have expertise in group facilitation. Notably though, many of the skills needed to conduct focus groups are also important process facilitation skills, e.g., encouraging all participants to express themselves; preventing one or a few persons from dominating the discussion; and making sure all important topics are addressed (Krueger, 2000; Puchta & Potter, 2004; Mertens, 2004).

Engaging in a participatory, consultative role requires comfort with maintaining ongoing, collaborative relationships with clients, strong interpersonal skills, and the ability to relinquish control. The objective is that evaluators help organizations learn through inquiry, reflection, dialogue, and action planning. In this process trust, respect, and positive interdependence are vital (Preskill, 1994a; Preskill & Torres, 1999; Torres, 1991). Establishing these qualities requires communicating with a variety of audiences in relevant, stimulating formats and styles. It also requires that evaluators be able to help with conflict resolution. In particular, working sessions may bring together individuals and/or groups who are at odds with each other.

Review the process skills and guidelines for facilitating working sessions presented below and determine if you feel confident to implement them. If not, you may want to solicit the help of another evaluation team member, undertake training, and/or consult additional resources on group facilitation (see for example, Hunter, Tailor, & Bailey, 1995; Kinlaw, 1996; Preskill & Torres, 1999 [Chapter 2]; Schwartz, 2002; Webne-Behrman, 1998).

Guidelines for Facilitating Working Sessions

- Know your own values, beliefs, and assumptions on the topic at hand, and then check them at the door.
- Explain your role as the facilitator—to guide the process, not the content of the work.
- Help group members get to know each other with introductory exercises (e.g., have participants introduce themselves and explain their role and most satisfying experience to date with the evaluand).

(Continued)

(Continued)

- Review or ask the group to establish norms for how all of you will work together as a team (e.g., everyone participates, speakers are allowed to finish without interruption, etc.).
- Considering the topic, your objectives, and your knowledge of the group, choose the most appropriate process techniques to engage the group productively (e.g., individual recording of responses to a question/issue followed by round-robin sharing out; group categorization of brainstormed items into themes or patterns; tossing of an object or passing of a "talking stick" to identify who will speak next and thus facilitate full participation).
- Encourage diverse viewpoints and perspectives to surface.
- Call attention to the group process as needed:
  - Watch the time and remind the group where they are on the agenda.
  - When the discussion has evolved away from the objectives at hand, call the group's attention to this and invite them to refocus.
- Note who in the group is participating; invite responses from others as needed.
- Convey both interest and respect in your responses to individuals' input.
- Acknowledge and address the feelings and needs of the group as they emerge.
- Be sensitive to the possibility of underlying agendas or conflicts among participants; diplomatically raise questions to surface and resolve them.
- Be willing to refocus or change the agenda as might be needed.
- Encourage participants to take responsibility for ideas, actions, and statements they make.
- Paraphrase comments; synthesize and integrate emerging ideas and developments for the group.
- Build consensus.
- Balance dialogue with decision making.
- Plan and articulate next steps.
- Ask for feedback about individuals' experiences with the group's process.
- Incorporate what you learn about both group process and substantive content into your next opportunity to work with each group.

■ **Build support for participation in working sessions.**

Some groups and organizations may not be particularly familiar with working sessions to plan evaluation activities and/or discuss findings. You can help prepare stakeholders to collaborate by building in time for working sessions from the outset of the evaluation. When stakeholders know they will have an opportunity to participate in planning the evaluation, to react to findings and develop action plans, they are less likely to feel threatened by the evaluation process as a whole. Figure 4.3 shows an information sheet used by FERA, Inc., a Michigan-based evaluation consulting group, to explain the purpose and benefits of their "Stakeholder Data Interpretation Workshops."

On the other hand, Case Example 4.7 illustrates how working sessions, not originally planned for, were instrumental in expanding use of findings from an evaluation in Australia. The message from this case is for evaluators to be open to new strategies that facilitate interaction and use throughout the evaluation.

FERA

Formative Evaluation Research Associates

A FERA Stakeholder Data Interpretation Workshop

Question: What is a data interpretation workshop?

Answer: A data interpretation workshop is an opportunity for program stakeholders to come together to engage, reflect upon and interpret data, and to develop implications from evaluation data about their program.

Question: Why conduct a data interpretation workshop?

Answer: It allows program stakeholders, who, by definition, care about the program, an opportunity to help interpret the data before the evaluator offers her/his sense of the highlights, conclusions, and, if appropriate, recommendations. It creates an opportunity for stakeholders to go through this exciting process with the evaluator and taps their best thinking about the data and its relationship to their program. It creates some space for guided reflection.

Question: When is it conducted?

Answer: It can be conducted at several points after data have been collected and initially analyzed, but before a final report has been prepared. For example, it can be conducted as soon as data summaries have been prepared, but before the data have been organized and displayed in tabular or graphic form. It can be conducted after the data have been organized for presentation, but before a draft report has been prepared. It can be done after a preliminary report has been offered, but before it has been finalized. Conducting a workshop at each of these points has its pros and cons. This decision is best made in consultation with the client.

1810 Cooley - Ann Arbor, MI 48103 - Phone: 734/994-9060 - Fax: 734/998-1378
www.feraonline.com   (*Over*)

Figure 4.3   Information Sheet About Working Sessions to Interpret Evaluation Findings

SOURCE: Used with permission of FERA, Inc.

Question: Who should attend the workshop?

Answer: If stakeholders were identified at the outset of the evaluation to help design it, then these folks should be involved along with any others who have become key stakeholders. If they weren't involved, then key stakeholders, e.g., service providers and other key staff, the program director, board members, funders, and clients or customers are possible participants. This decision depends on several factors, e.g., the position of the program in the organization and the focus of the evaluation.

Question: How long does a workshop take?

Answer: The timeframe is flexible, but usually a minimum of at least three hours is necessary and sometimes a day is necessary, depending on the number of objectives. Possible agenda items include: highlighting the data, interpreting it more thoroughly, drawing conclusions from the data, developing recommendations, and finally creating action plans to implement the recommendations. Sometimes this process is segmented over several days or weeks and task groups are formed to focus on some part of the agenda.

Question: Who leads the workshop?

Answer: Decisions about the content of the material to be offered and the process of the workshop are best worked out with the client. The evaluator usually facilitates the process. However, the evaluator, because of her/his relative independence and familiarity with the data, is also a key contributor to the interpretations that occur during the workshop. Sometimes two FERA staff members are used in the process.

Question: What techniques are used to facilitate the process?

Answer: A number of meeting management factors and group process techniques are used. Some of these key ingredients are: round robin introductions; sharing and clarifying expectations, roles, and responsibilities for the experience; an agenda; a rough schedule; a designated facilitator and recorder; attention to comfortable seating, usually in a square or rectangle, and good lighting; and finally, making sure the appropriate equipment is available, e.g., computer, overhead projector, newsprint, notepads, etc. Some of the appropriate group process techniques that democratize the work, stimulate reflection, and foster consensus include: (1) centering or focusing techniques used to help participants relax, clear their minds, and orient their energy toward the task at hand, (2) providing time for review of the data and note-making and or filling out trigger sheets to cause reflection on the data before discussion (a modified IGI or instrumented group interview), (3) facilitating open and shared discussion, and (4) the nominal group process, and conflict resolution techniques.

Figure 4.3 *(Continued)*

CASE EXAMPLE 4.7

Expanding Evaluation Use With Working Sessions Across Multiple Sites

The Centre for Program Evaluation (CPE) at the University of Melbourne undertook an evaluation of careers advice provision in educational organizations (schools, community education centres, prisons, etc.) across the State of Victoria, Australia (Owen, Day, & Joyce, 1991). A steering committee of key stakeholders was set up to guide the study and receive findings from the evaluation team.

A feature of the intervention was the use of a new computer database that was designed to allow careers advisers and end users (e.g., students in secondary schools) to access information about possible jobs and courses in higher education. The use of the computer database meant changes to careers education, and led to practices in schools and other educational institutions in Victoria that were innovative compared to what was happening in other States.

As the six-month study neared its conclusion, it became apparent that policy makers in these States had become interested in the impact of the program. This meant that the range of interested parties had increased during the period of the study, and there was pressure on the evaluators to meet the information needs of an expanded audience.

The evaluators solved the problem of additional stakeholders by holding a seminar at the end of the study to which the original steering committee and policy makers from other States were invited. After the presentation of findings, several working groups were convened to develop recommendations that related to their own jurisdictions. The evaluators acted as facilitators for this event. This enabled those in other States that were thinking of implementing the new program to work on recommendations useful for their purposes. At the same time the steering committee was able to work on guidelines to consolidate the program in Victoria. The program became widely used across Australia. The influence of the findings was far greater in terms of scope than originally envisaged.

SOURCE: Program described with permission of Centre for Program Evaluation, The University of Melbourne, Parkville, Australia.

■ **Specifically tailor each working session for your participants and carefully plan it to achieve clear objectives.**

Organization members typically complain not only about the number of meetings they must attend but also the meetings' ineffectiveness. An ineffective working session can delay the progress of the evaluation, add to costs, and/or undermine support for the evaluation. Each working session you schedule should have a clear purpose. The time that organization members devote to attending the session must be time well spent both for you and for them. You should have a clear idea of what you want to accomplish with each working session and carefully plan for it. This requires knowledge about the background of participants in the working sessions, for example,

- Their role(s) and responsibilities with respect to the evaluand
- Their prior knowledge about and participation in the evaluation activities
- Their history of working with each other
- Particular issues or concerns they may have about the evaluation

In some cases, you may be working with a single (or several) evaluation stakeholder(s) who—acting as key informants—can help you understand a group's background and design an effective working session. In any case, it is important to get feedback on your plans for the working session before finalizing them. With working sessions, in particular, the payoff from careful planning cannot be overstated.

■ Do your best to get key stakeholders at the table.

More often than not, working sessions are most productive when all of the key players are involved. Based on your identification of stakeholders for the overall evaluation endeavor (see Chapter 2), participants to be involved in any particular working session may be obvious. Considering the topic of your working session, though, it is a good idea to review your participant list with these questions in mind:

- What individuals or groups can inform this topic or issue?
- What individuals or groups are directly involved with or have a vested interest in this topic or issue?
- What individuals or groups will be affected by the (possible) outcomes of this working session?
- What individuals or groups otherwise have a right to be included in this working session?

Once you have identified the individuals to invite to your session, you may find it challenging to schedule a common meeting time. This could require delaying the session, and/or conducting more than one session. Decisions about various aspects of working session logistics are best made in consultation with primary stakeholders, and in terms of how you can optimally meet the overall objectives of the evaluation and the specific objectives of the session. Examples of decisions you will need to address are: which individuals must participate in order to accomplish the working session objectives; when the working session needs to take place; and whether or not to conduct more than one session. In some cases, it may be more important to delay a session until all key stakeholders can participate; in others, delaying the session may obviate the need for it.

■ **Determine what information or documents participants should receive ahead of time.**

Sometimes working sessions can be particularly productive when they bring individuals together once they have had a chance to review particular evaluation documents. Typically, only very limited time should be used in a working session for participants to individually read and review program or evaluation material. Providing material ahead of time may sometimes be done mostly as a courtesy. But, in those cases where the success of the session depends upon individuals' first reading and reacting to the materials, make sure you stress that they do so.

■ **Consider conducting working sessions as part of other regularly scheduled meetings.**

In many instances, having organization members attend a working session means they must add another meeting time to already busy schedules. It may be possible to devote some of the time of regularly scheduled meetings to the evaluation. For example, groups of stakeholders may already meet by virtue of their membership on task forces or committees. Further, these task forces may have responsibilities related to the evaluation, such as developing goals or recommendations for a particular program. Most programs or organizations hold staff meetings at regularly scheduled times. It is often possible to negotiate for some of the agenda time of these meetings. Although this strategy may not provide as much time as you would like, it can be used in combination with other meetings dedicated to the evaluation work. In many situations, using both types of meetings (those dedicated to the evaluation and those that are part of other regular meetings) provides a way to maintain contact throughout all phases of the evaluation without requiring too much of stakeholders' time.

■ **Provide sufficient background information at the beginning of the working session, and close the session with a clear outline of what is to follow.**

An individual working session—or the first in a series of working sessions—should begin with background information about the evaluation. Although some participants may be completely familiar with the evaluation because of prior involvement, others may not be. Background information might include information about the evaluator; the purpose of the evaluation; how it came about; the evaluation methodology; the current status of the evaluation process; and how the session itself fits into this process. Participants should then be given the opportunity to ask questions. The point is to resolve any issues or concerns that participants may have about the evaluation prior to beginning the work of the session. With anxieties laid to rest, stakeholders are able to participate fully. Similarly, the session should end with a clear outline of what will occur next and who will be involved.

■ **Spend time at the outset of the working session to reach common understandings on basic issues/information about the evaluand.**

Once the purposes of the evaluation work and of the particular working session are understood within the group, it may be important to spend time getting everyone to a common point of reference on basic issues or information related to the object or program being evaluated. Reaching this common understanding will facilitate subsequent dialogue and save time. Sometimes program staff do not always share the same understanding or view about particular aspects of their program. Figure 4.4 shows the agenda for a working session largely devoted to reaching a common understanding of both the evaluation purposes and the program's logic model.

■ **Use worksheets to organize the activities of a working session.**

Worksheets can help focus a working session. Evaluators may find it difficult to maintain a focused discussion among people who work together and otherwise have many things in common—particularly if they have had little opportunity to come together, socialize, and/or otherwise discuss issues of concern to them. Even a very simple worksheet can provide a framework for focusing the group. Worksheet 1 provided in Chapter 2 to identify an evaluation's audience, as well as the worksheet shown in Figure 6.2 to help stakeholders process evaluation findings, might be used in a working session.

There are particular advantages to asking participants in a working session to write down their perceptions of a situation before sharing them publicly. Doing so provides time for individual reflection before group discussion and lessens the possibility that stakeholders will screen their thoughts at the same time they develop them. After participants are given several minutes to write, you can ask them to share what they have written. As each person speaks, his or her responses can be recorded on a flip chart or overhead transparency that is visible to the whole group. Hopefully, participants will share their perceptions completely, but they do have the option to omit something they have written. Some may feel emboldened when they hear perceptions similar to, or even different from, their own.

■ **Develop ground rules about the confidentiality of the working session.**

Sometimes sensitive or controversial issues surface during working sessions. One key advantage of working sessions is that they can provide the opportunity to resolve programmatic or organizational issues. It is a good idea to set some ground rules about maintaining confidentiality around what is discussed during the session. This can be done at the outset, particularly if you are aware that sensitive topics may surface. In cases where they have come up unexpectedly, confidentiality concerns can be addressed with the group during or at the end of the session.

Working Session on Program Components and Evaluation Plan

Participants

Principal Investigator

Co-Principal Investigator/Evaluator

Co-Principal Investigator

Co-Principal Investigator

Co-Principal Investigator

Project Director

Staff Developer

Facilitator

Research and Evaluation Consultant

Objectives

Reach consensus on

- Defining the research and evaluation activity for the project, and the purposes of each
- Stakeholder groups (individuals, groups, organizations affected by the planning, activities, and/or findings of the research/evaluation)
- Evaluation plan and first level of detail on methodology

Develop next steps on

- Carrying out the evaluation plan, including roles and responsibilities
- Stakeholder involvement

Agenda

1. Review and revision of program's logic model to establish common language and understanding of major program components

2. Review and revision of illustration showing stakeholders

3. Focus group process to establish purposes of the evaluation

4. Group input to link evaluation purposes with primary and secondary stakeholders

5. Review of existing evaluation plan in terms of purposes established

6. Refinement of evaluation methods/activities as appropriate, including stakeholder involvement

7. Agreement on next steps
   - Research/evaluation plan revision
   - Communication with stakeholders
   - Roles/responsibilities of core team

Figure 4.4   Example of Agenda for Working Session to Reach Shared Understanding of Program and Evaluation Elements

- Consider expending evaluation resources on conducting action-planning sessions rather than on producing a final report.

A useful alternative to producing a final evaluation report is presenting evaluation findings at working sessions with stakeholders. The sessions can be expanded to develop implications of the findings as well as plans for acting on them. This approach can lead to quicker use of evaluation findings and can be particularly appropriate when there is no need for a written report. (See Case Example 3.4.) Sometimes, both evaluators and clients expect a comprehensive written report—more out of precedent than real need. Besides being expensive and time consuming to produce, written reports can leave organizations with fine documentation of the evaluation itself but little in terms of guiding their next steps. As Abma (1998) points out, typical evaluation reports are not especially useful for promoting dialogue among stakeholders. One possibility is to conduct action-planning sessions based on a presentation of findings and produce a brief report. The report can document the evaluation process, including the outcomes of the sessions.

- Follow up with the stakeholders who may not have been able to attend a working session.

One of the chief benefits of working sessions is that they give participants a chance to hear each other's perceptions and perspectives under what are (ideally) nonthreatening circumstances. Resolution, newfound cohesion, or at least better understanding are often the results. Stakeholders who are unable to attend will not have had a chance to be part of these kinds of change processes. So, besides their possibly feeling left out, having to catch them up at a next session can offset the tempo of the group. It's a good idea to make sure that you or someone else in the organization follows up with them as soon as possible afterward. Doing so may create the opportunity for productive one-on-one interaction with a stakeholder.

CAUTION FOR WORKING SESSIONS

- Working sessions can bring together groups/individuals who are in conflict.

Conducting working sessions with groups or individuals who are in conflict can pose a challenge, even for evaluators who are skilled in group facilitation. Ultimately there is no way to predict or control what will develop during a working session. At best, conflicts that emerge can lead to resolution, and stronger cohesion and focus within a group; at worst, they can derail the entire evaluation endeavor.

Synchronous Electronic Communications

A chief requisite for collaborative, learning approaches to evaluation is interaction, a significant amount of which is best if face-to-face. Sometimes this can be impractical, even among evaluators and stakeholders who work in the same towns and cities. Recent technological advances have made synchronous electronic communications—via Internet chat rooms, teleconferencing, videoconferencing, and Web conferencing, for example—more accessible and feasible than ever. These forms of communication allow participants to exchange messages in real time through an electronically networked environment without being in each other's physical presence. It is estimated that by 2010, 70% of the U.S. population will spend ten times longer per day interacting virtually (Gartner Group, Inc., 2000).

This is an important development for evaluation practice, given difficult economic times when tight budgets limit travel and meeting expenses. And, there is hardly anyone in today's workforce who could not productively use the time they would otherwise spend traveling. It is also true that electronic communications often work best when participants have first had the opportunity to meet and work together in person.

As interactive electronic communication increases among different realms of professional activity, evaluators need to assess the strengths and liabilities that various venues hold for different aspects of evaluation work. In comparison to face-to-face meetings, synchronous electronic communications can have these benefits for evaluators and stakeholders:

- Real-time collaboration when face-to-face meetings are impractical or impossible
- More informed and timely decision making about program and evaluation activities
- Quicker dissemination of findings
- Inclusion of stakeholders who might not otherwise be able/available to travel to a meeting
- Increased opportunities for interaction and collaboration
- Increased resources for expenditures on other critical aspects of the evaluation through savings in travel time and costs

Drawbacks include

- Lack of access to or experience with requisite technology for all desired participants
- Reliance on technology, which can fail and result in an immediate end to the communication
- Typical need to disseminate meeting materials ahead of time

- Reduced opportunity to facilitate full participation within the group
- If overused, lack of opportunity for mutual understanding and community building unique to face-to-face meetings
- Not necessarily suitable for stakeholders unfamiliar with communicating electronically
- Limited use for stakeholders in widely variant time zones

The more a communication medium simulates the qualities of face-to-face interaction, the more potential it has for fostering and building collegial and interactive learning opportunities. In most cases, when well designed for specific purposes, synchronous electronic communications benefit evaluations. By choosing carefully among the venues available—chat rooms, teleconferences, videoconferences, Web conferences—and using them in conjunction with face-to-face meetings, you can use these means of communication to significant advantage during the course of an evaluation.

Well-crafted, face-to-face meetings provide focus, structure, and follow-up. Doing so is especially important for all types of synchronous electronic communications, as described below.

Guidelines for Synchronous Electronic Communications: Chat Rooms, Teleconferences, Videoconferences, Web Conferences

Before

- For first-time use, try out the technology with a trial run. Glitches in getting all participants connected can delay or completely derail the meeting.
- Consider making the first use of synchronous electronic communications deliberately short and relatively simple.
- Identify a person or persons responsible for designing and facilitating the meeting.
- Establish clear outcomes for the meeting and an agenda to reach them, including the processes that will be used (i.e., asking the participants for examples, opinions, ideas, or responses to specific pieces of information; to brainstorm; to reach consensus, vote, or make a specific decision).
- Distribute the agenda, a list of participants, the date and time of the meeting, technical instructions for accessing the meeting, and any supporting documents ahead of time. (Note that documents presented during a Web conference may or may not be distributed ahead.)

(Continued)

(Continued)

- If any preparation is necessary, provide clear instructions about what participants are to do prior to the meeting.

During

- Begin and end the meeting on time.
- If needed, start the meeting with some type of roll call to determine who is participating.
- The facilitator should introduce the meeting by reviewing its objectives and starting with the first agenda item. Check that all participants understand what is to be accomplished during the meeting.
- Throughout the meeting, the facilitator keeps the meeting focused, helping to make sure that one topic is discussed at a time, and that all participants have a chance to be heard.
- At the close of the meeting, summarize outcomes, unresolved issues, and next steps.

After

- Either at the end of or following the meeting, ask participants to provide feedback about both the logistics and content of the meeting.
- Follow up with a written summary that includes information on any questions/issues not answered during the meeting. Also be sure to thank participants.

The sections that follow discuss each method—chat rooms, teleconferencing, videoconferencing, and Web conferencing—in detail.

Chat Rooms

A chat room is an area on the Internet where two or more people can have a typed conversation in real time. In a chat room, the messages you type are shown instantly to every other member of the room. Messages typed by other people are shown immediately to you.

Chat rooms use channels to transmit text between groups of users. Chat room software is available for free from most Internet service providers. Participants in a chat must be registered users with one of these programs. Chat rooms can also be set up on a Web site.

Chat rooms allow group members to participate in impromptu and routine conversations about data, plans, and implementation of results. They are useful for knowledge building, idea generation, giving and receiving feedback, and linking people and ideas. Since social class, race, and gender are not immediately evident, chat rooms that are text-based may "equalize" the interactions, thus allowing for more effective communication. The text exchanged among participants during a chat can be saved to a text file for documentation, later review, and/or analysis.

Chat rooms are not the best choice for complicated discussions where conflicting opinions may surface and need to be resolved. Rather, they are more suited for routine conversations about data collection or evaluation procedures. Case Example 4.8 describes the effective use of a chat room for gathering input on an evaluation design from a team in their third year of working together on the same project.

CASE EXAMPLE 4.8

Chat Room Dialogue Among Members of a Seasoned Evaluation Team

Members of a five-person evaluation team, beginning their third year of a five-year project, used a chat room dialogue to develop a draft set of evaluation questions. Beforehand, participants were asked by the team's coordinator to think about program areas that the evaluation might help inform for the coming year. It was mid-October, and she requested that they also review the evaluation findings from the previous year, which had been compiled in a summary report the previous July.

At the start of the chat, the facilitator invited participants to respond with a single evaluation question or focus area. In the e-mail she sent out confirming the date and time for their chat, she suggested that they use the same round-robin method to solicit everyones responses as they had in previous in-person meetings.

The first participant who was ready to reply entered "HU" for "hand up." Several others also did so at the same time. As their names appeared on the screen, the facilitator made a note of their order. She then asked each person (in the order that they "raised their hands") to respond by typing in a single evaluation question or focus area. When each person had responded once, the facilitator invited a second round, and repeated the process until no one had any more evaluation questions to list. The facilitator then asked for further questions/reflections/thoughts about what had been said so far, giving everyone a chance to reply. She closed the chat by reminding the team that she would compile all of the responses, draft a set of evaluation questions, and send them out in an e-mail attachment. This task was relatively easy, because all of the text generated by their responses was now available in a Word file on her computer. Their next meeting would be in person, to prioritize and refine the questions and begin a dialogue about data collection methods.

The following excerpt (Fetterman, 2002) provides another example of chat room use in an evaluation, describing how empowerment evaluation teams use them:

> Team members frequently sent brief notes to each other to determine if another team member was still awake late at night working on a draft report or sent special alerts during the day after a particularly noteworthy classroom observation or meeting.
>
> For an extended discussion or a discussion with more than one team member our research groups generally opened private chat rooms . . . to maintain confidentiality and minimize interruptions. (pp. 33 and 34)

Implementation Tips for Chat Rooms

■ Keep the text that you write clear, concise, and focused.

■ When using chat rooms with a variety of stakeholders over a period of time, establish and disseminate specific guidelines and conventions to help chat room dialogue function smoothly.

■ Avoid repeated use of chat rooms, without opportunities for communication via telephone and face-to-face meetings.

CAUTIONS FOR CHAT ROOMS

■ Chat rooms are not good choices for individuals who have visual impairments, or are not comfortable with written forms of expression.

■ Chat rooms provide little opportunity for receiving social cues and, like e-mail communications, can result in misunderstandings.

■ Some individuals may feel inhibited in their responses knowing that their words are being captured in a computer file.

Teleconferences

Teleconferences have the advantage of easily bringing a geographically diverse group of stakeholders together to participate in a conversation or to hear information at the same time. Teleconferences can be arranged in a variety of ways—for example, through telephone equipment that will make three-way calls and through communications service providers that provide a single number (usually toll-free) for numerous participants to call. With the use of high-quality speaker phones, the teleconference can include as many participants from any one site as can reasonably be accommodated and heard in a meeting room.

Teleconferences can be especially useful for discussing and getting feedback on evaluation documents (e.g., drafts of plans, data collection procedures, reports) that are distributed and reviewed by participants prior to the call. Without them having to be physically present, a teleconference allows everyone to hear each other's feedback. Case Example 4.9 describes how a teleconference was used as a follow-up to a face-to-face meeting of two collaborating organizations, located on opposite coasts of the United States.

CASE EXAMPLE 4.9

Teleconference Follow-Up to a National Meeting

The leadership team of an East Coast/West Coast collaboration formed to support educational reform in 20 elementary schools met to review midyear program evaluation findings. Their meeting took place on the East Coast, where the 20 schools are located. The purposes of the meeting were for the leadership team to reach a shared understanding of implementation status in the schools (based on interim evaluation findings), and to make any necessary adjustments in support provided to the schools. Findings shared at the meeting indicated that teachers were having difficulty integrating new instructional programs with the ones mandated by their districts. The meeting resulted in a rough outline of an action plan for strengthening support to teachers. Two members of the team volunteered to flesh out the plan with specific details. Another two team members were charged with contacting school principals to determine the feasibility of engaging teachers in further staff development. The team also agreed to hold a teleconference in two weeks, once a more detailed draft of the plan had been distributed. The team members contacting principals anticipated that they could complete their task within two weeks as well.

The teleconference took place as scheduled. Everyone had received a new version of the plan and reviewed it prior to the call. Before soliciting reactions to the plan, the team heard what had been learned from principals about the feasibility of further staff development. The meeting's facilitator asked that each person consider this new information as they provided their reactions to the plan. The call lasted 75 minutes, but by its end a second draft of the action plan had been developed, with a significant revision in strategy. Rather than with traditional staff development sessions, support to teachers would be provided through additional visits by coaches who worked with teachers individually. The teleconference was an effective way for this team to maintain the momentum of the action planning they had started at their annual midyear meeting. As a result, they developed a significantly better plan to support teachers, and with time to implement it during the remainder of the school year.

⇨ *Implementation Tips for Teleconferencing*

- ■ Limit the teleconference call to no more than 90 minutes to avoid participant distraction and/or fatigue.

- ■ When people speak, ask them to say their names before speaking so that others know who is talking.

- ■ Depending on the format of the call, agree upon the amount of time to speak before asking others to engage in the conversation. (If participants are making presentations to each other, 5 to 10 minutes is appropriate. If participants are sharing thoughts and ideas, 30 seconds to 1 minute is appropriate.)

- ■ To assure full participation, call on each participant in turn to respond to specific questions or issues raised.

- ■ Take notes during the call.

CAUTIONS FOR TELECONFERENCING

- ■ Listeners may be distracted by office interruptions, by e-mail messages, or by other noises.

- ■ It's not always clear who is paying attention during the call—some people might even leave the call without your knowing it.

- ■ Speaker phones vary in quality and do not always capture participants' voices well enough to allow for a fluid, multidirectional conversation.

Videoconferences

Videoconferencing is a meeting between people at two or more locations, and uses a system of monitors, microphones, cameras, computer equipment, and other devices. Video, audio, and data can be exchanged via videoconferencing. The group interactions that can occur during a teleconference or videoconference can lead to increases in creativity, democratic deliberation, constructive criticism, and learning from the evaluation process. Relative to other forms of synchronous electronic communications, videoconferences can make communication more personal, allowing participants to see each other's facial expressions, hand movements, and other gestures. This can help establish and maintain rapport between the evaluation team and stakeholders.

Videoconferencing can be arranged in two ways: through specialized equipment using dedicated high-speed telephone lines; or through the Internet using free or inexpensive software and inexpensive video cameras. The former is both more expensive and more reliable. It can be arranged through companies specializing in this service, and requires a technician at each site. Many universities and large organizations have the capacity for this type of videoconferencing. Internet videoconferencing is subject to jerky or halting images, depending on the level of Internet traffic and the speed of participants' connections.

Videoconferencing can be used with evaluation clients and stakeholders in place of any face-to-face meeting that you would otherwise have. Given its major advantage—it's the most like a face-to-face meeting—and its major disadvantage—the financial and/or technical resources it requires—you will want to use it when stakeholders are geographically dispersed and for the most significant phases of your evaluation work, e.g., to

- Establish an evaluation's purpose and identify evaluation questions.
- Get input on and revise the evaluation plan.
- Present and discuss preliminary findings.
- Interpret results and do action planning.

Case Example 4.10 describes how The Evaluation Center at Western Michigan University used videoconferencing to bring together stakeholders across different regions of the United States and extend their dialogue well beyond the final evaluation report.

CASE EXAMPLE 4.10

NSF-Sponsored Videoconference to Promote Evaluation Use

Western Michigan University's (WMU) Evaluation Center used videoconferencing in their sustainability evaluation of the NSF-funded Advanced Technological Education (ATE) Program. The ATE program promotes improvement in technological education at the undergraduate and secondary school levels by supporting curriculum development; the preparation and professional development of college faculty and secondary school teachers; internships and field experiences for faculty, teachers, and students; and other activities. The purposes of the evaluation were to (1) define sustainability as used by the ATE program; (2) identify key elements essential to sustaining an ATE project; and (3) determine the viability of the ATE program's efforts toward sustainability. The evaluation methods included a review of literature, annual Web-based surveys of ATE-funded projects, and one-to two-day site visits to 13 projects by evaluation teams of two to three persons.

In all, reporting for the evaluation consisted of a comprehensive final report, executive summary, a PowerPoint presentation, and a brochure providing guidance for improving sustainability. The evaluators undertook the additional step of a videoconference because NSF wanted to try further mechanisms to reach

(Continued)

CASE EXAMPLE 4.10 (Continued)

a larger audience. Too often primary audiences fail to read and use the long reports that evaluators prepare.

The videoconference was held following dissemination of the final report. Its overall purpose was to engage evaluation users in dialogue about the evaluation findings, and specifically to: (1) try out the video conferencing forum; (2) disseminate sustainability findings and recommendations; (3) share perspectives

Agenda

Videoconference on Sustainability for ATE

Tuesday, February 18

12-2 EST

11:30	Sites Make Connections
11:50	All Sites Connected
12:00	Roll Call
	Introductions and Overview (Arlen Gullickson)
12:15	Sustainability From the Evaluation Project's Point of View (Frances Lawrenz and Nanette Keiser)
	Paper available at ate.wmich.edu, Evaluation Products, Issue Papers
	PowerPoint will be available under Presentations by February 14
12:25	Sustainability From an Overall Point of View (Thomas Bailey)
	PowerPoint will be available under Presentations by February 14
12:35	Sustainability From the Centers' Point of View and Sharing of Best Practices
12:35	Advanced Technology Environmental Education Center (Ellen Kabat, PI)
12:45	AIM: Advanced Integrated Manufacturing Center (Monica Pfarr, PI)
12:55	Maricopa Advanced Technology Education Center (Michael Lesiecki, PI)
1:05	SC ATE Center of Excellence/National Resource Center for Engineering Technology
	Education (Elaine Craft, PI)
1:15	Sustainability From NSF's Point of View (NSF)
1:30	Open Discussion (All)
1:45	Evaluation and Wrap-Up

Illustration 1 Sample Videoconference Agenda

and best practices for sustainability; and (3) obtain feedback on how to frame reports and other evaluation products to make them more useful. Representatives from four large-scale ATE projects called Centers were invited to participate. The agenda for the two-hour videoconference is shown in Illustration 1. Conference participants provided both formal responses, and dialogue based on other participants' statements. The documents referenced and used during the videoconference were made available to participants prior to the videoconference. All participants were expected to have read the full report prior to the conference.

Once connections had been established and introductions were made, the lead evaluators for the sustainability study made a ten-minute PowerPoint presentation on the evaluation's findings. Immediately following, another ten-minute PowerPoint presentation was made by a sustainability expert from Columbia University, describing sustainability from an overall point of view. Then each of the four centers had ten minutes for those attending at their sites (e.g., center PIs, business/industry representatives, center staff) to share their points of view and best practices for sustainability. The Centers had been asked to prepare their remarks in advance.

A snowstorm in the DC area prevented NSF representatives from participating. Otherwise, they would also have made a presentation on sustainability from their point of view. The next 30 minutes of the meeting was devoted to open discussion. Here, a round-robin approach was used to hear comments and questions from each of the Centers. Fifteen minutes at the end were used to assess and close the meeting, again using a round-robin approach so that all participants were heard.

The videoconference was considered to be highly successful—in several ways. First, the funded Centers held a meeting several months later on sustainability and used the ideas and issues as presented in the paper and videoconference as a springboard for further discussion. They followed this event with a second meeting at the annual Principal Investigators meeting in Washington, DC in the fall of 2003. Second, a videotape had been made of the videoconference itself, which NSF viewed. NSF reactions to the videoconference indicated that the issues discussed helped sensitize the Foundation to a more expanded view of sustainability. Third, with NSF support, WMU extended the sustainability study to address new points raised in the videoconference discussion and provide more in-depth understanding of sustainability issues.

Finally, WMU has converted the videoconference to digital format and electronically linked parts of it to related points within the text of the original final report. This linked version of the report has been made available on WMU's ATE Web site. The costs for the videoconference were additional to the original funding. However, the feedback obtained, the buy-in by participants, and the specific actions taken as a result of it more than compensated for the additional costs.

SOURCE: Case described with permission of The Evaluation Center, Western Michigan University.

⇨ *Implementation Tips for Videoconferencing*

■ Plan and budget for videoconferencing at the outset of your evaluation work. Determine what technical and financial resources you have to support videoconferencing, and choose the optimal method accordingly.

■ Establish an overall facilitator, and a facilitator at each site.

■ Schedule the videoconference well in advance, especially when you will have several sites participating.

■ When choosing your clothing, avoid plaids, stripes, and prints. Pastel clothing is better than white, which may glare as a result of the lighting in the room. If you do wear white, keep a jacket or sweater on to give contrast.

■ Immediately before the videoconference, follow these guidelines:

  • Arrive 15–30 minutes before the videoconference is scheduled to start, to see that all locations are ready.
  • Make sure you have the confirmation or reservation with call instructions readily available.
  • Position the camera before the meeting begins.
  • Review the agenda for the videoconference.

■ During the videoconference, follow these guidelines:

  • Be courteous and allow people time to finish sentences. Always address the group as a whole by speaking toward the microphones and facing the camera.
  • There is a delay when using video. Give each person plenty of time to respond to questions or comments, and be sure they have finished before you speak.
  • Keep slides to a minimum during a presentation and only keep each one on camera for a short time to maintain interest. Allow questions about individual slides at the end of the presentation.
  • Be aware of your posture—if you need to stretch, the other participants will probably need to also.
  • In large groups, ask people to raise their hand to signal the camera operator that they would like to speak.
  • Remember, all locations view the speaker; the speaker only sees the last site from which a person spoke.
  • Mute the microphone when not speaking.

- Look into the camera when you speak. Doing this gives participants at the other site(s) the impression that you are making eye contact with them.
- Pause occasionally so others may make comments.
- Identify yourself as necessary.
- Keep others informed by announcing your actions. For instance, let others know when you are going to display a graphic so they don't try to transmit an image at the same time.
- Minimize extraneous noise. For example, avoid coughing into the microphone, shuffling papers, and engaging in side conversations.
- Be cognizant of which camera you are using. If you use the document camera to show a graphic, remember to switch back to the main camera when the discussion moves on to another topic.
- Reposition the camera periodically.
- If your videoconference runs more than one hour, include a break.
- Allow five to ten minutes at the end of your meeting to give participants the time to say goodbye and to arrange for any follow-up activities.

CAUTIONS FOR VIDEOCONFERENCING

- The most reliable videoconferencing technology can be costly to use, and may not be supported by your evaluation budget.

- Without the technical expertise of a videoconference service provider or information technology (IT) professionals, you may run into technical difficulties that can derail the conference.

- Videoconferencing is the most invasive of all synchronous electronic communications. As the conference proceeds, it can be easy to forget that you are visually in the presence of others. Not all people are comfortable with this level of interaction (Fetterman, 1997).

Web Conferences

Web conferences are meetings between two or more persons held via an Internet connection that allows them to view the same document or presentation on their computer screens simultaneously, along with audio communication. It is increasingly being used in business and industry organizations for training and collaborating on projects, resulting in significant travel cost savings (Kontzer, 2003). Using Web conferencing, Deere and Company employees are able to work "interactively, in real time. . . . And because workers can assimilate and digest more information they can both make decisions faster, and have more time to make complex decisions" (Carlo Pensyl, quoted in Microsoft Corporation, 1997).

The features of Web conferencing software vary. Most applications include a chat room feature where participants can write text that they all see simultaneously, and some also allow for video communication, making it much like a videoconference. The audio feature works through the Internet or can be set up via a teleconference using regular telephone lines. If audio communication is established through the Web conferencing software, some versions allow the facilitator or presenter to control it, determining whether or not and when participants can hear each other.

The video feature is available with some applications if individual participants have Web cameras. Again, there is variance among different Web conferencing applications, with some allowing all participants to see each other on small screens on their computers and others only transmitting one video image at a time (usually the presenter). The major difference from a videoconference is that participants join the conference from their computer desks rather than assembling at a single location. This makes it more convenient to set up and use. Web conferences can be scheduled in advance or arranged on the spur of the moment. In addition, Web conferencing allows a group of individuals to collaboratively edit the same document. That is, the document is set up as a single shared document that each individual, sitting at his or her computer, can edit. Or, groups at different sites can elect a single person as an editor, while the groups are discussing changes together.

In terms of evaluation communicating and reporting, Web conferences can be used for all of the same purposes that you might use a videoconference (see Case Example 4.10), but because they are easier to arrange and participate in, they can be used more frequently—e.g., for planning and training, presenting information, soliciting input and reactions, and editing evaluation plans and reports. Case Example 4.11 describes how a project team with evaluation responsibilities used Web conferencing to enhance ongoing collaboration and team functioning.

CASE EXAMPLE 4.11

Web Conferencing for Collaboration, Consensus Building, and Decision Making Across Diverse Perspectives

The formative and outcome evaluation activities for a federally funded educational reform initiative were significantly enhanced through Web conferencing. The evaluation team consisted of university and school district staff responsible for implementing the reform project, as well as an external evaluation consultant located about 300 miles away. The university faculty on the team represented various disciplines, including biology, physics, mathematics, and education. This diversity enriched the project, but it also meant that to be most effective the team needed to reach some shared understandings about significant aspects of their work. The evaluation consultant supported the team initially by facilitating a working session aimed at establishing shared language and perspectives on components of the intervention, the stakeholders involved, and, in particular, on the project's research and evaluation activity.

The team valued this facilitation, and felt it would be beneficial for it to continue throughout the project. The budget for the evaluation consultant included funds for only three trips to work directly with the team, however. Web conferencing provided an easy solution, especially since it happened that all team members had the same kind of Web conferencing software on their personal computers.

What follows is a description of two Web conferences held by the evaluation team. The first was a follow-up to the working session just described. In that session, the team had reviewed and discussed a draft logic model for the project. This resulted in several suggestions for additions and changes, which the evaluator subsequently made (in a PowerPoint version of the logic model). The team continued their work on the logic model through a Web conference where the evaluator presented the new version. Audio support for the conference was set up through a teleconference. The team provided further input, going into more detail about various components of the logic model (than they had in the previous onsite meeting) and surfacing new areas where there were variant perspectives on the project. In the discussion, issues were resolved and the evaluator made further changes to the logic model in real time—that is, during the Web conference. Everyone was able to see and concur that the changes were appropriate. All team members then saved a copy of the new logic model to their own computers for future reference.

For the second Web conference, the evaluator and her key contact within the team crafted an agenda to review the first set of interim findings for the project. All ten team members participated in the meeting from their offices. Again, audio support for the conference was set up through a teleconference. The evaluator presented the findings using a PowerPoint presentation on her computer that team members were able to see on their screens. She began the presentation

(Continued)

CASE EXAMPLE 4.11 (Continued)

with a slide showing the latest version of the intervention's logic model, pointing out the particular components that the interim findings addressed. After the presentation of the prepared slides, the evaluator facilitated a discussion about what conclusions were appropriate to draw based on the findings. She used a blank page of a word-processing document in the same way that she would have used a flip chart during a face-to-face meeting; that is, she recorded the conclusions as participants spoke, in the document viewed by everyone on their own computer screens. This discussion included several suggestions for remedial action based on particular findings. The evaluator was able to capture those suggestions as well. She converted the list of conclusions to a table and then created a second column where action steps related to each conclusion could be recorded. This was actually done during a scheduled 15-minute break. By the end of this two-hour session the team had generated a set of conclusions and action steps in a text document, which they each saved to their computers. Their next face-to-face meeting was devoted to working with this document to create a detailed action plan.

Both of these Web conferences resulted in productive collaboration within the evaluation team that ultimately benefited the project. The team was able to have additional aspects of their work facilitated by the external evaluator, which helped in bringing together their individual perspectives. Specifically, it enabled iterations of the logic model to be discussed and refined over time, resulting in consensus about and greater collective ownership and responsibility for the project within the team. Working with the logic model helped the team focus on what was most important in the project—in this case, specific outcomes for students and teachers. The logic model then served as a framework for reviewing and assimilating the interim evaluation findings, again focusing the team—on findings about program activities most directly related to student and teacher outcomes. As a whole, the team agreed that the Web conferencing enabled them to reach decisions about interim improvements to the project sooner than they would have otherwise.

Similar to other forms of synchronous electronic communications, Web conferences can be arranged in several ways, through companies specializing in this service or through the Internet using free or inexpensive software and inexpensive video cameras. One advantage of using a service provider is that they provide the technical support, rather than your having to sort it out yourself or get help from the IT department in your organization.

Implementation Tips for Web Conferencing

- Plan and budget for Web conferencing at the outset of your evaluation work. Determine what technical and financial resources you have to support it, and choose the optimal method accordingly.

- Plan each Web conference, deciding what features you will use based on the purpose of the meeting and the number of participants who will be involved. (For example, with a large number of people, it may be easier to have them contribute to a discussion using the "chat" feature rather than through their audio access.)

- Determine whether participants have the necessary hardware and software to participate in the Web conference. Set up a trial run to make sure everyone can get connected successfully.

- Schedule Web conferences for significant aspects of the evaluation work in advance.

- Make sure that each participant has received information about how to access the Web conference.

- For stakeholder groups that you work with regularly, consider using Web conferencing for ad hoc meetings.

- Immediately before the Web conference, follow these guidelines:
  - If using one, position your Web camera before the meeting begins.
  - Review the agenda for the Web conference.

- During the Web conference, follow these guidelines:
  - Keep slides to a minimum during a presentation. Consider inviting participants to ask questions about slides using the "chat" feature, and then responding to them via audio to all participants at the end of the presentation.
  - If you are using a Web camera, look into it when you speak. The same as in a videoconference, doing this gives participants the impression that you are making eye contact with them.
  - Pause occasionally so others may make comments.
  - Identify yourself as necessary.
  - Keep others informed by announcing your actions.
  - Be aware of what other participants are seeing. It can be frustrating if you, as the facilitator, are changing images on your screen too quickly.
  - If your Web conference is more than one hour, include a break.
  - Allow five to ten minutes at the end of your meeting to give participants the time to say goodbye and to arrange for any follow-up activities.

CAUTIONS FOR WEB CONFERENCING

■ Without the technical expertise of a Web conference service provider or IT professionals, you may run into technical difficulties that can derail the conference.

Personal Discussions

One-on-one conversations among evaluators and stakeholders are a natural part of any evaluation. They can involve the evaluator(s) and one or more parties to the evaluation. They may either be planned or impromptu, and they may be initiated by the evaluator or the stakeholder. They occur face to face or over the telephone. Indeed, they constitute one of the most significant elements of an evaluation. We make decisions about how to conduct the evaluation; we adjust those decisions; we communicate about the progress of the evaluation and its findings; we share ourselves and learn about others both personally and professionally—all through one-on-one conversations. Naturally, internal evaluators may have more opportunities to engage in one-on-one conversations with their stakeholders than external evaluators.

Frequent, substantive personal communications between individuals are a requisite for any learning organization. One-on-one conversations are one of the most powerful forms of communication for gaining insight, understanding, and new knowledge; and for developing solutions. Yet one of the major benefits of program evaluation is that it can help take decision making out of the realm of narrow discussions between selected parties. As evaluators, nothing can be more important than our ability to maximize the advantages and minimize the liabilities of one-on-one conversations we have with stakeholders.

⇨ *Implementation Tips for Personal Discussions*

■ **Plan ahead for how you will handle both prearranged and impromptu one-on-one conversations.**

One-on-one conversations with stakeholders are inevitable. Not all one-on-one conversations can be planned, especially those initiated by someone else. In some cases, you may have the opportunity to conduct a personal discussion with a busy stakeholder by virtue of being in the right place at the right time. You must be prepared to respond to such opportunities and requests in a way that maintains the integrity of the evaluation as well as rapport and trust between you and clients/stakeholders. As much as possible, try to anticipate any key one-on-one conversations that are likely to take place—especially around sensitive topics—and plan accordingly.

■ **Be aware of the political context of the evaluation.**

Most evaluators are adept at discerning the political context of their evaluations. That is, where is the impetus for the evaluation coming from? Is there any resistance to the evaluation and why? Who are its chief advocates, if any? Who has vested interests in favorable or unfavorable findings? Sometimes these questions are the object of evaluation design activities that uncover individuals' values, beliefs, and assumptions with respect to a program and its evaluation (see Preskill & Torres, 1999). You may also learn various aspects of the political context in one-on-one conversations with stakeholders. Being aware of where any sensitivities lie among stakeholders can help you anticipate the care with which one-on-one conversations should be handled. It can also help you gauge how much you will want to undertake group work with clients and stakeholders to resolve issues and defuse concerns.

■ **During the evaluation, provide the least amount of information that addresses the concerns of an inquiring stakeholder but still maintains an effective working relationship.**

As evaluators, almost all of us have experienced stakeholders approaching us informally with questions about how the evaluation is going and what our findings are. This can happen at any point in the evaluation and is more likely the longer we are around collecting data. It is understandable that stakeholders' natural curiosity and/or anxiety about the evaluation would prompt such questions.

Consider, particularly if it is early in the evaluation process, politely denying requests for information about findings, explaining that data have not been fully collected or analyzed and that it would be premature for you to articulate any conclusions. Still, there may be instances when you are approached later in the evaluation process by stakeholders. You may have not yet fully analyzed the data, but feel you must respond. It's a good idea to have thought ahead of time about some working hypotheses you can share, always stressing their provisional nature.

■ **Make efforts to make the content of one-on-one conversations known to other stakeholders.**

Case Example 4.12 recounts a situation where program participants who were not included in discussions held by the evaluator later challenged her findings as unrepresentative. At the close of each personal discussion (planned or unplanned), consider who else should be involved in the communication that took place. This might be a matter of informing others about decisions made or findings presented. It could be that the discussion has raised some issues about which you should get other persons' opinions. Often, it is quite appropriate to invite the client or stakeholder who has participated in the discussion to help you identify others who should be involved.

CASE EXAMPLE 4.12

Liabilities of One-on-One Conversations

An external evaluator was conducting a two-year formative evaluation of a nonprofit agency's training program for community volunteers. She requested biweekly meetings with the program's three trainers to discuss the evaluation findings as they emerged. Three months into the evaluation, however, the trainers explained they did not have the time to continue meeting because of the intense challenges they were facing in trying to implement the training program.

In response to interest expressed by the lead trainer, the evaluator invited him to meet with her biweekly for breakfast. There they discussed the program's progress and she shared her evaluation findings. They met regularly for six months.

When the evaluation report was delivered at the end of the year, the other trainers expressed concern that the findings seemed to represent the views of the lead trainer more so than theirs. They accused the evaluator of "siding" with the lead trainer and, as a result, discounted the evaluation findings.

To express their dissatisfaction, they wrote a letter to the agency's director claiming that the evaluation findings were not representative of their views. After a discussion with the evaluator, a decision was made to invite the trainers to describe their perspectives in a rejoinder that would be appended to the evaluation report. Even though no one did this, the evaluator's credibility was damaged, and her ability to carry out the second year's evaluation activities was compromised.

■ **Beware of the frequency of and participants in the one-on-one conversations you have throughout the course of the evaluation.**

You may find that during the course of an evaluation you tend to have more one-on-one conversations with members of one group of stakeholders than with another. Perhaps the teachers at one school are friendlier than those at another. At one program site, participants may even be more accessible due to some way in which a building is laid out. Or, as a matter of expedience, you may tend to spend more time with the evaluation client making procedural decisions about the evaluation than with others from whom you might get input. Be aware of the power and influence these discussions may be having on how you conduct the evaluation. Always strive to strike a balance across stakeholders in terms of exposing yourself to and making yourself available for one-on-one conversations. Case Example 4.13 describes a situation where one-on-one conversations with a program director, solicited by the evaluator, were used to alert the director of design problems in a three-day workshop.

CASE EXAMPLE 4.13

Saving the Day With Planned Debriefs

During a two-year evaluation of a global environmental studies program for middle school teachers from around the world, a three-day workshop was held to debrief them on the first year's activities and plan for the next year's work. Unbeknownst to the teachers, the program's director had invited several current and potential program funders to the workshop and had allocated a good deal of the workshop time to making presentations that would create support for the program. Almost immediately, the teachers began questioning the purpose of the workshop and expressed to each other and the evaluator their dissatisfaction and frustration. In the afternoon of the first day, the evaluator approached the director and suggested they meet to discuss each day's activities and subsequent evaluation findings. She explained that this would help keep the director informed about the teachers' satisfaction with how the workshop was being implemented. As a result of these planned discussions, the director made several adjustments to the three-day agenda and was able to avert what might have been a disaster.

■ **Be prepared to conduct one-on-one conversations with primary stakeholders during or following a site visit.**

Both you and primary stakeholders are going to want to take advantage of the opportunity for one-on-one conversations about the course (and possibly the findings) of the evaluation when you conduct a site visit. This is especially true if you are not readily available otherwise (e.g., conducting the evaluation in a location where you do not live and regularly work). The most obvious times for such discussion are at the beginning and the end of the site visit, but it can also occur throughout a visit.

Beginning discussions will likely focus on logistics of data collection. Discussions at the close of the visit can be more challenging because clients and stakeholders may want to know about findings from the data collection activities just completed. Without benefit of a complete analysis of the data, you may be able to disclose your working hypotheses while stressing their provisional nature. There may also be important issues on program implementation about which you feel clients and stakeholders should be informed immediately. The key is to allow yourself some time to formulate what you will communicate. Otherwise, particularly in the case of qualitative data collection activities, you may have a tendency to discuss those data (observations, interviews) you most recently collected. Alternatively, you might satisfy your hosts by setting a date in the near future when you will provide a report via telephone on your findings.

■ **Supplement written evaluation reports with planned one-on-one conversations with stakeholders.**

Once the evaluation has been completed, consider a planned personal discussion with busy stakeholders who may not find the time to read written reports. After completing and fully documenting an evaluation in a comprehensive written report, it seems incomprehensible to us that a stakeholder would not read the report. With experience, however, we learn and relearn that this is often the case. We must remind ourselves, as did Cronbach (1980), that "the evaluator's final, formal report is essentially an archival document, not a live communication. . . . Informal and oral statements are potentially far more influential" (p. 185). The key to the success of these communications is to plan them—not unlike the way in which you plan formal verbal presentations. What main points do you want to get across? Do these points provide a balanced representation of the findings?

These kinds of discussions can take place with the personal delivery of the evaluation report to stakeholders. At this point, you have the opportunity to emphasize sections of the report—perhaps tables or illustrations of key findings. By also reviewing how the report is organized and what it has to offer, you can increase the likelihood that the recipient will refer to it in the future.

■ **Keep records of one-on-one conversations to ensure the accuracy of further communication about what has been discussed.**

Important, frequently critical issues about an evaluation are addressed and/or resolved during one-on-one conversations. It is essential to keep your own notes about the contents of such discussions and perhaps to follow up with a written account of your understanding of the communication. Further, by writing down what was said and decided, you are much more likely to communicate this information to others accurately. Credibility with stakeholders can be damaged if they do not all receive the same information.

CAUTIONS FOR PERSONAL DISCUSSIONS

■ **The contents of personal communications are frequently based upon selective recall.**

Of all the forms of communicating during the evaluation process, the contents of personal discussions are the least likely to be planned. Try as you might to avoid them, there will be instances when personal discussions about important issues occur in an unplanned manner. Often, discussions occur without the benefit of notes or other documentation about the evaluation. Hence, what you have to say is subject to your own selective recall. You may remember only those aspects of the evaluation you have most recently dealt with or only those findings most salient to you.

■ **Informally communicated information is less likely to be recommunicated accurately.**

Further complicating the circumstances of informal personal discussions, the content of what is discussed may not be accurately recommunicated from one stakeholder to another. As one person recounts a conversation with you, the evaluator, to another person, important elements, including contextual and mitigating factors, can be lost. Obviously, you have no control over how stakeholders communicate with each other.

■ **It will not always be possible to document or follow up to reconfirm the contents of (and/or decisions made during) one-on-one conversations.**

Important agreements or decisions may be reached during one-on-one conversations between you and a stakeholder. Yet, it will not always be possible to reconfirm in writing or otherwise follow up on the conversation before some action is to be taken based on decisions made. With only two parties present, the likelihood of misunderstanding or misinterpretation is often greater than if more persons had been involved. Depending on the situation, actions taken, by either you or the stakeholder, based on miscommunication, can be difficult to remediate.

S U M M A R Y

In this chapter we have described a variety of communicating and reporting strategies that can be used to engage stakeholders and other audiences, and enhance their learning from an evaluation. The strategies presented are either potentially or fully interactive.

As potentially interactive, we have suggested that verbal presentations are most effective when visuals (PowerPoint presentations, transparencies, flip charts, video presentations) are used to enhance understanding. Further, the level of audience interaction can be increased by involving audience members in asking questions and inviting responses to the presentations. We have also described the use of posters and poster sessions as a means for engaging audiences in learning about and understanding an evaluation's process and outcomes.

To fully engage with stakeholders around evaluation processes and findings, we propose that evaluators use working sessions; various forms of synchronous electronic communications (chat rooms, teleconferences, videoconferences, and Web conferences); and discussions with individuals. These interactive strategies have the greatest potential for facilitating individual, group, and organizational learning among stakeholders.

CHAPTER

Creative Forms of Communicating and Reporting

Creative forms of communicating and reporting, including photography, cartoons, poetry, and drama, are increasingly being used by evaluators to present evaluation findings to a variety of audiences (in addition to the case examples provided in this chapter, see Brady, 2000;

Denzin, 2000; Greene, 2001; Harper, 2000; McCall, 2000; Richardson, 2000). Creative formats facilitate personalized representation and interpretation of evaluation findings on many levels. First, photography, cartoons, poetry, and drama are particularly good at capturing multiple voices, allowing program participants to "do their own talking" (Denzin, 1994, p. 503), and allowing "the world being described to speak for itself" (p. 507). Second, evaluators' perspectives are represented through their data analyses and presentations of the findings (often developed in collaboration with stakeholders). Third, each person—who then views the photographs or cartoons, reads the poems, or participates as an audience member of a dramatic performance—creates his or her own meaning and interpretations as the person engages in the dialogue, reflection, and visual, oral, and kinesthetic stimulations these formats encourage (Altheide & Johnson, 1994).

Photographs, cartoons, poetry, and dramatic performances are particularly useful for communicating tacit knowledge, including insights, apprehensions, hunches, impressions, and feeling (Guba & Lincoln, 1982). *Photography* can help convey the context of an evaluand, and/or reveal aspects of implementation or outcomes that might otherwise be overlooked by traditional data collection methods. It can help cross language barriers that may inhibit participants' ability to express their opinions or assimilate written information.

Cartoons illustrate simple or symbolically complex issues in an accessible and concise format. The message(s) or theme(s) of evaluation findings can be conveyed via cartoons in the same way that political cartoons are used to reveal the perspective or viewpoint of their creator. Cartoons can also convey evaluation information to audiences with low reading levels.

Poetry can illuminate the emotions, contradictions, and complexities of evaluation contexts. "Poetry and literature . . . were invented to say what words can never say and, through what they say, we can come to understand what we cannot state" (Eisner, 1990, p. 90). Poetry can be used to integrate the experiences and perspectives of multiple stakeholders (program staff, participants, funders, evaluators, etc.) into a collective voice.

Through orally spoken and written text (script), *drama* recreates lived experience—combining realism, fiction, and poetic genres (Richardson, 2000). It can also help create a balanced representation of the perspective of multiple stakeholders. All of these formats can promote dialogue, reflection, and learning based on evaluation information in a group setting.

In addition, these creative formats share a number of commonalities, with respect to evaluation communicating and reporting in particular. Generally, photographs, cartoons, poetry, and drama

- Can increase the accessibility of evaluation information for particular audiences.

- May be more culturally or audience-appropriate in some cases than in others.
- Are most typically used for conveying findings based on qualitative data collection methods (e.g., interviews, observations, document analysis).
- Are particularly powerful when used as a basis for interaction with program participants and stakeholders to interpret and discuss their meaning.
- Warrant special efforts to communicate the methods used for their creation and to obtain stakeholder feedback prior to dissemination
- Add costs in terms of time and budget to a typical evaluation endeavor.
- Are best used in conjunction with traditional formats (e.g., written reports and summaries).

Use of these creative formats has a particular advantage for evaluation practice. When evaluators experiment with different methods for communicating and reporting, they may find that their approach to more traditional formats improves because they understand the evaluation information more "deeply and complexly," having tried to craft it into a variety of creative forms (Richardson, 1994, p. 524). "By writing in different ways, we discover new aspects of our topic and our relationship to it," and are more aware of the communication choices we are making when creating an evaluation document (Richardson, 2000, p. 923). The remainder of this chapter presents detailed information on using photographs, cartoons, poetry, and drama for evaluation communicating and reporting purposes.

Photographs

The purpose of using still photography in evaluation is to represent the realities of program participants, as they exist at one point in time. For communicating and reporting evaluation processes and findings, photographs have a tremendous capacity to convey context, provide complex information, stimulate discussion, and promote self-reflection. Relatively inexpensive digital technology makes photographs available, without processing, that are easy to edit, insert in documents, and transmit electronically.

Evaluators who use photography to communicate and report findings often achieve a more personal knowledge of the phenomenon being studied, enabling them not only to describe and analyze, but also to communicate understanding. Case Example 5.1 describes how having photographs helped one evaluator provide a more accurate and balanced report than might have otherwise been possible.

CASE EXAMPLE 5.1

Influence of Photography on Evaluator Perspective

Findings from an evaluation of a summer camp for gifted adolescent students revealed numerous problems with its administration. The four-week summer camp provided classroom and experiential learning in marine biology taught by university faculty. Chief among the findings were the difficulties caused by the availability of only one sign language interpreter among the dormitory and teaching staff. This person was expected to be available at any time that the youth were awake or in the classroom. In addition, none of the university faculty had had prior experience with, nor were they provided any training or orientation to, working with deaf or adolescent youth, or with a sign language interpreter. Consequently, the classroom time reflected a lack of discipline, and the staff felt a high level of frustration.

In the two weeks she spent on site at the camp, the evaluator used photography to document the camp activities and experiences of the youth. Experienced herself in deaf education, the evaluator's sensitivity to these problems was particularly acute. During the evaluation process, she engaged with the camp's administrators to provide formative feedback as the findings emerged. In writing the final report, her first inclination was to focus on all the turmoil that she had seen and that had been expressed by the staff. However, a look through the pictures that had captured the enthusiasm on the faces of the youth—at the beach, conducting experiments, laughing, and playing—reminded her that some good things had happened. The gifted deaf adolescents themselves seemed to be fairly immune to the travail that was being experienced by those running the program. In viewing and reflecting upon the photographs, she was able to give a more balanced report of the weaknesses and strengths of the camp. The program did receive funding for the following year, and was implemented with remarkable improvements, including the hiring of a fully fluent dormitory staff, two interpreters for the classroom, and a science teacher from a residential school for the deaf.

SOURCE: Personal communication, Donna Mertens, 2004.

Using photographs in communicating and reporting evaluation processes and findings is particularly effective when

- Visual information is of primary interest.
- Information about the program looks different to various people.
- It is important to understand and describe the subjective nature of participants' experiences.
- The evaluation is focused on discovering and describing the unexpected, unobtrusive, secondary effects of the program.

- Studying program implementation is important.
- The evaluator is interested in counting, measuring, comparing, qualifying, or tracking artifacts or information that can be captured visually.
- The evaluator wishes to develop a framework for understanding and classifying some of the important events that occur during the course of a program.
- The evaluator wishes to illustrate the activities of a single participant in a program.
- Language or cultural barriers may inhibit participants' ability to verbally express their opinions, and/or easily assimilate information in written reports.

When used to convey interim or final evaluation results in a written report or a visual presentation (see Case Example 4.2), photographs provide an opportunity for stakeholders to construct their own meaning of the findings. The photography can be a catalyst for dialogue that stimulates audiences' participation in interpreting important events and experiences, enabling the findings to be used for developing action plans. Case Example 5.2 illustrates how using photography as both a data collection and reporting method led to new insights about the program and a revision of the next year's evaluation plan.

CASE EXAMPLE 5.2

Using Photography to Collect Data and Communicate Evaluation Findings

Parent University is a parent involvement program for elementary school children and their families in a small town in rural South Georgia, where there are few community resources. The program is designed to maximize the opportunity for creating and maintaining parent involvement in their children's school success. In creating healthy norms for parent involvement, it was important that the school create a welcoming environment where parents and children could learn together and have fun doing it. The more families the school can expose to the same information and experiences regarding parent involvement, the better chance it has of creating and maintaining a healthy community norm. During FY 2003, the program sponsored 25 parent activities involving 2,064 participants. During a typical session, children attend a story time and activity to learn about the value of money. Meanwhile, their parents learn about family financial strategies from local bankers. This strategy gives family members a shared learning experience that is developmentally appropriate, providing a foundation for many important family discussions.

(Continued)

CASE EXAMPLE 5.2 (Continued)

An evaluation of Parent University was undertaken to determine how it has helped parents get involved in their children's school success. Throughout the program's implementation, photos were taken during regularly scheduled activities to depict the real-time interactions among school administrators, teachers, parents, and children. The photos (see below) were included in the evaluation's final report and were used to facilitate a discussion about the findings with various stakeholder groups and to develop a three-year strategic plan. The program's external evaluator, Mary Cofer, believes that the photos provided a series of "poetic glimpses into the inner workings of the program that could not be adequately conveyed by words alone." (To view these photos in color, go to http://www.sagepub.com/escr.)

Parents learn about money management.

Children learn about money value.

The game of Bingo is a family activity.

(Continued)

CASE EXAMPLE 5.2 (Continued)

Children help parents with computer learning.

Family fun can be intergenerational.

Siblings of all ages lend a helping hand.

During the discussions it became obvious that members of the collaborative were impressed that the photographs revealed program qualities that were not being reported otherwise. "Until we looked at the photos, we were not aware of the extent of inter-generational participation and support for the program. This support system is an important one for school success." As Cofer further explains, "the simple act of viewing the visual images of a program at work generated new revelations of knowledge and understanding. Each person saw the photos from a new and different perspective and pointed out aspects of which others were unaware." For example, in some of the photos it appeared that the children were helping parents learn about computers. Other photos revealed parents helping children learn.

In developing the three-year strategic plan, Cofer reports that the "photos were instrumental in raising the level of discussion regarding programmatic and evaluation issues. As a result, we will refine the evaluation instrument to include more questions designed to broaden the scope and deepen the nature of information collected. There will be questions that ask about the parents' school involvement and community involvement that go beyond just attending the Parent University program activities."

The ways in which photography was used in this evaluation facilitated both individual and group learning. Including the photos in the evaluation report increased individuals' understanding of the program's context and outcomes, and using the photos to communicate the findings to audience members in a large-group setting created the opportunity for members to collectively interpret the findings and to co-construct new meanings about the program, which ultimately influenced the next year's evaluation plan.

SOURCE: Case described with permission of Evaluation Enterprises, Inc.

Implementation Tips for Using Photography in Communicating and Reporting

■ **Consider the appropriateness of photography for your evaluation participants.**

Photography may be especially useful for communicating and reporting with the following stakeholders and audiences:

- A wide variety of program participants, including youth, those who do not speak the dominant language, and those who have seen or participated in only select parts of a program
- Program administrators and staff, both those widely involved in the program and those in tangential roles
- Program staff and participants in similar programs
- Funders who have limited contact with the program/participants
- Potential funders/donors who have limited knowledge of the program
- General public with an interest in the program's activities and impact

Photographs are widely used in professional reports and documents of all types throughout the world. Nonetheless, it is important that before deciding to use photography, you make sure participants are comfortable having images of themselves and their environments recorded and disseminated. Numerous cultures across the globe (e.g., the Amish in America, many Indian pueblos of the American Southwest, inhabitants of remote areas of Nepal) have prohibitions against photographic or other recordings of visual images.

■ **Plan your use of photography for data collection and reporting.**

As described in Case Example 5.2, photography can serve as both a data collection and reporting method. When using photography, it is important to consider what will be photographed before the first photos are taken. Much like the decisions that guide evaluators in determining whom to interview in qualitative studies, the key factor in deciding whom and what to photograph rests on the desire to represent program participants' and stakeholders' perspectives and realities. Evaluators should consider the following sampling questions (Templin, 1981, 1982): Is this photographic evidence representative, and of what? Whose differing perspectives are represented? Does this sample of photographs represent to others what you had in mind? Another important question to consider is, Which individuals or groups do not appear in the photograph(s), and why?

Sampling techniques include the following:

- Time sampling, where people are photographed at regular intervals
- Blanket sampling, where the photographer attempts to photograph as much of the events and people as possible

- Shadow sampling, where an individual is accompanied by you as evaluator/photographer throughout a day, periodically taking photographs
- Snowball sampling, where participants are asked who or what should be photographed in an attempt to capture issues as they arise

In addition to following a particular sampling plan, be prepared to take photos when unique opportunities present themselves—it is not always easy to predict what will happen in any program or organization being evaluated. You will also want to create a system to track and organize your photographs. Maintaining a log listing the time, place, date, and frame for each photograph makes them easy to locate and identify for later use.

An example of an organized and well-planned approach is Wynne's (1993) book *A Year in the Life of an Excellent Elementary School*. After spending several years studying effective schools, he developed a schema that outlines the characteristics of an effective school. The framework lists general categories or principles, followed by increasingly specific and refined activities and practices. For each category he then identified observable behaviors that are evidence of traits or characteristics. Once he completed the framework, he began taking photographs illustrating the presence or lack of the particular traits identified. Wynne used photography in his book to provide teachers with visual, not just written, evidence that educational reform can work and that teachers do accomplish many reform goals.

■ Support photography with other forms of data collection.

Some audiences may feel that photographs are not sufficiently representative. Various writers on photography caution that because photographs represent only one point in time, they reflect "an array of casual fragments—an endlessly alluring, poignantly reductive way of dealing with the world" (Sontag, 1977, p. 80). The observation that photographs "destroy reality and interfere with the accuracy of possible generalizations from the findings" (English, 1988, p. 9) suggests there is a certain truth "out there" that cannot be ascertained from photographs. When used as a data collection method, photography should be supported with other forms of data collection (e.g., interviews, surveys, observations, measures of student achievement) that address your evaluation questions.

■ Consider using photographs primarily as a reporting method—to facilitate audience understanding of the program, its participants, and/or context.

Photographs add to the visual appeal of written reports and invite readership. A single photograph, or several, illustrating a program's context and/or participants can be included in an evaluation report, summary, or a newsletter to help the reader accurately visualize the evaluand. In this case, accuracy and representativeness of the photographs are of concern, but not to the same extent as when photography is used specifically as a data collection method. As will be discussed later, you will want to obtain feedback and consensus from primary stakeholders about the validity of any photographs selected for inclusion in written documents.

Figure 5.1 shows a single-page summary of a study that identified success factors of a downtown revitalization effort in Charlottesville, Virginia. The single color photograph significantly enhances the information provided in the summary by showing readers at least one outcome of the revitalization. Much more text would have been needed to convey the contents of this single photograph. Further, the photo adds to the overall visual appeal of the summary. (To see this figure in color, go to http://www.sagepub.com/escr.)

■ Negotiate permission to photograph.

As the evaluation design is finalized, discuss with key stakeholders why and how photography will be used in the evaluation study. It is important to get written permission for the use of photographs from program participants (or their families in the case of minors). This should be sought and obtained before the first photograph is taken. Many programs and organizations routinely obtain permission from parents for their children to be photographed. Figure 5.2 shows an example of a parental consent form for photographs, videotaping, and publication (including Web site) for use by the organization that administers the program being evaluated.

You should discuss with decision makers two other important issues: who will have access to negatives or digital files, and how you should handle the possibility of particular individuals not wishing to be photographed. It is important to respect different people's cultures and attitudes about being photographed. If groups or individuals decline to be photographed, it is critical that their wishes are respected.

■ Use several photographers to get multiple perspectives.

One criticism of photography has been that photographs ultimately represent what the photographer deems important. This often leads to the question, what photographs were missed or purposely not taken? To address this issue, you may wish to work with a team of evaluators or ask program participants to take photographs during the evaluation study. One option is for participants to use their own cameras or inexpensive, one-time-use cameras. The photographs they take can be used in conjunction with yours to discuss different perspectives represented in the various images.

CHARLOTTESVILLE, VIRGINIA: REVITALIZING THE HEART OF THE CITY

PROGRAM DESCRIPTION

The City of Charlottesville constructed an eight-block pedestrian mall between 1975 and 1985 to provide a catalyst for the revitalization of the central city, to stabilize the downtown retail market and to improve the quality of the physical environment on East Main Street and in the downtown area.

The research has focused on an analysis of the factors surrounding the mall's development and the lessons learned in an effort to explain the success of Charlottesville's downtown revitalization.

KEY RESEARCH QUESTIONS

- Was revitalization of the downtown successful and what were the key indicators? Sales and property values? Soft indicators of use? Opinions?
- What processes and actions led to the success of Charlottesville's downtown revitalization?
- How does one compare and convey the elements of success?

MOST IMPORTANT FINDINGS

- Successful downtown revitalization requires a substantive vision and long-term, effective persistence.
- Planning and implementation require a complex interplay among public officials, private investors, private users of facilities and purchasers of goods and services, non-profit organizations, and interested citizens.
- Downtown revitalization depends on creating a place with numerous parts that attracts many people at different times of day and week, month and year.
- Preservation of historic resources is a necessary ingredient to creating or retaining a place where many people choose to be.

IDEAL AUDIENCES FOR RESEARCH FINDINGS

- Local and regional: government officials, businesses, developers, property owners, citizens
- National: other cities and centers of metropolitan areas, planners and urban designers

World Class City

Figure 5.1   Example of Summary Report With Single Photo Depicting the Evaluand

SOURCE: Used with permission of City of Charlottesville.

Film and Media Permission Form

Dear Parent:

Please complete this form to give consent for [name of program/organization] to take photographs/videos of your child.

I am the parent and/or legal guardian of _____ (first and last name of child), born on __/__/__ (date of birth of child), and am giving [name of program/organization] permission to use:

_____ A photograph/video of my child

_____ A photograph/video taken by my child

_____ My child's first name

[Name of program/organization] has my permission to use the above for evaluation, educational, public relations, publishing, and public awareness purposes (including, but not limited to, the [name of program/organization] Web site). By this authorization I agree that I shall not receive any fee and that all rights, title, and interest to the photographs/videos and use of them belong to [name of program/organization].

_____
Signature of Parent or Guardian

_____
Printed Name of Parent or Guardian

Relationship to Child:

_____

Date: _____

Figure 5.2   Example of Parental Consent Form for Photographs, Videotaping, and Publication

---

■ **Be aware of participant reactivity, as well as the use of photography to establish rapport in the field.**

Reactivity refers to the influence of your presence on the behavior of program participants. It raises issues about whether the participants' actions are part of their ordinary behavior or are influenced by your presence with the camera. Becker (1979) and Collier (1967) argue that the camera reduces reactivity because it validates the researchers' right to be there. Although the presence of a camera can be obtrusive, we have found that people generally like to be photographed.

The camera can even help establish relationships between you and the participants. When one of the authors first started taking photographs at the Saturn School in St. Paul, Minnesota, some of the students approached her and asked her what she was doing (see Preskill, King, & Hopkins, 1994). This enabled her to begin a conversation about her role and the students' perceptions of how things were going. Eventually, they grew used to her presence in the school, camera and all, and rarely paid attention to her efforts to photograph them, thus reducing the potential for reactivity.

Similarly, Fetterman (1998, 2002) describes the use of digital photography as an icebreaker "to help gain access and familiarity with people in the field" (2002, p. 37). In one instance, "community members could see themselves immediately and if they did not like the picture, it could be erased and reshot moments later. This helped to establish rapport" (p. 31).

■ **Determine how you will analyze photographs used for data collection.**

Analyzing photographs is similar to analyzing qualitative data. Use several analysts, edit analytically, examine random samples, and perform content analyses (Wagner, 1979). As the evaluation progresses, you can work back and forth between the data (photographs) collected, developing more elaborate and complex theories, interpretations, and judgments related to the study's evaluation questions. Ultimately, the photographs can be arranged in categories that relate to emergent evaluation themes, conceptual frameworks, and key evaluation questions. These analyses can then be integrated with the participants' stories and other evaluation data that have been collected.

Photographs can be used in an evaluation to strengthen stakeholder involvement, to focus on group learning, and to stimulate dialogue among program participants. In this case, stakeholders participate in the analysis, guided by your questions. They are asked to view, analyze, interpret, and perhaps judge the images according to themes and patterns they discern in the photographs. The inferences you and the participants make when analyzing the photographs should be included in verbal or written evaluation reports with the photographs.

■ **Solicit stakeholder feedback.**

Whether or not you involve stakeholders in the analysis and selection of photographs to represent the evaluand and/or evaluation findings, it is important to solicit their feedback on your final selections. Even when participants have given permission to be photographed, they may later be surprised (pleasantly or unpleasantly) to see photographs including them in an evaluation document.

■ **Provide details about your sampling and analysis methods.**

Written reports containing photographs should provide documentation, such as contact sheets, sampling plans, photographing protocols, and photo interviewing protocols—as well as details about your analysis methods. Doing so gives readers access to information about the validity of the photographic evidence. When you have used one or several photographs to portray elements of the evaluation context, you may want to include details, such as its date and location, in a caption.

■ **Prepare photographs for discussion with and feedback from program participants.**

To facilitate discussions with stakeholders regarding the evaluation's process and findings, photographs should be produced in 5" × 7" or 8" × 10" sizes. Then they can be mounted on foam core board or other sturdy material available at any art supply store. The number of photographs and how they are mounted depends on the purpose and scope of the discussion desired. It is also possible to mount many images (4" × 6" or larger) on a wall in the school or organization as a gallery display. Alternatively, digital photos can be projected from your computer. When you have program participants view all of the photos at the same time, this can be followed with a discussion about what they saw, as described earlier.

Cartoons

Cartoons are another form of visual representation that evaluators can use for communicating and reporting. They draw on the viewer's visual literacy, the ability to look at an image "carefully, critically, and with an eye for the intentions of the image's creator" (Thibault & Walbert, 2003). Traditionally, cartoons are black and white or color drawings, depicting: (1) humorous situations, often accompanied by a caption; (2) current public figures or issues portrayed symbolically and often satirically (political cartoons); and (3) basic information in a simplified format. Despite the fact that cartoons have been a form of communication, entertainment, and social and cultural commentary for over 100 years, they are the least used among the creative formats for evaluation communicating and reporting. Although, evaluators have used cartoons to depict evaluators and aspects of evaluation processes in works primarily written for other evaluators (see Patton, 1997; Stake, 2004).

Modern-day comics began in 1896 when Richard Felton Outcalt created what is recognized as the first comic strip or comic book. His work often appeared in the Sunday supplements of newspapers. Throughout the years, comics have reflected a variety of issues and concerns. For example, in the United States, after the stock market crash in 1929 and during the Great Depression of the 1930s, many of the comics were escapist and hope-oriented. The resulting emphasis on superheroes continued through World War II. Also during this time, *Brenda Starr*, the first cartoon strip written by a woman, appeared in Chicago in 1940. Further reflecting society's concerns in the 1950s, comics often focused on issues of prejudice, juvenile delinquency, and the Cold War. Comics continue today to be a voice for various groups of individuals (e.g., political parties, the underclass, rural communities, young families, the lovelorn).

Cartoons are widely used in public awareness and learning materials to convey information to children and low-level adult readers. For example, meal programs for the homeless in Rhode Island have used place mats depicting information about community services in cartoon form, designed for non-readers and low-level readers (Office of Vocational and Adult Education, 1994, p. 39). Another example is seen in an annual report of the adult education and training division of the Grassroots Educare Trust (1993), an organization that helps South African communities provide preschool education and healthcare. The entire section of the report describing its resource center is provided in a cartoon format consisting of 23 drawings presented over four pages. Each depicts a different activity of the center and is accompanied by one or two sentences describing the nature of the activity. This presentation format was consistent with the Trust's goal of adapting its training materials to the needs and literacy levels of the peoples it serves.

Cartoon images can be used by evaluators to provide audiences with an informal, visually oriented understanding of program impact. They can also be used to provide anecdotal scenes of program implementation. As with photographs, cartoons can be particularly useful when language or cultural barriers may inhibit participants' ability to easily assimilate information in written reports. "Cartoons afford evaluators an opportunity to present findings in an illustrative and succinct way to attract the attention and interest of readers to an evaluation report" (Chin, 2005, p. 42). In the 1980s, Phoenix Union High School used a brochure with a cartoon depiction of students in a stalled car; it was aimed at students who might be thinking of dropping out of school. The brochure presented findings from an evaluation study that revealed the experiences and opinions of students who had dropped out and subsequently returned to school (Hathaway, 1982). As a visual form of presentation, cartoons can address simple or complex issues and findings, communicating them in a highly accessible and concise manner. What newspaper write-ups attempt to express in 12 pages, the cartoon does in a pithy one-liner. Little wonder then that the first thing most of us like to look at when we pick up a newspaper is the cartoons (Austa, 2003).

⇨ Implementation Tips for Using Cartoons in Communicating and Reporting

■ **Consider the appropriateness of cartoons for your evaluation stakeholders.**

Cartoons may be especially useful in communicating and reporting to the following stakeholders and other audiences:

- Program administrators and staff involved in the program's design and implementation
- Youth
- Parents, guardians, caregivers, and teachers of participants
- Stakeholders with low-level reading ability
- Funders who have in-depth experience with the context of the program and its participants

Cartoons may not work well for audiences who would view them as detracting from the credibility of the evaluation work. This could include funders, or corporate, government, and other audiences who have almost exclusively received traditional, text-rich evaluation reports. It is also important to be aware of the cultural perspectives of audiences when using cartoons to depict situations that are meant to be humorous. What is acceptable or interpreted as humorous in one culture may not be so in another culture.

■ **Determine how you will select topics or findings for illustration with cartoons.**

As described in Case Example 5.3, Chin used specific interview questions to identify humorous situations experienced by staff and participants in her evaluation of a reading program for an elementary school. She then created four cartoons based on the interview data.

CASE EXAMPLE 5.3

Using Cartoons to Report Evaluation Findings

Chin (2002) used cartoons to communicate and report findings for her evaluation of a reading program in a Florida elementary school. To help her develop this approach, she asked an additional interview question of some teachers, parents, and students to elicit "amusing sidelights or funny incidents" that were experienced in the program. What she found was that while the participants' examples were indeed funny, they also represented the benefits, critical issues, and challenges in implementing the program. From the interview data, her classroom observations, and reflective role-play analysis she used "cartoon transcreation" to develop four cartoons depicting the key evaluation themes. Chin (2003) defines this process as "the creation of cartoons from data and other source(s) pertinent to the study with the purpose of representing findings based on humor, gentle conveyance, and/or elicitation of awareness on matters deemed important to readers" (p. 295).

Illustration 1 Cartoons

SOURCE: © 2002 Chin Mei Chin

(Continued)

CASE EXAMPLE 5.3 (Continued)

Chin drew three of these cartoons and commissioned an artist, Bill Otersen, to draw the fourth cartoon because she felt the complexity of drawing required was beyond her skill level. The fourth cartoon illustrates the repetitive nature of the reading program and the teachers' and students' feelings about the 90-minute classroom sessions. About 40% of teachers found this amount of time to be appropriate, and an equal percentage found it to be too long.

Chin included the four cartoons in her final evaluation report (2002) and subsequently surveyed and interviewed members of the school community about their reactions to them (2003). Out of 15 respondents, only one unfavorable reaction was recorded. Among the respondents' reasons for liking the cartoons were that they provided visual pictures that explained the findings; helped the reader in remembering the findings over time; conveyed the findings even for those who could or would not read the entire report; allowed the reader to "feel the attitudes" of the characters; were accurate depictions of the program; added interest, appeal, and variety; attracted and kept reader attention; and were amusing (2003, pp. 142–143).

SOURCE: Case described with permission of Chin Mei Chin.

An alternative to this approach is to use cartoons to illustrate the main findings or issues identified through routine data collection and analysis in the evaluation. The issues, topics, themes, or findings need not necessarily involve humor. The purpose of the cartoon illustrations could be to provide a visual image with some of the same benefits of photographs—for example, to address different learning styles, to depict context, to communicate with low-level readers, to bridge language barriers, and to stimulate dialogue and reflection among stakeholders about the findings illustrated.

■ **Determine how you will create your cartoons.**

There are three basic alternatives for creating cartoons: (1) draw them yourself; (2) create them on the computer with art/drawing software, or by using or adapting clip art available from software programs or on the Internet; or (3) hire a cartoonist or graphic artist. Drawing skills are often all that is necessary to create simple cartoons. Cartoonists use the three principles of the cartoon code: leveling, sharpening, and assimilation (Harrison, 1981). *Leveling* refers to techniques for simplifying what is seen; for instance, using black and white instead of color, dropping insignificant details, and using as few lines as possible. With *sharpening*, figures in the cartoon stand out from the background. Cartoonists use *assimilation* by exaggerating features or expressions to help the viewer grasp the feelings or circumstances being portrayed. Numerous resources are available on drawing cartoons (see for example, Blitz, 2001; Hart, 2000; Tatchell, 1990).

The principles just discussed can be applied to artwork you draw manually, or on your computer with the appropriate software. Most word-processing programs also include clip art drawings that might be suitable for conveying evaluation findings or themes. With skill in the use of artwork software, these images can be modified to suit your purposes. An endless variety of clip art drawings is also available on the Internet. You should proceed cautiously, however, in using ready-made artwork, which may or may not accurately convey the message you intend.

Finally, you may decide to hire a cartoonist or graphic artist to create your cartoons, providing detailed instructions on the concepts and ideas to be depicted. In this case, you will need to find room in your evaluation budget to cover the cost of hiring an illustrator.

▥ Write simple call-outs and captions for your cartoons.

Though cartoons are obviously a visual medium, it is the combination of pictures and text that most often conveys the complete message of the cartoon. Most comic strips are written in language suitable for elementary and middle school readers (Lin, 2003). The text that accompanies cartoons for depicting evaluation information and findings should be similarly simple.

▥ Solicit participant feedback.

There are at least three important reasons to obtain feedback on cartoons from program participants. First, participant feedback provides a validity check on how well the cartoon conveys the intended message, particularly because there is a large interpretive element with cartoons. Second, caricatures of individuals or situations as depicted in cartoons could be deemed offensive, insulting, or inappropriate within the context of any particular culture that participants represent. Finally, whether intended or not, program participants may think they see themselves depicted in a cartoon that you create. If so, they may think that promised confidentiality has been violated. Naturally, if this were the case, it would need to be resolved through revision of the cartoon, and/or clarification and negotiation with the participants.

▥ Use cartoons in combination with other communicating and reporting formats.

While cartoons can enhance one's understanding of the evaluation's findings, they also require additional information and explanation to ensure that the intended message is being received. Using cartoons in conjunction with formal written reports, newsletters, executive summaries, and other text-based formats increases the reader's understanding by adding a visual element to the information being presented. The text provided should include methodological details about how the cartoons were created, their intended meaning, and if possible, participants' reactions to them.

Poetry

Qualitative researchers in the fields of anthropology, sociology, and education have sought to present their findings in ways that "make a difference in the lives of those whom they represent and those who are the audiences for the presentation" (Goodyear, 2001). Poetry addresses this goal by creating a sense of the reality of "being there," offering a vicarious experience to the audience and aiding them in understanding the "nuances and subtleties of conflict and agreement in *this place and at this time*" (Lincoln, 1990, p. 73, emphasis in the original).

The use of poetry to communicate evaluation processes and findings is often derived from a practice called "poetic transcription" that "involves word reduction while illuminating the wholeness and interconnectedness of thoughts" (Glesne, 1999, p. 183). That is, a poem is created by using the interviewees' words or phrases. When read, the poem reflects more than the individuals' words—it represents the combination of the evaluator's interpretation and the participants' voices (Glesne, 1997). Figure 5.3 provides a poem created by one of the authors using the words of corporate training and development staff to represent their vision of an ideal evaluation system. It captures both the multitude of participant voices and the complexity of a well-functioning evaluation system.

Poetry provides another way of perceiving meaning from the text, and can be especially effective in communicating the tacit and the implicit. Poetry helps articulate contradictions, sensitive topics, emotional reactions, and challenges in the setting. It can make evaluation results more accessible by using participants' language and avoiding evaluation or other academic jargon. The use of poetry for communicating and reporting may

- Convey meaning about social/organizational complexities of evaluation contexts.
- Educate and promote learning both during an evaluation and in reports or other documentation.
- Create opportunities for dialogue that enhances learning from the evaluation.
- Provide an accessible medium for communicating individual and collective experiences (MacNeil, 2000).

An Ideal Evaluation System for the CEDT Organization

Questions, information, feedback, stakeholders
use, improve, modify, make decisions, and communicate
collaborative, customer focused, teams
values—mine, yours, the organization's
specific, clear, targeted, relevant, consistent, trustworthy
Level 1, Level 2, Level 3, Level 4
qualitative, quantitative, multiple methods
reflective, talk, face-to-face, buy-in
technology, analysis, database, user-friendly, accessible, linked
reports, canned, customized, summaries, desktop
summarize, make changes, flexible
integrated, whole, systemic, bridge, connected, continuous
committed, supported, embedded, resources, line of sight
new ideas, suggestions, lessons learned, change, celebration

Figure 5.3   Example of Poem Reflecting Multiple Participant Voices and Evaluator Analysis and Interpretation

SOURCE: Used with permission of Sandia National Laboratories.

Case Example 5.4 details how a poetic transcription of language from focus group interviews promoted dialogue and understanding about program participants' experiences, as well as about evaluation practice.

CASE EXAMPLE 5.4

Using Poetry to Communicate Evaluation Findings

For an evaluation of a government-funded, self-help program, MacNeil (2000) took language from focus group interviews and constructed a poem that was intended to provoke readers of the report "to engage in a process of reflective meaning making about the program" (p. 359). The program hired successful recipients of mental health services to provide peer support to people in psychiatric institutions. Using an open-coding approach to the qualitative data analysis process, she "highlighted the descriptive, metaphoric, poetic, or emotive clusters . . . embedded in the quotations, and then extrapolated and reassembled these clusters into a poetic narrative that conveyed the particular central theme for the evaluation finding" (p. 361). The resulting 44-verse poem represented seven connected themes found in the data, one of which was related to the employees' role identity (p. 364):

(Continued)

CASE EXAMPLE 5.4 (Continued)

Poetic Representation of "Role Identity"

Which side of the line am I on?

> a psychiatric survivor
> a full-time worker
> running support groups
> getting a paycheck

> > learn to play politics
> > case management
> > covering for staff
> > keeping my distance

> > > mixing oil with water
> > > walking a fine line
> > > a political dance
> > > a dance with the system

> > > > I don't want to sit in staff meetings
> > > > but where is the voice?
> > > > why doesn't anyone ask?
> > > > have your tried this?

The entire poem was included in the final evaluation report. When McNeil shared the report with the client who commissioned the evaluation, her reaction was very positive. "She thought the poetic transcription, 'would be useful in shaping understandings about the inherent challenges and contradictions of the position.' But she also wondered whether others she would be sharing the report with would understand or value the representation" (p. 364). As a result, MacNeil and her client decided to present the evaluation's findings at an annual retreat. Early on the day of the retreat, just prior to its start, she asked some of the employees to read the poem "with a critical eye to see if it held up for them . . . and consider reading it aloud at the end of the day. They were enthusiastic about the offer and snuck away with the piece during the afternoon for a private rehearsal" (p. 364). At the end of the day, the employees read the poem to their colleagues and supervisors. "It was quite a striking performance. The room was deadly quiet while the readers intently focused—smiling, grimacing, and accentuating at all the fitting moments. The audience members nodded in agreement verse after verse and delivered a resounding round of applause upon completion of the reading" (p. 364).

When the reading was over, MacNeil asked the audience to comment on the poem. They responded that "the poem put their work, thoughts, and experiences into an accessible medium." One participant best summed it up in stating, 'It makes people think differently about what we are doing because you have transformed very complicated issues into simple content that illuminate raw realities'" (p. 365). Other stakeholders felt that the poetic transcription "validated their roles . . . made them view their jobs differently . . . helped to unify them as a group, and built on their courage to continue working in this challenging position" (p. 365). In sum, MacNeil believes that the content of the poem "made readers re-think what it meant to be an employee . . . and influenced the meanings and values held by the different stakeholders about the evaluand, and raised higher moral and political issues for reflection about a dimension of the program" (p. 365).

Finally, "by promoting discussions among readers about processes and products of evaluative inquiry, the poetic transcription provoked reflective dialogue about evaluation practice" (p. 365). Stakeholders "talked a lot about how important the poem was in its ability to communicate in a language different than traditional evaluation reporting" (p. 365). MacNeil reports that the poem stimulated discussions about what is knowledge, what is evaluation, and what are underlying assumptions of various methodologies.

SOURCE: Case described with permission of Cheryl MacNeil.

Implementation Tips for Using Poetry in Communicating and Reporting

■ **Consider the appropriateness of poetry for your evaluation stakeholders.**

Poetry may be especially useful for communicating and reporting with the following stakeholders and audiences:

- Program participants, administrators, and staff, especially those who have participated in case studies or provided qualitative data such as interviews
- Stakeholders of programs related to education, social services, arts and culture
- Audiences whose cultural/social traditions value verbal communication

It is important to remember that some audiences may not readily understand or value poetic representation or its role in evaluation. Given that poetic forms of representation are not typical in most evaluations, audiences may be surprised when you use these methods. You will want to consider how poetry might be received by your particular stakeholders and other audiences, and how you will explain why it is being used. There may be better times than others, or with certain groups, that poetry may be more acceptable and appropriate. Some audiences may see poetry as highly aesthetic or elitist and react negatively. Others may consider formal presentations and final reports as the only legitimate venues for evaluation information and dismiss poetry as too informal or "unscientific."

■ **Determine how you will construct poems to represent key findings, themes, or issues in the evaluation data.**

After conducting a thematic or content analysis of the data, using "poetic transcription" a poem can be developed from key words, excerpts, or phrases from the data that stand out—that appear particularly poignant, insightful, or compelling. Case Example 5.5 presents a poem using interviewees' direct words, which was then refined by the interviewees themselves.

CASE EXAMPLE 5.5

I Want to Help My People: Reflections From Community Health Representatives Serving a Northern Plains Indian Nation

What is it like to work as a community health representative on a Northern Plains reservation? To stay up all night listening to unfolding storm reports, making emergency disaster plans for your own family and for your whole community? To know your community's elderly so well you plan your long rural routes around their schedules for getting up in the morning? To stop at the houses where you know the availability of heat is in question when temperatures plunge, and scrounge for electric fans when they soar into the 100s? To often speak in the native language of your people as you advise your elderly neighbors about avoiding frostbite in the winter and heat exhaustion in the summer? To use "drive time" searching your own heart and mind for health, bound in emotional, spiritual, physical, and mental balance? To witness with a heavy heart the rising devastation of "new" illnesses, like diabetes, among your people? To grieve over the loss of young relatives and neighbors from vehicle crashes and suicides? Yet, to feel a warm glow when neighbors you have encouraged to stop smoking, stop drinking, eat healthier foods, start getting out and walking, or start back to school—gradually and with some setbacks—take those steps?

The following poem, *I Want to Help My People,* provides one answer to these questions, reflecting the dedication of community health representatives (CHRs) to their communities' health in all dimensions—mental, spiritual, physical, and emotional. CHRs are American Indians and Alaska Natives specially trained, but employed and supervised by their tribes and communities. They are paraprofessional health care providers who know the dialects and the unique cultural and social aspects of their people's lives (Indian Health Service, 2002). CHRs are deeply engaged in promoting health and preventing disease within their own communities, making possible early intervention and case finding so that patients get the care they need earlier in the course of their illnesses, and helping to prevent chronic illnesses as they encourage physical activity and healthy eating. CHRs often work long hours and serve their communities on a 24-hour basis (Indian Health Service, 2002). Today approximately 1,400 CHRs serve in about 400 tribally managed programs.

I Want to Help My People

A Poem by Lakota & Dakota Sioux Community Health Representatives

John Eagle Shield, Gerald Iron Shield,
Elaine Keeps Eagle, Virginia Leaf, Dawn Satterfield,
Sally Taken Alive, Jolene White Bull Codotte

"I am a representative of my community."
"I am a representative for health."
"I believe in my Creator."
"I see it as a calling."
"This is what I'm supposed to do."
　"I want to help my people."

"My own life has to have balance or nobody will believe me."
"I'm not better than anybody else."
"I ask for forgiveness."
"I have to have a clean frame of mind."
"I pray to say the right things."
　"I want to help my people."

"It's this idea of helping people."
"People trust me."
"They come to me in need."
"I'm there for everyone."
"We're the 'in-between' people."
　"I want to help my people."

"The eagle sees everything that's going on."
"Our ears are always open."
"Like bees, we're busy, trying to make things right."
"Sometimes we see things that make us sad."
"I can be fierce like a bear . . . trying to protect."
　"I want to help my people."

"We have feelings, too."
"I wish they knew how much we care."
"I say, 'We're here for you but please meet us halfway'."
"Some people thank us from the heart."
"Our elders—they understand."
　"I want to help my people."

"From the job came a concern for my people."
"I didn't know my people were so sickly with diabetes."
"People on dialysis talk to me—'If I had only known. . . .'"
"We've got to think about our children and grandchildren."
"We need prevention here."
　"I want to help my people."

"We try again and again—then there's a little change."
"She gets outside and starts moving around."
"Just yesterday, he got off insulin and onto a pill."
"We did it! She switched to diet pop!"
"That's rewarding . . . rewarding. . . rewarding. . . ."
　"I want to help my people."

"We should tell our youth, "No, diabetes doesn't have to happen to you."
We know how to prevent these long-term illnesses.
Let's commit again to our traditional ways of living,
A life of balance, of people walking together on the same path.
Coming together in a good way.
　"I want to help my people."

"I think of all the things I want for my community."
"I think of the animals that fly, swim—that survive . . ."
"I want our people to stand and be proud like the eagle."
"I think of the patience of the turtle."
"I remember the strength of the buffalo."
　"I want to help my people."

NOTE: Dedicated to Eugene Parker, a veteran CHR who put the needs of his community before his own. Used with permission. Contact: John Eagle Shield, 701-854-3856, Standing Rock Lakota Sioux Nation.

(Continued)

CASE EXAMPLE 5.5 (Continued)

The poem was written using the direct words of CHRs from two sources: (1) focus group interviews where they described the most important aspects of their roles as CHRs, what they wished people to know about their work, and the effect diabetes has had on their people; and (2) refrains from other area CHRs heard by the interviewer in her role as their instructor for courses about diabetes. A group of five CHRs then refined the poem and dedicated it to a colleague before his death in 2001.

Evidence for the poem's validity was seen in 1999 when over 700 participants closed a national conference on diabetes among American Indians, standing on their feet repeating, "I want to help my people." During the conference, John Eagle Shield had read the poem, and described the dedication of the Standing Rock Nation's CHRs and their program's collaboration with diverse partners to improve diabetes outcomes.

SOURCE: Case described with permission of Centers for Disease Control and Prevention, Division of Diabetes Translation, National Diabetes Prevention Center.

Another approach is to create the poem based on your own understanding of the program and analyses of the data. Case Example 5.6 describes this approach and audience members' positive responses about the utility of the poetry.

CASE EXAMPLE 5.6

Positive Audience Reaction to Poetry Based on Evaluator Interpretation

Goodyear (2001) created poems to represent the findings of two large-scale surveys of risk behaviors regarding HIV/AIDS among youth. She generated poems based on her understanding of the prevention program and the findings from the studies' data. The poems are not poetic transcriptions, but rather they are interpretations that were grounded in the survey responses and informed by five years of observations and multiple methods of data collection related to the specific HIV/AIDS prevention program.

In order to create the poems, Goodyear exposed herself to many forms of poetry, mostly the type that is informed by issues of class and race and is part of a new movement to make poetry more performative and politically relevant.[1] To understand the performative aspect of poetry, she attended multiple live poetry readings—also known as poetry slams—and watched videotaped performances of poems.

The poems were presented to audiences in combination with other traditional presentations of data (graphs, narrative text, etc.), and depicted the emotionally compelling human aspects of participants' experiences alongside the more neutral, general descriptions of program issues, trends, and outcomes. The following is one of the poems. Its topic is parent-child communication, from the perspective of a parent:

> III.
> Every time she comes home, I feel the gap.
> I don't ask; she won't tell.
> Is it a generation gap? A communication gap?
> No, the gap is that space between.
> Not between my child and me,
> Not between her age and mine,
> her values and mine, her goals and mine.
> It's the space between silence and understanding
> Between fear of telling and fear of knowing
> A wide gaping hole, with no bridge, just depth.
> An outstretched hand or a turned back.
>
> Today I asked what she did in school.
> She said, "We talked about AIDS."
> Did my surprised look come from her answer
> or because she answered?
> A pause, then, "What did you learn?"
> My response, an outstretched hand,
> begins the construction of a bridge.

After hearing the poems, audience members were asked to discuss their understandings of the information presented, what action they might take based on that information, and what they thought of the poetry as a means of communicating the studies' findings. Their responses validated this use of poetry. They thought the poems could be used to: (1) highlight cultural perspectives within the program; (2) convince a skeptical audience to participate in the program; (3) inform future research and generate new hypotheses; (4) energize audiences in ways they thought conventional presentations do not; and (5) take action on behalf of the program. Audience members also said that the poems added contextual, emotional, and personal information about the program. For example, one person reflected that the poem's message about the importance of parents using different modes of communication when talking with their kids about HIV/AIDS role-modeled that challenge for him. He believes that the poem communicated how to do this more effectively than a more traditional reporting format would have been able to do.

SOURCE: Case described with permission of Leslie Goodyear.

NOTE: 1. See for example, *Poemcrazy* by Wooldridge,1996; *Joker, Joker, Deuce* by Paul Beatty, 1994; the Nuyorican Poets Café anthology *Aloud,* 1994; *The United States of Poetry,* a Washington Square Films production for ITVS, 1996.

■ **Share poems with a sample of evaluation participants for feedback prior to dissemination or publication.**

Participant feedback is necessary to make sure that poems used in evaluations capture issues and findings with validity. You will want to ask a variety of stakeholders to read and comment on the poetry as you develop and refine it.

■ **If poems are being presented in a working session or verbal presentation, consider asking stakeholders to read the poems aloud.**

Having stakeholders read the poems aloud to others can be quite compelling as a form of communicating and reporting. Those listening may be more inclined to believe the findings when they are delivered by those inside the program, especially if they know them personally. An evaluator reading the same poems might not have the same impact. In addition, those who read the poems may come away with a greater commitment to using the findings, since they have been so intimately involved in communicating the evaluation's results.

■ **Facilitate discussion about the poetry by asking for participant reactions.**

Like photography and artwork for the viewer, the meaning and value of poetry varies by the listener or reader. To explore the variety of meanings stakeholders may derive, you can facilitate a discussion based on questions like the following:

• What about the program is this poem revealing to me? Is it anything I had not known before?
• What does my reaction/response to this poem reveal about me in relationship to the program?
• From hearing (or reading) this poem, what has become more real?

■ **Use poetry in combination with other communicating and reporting formats.**

While poetry may add important insights into the evaluation's findings, it is not a stand-alone strategy for communicating and reporting. Goodyear (2001) found that evaluation audiences were interested in presentations of evaluation findings that combined representational forms—e.g., graphical representations of trends, presented in conjunction with poetry that highlighted the perspectives of program participants (see Case Example 5.6).

Poetry should always be accompanied by additional text detailing important contextual information to assist audiences in understanding the role and value of poetic representation. Written reports should include methodological details about how the poems were created so that audiences can judge their credibility and representativeness. And, as with cartoons, information about the meaning of the poems should also be included. If using poetry in a verbal presentation, it is also important that the evaluator either provide some interpretation as part of this presentation, or that he or she facilitate a dialogue with audience members about possible interpretations.

Drama

Dramatic performances provide evaluators with an innovative method for promoting dialogue, increasing interaction among and across stakeholder groups, and creating opportunities for informed decision making through the presentation of research and evaluation findings. Similar to verbal presentations, working sessions, and synchronous electronic communications, dramatic presentations provide participants opportunities to discuss and reflect on evaluative information in a group setting.

Dramatic presentations can synthesize a broad collection of research and evaluation findings; respond to the emergent needs and concerns of specific audiences; and address issues that shape organizational dynamics and individual behavior (Boal, 1992, 1998; Center for Research on Learning and Teaching, 2002; Kardia, Miller, & Steiger, 2004). Presenting evaluation findings through interactive formats enhances audiences' access to and understanding of a program's context and impact "by providing a deep sense of the lived experience of program participants using literary and dramatic devices" (Patton, 2002, pp. 102–103). As an interactive communication format, drama addresses visual, auditory, and kinesthetic learning styles.

Dramatic performances are flexible in their design and provide evaluators with a visually and inter- and intrapersonally evocative approach to presenting evaluation information, including communicating to the audience the important aspects of a program's context and activities; evaluation data summaries and quotes from participants; or recommendations and evidence of program impact. Dramatic presentations may be combined with working sessions or verbal presentations to set the context for the performance and provide a structured format for group discussion of evaluative information. Case Example 5.7 describes three formats for dramatic performances that have particular utility for evaluators: (1) traditional sketch, (2) interactive sketch, and (3) forum theater workshop (Center for Research on Learning and Teaching, 2002; Kardia, Miller, & Steiger, 2004). Each involves some degree of audience participation. In particular, the interactive sketch and forum theatre formats provide a means for evaluation use and action planning.

CASE EXAMPLE 5.7

*Using Research-Based Dramatic Performances to
Spark Dialogue, Promote Inclusivity, and Effect Positive Change*

The Center for Research on Learning and Teaching (CRLT) at the University of Michigan offers, as part of its programs and services to the university community, the CRLT Theatre Program and the CRLT Players, a theater troupe of local professional, staff, and student actors. Using research and evaluation information on the experiences of instructors and students in higher education, the CRLT Players develop and present sketches that engage audience members in discussions about issues of pedagogy, diversity, and inclusion.

The CRLT Theatre Program

- Disseminates research about teaching and learning issues to faculty and graduate students.
- Engages audiences in an interactive format.
- Focuses more on solutions than problems.
- Adapts to the particular needs and concerns of the audience.
- Addresses issues that shape classroom dynamics and student behavior.

The CRLT Theatre Program uses three theatrical formats for its CRLT Players productions: (1) the traditional sketch, (2) the interactive sketch, and (3) the forum theatre workshop.

Traditional Sketch

A traditional theatrical sketch performance evokes assumptions, motivations, feelings, experiences, themes, or metaphors related to a specific topic. The sketch is usually developed from original research or evaluation data (especially interviews and focus groups) but may also reflect findings in research, evaluation, or academic literature. The actors may be characters or may represent abstract themes or metaphors. A trained facilitator guides the discussion between audience members after the traditional performance of the sketch (the audience may be arranged as one, larger group or subdivided into multiple, smaller groups). The actors do not engage in the post-performance discussion. Examples of CRLT Players traditional sketches include inspirations and challenges about teaching and learning based on interviews with award-winning professors at the University of Michigan (UM); and perspectives on diversity from students, faculty, and administrators at UM.

Interactive Sketch

Using a solid foundation of research and evaluation findings on the experiences of instructors and students in the classroom, the CRLT Players develop and present provocative vignettes in order to engage audience members in thinking and talking about issues of pedagogy, diversity, and inclusion in the classroom. Each sketch reflects theory and practice about a given topic. The number of actors varies by sketch.

Sketches draw the audience into the scene with a mix of comedy and drama and are designed to portray the complexities and challenges of everyday classroom situations. Following each sketch, the audience dialogues with the actors, who stay in character. A trained facilitator guides this discussion and provides professional expertise and research-based information about the topic at hand. The facilitator also poses questions to and solicits questions from the audience. After the facilitated discussion, the actors repeat the sketch, incorporating audience members' suggestions and examples of "good practice" into the scenario.

Examples of CRLT Players interactive sketches include gender and the climate that women students experience in science classrooms, disability in the classroom and the many issues surrounding visible and hidden disabilities, and anxiety in a clinical setting and how instructors can help students learn and succeed in the complex clinical environment.

Forum Theater Workshop

In a forum theater workshop a facilitator presents a general topic for discussion. The topic may include presentation of research/evaluation findings or just open solicitation of issues of concern from the participants. The topic of discussion may be predetermined or decided as part of the facilitated conversation during the meeting.

In this format each participant serves as both an actor and an audience member. Participants create mini-scenes of situations, contexts, or scenarios about the specific topic based on their own experiences. They may do this in pairs or in small groups of up to six to eight people who will act out the mini-scenes. The participants who are the audience for each mini-scene then step into different roles to try a variety of approaches and strategies related to the topic of the scene or to expand the topic to reflect their experiences/perspectives. Each audience member can step into any actor's role at any point in a scene, and a scene may be repeated any number of times to enable the maximum number of participants and strategies to emerge.

While the interchange of actors and audience members occurs, the facilitator elicits discussion and reflection about each mini-scene. Forum theater technique creates opportunities to discuss the pros and cons of the approaches and strategies, how the theater technique has influenced participants' understanding of the topic and their emergent insights, and to develop plans for implementing and evaluating future changes. The forum theater technique has been used by the CRLT Theatre Program to promote discussions among faculty, administrators, and graduate students about issues related to quality pedagogy, increasing student engagement, and creating supportive classroom environments.

SOURCE: Case described with permission of the Center for Research on Learning and Teaching at the University of Michigan, Ann Arbor.

A *traditional sketch* format lends itself to the presentation of complex programmatic issues and impacts on stakeholders, organizations, and communities. Case Example 5.8 provides an example of how a traditional dramatic performance was used to report findings from a program evaluation conducted for a science department in a higher education setting (Greene, et al., 2003). The performance script was crafted from data collected in interviews, observations, and documents.

CASE EXAMPLE 5.8

Using a Dramatic Performance to Report Evaluation Findings Within a University Context

A team of evaluators that included graduate students and faculty was commissioned to design and conduct a program evaluation for a university science department. The science department had received a multiyear grant to increase the diversity of its science majors, and to revise the curriculum to involve more active student learning and be more inclusive of all students. The evaluation focused on describing the nature of diversity, equity, and justice in the program; the educational experiences and perspectives of the program participants; and the connection of the program to the overall campus community.

As part of the evaluation reporting process, the evaluation team developed a performance script crafted from data collected in interviews, observations, and documents. It was developed to accompany more traditional forms of communication, i.e., the standard technical report. The team wanted to communicate not only the substantive findings, but also the emotions, nuances, and lives of the participants through the performance format.

The script consists of a narrator that sets the context for the performance and six composite characters representing students and faculty, male and female gender, and a variety of racial/ethnic, cultural, and socioeconomic backgrounds. During the performance, the characters speak to each other in interactive dialogue about issues related to diversity and science education, meant to convey the complexity of diversity in the higher education context. Some characters have brief monologues, but most of the script is interactive between two or more characters. Typically, two characters react to each other and other characters join in the conversation, adding their perspectives and experiences to the conversation. For example, two students discuss how they like to learn and whether their science courses support how they best learn. A faculty member interjects issues related to curriculum change and the difficulty in getting faculty to expand their teaching pedagogy, while another faculty member focuses on teaching content as the primary concern in science education. The performance has been done in various settings as described below. Members of the evaluation team have served as the actors for some presentations; at other presentations the evaluation team has recruited audience members to perform as actors.

The performance was presented to members of the science department grant team during the second year of the evaluation implementation. The performance was also designed for use in public forums on the college's campus to promote ongoing discussion of the evaluation issues and findings. The performance format was chosen by the evaluators to make the public forums engaging and to promote dialogue among the audience about their interpretations and experiences related to diversity.

SOURCE: Adapted from Greene, Chandler, Constantino, & Walker (2003).

Evaluators might use the *interactive sketch* format to present a program's context from a variety of stakeholder perspectives, each perspective represented by a different character (actor) in the sketch. The actors may be professional actors, members of the evaluation team, program staff, or other stakeholders in the evaluation. Following the sketch the audience interacts with the actors, who stay in character. A facilitator guides the discussion, responding to questions from the audience and interjecting further information about the evaluation findings as appropriate.

The *forum theater* technique, combined with a working session, fosters stakeholder analysis of and reflection on evaluation data, and serves as a mechanism for participants to try out strategies for change in a dynamic and synergetic process, as described in Case Example 5.8. It can also be used as a method of inquiry. Case Example 5.9 describes the use of forum theater to explore perspectives about student assessment in a school setting in Denmark. Through audience participation and interaction, this technique allowed the social construction of realities in a school setting to emerge.

CASE EXAMPLE 5.9

Using Forum Theatre to Explore Perspectives on School Assessment in Denmark

A faculty member at the University of Southern Denmark, working with the Dacapo Theatre Company, used dramatic performance—in particular forum theatre—as a means of inquiry into assessment practices in school settings (Dahler-Larsen, 2003). (The Dacapo Theatre Company consults with public and

(Continued)

CASE EXAMPLE 5.9 (Continued)

private organizations to better understand the processes of change.) In this case the purpose of using a forum theater technique was to promote interactive, improvisational, nonthreatening discussion as individual members of the audience took over performance roles or added new ones to try out alternative strategies related to the issue of assessment. Audience members shared their individual experiences and ideas about the topic, and saw firsthand how their strategies and advice play out in a dynamic, ever-changing context.

The faculty member and Dacapo Theatre members wrote and performed three short plays for a mixed audience of principals, teachers, pupils, and parents. The plays focused on: (1) a principal discussing with teachers how to assess social competence among pupils; (2) a teacher reporting back to a pupil and parent about the outcome of an assessment of the pupil; and (3) a principal and group of teachers discussing the use of assessments at a parents' meeting. In the third play the audience acted as the parents participating in the meeting.

The performance was videotaped, and the faculty member used the videotape to analyze the nature of the audience participation and their perceptions of the use of assessment in the school setting. In this dramatic setting, issues of power, interest, self-image, emotional commitment, frustration, and fear were surfaced in the audience's participation and comments during the performances. The forum theater drew out a variety of assessment issues including criteria for judging social competence; individuals adapting assessments in ways that were not anticipated; pupils, parents, and teachers using assessment findings to define the pupils' educational present and future; and misuse of assessment data to further individuals' personal agendas.

While the faculty member had originally conceived the purpose of the forum theater event as a mechanism for the audience to discuss the effects of assessment in the school setting, the audience often drew the conversation to issues of hidden political agendas, and to conflicting beliefs about appropriate behaviors and decision-making processes in the school. The audience was highly engaged in the performances; participants raised issues and improvised strategies related to their perceptions of the motivations and impact of assessment in their school. The balance of improvisation of the audience and preparation of the performance allowed particular issues to be raised by the script of the plays (e.g., assessment of students and the use of those assessments by administrators and teachers) while allowing other contextual issues to emerge from the audience members' interaction with the plays (e.g., disagreement about who makes decisions related to school policies and procedures).

SOURCE: Case described with permission of Peter Dahler-Larsen.

⇨ *Implementation Tips for Drama*

■ **Consider the appropriateness of drama for your evaluation stakeholders.**

Drama may be especially useful for communicating and reporting with the following audiences:

- Program administrators and staff involved in the program's design and implementation
- Other stakeholders who have experiences related to the program's focus/purposes
- Youth
- Stakeholders of evaluands related to education, social services, arts, and culture
- Stakeholders and other audiences who are available to attend a performance

While drama can be a particularly engaging format for presenting evaluation findings, some audiences may negatively dismiss it as "child's play." Others could feel alienated by theater because of prior experiences with highly aesthetic, abstract drama that distances the audience from the actors and the events on the stage. Humor in the theatrical performance can enhance audience interest by releasing tension around controversial issues and allowing audience members to ask questions or offer suggestions without fear of saying the "wrong thing." However, humor can also cause audience members to view the performers as broad caricatures removed from their daily experiences and informational needs.

■ **Consider your options for creating the script for the theater performance.**

In developing the text (or script) for the theater performance, the evaluator should consider the following questions:

- Should the performance be a verbatim conversation from interview or focus group transcripts or a dialogue created by arranging excerpted quotes?
- How many of the participants in the data collection/evaluation should be represented in the performance?
- What criteria will I use to choose whom to represent in the performance? By stakeholder group? By level of involvement in the program? To show a variety of impacts of the program? To represent positive and negative aspects of the program?
- If the script will be a dialogue created from excerpted quotes, should those quotes only be attributed to the individual who said them, or should I create composite characters?

- Should the performance highlight the most significant or dramatic aspects of participants' experiences, or should it cover the range of experiences during the entire time frame of the data collection?
- Should I develop the sketch as a typical conversation that took place during the interviews or focus groups, or should I include information gathered through observations, surveys, and document review (including quantitative statistics and demographic information)?
- Should I include myself as a character in the performance? If so, should I fictionalize my dialogue or take it verbatim from transcripts?

■ **Select those who will perform the theatrical piece and make sure they are thoroughly familiar with the evaluation study.**

The actors for a dramatic performance depicting evaluation findings could be professionals, members of the evaluation team, program staff, or stakeholders. Case 5.10 describes the work of an evaluator who developed and performed a traditional dramatic piece to depict the evolving experiences of the program's participants (Goodyear, 1997, 2001).

Whoever participates in the performance needs to have a solid grounding in the evaluation. When audience members ask questions or provide suggestions, having a thorough knowledge of the evaluation context, the evaluation design, the data collection processes, and the findings and recommendations enables the actors and facilitators to provide informed and reliable responses, especially when improvising. Training sessions where the actors and facilitators review the evaluation data and discuss the implications of the data are vital preparation for any theatrical performance.

■ **Set the context for the performance.**

A primary responsibility of the facilitator of the performance is to provide the audience with an overview of the evaluation's purpose and methods, and in particular the methods used for creating the performance script (see Case Example 5.10). The overview might also highlight issues and findings reflected in the performance or, alternatively, might generally define the primary evaluation issues, without presenting actual findings. In this case a fuller treatment of the findings might be incorporated into a discussion with audience members following the performance.

CASE EXAMPLE 5.10

A Dramatic Piece on the Experiences of Project Participants Performed by the Evaluator

Goodyear (1997, 2001) created a dramatic performance by choosing excerpts from the transcripts of individual and group interviews that were part of her evaluation of an HIV/AIDS prevention program. She arranged the excerpts in the form of a hypothetical conversation among three of the participants, and chose to perform all the characters in the performance herself, forcing the audience to imagine the participants. An important goal of the performance was to create a piece that drew the audience into a discussion of the evaluation's issues, while also providing key information about the evaluation design, data, and findings to frame that discussion.

The dramatic performance was meant to portray the experiences of the project participants as they discussed them during the program's volunteer training and subsequent interviews, representing the movement within the participants' discussion from their initial ignorance and fear regarding HIV/AIDS to their articulation of the understanding of which roles within their lives can contribute to the prevention of HIV/AIDS. Through the presentation of the performance, the audience was brought along on this journey.

The performance began by distributing a written description of the program and an overview of the evaluation design (case study) and the performance. Goodyear read a scripted introduction that reiterated the description of the performance, the data collection process, and how the transcribed data informed the script development. She then read quotes from the women, moving back and forth across three chairs to represent different participants. At the end of the 15-minute performance, Goodyear facilitated a discussion with audience members about the evaluation findings and the performance itself. In response to the performance, audience members stated that they thought the performance conveyed a lot about the women, but nothing about the program; stories about the participants, but nothing evaluative. Other audience members suggested that such a performance conveyed the women's struggle to come to grips with difficult issues and the development of these individuals as they shared their interactions with others, "the living example of how the program works" (Goodyear, 2001, p. 177). Speaking to the form, an audience participant reflected that "performance is not only a vehicle to communicate findings, its artistic beauty has intrinsic value" (Goodyear, 2001, p. 182).

SOURCE: Case described with permission of Leslie Goodyear.

While it is important to provide a context for the theatrical performance, avoid distributing lengthy written documents at a performance (or having the facilitator recite lengthy lists of findings or recommendations). Audience members may be distracted with "reading," rather than viewing the performance if given written documents just prior to the dramatic event.

■ **Create a physical space for the theater performance that maximizes audience and actor interaction.**

A raised, well-lighted stage, surrounded by rows of chairs, and use of remote or handheld microphones enhances the implementation of any theatrical performance. Renting stage time and equipment at a local theater, reception hall, or school auditorium is an efficient way to provide a theater setting for the performance for large or small audiences. If the theatrical performance is to take place at the organization being evaluated or at a funder's office, audio equipment (microphones, speakers) can be rented from private suppliers (or purchased at relatively reasonable rates if an organization or evaluation team expects to use theatrical performance as a regular communication and reporting strategy). For small audiences, using staggered circular configurations of chairs eliminates the need for a raised stage.

■ **Use dramatic performances in combination with other communicating and reporting formats.**

As part of the same work cited earlier, Goodyear (2001) asked various audiences (the program's stakeholder audiences, including local and regional program staff; program evaluators at a national evaluation conference; and other audiences at academic conferences) to react to two different forms of representation of the same evaluation findings (dramatic performance and written text). Most of the audiences were interested in a combination of dramatic performance and more conventional formats in order to understand the human and emotional aspects of participants' experiences alongside a traditional representation of evaluation findings that addressed the generalizability of the findings, the methods by which data were collected, and the overall evaluation findings.

The information different audience members take away from a dramatic performance related to evaluation issues and/or findings is likely to vary greatly, based on their: (1) role in the evaluand and the evaluation process, (2) level of interest in the data being presented, (3) level of engagement in and the extensiveness of the discussion, and (4) level of involvement in decisions related to the evaluation's findings and recommendations. Providing all audience members with a written document summarizing the evaluation, for example an executive summary, will ensure that all participants have consistent and reliable information on which to draw at a later date.

■ **Consider using technology-based formats to increase audience access to dramatic performances.**

Video recordings of dramatic performances can be made and disseminated or transmitted live through videoconferencing, allowing audiences to view the dramatic performances remotely, at their convenience, or in coordination with other evaluation meetings or events at a variety of locations. Video recordings can also be disseminated via Web-based technology where audiences connect to a Web site and view the dramatic presentations through the Internet.

CAUTION FOR CREATIVE FORMS OF COMMUNICATING AND REPORTING

■ **Creative forms of communicating and reporting can be time- and resource-intensive.**

Although we mentioned this point at the beginning of this chapter, it bears further consideration. For many evaluators the creative and intriguing formats presented here are a new approach to communicating and reporting. Although the implementation tips we offer are designed to support you, incorporating most any of these formats into your regular practices will require additional time, and in many cases, money! Taking photographs requires an investment in equipment, film, and processing that may not be part of the typical evaluation budget—nor would the costs for hiring an illustrator to create cartoons. While poetry may add little in direct expenses, hiring actors for dramatic performances to depict evaluation findings could be especially expensive.

Another consideration is that, just as these may be new formats for evaluators, they will be new to most evaluation stakeholders and audiences—requiring additional time to explain the approach, request permission for photographs, solicit participation in the development and performance of poetry and dramatic pieces, and obtain feedback.

S U M M A R Y

In this chapter we have explored a variety of creative forms of communicating and reporting evaluation information. Photography, cartoons, poetry, and drama are particularly useful for representing participants' multiple perspectives and experiences in ways other forms of communicating and reporting may not. Through these formats, evaluation audiences are given the opportunity to develop a deeper understanding of complexities and nuances in the evaluation's findings. Finally, these creative approaches are well suited for involving stakeholders in the co-interpretation of findings, which supports learning and the greater possibility of evaluation use.

Additional Considerations for Communicating and Reporting

This chapter addresses a variety of considerations, additional to what we have covered in the previous chapters on planning for and using different strategies to facilitate and maximize learning among stakeholders and other audiences. They are: communicating and reporting for diverse audiences; communicating negative findings; integrating quantitative and qualitative methods; developing recommendations; and multisite evaluation. Evaluators routinely encounter opportunities and issues related to these topics, and they have implications for both the content of and the processes for delivering evaluation communications and reports. This chapter follows the format of Chapters 3, 4, and 5, providing explanations of the topics, implementation tips, and cautions where appropriate.

Communicating and Reporting With Diverse Audiences

The cultural diversity of evaluation stakeholders is steadily increasing as evaluation has become a truly global activity. Regional and national evaluation associations have grown from five prior to 1995 (representing the United States, Canada, Australia, Central America, and Europe) to almost 50 today that span the globe from Egypt to Sri Lanka (Russon, 2004). Members of the American Evaluation Association currently represent 59 countries outside of the United States; and, between 2000 and 2004 approximately 10% of the proposals submitted annually to the AEA conference were from individuals outside of the United States (Kistler, 2004). These trends suggest that (1) evaluations conducted in more and more diverse cultures may be led by evaluators from the same cultures; and (2) there is likely a growing market for cross-cultural evaluation where evaluators practice in cultures or countries different from their own.

It is well known that the United States—where likely the greatest volume of evaluation activity takes place—is one of the most culturally diverse countries in the world. Categories of race/ethnicity used for the 2000 U.S. census number 20, a 43% increase over the 14 categories used in 1970 (www.ameristat.org). Evaluation is not only reaching more and more audiences in terms of cultural diversity, but also audiences of a wider age range. Not all evaluators and evaluation users are adults. For example, youth-led research, evaluation, and planning is a growing sector of the profession (see Checkoway & Richards-Schuster, 2003; Sabo, 2003).

Stake (2004) points out that frequently evaluators are operating "out-of-culture":

Cultures have their own traditions, languages, values, organizational structures, aesthetics, and mannerisms. The evaluator belongs to one or more cultures ethnically, but also to the culture of a department, a coterie, a profession. The evaluand's staff and stakeholders share some cultures, yet subdivide into subcultures and sub-subcultures. (p. 20)

The issue of evaluators' cultural competence is not new (see for example, Office of Substance Abuse Prevention, 1992), but of late is receiving more and more attention within the profession (see Endo & Joh, 2003; Hopson, 2003; Mertens, 2004; Preskill & Russ-Eft, 2004; The California Endowment, 2003; Thompson-Robinson, Hopson, & SenGupta, 2004). The American Evaluation Association's Guiding Principles for Evaluators addresses cultural competency in the following item of Section D, Respect for People:

D. 5. Evaluators have the responsibility to identify and respect differences among participants, such as differences in their culture, religion, gender, disability, age, sexual orientation, and ethnicity, and to be mindful of potential implications of these differences when planning, conducting, analyzing, and reporting their evaluations.

From the standpoint of communicating and reporting, evaluators must design their communications and reports to maximize stakeholders' participation as contributors to evaluation activities and users of evaluation findings. Participation and use should not be limited by communications and reports that stakeholders do not understand (due to diversity in age, language, educational levels, etc.), or reject because they are insensitive to the cultural orientations of stakeholders. And indeed, as discussed in Chapter 2, evaluators have long been advised to match their communicating and reporting work to audience needs and characteristics. The following implementation tips address fundamental aspects of communicating and reporting for diverse audiences.

Implementation Tips for Communicating and Reporting With Diverse Audiences

■ **Use a fully participatory approach with diverse evaluation stakeholders.**

One of the best ways to assure that your evaluation work is sensitive to diverse stakeholders is to solicit their participation in all its phases. Convene a broadly representative evaluation team or advisory group that functions from the very outset of the evaluation through delivery of the findings and support for action planning. Case Example 6.1 describes how input from a national evaluation's advisory committee, consisting of tribal members from Native communities, refocused an evaluation's early, unsuccessful efforts to report findings.

CASE EXAMPLE 6.1

Communicating and Reporting With Native Communities

In the past, research and evaluation studies have been used to demonstrate deficits in Native communities, or as some tribal members say, "To show us what's wrong with us." They have been perceived as ways to embarrass the community. Native communities are more likely to welcome program evaluation if encouraged to take an active role in deciding how and where the data should be used. Also, the community should decide if the data are to be reported in such a way as to reflect the unique characteristics of their tribe, or if the data should be aggregated, thereby protecting their confidentiality.

In a symposium on research and evaluation methods, Running Wolf et al. (2002) described an instance of how communicating and reporting should *not* be done with Native communities. As a part of a national evaluation, early efforts to provide feedback to one tribe were unsuccessful. The results were presented in a traditional research conference format, and tribal members were not receptive to this type of presentation. The evaluation advisory committee, which consisted of tribal members, suggested going back to the community and presenting small portions of the findings to small groups over several sessions. This allowed the community to better understand the information and discuss what to do with it. When working in Native communities, it is especially important to recognize that the data belong to the community and it is theirs to decide how and where to use it.

It is also important to consider both literacy and readability when preparing reports for Native communities. English may not be the first language for the tribal council members or other community planners. So, lengthy reports laden with text and numbers are not as well received as one- or two-page reports with visual representations (e.g., pie charts and graphs). Finally, it is important to inform the community about how the data can be used—for example, whether to make program changes and/or to apply for further funding.

SOURCE: Patty Emord, personal communication, 2004.

Involving diverse stakeholders, not only in the development of communications and reports, but also in their presentation, is important. In particular, stakeholders should participate in developing conclusions and recommendations so that they are framed in light of local culture, values, or beliefs. The following two cases illustrate this point. Case Example 6.2 describes a situation from a quarter of a century ago, still useful in showing the critical importance of having stakeholders involved in the release of evaluation findings. Case Example 6.3 illustrates the need for sensitivity to and inclusiveness of local culture throughout the evaluation process.

CASE EXAMPLE 6.2

Need for Local Involvement in the Dissemination of Evaluation Findings

In 1980, a very sensitive report on alcoholism in a Native Alaska village was released to the general media (cf. Manson, 1989). In addition to a number of other serious errors in protocol, the information from the study was presented at a press conference thousands of miles away from the village where the study was conducted. This precluded any participation by local people and allowed the whole situation to be presented out of context. Once again, an Indian community experienced a great deal of shame because the information released implied that nearly all the Indian adults in the community were alcoholic. Although the actual situation was quite different, there was no way to moderate what was presented.

It is good practice to have local people involved in any release of information, either in person or through a cover letter signed by an agency representative. This once again demonstrates the need for community people to be intimately involved in any evaluation effort. It not only ensures that the most accurate information is presented, but also precludes the perception that the community is once again the subject of outside interventions and is not capable of resolving local issues.

SOURCE: Beauvais & Trimble, 1992, pp. 195–196.

CASE EXAMPLE 6.3

Need for Local Involvement in Evaluation With Marginalized Communities

In his work with the Village Schools Project (VSP) of the Nyae Nyae community of Namibia (southern Africa), Rodney Thompson had the opportunity to review previous research and evaluation reports about the project. The VSP provides instruction for lower primary Ju|'hoansi students of this rural, marginalized area, "with a history of oppression and abject poverty that is largely unparalleled by other groups in the country" (Hopson, 2001, p. 378). Hopson's interviews with program staff and community members about one evaluation report on teaching and learning revealed that they felt findings from the evaluation's interviews were reported inaccurately, reflecting a "general disregard for the participation and consultation of key members of the staff and community" (p. 379). In all, "a significant number of persons in the community were omitted from the evaluation learning and capacity-building process, little knowledge was shared and understood from the Nyae Nyae about the purpose of the evaluation, little instrumentation and documentation was left behind, results were not shared with the community, and no one knew exactly who provided information to the evaluator" (p. 379). This circumstance makes obvious the need for evaluation thinking and design that incorporates local knowledge and ownership into the whole evaluation learning and capacity-building process (Hopson, 2001).

SOURCE: Case described with permission of Rodney Hopson.

■ **Form teams of evaluators to include those from multiple cultural contexts.**

While evaluators may be aware of how their social location (i.e., lived experiences, as determined by class background, racial and ethnic identity, educational background; see Hopson, 2003) differs from that of the people involved with the evaluand, this awareness does not necessarily translate to effective evaluation practice with diverse populations. If possible, it is best to include evaluation team members who have the same cultural perspective as the evaluand's participants. They can guide the evaluation design, data collection, analysis, and communicating and reporting to help assure its appropriateness for and sensitivity to local contexts.

■ **Identify the dominant language(s) among evaluation stakeholders and provide all communications and reports in this language or languages.**

The UCLA Center for Health Policy Research used a pre-letter in five languages to alert California households about their selection to participate in a telephone survey. As shown in Figure 6.1, it was formatted on both sides of an 11×17 page and folded in half to create an 8.5×11 booklet. The front and back pages provided the letter in English and in Spanish. The space of the two inside pages was divided into three columns containing the letter in three Asian languages.

Similarly, the World Bank's Operations Evaluation Department provides the executive summaries of many of its reports in multiple languages. Their report on the country assistance evaluation for Russia covering the period from 1992 to 2001 (The World Bank, 2003) is a bound report with an executive summary included in the front. Each page of the executive summary is divided into two columns where its contents are presented in English and Russian. This dual-language version is immediately followed by a second version of the executive summary, again divided into two columns, one for each of a Spanish and a French translation.

When providing translations of the contents of evaluation communications and reports, in most cases you will want to have them done by a native speaker of the language. Then, the translations should be piloted by at least one (if not several) member(s) of the target audience. In the United States, the home language of many students is Spanish. This makes it necessary to create English and Spanish versions of letters to parents requesting permission for their child(ren)'s participation in data collection activities. (Spanish versions of data collection instruments for use with children are often needed as well.) Typical Spanish translations made by nonnative speakers are written in a language style more formal than native speakers use, and can reduce parents' understanding of what is being requested. As with any written communication, when the audience does not understand it, they are far less likely to respond or provide valid information.

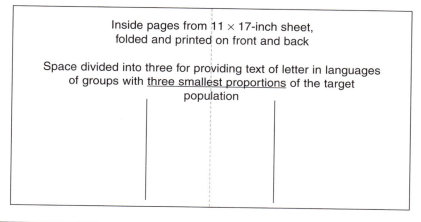

Figure 6.1   Example of Format for Survey Pre-Letter in Five Languages

■ **Use language appropriate for diverse participants and reflective of their voices.**

The fifth edition of the APA's *Publication Manual* (2001, pp. 61–76) provides guidelines for avoiding bias against persons on the basis of gender, sexual orientation, racial or ethnic groups, disability, or age. While these guidelines (see Table 6.1 for a summary) apply to writing articles published in academic journals, they are useful for both verbal and written communications throughout an evaluation.

Insensitivity to diverse cultures and perspectives can also surface if the language in which the evaluation questions, data, and results are cast does not reflect the language of diverse stakeholders and "the concepts, experiences, and value stances this language captures" (Hopson, 2001, p. 2). Evaluators can make their work more inclusive of this language in at least three ways. First, use a participatory approach and second, if possible, include members of the culture

Table 6.1   Summary of APA Guidelines to Reduce Bias in Language

Guideline 1. Describe at the appropriate level of specificity.	Generally, it is better to be more specific rather than less. Being specific avoids stereotypic bias. For example, specify "children at risk for early school dropout," rather than "at-risk children."
Guideline 2. Be sensitive to labels.	Preferences for what people prefer to be called change over time. Ask stakeholders which designations they prefer, particularly when preferred designations are being debated within groups.
Guideline 3. Acknowledge participation.	Replace the impersonal term "subjects" with "participants," "individuals," "high school students," "children," "respondents," as appropriate. Avoid the passive voice when referring to participants' actions. The passive voice implies being acted upon.
Gender	Use gender-neutral language, including alternatives for the generic "he" when referring to everyone, everybody, someone, or somebody.
Sexual Orientation	Use "lesbian" and "gay" rather than "homosexual," which has been associated in the past with negative stereotypes.
Racial and Ethnic Identity	Ask stakeholders about preferred designations and avoid terms that are perceived as negative.
Disabilities	Put people first, not their disability ("person with (who has) a disability" rather than "disabled person"). Preferred expressions avoid the implication that the person as a whole is the disability.
Age	Be specific in age ranges. Use "boy" and "girl" for people of high school age and younger. Use "young man" and "young woman" and "male adolescent" and "female adolescent" as appropriate. For persons 18 and older, use "men" and "women". "Older person(s)" is preferred to "elderly."

SOURCE: Adapted from *Publication Manual of the American Psychological Association* (2001).

whose programs are the subject of the evaluation on the evaluation team. Third, consider alternative formats for communicating findings, such as poetry and drama, which directly incorporate the language of participants (see Chapter 5).

■ Avoid primarily relying on written communications.

Written communications are particularly subject to the social location (see above) of the writer. You will want to seek, whenever possible, opportunities for interacting with diverse populations in order to communicate about evaluation processes and findings. Case Example 6.4 describes the effective use of oral communication combined with visuals to collect data from illiterate farm workers.

CASE EXAMPLE 6.4

Effective Use of Oral Communication and Visuals With Low-Level Readers

Conner (2004) describes an HIV/AIDS education program for Latino farm workers and its evaluation. The excerpt below explains how the evaluators used an oral survey with visuals to collect data from participants.

Preliminary work on the evaluation made it clear that most of the farm workers had very limited Spanish reading ability but had also a reluctance to admit this limitation to others, whether they were members of the program, evaluation team, or fellow farm workers. The evaluation surveys were designed with these realities in mind. A self-administered written survey was not used; an oral survey was used instead, with written questions and answer options, supplemented by a large-scale visual representation of each set of answer options. This process allowed men who did not read Spanish well to follow the written questions and response options by listening to the evaluation staff member. Participants were then able to match what was said to what was on the sheet in front of them. All information on the paper was duplicated exactly on the flip chart sheet for use as a visual guide. If necessary, then, men could "icon-match" instead of read, keeping their literacy level private and answering the questions accurately. Even men able to read sometimes found the icon-matching approach easier when coupled with the oral presentation of all questions and answer options (e.g., with thinking such as "the second option that he read and that's on his chart is the one I'm picking for my answer"). In terms of fostering multicultural validity, a significant benefit of this written-oral-icon approach is that, once refined and pilot-tested, respondents can quickly and almost unconsciously understand and use it. Many of us unconsciously match icons already. For those persons who are uneasy about their literacy level, the approach provides a way to step around literacy problems that does not intimidate or denigrate but instead affirms and assists.

SOURCE: Conner (2004, pp. 60–61).

In a very different context, Case Example 6.5 describes how a verbal presentation using simple, clear graphs of quantitative data helped parents understand evaluation data in ways they previously had not. It shows how interactive learning based on evaluation findings can be important among people of different backgrounds.

CASE EXAMPLE 6.5

Making Quantitative Findings Accessible

California Services for Technical Assistance and Training (CalSTAT), is a special project of the California Department of Education's Special Education Division that helps schools and families educate children and young adults with special needs. CalSTAT administers a State Improvement Grant (SIG) from the Federal Office of Special Education Projects, designed to support California in improving its special education system. Each year, progress made toward achieving the objectives of California's SIG is assessed and reported.

A primary audience for the SIG annual progress reports is the Partnership Committee on Special Education (PCSE). The committee is a broadly diverse and representative group of individuals involved in, or concerned with, the education of children with disabilities. The PCSE provided significant input for the development of the state improvement grant, and guides its implementation.

The SIG evaluator, Cheryl "Li" Walter, Ph.D., has been very intentional about making the results of the annual progress monitoring understandable to the wide variety of individuals (over 100) who comprise the PCSE—state department of education staff, staff of related agencies and associations, teachers, parents, school district personnel, special education consultants, and university faculty. Members of this group vary considerably in their exposure to, familiarity with, and use of tables, graphs, and other means of displaying quantitative evaluation data.

System Objectives—Students Integrated With Their Peers

k) To improve the **equity of placement** across ethnicity and socioeconomic status by disability

In '99–'00, there was a 10.7-percentage-point disparity between the ethnicities with the highest (African American) and lowest (Asian Pacific Islander) proportions of students in special education. This disparity decreased to 10.2% in '00–'01.

l) To increase the amount of time that California's students with disabilities spend **in the general education environment**

There has been a shift in how this data element is reported in CASEMIS, from the percentage of instructional time spent in the general education program, to the percentage of time a student is outside the regular classroom for special education instruction or services. While it was initially thought that this would not disrupt the measure over time, there have been unanticipated differences in the data that have impacted the overall measure and necessitated re-calculation. Thus, these figures are different than what was reported previously.

There was a steady increase in the percentage of CA's special education students spending 80% or more of their time in the general education environment (from 49 to 53.3 to 55.8) between '98–'99 and '00–'01.

m) To decrease the percentage of students with disabilities **expelled or suspended**

This data element was recently added to CASEMIS. Because there is a grace period of one year during which new data elements are optional, reliable data were not available before '00–'01. At this point, the data for this objective are being analyzed, and it is anticipated that they will become available in May of 2002.

SOURCE: The data for these objectives come from the CA Special Education Management Information System (CASEMIS).

Illustration 1

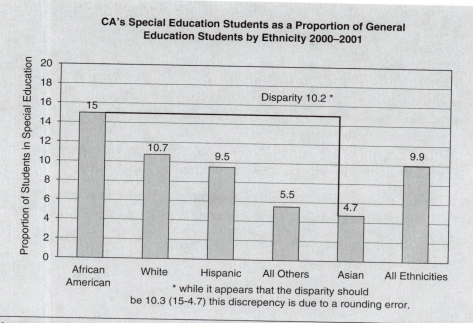

CA's Special Education Students as a Proportion of General Education Students by Ethnicity 2000–2001

Illustration 2

Her reports are straightforward, written in plain language, with the majority of text in 14-point type (see http://www.calstat.org/sig_progress_01.pdf). As shown in the excerpts below, the main body of the reports consists of the objectives of the state's improvement grant, integrated with narrative commentary on the progress made (see Illustration 1), followed by charts of data (see Illustration 2).

Although helpful, the very best opportunities for helping assure that audiences understand evaluative information are not in the design of reports, but in opportunities to interact with them. A particular experience in presenting these findings to a meeting of the PCSE illustrates this point. Walter preceded her presentation of the chart shown in Illustration 2 with another chart to help the audience understand the concept of proportions. It was a two-bar histogram showing the total number of students in California schools in one bar, and the total number of special education students in the other bar. Then, shortly into her explanation of Illustration 2, Walter got a cue from her colleagues that the time available was up, and she should conclude the presentation. Her audience (in particular a group of parents) objected, exclaiming, "We were just beginning to understand this!" Walter was allowed to continue. After the presentation, several participants approached her with feedback: "For the first time, we are really getting this. Thank you!"

Over the five years that these progress reports have been available, Walter feels that the collaborative partners "really understand the data." They are now ready to take their work further by sharing the findings with schools and school districts, and teaching them how they can compile these kinds of data for use in their own decision making and improvement efforts.

SOURCE: Case described with permission of California Services for Technical Assistance and Training, and California Institute on Human Services.

The wide variety of formats currently available to evaluators for communicating and reporting has significantly increased their accessibility to diverse audiences. In Chapter 3 we provide detailed information on document design and layout, and the use of tables and figures. In Chapter 5 we cover creative formats—photographs, cartoons, poetry, and drama—which may have special appeal for audiences from various cultures and age groups. In particular, the visual images provided by still photography and cartoons, as well as videotapes (see Chapter 4) can transcend the barriers of differences in language and reading abilities. Further, as Case Examples 6.3 and 6.5 show, interactive learning can be particularly important among peoples of different cultures and backgrounds.

■ **Select photographs and video footage that are representative of stakeholders' race/ethnicity, socioeconomic status, age, sex, and gender.**

Accurately representing the characteristics of evaluation participants and stakeholders is necessary to illustrate the context of evaluation activity—a powerful benefit of using visual representations. See Chapter 5 for more information on sampling and analysis of visual images.

■ **With heterogeneity among evaluation stakeholders, allow additional time for communicating and reporting activities.**

The more diverse your evaluation stakeholders are, the more time many aspects of evaluation work will require. For example, more than usual amounts of time will likely be required for creating different language translations; soliciting feedback on draft versions of reports and communications; and interacting with stakeholders to interpret, draw conclusions from, and develop action steps based on evaluation findings.

CAUTION FOR COMMUNICATING AND REPORTING WITH DIVERSE AUDIENCES

■ **Despite your best efforts in any given instance, your communicating and reporting efforts may still not be as respectful and sensitive to diverse audiences as they could be.**

Inherently, our own long-standing cultural background, experiences, and practices exert a powerful influence over our evaluation work. Developing cultural competence is an active and ongoing process. For evaluators it comprises an intent rather than an achieved state of being (Sue & Sue, 2003). As Symonette (2004) shares, "Through my work and praxis, I have been striving to walk the convoluted pathways towards being and becoming a culturally competent evaluator and evaluation facilitator. The focus has been on dynamic flows rather than a particular destination status, on a lifelong process rather than a position or product" (p. 95).

Communicating Negative Findings

There is little question that an evaluator's job would be much easier if evaluations always resulted in good news. The reality, however, is that we often must report findings that are not positive—that show little merit or worth or express the need for minor improvements, substantial changes, or discontinuation. We may also be called on or compelled to report results that describe unethical practices or illegal activities.

At some time, all evaluators must face the challenge of explaining negative findings to stakeholders. Evaluators have an ethical responsibility to facilitate stakeholders' understanding of negative findings in an effort to guide them toward future decisions and actions. These are not simple issues, and there is no one solution for making this an easy task. Yet there are strategies an evaluator can use to help stakeholders listen and learn from evaluation studies. Case Example 6.6 illustrates a situation where an evaluator was able to use several of the implementation tips described below.

CASE EXAMPLE 6.6

*Presenting "Negative" Findings in a
Context of Continuous Improvement*

Two years ago, the Sunport Neighborhood Center was established in conjunction with two city schools to serve as a liaison among the school district, the city, and the neighborhoods. The program's three components were a community after-school program, a crime prevention program, and a senior block worker program. The goal of these programs was to promote a sense of community, pride, and ownership in the neighborhood.

As the program was entering its third year, there was a request to increase the funding of the existing center programs and to expand the number of neighborhood sites in the city. An evaluation was deemed necessary to determine the impact of the present neighborhood center programs and to verify the need for expansion. A secondary purpose of the evaluation was to make formative improvements to the current center programs. The primary audiences were the city's police department, crime prevention association, community education department, and its advisory council. The evaluator was an internal city staff person.

The internal evaluator knew that this evaluation had audiences that would be concerned about any negative findings that could possibly emerge. She was well aware of the political nature of this endeavor. She decided to have the stakeholders respond to a series of "what if" questions relating to the possibility of

(Continued)

CASE EXAMPLE 6.6 (Continued)

negative findings. This discussion helped prepare the program's administrators and other primary audiences for dealing with the findings, both positive and negative, in a constructive manner.

During the evaluation negotiations, the evaluator requested that the administrators meet with her weekly to discuss the emerging findings. Again, she felt the administrators needed to be aware of potentially serious issues before these were reported in the final report. In this way, the evaluation's audiences could begin deciding whether or not or in what ways the program should be altered and expanded. If they waited to learn of "negative findings" in the final report, valuable time and energy might be wasted and the political ramifications could be serious.

Even though the weekly debriefings were a productive and effective way of dealing with the program's deficiencies as findings emerged, the evaluator was concerned about reporting these negative findings in a fair and balanced way in the final report. She decided to address each key question that guided the study by describing the findings that were positive and descriptive of program successes. The heading to this section was titled "Things That Are Working Well." As a way of introducing the negative findings, she chose the heading "Work in Progress." Here she summarized the key issues and used the interviewees' and survey respondents' words to articulate the concerns program users had with the program. Employing this approach allowed the program constituents to speak directly to the reader, thus minimizing the evaluator's voice. The effect of this method was quite successful.

From the weekly debriefings, the program administrators knew that the evaluation would likely uncover issues requiring attention. They were able to read the report's positive comments as successes and the negative findings as action plan items, viewing the continued refinement of the program as part of an ongoing learning process. Instead of seeing the negative findings as failures, they were able to put them into a context of continuous improvement.

Implementation Tips for Communicating Negative Findings

■ **From the outset, position the evaluation within a learning context.**

Few evaluations have a strictly summative purpose. And in fact, few decisions to terminate programs are made primarily on the basis of negative evaluation findings. In reality, most evaluations have both formative and summative purposes. Increasingly, funders are requiring not so much that grantees prove that a program results in indisputably positive outcomes, as that grantees show how they are working to assure that requisite program implementation takes place.

Nonetheless, when evaluations are required for accountability purposes, program and organizational staff tend to view them in a summative light.

They may not realize that an evaluation need not (nor should it) focus solely on the bottom line of intended outcomes. For one thing, it is difficult to attribute positive or negative outcomes to a program without knowing that implementation has actually taken place. Evaluators can educate clients about the importance of examining implementation and highlight the collection of data about the program's operations as a specific benefit of the evaluation.

■ **Involve stakeholders and program participants in the evaluation's design, data collection, and analysis activities—and communicate throughout the evaluation.**

Stakeholders and program participants will be much more likely to accept difficult feedback if they have been involved in conducting the evaluation. Ownership of the evaluation processes builds their belief in the data's validity and the findings' credibility.

Findings that focus on issues and concerns are much harder to accept and use constructively if they come as a surprise. This scenario can be avoided by using a variety of strategies to communicate with stakeholders throughout the evaluation. The best way to ensure that will happen is to develop and follow a communicating and reporting plan for the evaluation (see Chapter 2).

■ **Keep stakeholders' perspectives in mind.**

As evaluators consider what to say and how to say it, they must always keep in mind what it is like to be on the other side of the evaluation. It is important to remember that it is sometimes difficult to face a lack of success. The reaction to such news might be to find fault with the evaluation or simply to disregard it, rather than accept the verdict that change is necessary or that the organization has failed to meet its goals. These communications must take place, but with special attention to protecting individuals' dignity and maintaining the evaluation's credibility.

■ **Assist stakeholders in processing negative findings.**

Help clients and stakeholders see their program or organization as a whole rather than spotlighting specific parts where findings are unfavorable. By facilitating a discussion that focuses on understanding how various aspects of an organization contribute both favorably and unfavorably to particular outcomes (through the use of a logic model, for example; see the section on final reports in Chapter 3), you can help clients develop realistic solutions. In this way, you directly contribute to organizational learning.

Figure 6.2 shows a form that can be used to facilitate a working session where stakeholders review evaluation findings and then think about contributing

Working Session on Evaluation Findings

Program Component/Area:
What are some factors/circumstances that may explain these findings?
What are we doing this year to sustain and/or improve these findings?
What more can/should we consider doing?

Figure 6.2   Example of Worksheet to Help Stakeholders Process Evaluation Findings

factors, activities already underway to sustain or improve the situation, and additional action that might be taken. This form can be used in a situation where small groups of stakeholders review findings for different program areas, capture their reflections on the form, and then share out in a large-group discussion that addresses all of the evaluation findings. This process helps program/organizational staff members see findings in the larger context of both the constraints they face and the opportunities available to them, as they use evaluation findings for program improvement.

■ **If possible, stay engaged beyond the immediate evaluation effort to work with stakeholders on using evaluation findings.**

Most evaluators will want to help stakeholders think about how they can use evaluation findings for both formative and summative decision making. Staying engaged in this process helps stakeholders make the most out of the evaluation—particularly when the purpose is for program or organizational improvement. Some clients and stakeholders will welcome the opportunity to have you facilitate action-planning sessions designed to develop strategies for implementing change. In many cases, doing so can help take the focus away from any negative feelings associated with the evaluation findings, and direct it toward making the situation better. A separate action-planning session might follow the process just described where stakeholders begin to identify possible courses of action. It could begin with helping stakeholders reach consensus about actions to take, and then move into identifying the details of who, how, where, and when for each action to take place. (For more on working sessions with stakeholders, see Chapter 4.)

■ **Present positive findings first.**

By presenting positive findings first, receptivity to the evaluation as a whole may be enhanced. Then discuss the negative findings, always referring back to what the program is doing well. It is especially important to do this in a written report, which may be read and assimilated without interaction with you or others in the organization.

■ **Avoid using the words "positive" and "negative."**

Wording such as "accomplishments" and "objectives still in progress" or "successes," "things to work on," or "needs improvement" might be less threatening to stakeholders. Use of this language would be most appropriate for formative evaluations, developing programs, or programs undergoing change. Be acutely aware of the language you use to report what is working well and what is not. Figure 6.3 shows an example set of icons and labels to associate, as appropriate, with the various findings of an evaluation. In

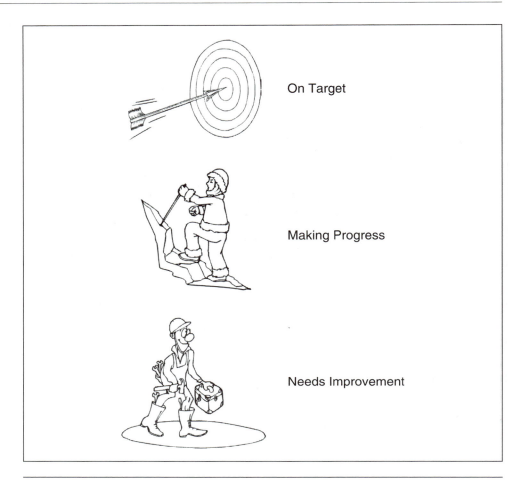

On Target

Making Progress

Needs Improvement

Figure 6.3   Examples of Icons and Labels to Associate With Formative Evaluation
            Findings

addition to guiding readers through a report and helping them assimilate
findings, the icons add visual appeal. (To see this figure in color, go to
http://www.sagepub.com/escr.)

CAUTION FOR COMMUNICATING NEGATIVE FINDINGS

■ **Ultimately, there is no way to control the reaction of clients and
stakeholders to unfavorable evaluation findings.**

Although you are careful to distinguish personnel from program
evaluation, findings do reflect on individuals' performance. It is unre-
alistic to expect that everyone will consider unfavorable findings a
learning opportunity.

Integrating Quantitative and Qualitative Methods

The combination of quantitative and qualitative data collection methods enhances the utility and accuracy of evaluations by capturing a more complete portrayal of events and participants (Caracelli & Greene, 1997; Chen, 1997; Datta, 1994, 1997; Farley, 1991; Fielding & Fielding, 1986; Greene & Caracelli, 1997; Hedrick, 1994; House, 1994, 2001; Mark, 2001; Mark, Feller, & Button, 1997; Reichardt & Rallis, 1994a, 1994b; Rossi, 1994; Smith, 1986, 1994, 1997; Smith & Heshusius, 1986). A mixed method approach can also provide more flexibility for adapting the evaluation's design and implementation when contextual variables, political administrations, agency management, program participants, and implementation sites change (Mark et al., 1997). Mixed method evaluations can be more relevant by being grounded in local participants' experiences while providing some generalizability to other contexts; more useful in identifying both typical and atypical cases; and more insightful about causal connections than single method evaluations (Greene & Caracelli, 1997).

Qualitative data collection methods include

- Onsite observation
- Semistructured and unstructured individual and focus group interviews
- Archival and historical document review
- Videotaping, photographic recording, and analysis

Quantitative data collection techniques include

- Creation of databases on program attendance
- Census data and economic/sociological factors
- Structured interviews
- Closed-ended survey questions
- Student achievement test scores

Datta (1994) provides a convenient summary of the lessons taught by each approach:

What the Qualitative Approach Has Taught Us
- The importance of involving stakeholders
- Taking multiple perspectives into account
- Looking at events/programs within a particular context
- Studying meaning and history
- Emphasizing implementation and process

- Explaining variability rather than dismissing it as error
- Looking for patterns
- Focusing on the user and use

What the Quantitative Approach Has Taught Us

- The importance of paying attention to policy questions
- Emphasizing design power and sensitivity
- Using multiple measures
- Seeking rival hypotheses
- Looking for interactions
- Making clear what methods were used in the conduct of the evaluation

By combining both qualitative and quantitative data collection and analysis methods, evaluators are better able to develop a more comprehensive understanding of the complex social context of the programs or organizations under study (Datta, 1994; House, 1994; Mark et al., 1997; Reichardt & Rallis, 1994b). Moreover, combining methods is likely to expand audiences' understanding and use of evaluation findings because audiences have different ways of knowing, which may be more compatible with either qualitative or quantitative information.

Many evaluators have a predisposition toward the use of one approach over another (Rossi, 1994; Smith, 1994). Yet preference for one method does not suggest "exclusivity, lack of rigor, or the complete absence of any other approach" (Fetterman, 1989, p. 1). Instead of focusing exclusively on the philosophy or the intrinsic value of any approach, evaluators should allow the nature of the evaluation problem and the audience to determine the best way to collect data and present findings. What follows are some of the ways to effectively integrate qualitative and quantitative data in evaluation reports and the challenges faced in doing so.

Implementation Tips for Integrating Quantitative and Qualitative Methods

■ Form teams of evaluators to provide expertise in both qualitative and quantitative data collection, analysis, and reporting.

Based on their training, epistemological orientations, and personal styles, many evaluators are more experienced in using either quantitative or qualitative methods. Today's generally accepted (if not expected) practice of combining the two approaches can pose a problem if you are more comfortable with one over the other. Collaborating with other evaluators who can complement your expertise provides clients and stakeholders with a more holistic, integrated view of their programs or organizations.

■ **Develop a framework that can guide the integration of qualitative and quantitative findings, and focus the report.**

Integrating findings from qualitative and quantitative data provides audiences with a rich and powerful report. A conceptualization or framework can be established to guide the integration of all data. Qualitative and quantitative findings also can be arranged according to the original set of evaluation questions the data were collected to answer. This process involves sorting discrete sets of findings (different tables showing quantitative survey results, sets of coded interview transcripts) according to the evaluation questions and then integrating them during the writing process.

However, you may find that, as a framework for reporting findings, the evaluation questions do not offer the greatest explanatory power. Another overarching framework may have revealed itself during data collection and analysis. The next two case examples illustrate this point. Case Example 6.7 summarizes an evaluation where a framework of systemic reform elements was used to guide the data analyses and reporting (Barley & Dodson, 2000). Case Example 6.8 describes an evaluation where findings were organized in terms of the program's larger context, its implementation, and its outcomes.

CASE EXAMPLE 6.7

Integrating Quantitative and Qualitative Data in a Mixed Method, Multiyear Evaluation

An evaluation of a multiyear K–12 systemic reform initiative in 22 districts in a midwestern state used a quantitative and qualitative mixed method approach. Data were collected annually and included criterion-referenced state assessments in mathematics and science; focus groups and individual interviews with key stakeholders in each district; surveys of teachers; demographic information on student populations; curricula and other school improvement materials; and site visit transcripts. Additional data were collected at annual initiative meetings of representatives from each of the 22 districts.

This collection of mixed method, multiyear data was organized into a "portfolio" for each district, according to six elements of systemic reform: curriculum, parent-community involvement, classroom practice, professional development, administration and leadership, and system change. The evaluation team created a five-point rubric for each of the six areas of reform with descriptions for the "old

(Continued)

CASE EXAMPLE 6.7 (Continued)

system" (scored as a 1) and an "exemplary" system scored as a 5. The descriptions were drawn from systemic reform literature, the mission and goals of the systemic reform initiative, and the professional experience of the evaluators.

Teams of two evaluators (from a four-member team) reviewed each portfolio and rated the districts according to the rubric. They developed a comprehensive report that integrated qualitative and quantitative findings in a concise, easy-to-assimilate format with text and visuals. The report included single pages for each of the six elements showing the average rating across the 22 districts, and the frequency for each rating level. The report also provided descriptions of each school reform element by district using specific examples drawn from district outcome data sources, interview and site visit transcripts, and district demographics. Bar graphs and boxed portions of text set off quantitative and qualitative data on each page.

To explore the connections between the rated levels of reform on the six elements and other district variables, the evaluation team further grouped the 22 districts into three categories: low reform, moderate reform, and high reform. These ratings were compiled into tabular form to show the relationships between reform status and other variables (student achievement increase/decrease, program type/funding amount, district demographics, etc., as well as illustrative examples from district-level data and teacher feedback). Because the report was organized under the framework of systemic reform elements, it was appropriate for dissemination to not only the initiative's national funder and the participating districts, but also to other stakeholders engaged in K–12 systemic reform initiatives, science and mathematics reform, community involvement initiatives, curriculum and assessment reform, and K–12 leadership development.

SOURCE: Case described with permission of Zoe Barley.

CASE EXAMPLE 6.8

Integrating Qualitative and Quantitative Data in a Final Report

This case concerns the evaluation of an after-school enrichment program for primary-grade students who were limited-English proficient. At the outset of the evaluation, the following questions were posed to guide evaluation activities:

- Was the program implemented as specified? If not, what circumstances contributed to changes in implementation?
- How do stakeholders (students, staff members, community volunteers, parents, etc.) view: (1) their participation in, (2) the implementation of, and (3) the success of the program?

- To what extent have parents participated in the program?
- Has parental attitude toward success in school improved?
- Has parental involvement in other school activities increased?
- Have the students participating in the program improved their language proficiency and reading skills?
- What unanticipated impacts of the program—positive or negative—have occurred?

As shown in the following table of contents for the final report, both qualitative (interviews, observation) and quantitative (surveys, standardized tests) methods were used to address these questions.

A framework for the report was established that described the program's larger context first, then its implementation, and finally its outcomes. Throughout the report, qualitative and quantitative findings were integrated for each aspect of these three major areas. This integration provided a comprehensive and holistic picture of the program that facilitated the development of recommendations focused on improving the program after its first year of implementation.

Table of Contents

Final Report

Introduction
Overview of the Program
The Inquiry Process
    The Evaluation Team and Its Approach
    Evaluation Design and Methods
        Interviews
        Individual Interviews With Staff/Stakeholders
        Structured Interviews With Students
        Focus Group Interview With College Students
        Individual Interviews With Parents
        Surveys
            Teachers With Students in Program
            Other Instructional Staff
            Volunteers
        Site Visits/Observations
        Standardized Tests
        Dissemination of Results
        Presentation of Interim Findings
        Year-End Report
Context and Implementation of the Program
    The Program's Larger Context
        Lincoln Elementary School

(Continued)

CASE EXAMPLE 6.8 (Continued)

Sebastian College
Crestview Public Schools
Community at Large
Implementation of the Academic Success Program
    The Students
    Student Selection
    Staff
    Program Activities
        Getting Started
        Snacks
        Computer Use
        Reading Activities and Educational Games
        Art Projects
        Further Discussion About Program Activities
Program Outcomes
    Student Progress
        Brigance Inventory of Basic Skills
        Classroom Teacher Assessments
        Sebastian College Student Assessments
        Parent Assessments
    Student Benefits
        Positive Alternatives and Attention
        Computer Literacy and Enhanced Motivation
        Other Benefits
    School Use of Program Materials
    Sebastian College Student Benefits
    Volunteer Benefits
    Overall Assessments of the Program
        Teachers
        Parents
        Volunteers
        Program and District Staff
Conclusions, Interpretations, and Recommendations for Consideration
Summary of Outcomes
        Summary of Issues About Implementation and
           Recommendations for Improvement
        Future Evaluation Efforts

Another way to think about this approach is as a story line, where data are arranged in a manner that best tells the story. Keep in mind, however, that generally the story line or framework is useful only to the extent that it accounts for all the evaluation's findings.

Sometimes members of an evaluation team work relatively independently for parts of the evaluation. If each has focused on either qualitative or quantitative data collection activities, as may be the case in mixed method component designs, integration of the findings and the development of written or verbal communications may be difficult (Caracelli & Greene, 1997). This division of labor may reflect (the evaluators') individual training and disposition toward using particular methods. It can make integrating the voices of multiple authors with varying values about "what the world is like" even more challenging. Using the evaluation questions or some other framework as a guide can help minimize debate spurred by individual philosophical stances. For example, you may choose to use an analytical induction approach (where the data are considered as a whole regardless of the method/philosophical stance) to arrive at assertions and linkages among the assertions (Smith, 1997). The data should be organized in the way that best communicates findings to the primary audiences, not according to individual evaluators' methodological preferences.

- **Determine the primary audiences' preference for different types of data when deciding if one type should take center stage over another.**

How the data are combined is largely determined by the points you wish to make in communicating and reporting the findings (Datta, 1994; Reichardt and Rallis, 1994a). However, it is also important to be sensitive to ways of knowing that are familiar and convincing to the primary evaluation audiences. Although this factor bears consideration during the evaluation design, it comes up again when you consider the relative weight to be given each type of data in the report. Should one type of data take center stage over another? Should the findings from interviews (qualitative data) be presented as a facilitator or supporter of test scores (quantitative data) or vice versa? Some stakeholders may perceive quantitative data as more valid or accurate. If this is the case, you might present the quantitative data first, using tables and charts, and then bring in the qualitative data to further reinforce the quantitative findings. The important point is to present the findings in a way that gets and holds the audiences' attention. See Figure 3.23 for a form to solicit information about stakeholders' preference for quantitative presentations (charts and tables) vs. narrative descriptions.

- **Consider which communicating formats are most conducive to reporting qualitative and/or quantitative data.**

Formats such as memos, postcards, e-mail, bulletins, brochures, briefs, or newsletters may be used to present findings from qualitative and/or quantitative data. Because of their compact length and specified formats, the information presented must be focused and concise, but can be of any type. A postcard might report a key "quotation" from a series of in-depth interviews with program participants; a memo might contain a graph of program attendance over the past nine months. A bulletin could report key findings on one evaluation question using a pie chart to show a budget for the past year, a table of closed-ended survey responses, and quotes from program managers and staff members.

Graphs, tables, and charts can condense quantitative data into comparable and understandable pieces. Figures, illustrating how various components of a program relate to each other, can summarize findings from interviews. Interim and final reports may use these types of visuals, along with quotes from stakeholders or excerpts from documents, to present a full picture of the program or organization. Again, knowing the information needs and preferences of your audiences will help you choose the most effective format to communicate and report findings.

CAUTIONS FOR INTEGRATING QUANTITATIVE AND QUALITATIVE METHODS

■ **Evaluations that combine both qualitative and quantitative approaches can be resource intensive and time consuming.**

The more comprehensive and integrative the approach to an evaluation, the more it will cost and the more time it will take (Datta, 1994). Of course, these factors are best taken into consideration at the beginning of an evaluation. However, despite the best planning, using an integrated approach from the start means the evaluation will take longer (and possibly cost more) than originally anticipated. If an integrated approach is deemed too costly at the outset, using one method or the other to collect a limited amount of information may be a reasonable solution. In most situations, some information is better than no information at all.

■ **Despite your conviction that a combined approach is best, some clients and stakeholders may still prefer one approach to the other.**

Most evaluators appreciate the advantages of using both qualitative and quantitative methods. Clients and stakeholders, however, may not have this more balanced perspective (Smith, 1997). Despite your best efforts, they may insist on one approach to the exclusion of the other, particularly when they consider the high cost of qualitative methods. In some cases, you might convince clients and stakeholders of the merits of both methods and then conduct a particular evaluation accordingly. Yet, trouble may arise at reporting time if clients' and stakeholders' original preferences resurface.

Developing Recommendations

Recommendations are the formal linkage between an evaluation and its use. Supplying specific action-oriented recommendations has long been considered good evaluation practice (see Drezek, 1982; Hendricks & Handley, 1990; Hendricks & Papagiannis, 1990; Morris, Fitzgibbon, & Freeman, 1987; Patton, 1997; Sonnichsen, 2000; Stallworth & Roberts-Gray, 1987). While some clients may ask evaluators *not* to provide recommendations at the conclusion of an evaluation, most stakeholders do expect the evaluator to include them. Recommendations can be one of the most visible and important outcomes of the evaluation. As Patton (1997) explains, "Well-written, carefully derived recommendations and conclusions can be the magnet that pulls all the other elements of an evaluation together into a meaningful whole" (p. 324).

Figure 6.4 shows "key decision variables" for providing recommendations developed by Iriti, Bickel, and Nelson (2003). Variables to consider are the (1) evaluator's role; (2) evaluation's design; (3) use context; (4) evaluator's experience and expertise; (5) ethical considerations; (6) knowledge of costs and trade-offs; (7) internal capacity of the program; (8) quality, strength, and clarity of the findings; and (9) related literature of the field. The questions they pose for each variable are helpful in determining whether or not to make recommendations, as well as what kinds of recommendations are useful and appropriate.

Methods for developing recommendations may vary according to the extent of stakeholder involvement that is possible or desired. On one end of this continuum, evaluators develop recommendations and then present them to stakeholders. In this situation, the evaluator is often functioning in the role of expert authority or, as House (1986) puts it, as "philosopher-king" (p. 35). The two middle positions on the continuum involve stakeholders: (1) recommendations may be presented to them for critique and modification, or (2) recommendations may be developed collaboratively with stakeholders. On the other end of the continuum, stakeholders alone develop recommendations.

By involving stakeholders in developing recommendations, there is a greater likelihood that they will better understand the findings and see them as credible, and that the final recommendations will be meaningful, plausible, and useful. Describing an evolutionary view of program improvement, Stake (1985) explains that practitioners are "moved to act, to change an activity, to refrain from acting, or to resist acting, only when sufficient external demand or internal conviction arises" (p. 96). The focus here is on internal conviction. Stakeholders who internalize feedback about corrective action are more likely to take that action (Torres, 1994a, 1994b). This kind of ownership is key to individual and organizational learning. It requires that stakeholders be involved in drawing conclusions about what the evaluation findings mean and what action should be taken.

1. *Quality, strength, and clarity of findings*

    a. Are the evaluation findings valid and reliable?

    b. Are the evaluation findings reasonably comprehensive?

    c. Do the evaluation data converge to indicate specific course(s) of action?

2. *Evaluation design characteristics*

    a. What is the depth of the evaluation?

    b. What is the scope of the evaluation (comprehensive or limited to a few components)?

    c. To what extent are the client and stakeholders involved in the evaluation planning, implementation, interpretation of findings, and development of recommendations/course of action?

    d. Does the methodology include strategies to seek contradicting or alternative evidence?

    e. Does the methodology allow voices from all stakeholder groups to be heard?

    f. Does the evaluator clearly understand the value judgments implicit in the evaluation methods selected?

3. *Use context*

    a. Is the evaluation intended to be formative, summative, or a combination of both?

    b. What are client expectations (informal and contractual) about the provision of recommendations?

    c. Is the evaluation use plan focused on instrumental use, process use, political use, conceptual use, or some combination of these?

    d. Will evaluation findings be used to make a specific decision (e.g., renewal of funding)?

    e. Will evaluation results be used by internal program management or by external decision makers?

    f. Does the evaluator have a good understanding of the program's internal politics?

    g. Where is the program in the program "life cycle"?

    h. Are recommendations likely to be controversial internally? Externally?

    i. Do the clients understand that recommendations from this evaluation reflect only one source of information for decision making and that other information might lead to different recommendations?

    j. How stable is the relevant broader environment? Is the broader environment likely to change and thus have implications for any recommendations that would be made?

Figure 6.4   Key Decision Variables for the Provision of Recommendations

SOURCE: Iriti, Bickel, and Nelson (2003). Used with permission.

4. *Evaluator experience and expertise*

   a. Does the evaluator have intimate/extensive knowledge of the program context, history, and operations?

   b. Does the evaluator have evaluation experience in similar or analogous program contexts?

   c. Does the evaluator have specific content knowledge related to the focus of the program?

   d. Does the evaluator have experience making recommendations of the various types?

   e. To what extent is the evaluator aware of the role s/he is taking on as a result of various evaluation and evaluation-based activities?

5. *Ethical considerations*

   a. Are there any compelling inside or outside interests that could influence the evaluator's decision to make particular recommendations over others?

   b. Is the evaluation being conducted for purely political reasons?

6. *Knowledge of costs and trade-offs*

   a. Does the evaluator have a reasonable understanding of the cost of potential recommendations?

   b. Does the evaluation yield data on trade-offs between recommendations and other courses of action?

   c. Does the evaluator have a reasonably clear understanding of the assumptions and value judgments implicit in making various recommendations over others?

7. *Internal capacity of program*

   a. Does the program have good internal resources (time, staff, expertise) to use data for decision making?

   b. Does the program have good internal resources to do program design?

8. *Role of evaluator*

   a. Is the evaluator internal or external to the program?

   b. Is it an ongoing relationship or a one-shot contract?

   c. Is the role defined as "auditor," "assigner of value," "consultant," "facilitator," "counselor," "organizational developer," "other," or some combination of these?

9. *Literature in field of study*

   a. Does the relevant field of study have valid and reliable research findings that speak to the issue that is the focus of the recommendation?

Figure 6.4 *(Continued)*

➡️ *Implementation Tips for Developing Recommendations*

- **Make sure there is a clear linkage between recommendations and the evaluation findings.**

All recommendations should be firmly grounded in the evaluation findings. Recommendations should never go beyond the data. That is, while it might be tempting to make certain recommendations based on your observations, beliefs, or gut feelings, recommendations must be grounded in the data. After reading or hearing about a recommendation, one should be able to track that recommendation back to the data on which it was based.

- **If recommendations are initially developed by you, submit them to stakeholders for review, discussion, and modification.**

At the very least, you should give stakeholders the opportunity to review, discuss, and develop modifications to recommendations you initially developed. In drafting these recommendations, you should use your knowledge of organizational context, logistics, and constraints. Recommendations should be as realistic as possible and be presented as provisional, since it is important that the essence of the recommendation be maintained during the revision process. Here, you should listen carefully to understand why stakeholders do not see a particular recommendation as valid. Rephrasing it to take practical concerns into account may be the solution. Sometimes, you may have to remind stakeholders of the specific evidence that supports a recommendation you think is particularly important.

It is also important to recognize that recommendations have political consequences. Carefully consider the language and vocabulary you use around politically sensitive topics. Stakeholders should be asked to review the language and focus of final recommendations prior to disseminating them more widely.

- **Increase stakeholders' ownership of recommendations by developing them collaboratively.**

You can help stakeholders internalize evaluation findings by involving them in the interpretation process and then working with them to derive recommendations. (See Case Example 6.9.) The point is to bring the feedback that the evaluation affords as psychologically "close" as possible to those stakeholders who will be expected to make changes. Of course, you do provide the advantage of an outside and integrated perspective. To maintain this benefit, it is a good idea to develop some general ideas about recommendations before meeting with participants. These ideas should easily follow from your knowledge of the organization and analysis of the evaluation data.

CASE EXAMPLE 6.9

Developing Recommendations Collaboratively

The Healthy Living Foundation is a nonprofit organization, created in 1996, to help people make healthy life choices related to nutrition and exercise. The Foundation's primary goal is to decrease nutrition-related illnesses by helping people make wiser nutritional choices and by increasing their level of exercise. The Foundation does this by providing training, technical assistance, and educational materials to community service providers and community members.

Training is provided to four tiers of individuals (school personnel, students, parents, and service providers) in an attempt to involve the entire community in making healthy living choices. While training has been provided for several years, there has been little evaluation data collected. The purpose of the evaluation was to explore the ways the training services have affected participants' ability to eat healthier and engage in greater levels of exercise.

In concert with the Foundation's desire for the evaluation to be collaborative, participatory, and learning-oriented, 15 people were personally invited by the executive director to participate in the evaluation as advisory group members. These individuals were selected because of their involvement in a variety of the Foundation's initiatives and the belief that they would provide valuable insights into the evaluation plan's development and eventual recommendations. In addition to attending an evaluation focusing meeting and reviewing the data collection instruments, the advisory group was invited to attend a four-hour "Data Analysis and Interpretation Meeting." Prior to this meeting each advisory group member was mailed a binder that included the evaluation plan and the findings organized by the evaluation questions and presented in a series of charts and tables. Advisory group members were asked to review the findings and to come to the meeting prepared to discuss their reactions, ideas, and questions.

The evaluator began the meeting by thanking everyone for participating in this important phase of the evaluation process. She then reviewed the purpose of the evaluation and the original intended uses of its findings. She also described the ways in which the data were collected, and shared some of the logistical challenges experienced in obtaining the data. She explained that while her team had confidence in the results, caution should be taken in generalizing the results to the other sites not included in the evaluation. As the advisory group considered each table and chart, the evaluator asked the following questions to the entire group:

- What do these findings mean to you?
- What is especially interesting about these findings?
- What do you find surprising about these findings?
- What is not here that you thought would be here?
- What other questions do these findings raise for you?
- What are the implications of these findings?

(Continued)

CASE EXAMPLE 6.9 (Continued)

As participants offered their thoughts about the findings, the evaluator frequently asked if there might be additional, alternative explanations or interpretations of the findings. At the same time another member of the evaluation team took notes on her computer, capturing the majority of comments and questions made by the participants. Inevitably, the advisory group members began making recommendations. Since the evaluators wanted to make sure that all of the findings were discussed and interpreted prior to making recommendations (to avoid jumping to unwarranted conclusions), they offered to put the emerging recommendations on a flip chart for later discussion. After all of the tables and charts had been considered, the evaluator then asked participants to review the recommendations made earlier in the meeting, and to add additional recommendations. Once all of the recommendations were listed on several flip chart pages, she asked them to prioritize them, and indicate who might need to be involved in implementing the recommendations. In addition, a conversation about the costs of implementation highlighted the need to think strategically and to involve others in developing action plans based on the recommendations. At the end of the meeting, advisory group members expressed appreciation at being part of this process and indicated they had learned a lot about data collection and evaluation procedures generally. They also made a commitment to implementing the recommendations. The evaluators included the advisory group's recommendations in the report, as well as others the evaluators felt were necessary based on the evaluation findings.

■ **Consider grouping recommendations into categories.**

Particularly when there are a large number of recommendations, you might want to organize the recommendations into various categories. For example, recommendations could be sorted according to the following variables:

- Program area
- Cost (e.g., no cost vs. financial resources needed)
- Time frame (e.g., can be implemented immediately vs. requires a timeline for implementation)
- Approval or further input needed (e.g., can be implemented without additional input vs. required additional approval/input
- Organizational functions (e.g., administration/operations, product development, human resources, sales, marketing)

■ **Work with the stakeholders to develop action plans for implementing various recommendations.**

Evaluation recommendations do not typically contain information about how to carry them out. Yet, evaluators are in an excellent position to stay engaged with stakeholders to further learning and action from the evaluation. Based on your knowledge of the program or organization, the evaluation findings, and your working relationship with stakeholders, you may be asked to (or you may want to suggest that you) work with stakeholders in developing action plans for implementing the recommendations.

Action planning often begins when stakeholders are involved in the development of recommendations. You can record ideas that emerge at that time about specific actions to implement recommendations, and then return to them in an action-planning working session once the recommendations have been completed.

As an interim activity, the evaluator could help stakeholders see how different recommendations might lead to particular outcomes, changes, or consequences. Using an "if-then" approach in discussing key recommendations could help stakeholders better understand their assumptions about the program and the organization; trends and factors that should be monitored; and the conditions that may be necessary for supporting the implementation of specific recommendations (Patton, 1997).

You can structure an action-planning session around the following types of questions (Preskill & Torres, 1999):

- What priority should each recommendation be given (low, medium, high)?
- What reasoning is behind each prioritization?
- What values and assumptions are reflected in the reasons given?
- What actions are indicated in order to implement this recommendation?
- For each action,
  - What steps are necessary to carry it out?
  - What costs or other resources would be involved?
  - Where should responsibility for carrying it out lie?
  - What is a reasonable time frame?

■ **In multiyear evaluations, review the fate of recommendations previously made.**

Evaluators who have had the opportunity to conduct multiyear evaluations within organizations are in an excellent position to facilitate continuous improvement by reviewing the current status of recommendations from previous years that may still need attention. One way of doing this is to organize findings and recommendations around the evaluation questions in the final report. For each question, provide: (1) a summary of the findings; (2) a discussion of how the findings relate to the status of previously made recommendations; and (3) a new set of recommendations based on the current findings, as well as prior recommendations that are still appropriate for stakeholders to consider. Recommendations related to those from the previous year might be included as a restatement or revision of the original recommendation, or might begin with wording such as "Continue efforts to . . ." This approach can help program staff, in particular, maintain a sense of continuity about their improvement efforts, and contribute directly to organizational learning over time.

■ **Allow time for work on developing recommendations and plans for acting on the recommendations.**

Evaluation work is resource intensive. Many evaluators routinely scramble to complete evaluation work as scheduled. Significantly involving stakeholders in the development of recommendations and action plans may be a new practice for some evaluators, and one that comes toward the end of any given evaluation cycle. Hurriedly constructing recommendations for a draft evaluation report to meet a deadline can be tempting. One safeguard is to schedule time for the collaborative development of recommendations and action plans. These activities can be specifically included in the evaluation plan and timelines.

CAUTION FOR DEVELOPING RECOMMENDATIONS

■ **Occasionally, clients and stakeholders may insist that you provide recommendations that you alone develop.**

Some clients may feel that it is most appropriate for the evaluator to develop recommendations without their involvement. This circumstance is more likely to arise with summative than formative evaluations, and for external rather than internal evaluators. Finally, clients' previous experiences with evaluators who used more traditional, distanced approaches may influence this request.

Multisite Evaluations

Multisite evaluations assess a single program implemented at more than one site, or variations of a program, each implemented at a different site. Straw and Herrell (2002) describe three types of evaluations involving multiple sites:

- Cluster evaluation (initiated by the W. K. Kellogg Foundation to identify common program components associated with positive impacts)

- Multisite evaluation (typically required of federally funded demonstration programs to assess the effectiveness of different interventions within the same program area)
- Multicenter clinical trials (conducted to increase sample size and ensure that the intervention works in multiple settings)

Each type of multisite evaluation, whether formative or summative, exploratory or confirmatory, planned or retrospective, typically complicates the communicating and reporting processes. An evaluation that spans multiple sites may require several data collection and analysis strategies, along with a variety of communicating and reporting methods. Creating different reporting formats for different audiences and integrating findings across multiple sites can be a challenge.

Decisions about which communicating and reporting strategies to use depend upon available resources and time, the various audiences' particular needs, the political climate, how the program was implemented at different sites, and varying organizational cultures at the sites (Sinacore & Turpin, 1991; Hedrick et al., 1991).

Implementation Tips for Multisite Evaluations

■ **Help clients and stakeholders develop common goals and/or outcomes across sites.**

Multisite evaluators sometimes find that each site has a different approach to implementing the program in question. This situation poses a problem for reporting on the progress and/or outcomes of the program as a whole—a likely requirement of program funders. On the other hand, differences across each site can provide valuable information about program implementation and outcomes in different contexts. One solution is to help clients and stakeholders develop goals addressing at least part of what is being done at each site. Evaluators can collect data on these common outcomes as well as outcomes unique to each site. Collaboration across sites helps facilitate stakeholders' participation in all phases of the evaluations, from developing common outcomes to analyzing data and interpreting findings (Cook, Carey, Razzano, Burke, & Blyler, 2002). Federally funded programs that span multiple sites often require that some common measures be used by all sites. These measures help funders assess the effectiveness of the programs and examine variation in outcomes across sites (Straw & Herrell, 2002).

■ **Assess the political and organizational contexts of each site.**

Multisite evaluations hold special challenges in their design and implementation (Lawrenz & Huffman, 2003; Straw & Herrell, 2002). Multisite evaluators should consider the following questions:

- Is the program implemented at each site in the same way or in different ways? Who are the program participants and how are they included in/excluded from the programs?
- How are program staff involved in the evaluation process? What evaluation activities are sites expected to implement? Who will coordinate the evaluation activities at each site and across sites?
- What is the political climate at each site?
- What organizational policies, procedures, and/or traditions govern each site? How will data be collected and analyzed across sites?
- How is information typically communicated within each site?

Political and contextual differences at each site mediate how you will interact with each site. In short, understanding the organization's culture, including how members typically communicate information, is critical. Based on this understanding, you can negotiate the most effective communicating and reporting strategies with each site.

■ **Hold periodic meetings with staff from each site.**

Evaluations of multisite programs provide excellent opportunities for collaboration and learning among groups of professionals with common interests. Periodic meetings with staff from each site add value to multisite evaluations.

Cross-site meetings with program managers and staff can bring participants together to: (1) build their evaluation knowledge and skills, (2) facilitate sharing of issues and knowledge, (3) promote awareness of emerging ideas, (4) develop connections with other project staff and experts in the field, and (5) provide access to and information about new resources.

This point is illustrated in Case Example 6.10. Barley and Jenness (1993; Jenness & Barley, 1995) have implemented an approach called "cluster evaluation," initiated by the W. K. Kellogg Foundation (1989). Cluster evaluation provides a complex, rich data set derived from the involvement of stakeholders in the formation of the evaluation itself. Various programs clustered under one umbrella of funding use similar data collection strategies to assess common goals across program sites. Cluster evaluators, project staff, and funders share responsibility for data collection and analysis. Data collection occurs at both the project level and the cluster level. Individual project staff members conduct their own evaluations while at the same time assisting cluster evaluators in collecting data pertinent to the entire cluster.

CASE EXAMPLE 6.10

A Collaborative Approach to Cluster Evaluation

Directing the evaluation of two science education projects, funded by the W. K. Kellogg Foundation, each with 12 sites within a single state, the evaluators used a collaborative approach to designing, implementing, and disseminating the evaluation (Jenness & Barley, 1995). The collaborative approach included developing common cluster outcomes through consensus of the projects, the funder, and the cluster evaluators; and collecting site-specific data using common instruments developed by the cluster evaluators and adopted by each site. In addition to providing evaluation training and technical assistance to individual projects, the cluster evaluators held regular networking conferences where project directors, project-level evaluators, funding staff, and the cluster evaluators discussed individual project and cluster-level evaluation findings. These conferences often served as working sessions, whereby project directors would: (1) review the evaluation results, (2) develop working hypotheses, and (3) suggest additional data collection activities. In addition to the networking conferences, project staff "periodically submitted 'lessons learned' that were compiled and analyzed cooperatively by cluster evaluators and project staff" (p. 66). These lessons learned were often shared with other science educators throughout the state at local, state, and national gatherings. The evaluation's results were further disseminated through panel presentations, paper presentations, and poster sessions at the Michigan Science Teachers Association annual conventions.

The collaborative cluster approach encouraged ownership of the evaluation by the individual projects and increased the utility of the evaluation findings (individual and cluster level) by providing data grounded in the reality of individual projects but that also measured the overall impact of the cluster of projects. The collaborative development and dissemination of findings increased program capacity to develop evaluation strategies and use their own data to inform formative and summative decision making.

SOURCE: Case described with permission of Mark Jenness and Zoe Barley.

■ **Create site-specific reports as well as a comprehensive final report.**

Final reports that aggregate findings across sites are of limited use to individual sites. To provide findings about individual sites, evaluators may choose to produce site-specific reports. Cluster evaluators (see above) prepare site-specific reports based on cross-project surveys and other data collection efforts. These are shared with project staff. A final cluster evaluation report describes context, implementation strategies, and progress toward common cluster outcomes across the group of projects. It is shared with both the staff of individual projects and funders. Further, maintaining the confidentiality of site-specific reports can help staff at each site learn more readily from their successes and failures (Barley & Jenness, 1993). Having evaluation teams that focus on developing site-specific interim findings is another way to produce timely findings, as well as help to monitor the quality of evaluation implementation at individual sites (Leff & Mulkern, 2002).

■ **Enlist stakeholders at each site to help in the communicating and reporting process.**

If program staff have been involved in evaluation planning, question development, data collection and analysis, and generation of findings, they can help in the communication and dissemination process by producing memos, bulletins, e-mail, or final reports as well as co-presenting at meetings. Involving the staff not only expands communication possibilities when resources are tight but also increases staff ownership of the evaluation process and its findings. This collaboration enhances the use of the information in long-term program planning and development. It also enables staff to continue evaluation processes as part of day-to-day program functions through the skills and knowledge they have gained from their involvement.

■ **Use combinations of various communication formats.**

Using combinations of communication formats may be an evaluator's best strategy for reaching multiple audiences at multiple sites. Various combinations of communicating and reporting strategies are possible. For instance, you may (1) write one comprehensive final report encompassing all sites along with individual site mini-reports, or (2) use multiple conference calls and presentations at individual sites along with interim reports, or (3) use e-mail sent to communicate findings about all sites combined with site-specific bulletins. You must, however, be aware that communication that is too frequent and too varied can become confusing and intrusive. Conversely, communication that is too infrequent and too limited can impede the program staff's ability to use information and correct problems.

CAUTION FOR MULTISITE EVALUATIONS

■ **Different sites are likely to have unique communicating and reporting needs.**

Even when you develop a reporting plan delineating the timing, frequency, and content of reports at the outset of a multisite evaluation, as the evaluation progresses you may find yourself besieged by requests for information to meet individual sites' particular needs. If you respond to these requests, as you are likely to do, it can require considerable additional time and effort. You may also find that other sites will feel slighted, and/or will also desire additional reporting.

SUMMARY

In this chapter we have suggested that evaluators consider the cultural diversity of evaluation stakeholders, the implications of communicating and reporting for multisite evaluations, and the ways in which evaluation processes and findings can be communicated and reported respectfully and effectively. Recognizing that reporting negative findings can be challenging, we have identified several strategies for positioning negative findings as an opportunity to learn and grow from the evaluation. Strategies for communicating and reporting quantitative and qualitative findings have also been offered in this chapter. In addition, we have suggested that making effective recommendations is important when it comes to using the evaluation findings. To this end, we have provided several strategies for including stakeholders in the development of recommendations, and tips for how to organize and present different kinds of evaluation recommendations.

7

Issues and Opportunities for Evaluation Practice

CHAPTER OUTLINE

Topics Discussed

- Breadth and Depth of Skills Evaluators Need
- Evaluator Roles
- Time for Collaboration
- Misinterpretation/Misuse of Findings
- Organizational Readiness for Evaluation

Questions to Ponder

- ☐ *What skills do evaluators need for effective communicating and reporting?*
- ☐ *What roles do evaluators play?*
- ☐ *What are the issues and opportunities presented by the time required for meaningful collaboration?*
- ☐ *How can collaboration help with issues of misinterpretation and misuse of evaluation?*
- ☐ *What impact does an organization's readiness for evaluation have on evaluation practice?*

This book is not intended as a comprehensive treatment of evaluation practice. But because its topic is communicating and reporting—an aspect that permeates the entire evaluation endeavor—it has given us an opportunity to traverse the landscape that is the evaluation profession today. The breadth of this landscape is astounding. Ever-changing technological advances have ramped up the possibilities for effective communicating and reporting significantly over the past decade. We can be in almost constant communication electronically, around the clock, and around the globe. We can interact in real time over virtually any distance, and we can select among a variety of ways to do so. We can choose any combination of instantaneously seeing our text messages exchanged, seeing each other, and/or hearing each other. The opportunity for this kind of interaction, largely unconstrained by disparities in physical location, substantially increases the opportunities for learning that evaluation affords.

We are also increasingly attracted to getting together at the same time and in the same place to enhance mutual understanding and learning about evaluation processes and findings. Collaborative, participatory approaches to evaluation are more popular than ever—and are now far more the norm than the exception in evaluation practice. In 1994, Yvonna Lincoln advised us that the next generation of evaluation will move us *away from* conventional evaluation practice, and *toward* fresh, new, and more responsive models of inquiry" (p. 307). Evaluation practice, according to Lincoln, would be more activist and stakeholder oriented than ever before. We believe this time has come. Many evaluators, like us, have evolved their predilections for collaborative and participatory evaluation toward explicitly engaging stakeholders in reflection and dialogue to facilitate individual, group, and organizational learning.

Another area of the evaluation landscape that we explored in this book's comprehensive treatment of communicating and reporting are the more creative realms of expression covered in Chapter 5. Borrowing from anthropology and sociology, the use of photography to collect data and report findings has been part of some evaluators' repertoire for some time now. And with advances in digital technology, recording and reproducing both still photographs and the sound and motion of video are easier and cheaper than ever before. Interest in using cartoons, poetry, and drama for communicating and reporting evaluation information is increasing, particularly as evaluators seek ways beyond meetings and working sessions to engage with stakeholders, and at the same time meaningfully reflect stakeholders' voices and experiences.

Relatedly, current attention on evaluators' cultural competence stems from the desire to make evaluation culturally appropriate, meaningful, and useful for increasingly diverse stakeholders and audiences. Cultural sensitivity means attention to different people's national origins, traditions, values, abilities, orientations, and languages. It also means attention to different age cultures. Youth-led evaluation is emerging as a distinctive niche within the profession.

We have already touched on the things technological advances have made available to evaluators by way of synchronous electronic communications. The information highway of the Internet is no less traveled by evaluators and their constituents than by those in other professions. And with increasingly inexpensive computer technology, the options evaluators have for creating professional-looking, engaging, and useful evaluation products are innumerable.

Membership in the American Evaluation Association is higher than it has ever been. Evaluation associations are springing up around the globe. This is an exciting transdisciplinary profession. These days there are lot of things for evaluators to know about and to do. And there are some other issues, too. All this communication, interaction, engagement, collaboration, and creativity takes a lot of time. There can be a lot to manage within any one evaluation endeavor, which can invoke a variety of roles for the evaluator. At the same time, among all this evaluation activity and access, there are more and more opportunities for misuse and misinterpretation. And if that weren't enough, there is the issue of an organization's capacity and readiness for learning from evaluation. In the remainder of this chapter we address these issues by discussing the breadth and depth of skills evaluators need, the variety of roles evaluators play, time needed for meaningful evaluation practice; misuse and misinterpretation of evaluation processes and findings, and organizational readiness for evaluation.

Breadth and Depth of Skills Evaluators Need

The strategies for communicating and reporting covered in this book require numerous skill sets: organizational change, consultation, and facilitation; cultural competency; and both technical and creative skills.

Organizational Change, Consultation, and Facilitation

To facilitate individual, group, and organizational learning, evaluators need a broader range of skills than most evaluation training provides. In terms of essential knowledge and skills for any evaluator, Mertens (1994) identifies three main areas: (1) the traditional scientific research philosophy, design, and methodology; (2) evaluation theory and design; and (3) specific knowledge and skills in the discipline area(s) in which the evaluator practices.

Engaging in a participatory, consultative role requires comfort with maintaining ongoing, collaborative relationships with stakeholders, the ability to relinquish control, and at the same time help organizations learn through inquiry, reflection, dialogue, and action planning. In this process, trust, respect, and positive interdependence are vital. Figure 7.1 includes the phases of evaluative inquiry (Preskill & Torres, 1999) that we provided in Chapter 1 as an overview of our learning approach to evaluation. Here we present them in conjunction with the evaluator role and skills used to support learning through evaluative inquiry. That is, evaluators use a variety of consultative and process skills to: help establish and maintain a culture of learning, facilitate and sustain dialogue among stakeholders, and manage group processes. As shown, evaluators' skills in these areas draw on specific areas of knowledge about learning at the individual, group, and organizational levels.

While evaluators often learn research design, methods of data collection, and analysis skills in workshops and research and evaluation courses, they tend to receive little instruction on the nuances of the *focusing* or *apply learning* phases of an evaluation. That is, most evaluators are trained to be technicians in the design and implementation of the evaluation, but are not necessarily prepared for dealing with the interpersonal relationships needed for collaborative and participatory kinds of evaluation work. We will return to this topic after first looking at skills needed in three additional areas.

Cultural Competence

To effectively establish and maintain rapport with diverse stakeholders, evaluators must be sensitive to their multiple backgrounds, values, abilities, interests, and experiences. First, understanding how different cultures learn and process information is essential to effective communicating. As discussed in Chapter 6, we know that culture shapes the way we think and behave, as well as how we transmit knowledge to others. Communicating and reporting findings using multiple methods that address various audiences' ways of knowing will increase their understanding and use of evaluation. In many instances this can mean deviating significantly from the social science research paradigm that yields logically derived conclusions and recommendations with no acknowledgment of the underlying values of the evaluators and stakeholders involved.

Second, on a more interpersonal level, the ability to create dialogues with all stakeholders—but especially where underrepresented groups, minorities, and diverse voices are present—requires not only advanced skills in listening, facilitation, and negotiation, but also a willingness to share the authority of evaluation and responsibility for guiding evaluative processes with those who are participants in the evaluand.

Technical and Artistic Skills

Evaluators also need both technical and creative skills to take advantage of many of the different ways we can use communicating and reporting processes to support learning. On the technical side, evaluators can use skills

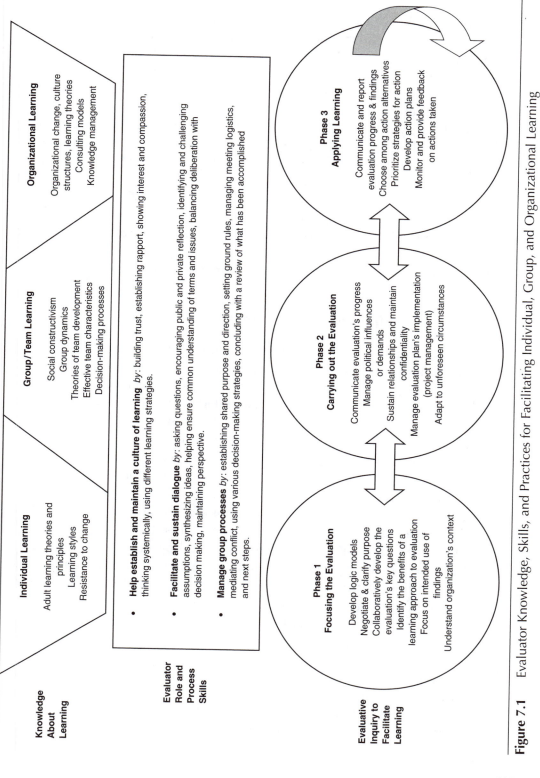

Knowledge About Learning

Individual Learning

Adult learning theories and principles
Learning styles
Resistance to change

Group/Team Learning

Social constructivism
Group dynamics
Theories of team development
Effective team characteristics
Decision-making processes

Organizational Learning

Organizational change, culture structures, learning theories
Consulting models
Knowledge management

Evaluator Role and Process Skills

- **Help establish and maintain a culture of learning** *by:* building trust, establishing rapport, showing interest and compassion, thinking systemically, using different learning strategies.

- **Facilitate and sustain dialogue** *by:* asking questions, encouraging public and private reflection, identifying and challenging assumptions, synthesizing ideas, helping ensure common understanding of terms and issues, balancing deliberation with decision making, maintaining perspective.

- **Manage group processes** *by:* establishing shared purpose and direction, setting ground rules, managing meeting logistics, mediating conflict, using various decision-making strategies, concluding with a review of what has been accomplished and next steps.

Evaluative Inquiry to Facilitate Learning

**Phase 1
Focusing the Evaluation**

Develop logic models
Negotiate & clarify purpose
Collaboratively develop the evaluation's key questions
Identify the benefits of a learning approach to evaluation
Focus on intended use of findings
Understand organization's context

**Phase 2
Carrying out the Evaluation**

Communicate evaluation's progress
Manage political influences or demands
Sustain relationships and maintain confidentiality
Manage evaluation plan's implementation (project management)
Adapt to unforeseen circumstances

**Phase 3
Applying Learning**

Communicate and report evaluation progress & findings
Choose among action alternatives
Prioritize strategies for action
Develop action plans
Monitor and provide feedback on actions taken

Figure 7.1   Evaluator Knowledge, Skills, and Practices for Facilitating Individual, Group, and Organizational Learning

in Web site design, development, and maintenance; operation of digital cameras and video equipment for recording and playing back visual images; photo and video editing; and operation of software and hardware for video and Web conferencing. Help is available from information technology professionals and service providers. But with advances in technology, the minimum level of technical expertise necessary for evaluators to be knowledgeable clients of technical services is also rising.

On the artistic side, for effective communicating and reporting evaluators can use skills in photography, drawing, videography, poetic transcription, graphic design, creation of PowerPoint slides, design and layout of documents, scene selection, and script writing. Outside services are available in some of these areas, too.

No one evaluator, or even sets of two or three, can expect to be skilled in all of the technical and artistic areas that their communications and reports might invoke. There are options: selectively learning in one or two areas over time, working in teams, and budgeting for technical and artistic support.

Education and Training Opportunities

Clearly, evaluators' education and training needs are expanding; fortunately, so are the learning opportunities available to them. Many evaluators have access to numerous professional workshops, seminars, and conferences. Both the American Evaluation Association (AEA) and American Educational Research Association (AERA) provide professional training opportunities associated with their annual conferences. Pre- and postconference workshops for AEA's conferences are quite varied. Topics include utilization-focused evaluation; consulting skills for evaluators; techniques for analyzing qualitative and quantitative data; the *Program Evaluation Standards;* return on investment; developing logic models; appreciative inquiry and evaluation; performance indicators; and multicultural and cross-cultural evaluation.

The conferences themselves present excellent opportunities for evaluators to learn from other evaluators reporting on their research on evaluation, as well as their professional experiences with particular evaluation projects. Discussions, networking, and camaraderie among colleagues outside the sessions can be equally productive.

Many of the AEA state and regional affiliates also provide monthly or quarterly presentations and annual conferences that further support evaluators' professional development. (For further information on AEA's affiliates, see www.eval.org.) The Evaluators Institute has had East and West Coast course offerings on a broad range of topics since 1996. Fielding Graduate Institute currently offers a certificate program in evaluation and organizational development specifically designed to enhance the evaluation skills of organizational development (OD) professionals, and the OD skills of evaluators. Claremont Graduate University also offers professional development workshops each summer on various evaluation topics. Outside of the evaluation and OD professions, professional development useful to evaluators can be found in the areas of public and media relations, public speaking, technical writing, graphic design, conflict resolution, project management, computers, photography, videography, and other media skill areas.

Evaluator Roles

In any given evaluation, evaluators serve in a variety of roles, particularly if they are interested in enhancing evaluation use and individual, group, and organizational learning. These roles involve: (1) initiating and maintaining group interest in, cooperation in, and commitment to an evaluation; (2) keeping clients' expectations realistic by assisting them in articulating their needs; and (3) facilitating stakeholder ownership of evaluative information and findings (Webber, 1987).

Evaluators whose work reflects collaborative, participatory, and learning-oriented approaches often find themselves acting as educators, consultant/facilitators, coaches, and interpreters. Each of these roles moves beyond the traditional notion of evaluators as expert-scientist-researchers and challenges the positivistic assumption that evaluation can provide clear-cut explanations of cause/effect relationships. In an educative role, evaluators cue in on "teachable moments" to develop a shared language, to inform about evaluation activities and processes, and to motivate primary users to participate in evaluation activities (Cousins & Earl, 1992). The evaluator creates processes where dialogue, reflection, inquiry, and the clarification of individual and organization beliefs and knowledge occur (Morabito, 2002; Preskill & Torres, 1999).

Many evaluators who work collaboratively with stakeholders also act as *consultant/facilitators* in an effort to increase the use of evaluation information. As an organizational consultant, the evaluator supports organizational improvement by promoting the clarification of program goals and outcomes; by providing evidence about progress and performance that informs decision making; and by advocating for the use of evaluation to provide ongoing feedback from multiple perspectives (Fitzpatrick, 1994; Morabito, 2002; Nee & Mojica, 1999; Owen & Lambert, 1998; Preskill & Torres, 1999; Wholey 2001). This evaluative work often takes place through working sessions facilitated by the evaluator.

The evaluator-as-*coach* poses questions that challenge program administration and staff to reflect upon their actions and how those actions are leading to the intended outcomes (Harmon, 1995; McColskey et al., 1995). They often work one-on-one with stakeholders in personal discussions to facilitate their understandings and decisions about the evaluand and the evaluation.

The evaluator who educates and facilitates may also serve as an *interpreter*. Evaluators who serve in this role are often concerned with revealing the underlying assumptions within particular programmatic or organizational contexts (Noblit & Eaker, 1987). Grounding their work in the experiences of participants, these evaluators' approach is holistic, historical, and comparative (Beardsley & Miller, 2002; Spicer, 1976). Typically, they observe and interview participants to construct an ethnography or case study of multiple perspectives and multiple realities. The evaluator's interpretation then serves as a tool for change as participants see aspects and interrelationships that are operative but were previously invisible to them. Sometimes evaluators use poetry or drama to portray their interpretations.

As evaluators take on these different roles, it is critical for them to fully understand their own values and assumptions underlying evaluation practice. Each of these roles requires not only a wider range of knowledge and skills for working effectively with stakeholders, but they push the boundaries of traditional evaluation practice, thus making them more vulnerable to ethical as well as practical challenges and debates.

Time for Collaboration

While collaboration in evaluation and indeed, in many organizations today, is encouraged and even required, working collaboratively with others requires a significant investment of time and energy. For an evaluation, most of this time is spent in the initial stages, when the evaluator(s) and primary stakeholders are gaining a mutual understanding of the evaluand and its intended effects (often through developing a logic model); developing the evaluation's purpose and key questions; and identifying stakeholders and other audiences who may use the evaluation processes and results. Many evaluators work with advisory groups or evaluation teams to develop the evaluation plan. To accomplish this often requires numerous phone conversations, e-mails, and meetings (either in person or through synchronous electronic communications). Scheduling of meetings alone can require a substantial effort.

Collaboration with stakeholders occurs during the data collection and analysis phase of the evaluation as well. Stakeholders are often asked to review data collection instruments and attend working sessions to co-interpret the data and develop interpretations and recommendations. Again, these meetings, while extremely beneficial to facilitating individual, group, and organizational learning and the overall usefulness of the evaluation's findings, are time consuming.

Yet, a continuous process of stakeholder involvement and discussion leads to greater interest and use of evaluation through more timely and meaningful exchanges of information. Improved, more refined communicating and reporting strategies have more impact on organizational learning. A learning process for evaluators and stakeholders alike develops. Then, when evaluative information has to compete with other information sources, interference from organizational resistance lessens. In the long term, the benefits of collaborating—better use of evaluation information, evaluator satisfaction, client understanding, and successful strategies for dealing with political and organizational complexity—may result in *less* time and other costs.

Misinterpretation/Misuse of Findings

In several of the cautions associated with various communicating and reporting strategies, we raised concerns about the misuse or misinterpretation of findings. Short communications (memos and e-mail, postcards) can be expedient, but may also lack desired confidentiality. That is, they may be visible to persons less involved with an evaluation who could misinterpret their meaning. Short communications and summaries typically contain limited information, which is more vulnerable to misinterpretation and/or misuse by any evaluation audience. And, while advances in technology have increased our ability to disseminate evaluation information easily and quickly, we also know that communications posted via e-mail or on the Web can be altered and misused without the authors ever knowing it.

Approximately one quarter of the respondents to our survey on communicating and reporting practices cited misuse or misinterpretation of formal communications as a main impediment to successful communicating and reporting. They described specific instances of misquotation, distortion, and oversimplification of findings. The research reported by Preskill and Caracelli (1997) further affirms the seriousness of this issue. In their study on evaluation use, they found that 50% of the respondents believe that both intentional and unintentional misuse of evaluation results are a major problem in the field (p. 220).

Developing collaborative relationships with organizations does take a great amount of time, energy, personal skill, and understanding. Yet for every situation the collaboration complicates, it has the potential for simplifying another one down the road. Take misinterpretation or oversimplification of findings as an example. Collaboration, interaction, and the establishment of trust with stakeholders are likely to favorably mediate many circumstances where misinterpretation could occur.

Organizational Readiness for Evaluation

Skills and experience, although essential, cannot eliminate some of the issues raised in this chapter. Clearly, it is difficult to find adequate time to fully analyze, develop, and communicate evaluation information, especially when enveloped by political and organizational agendas, and competing with a myriad of people, policies, and other information for stakeholders' attention. Under these circumstances, the prospect of implementing a new communicating and reporting strategy can be daunting. In some cases, the most we can expect of ourselves is to rely on past practice with the hope that we have enough time to communicate adequately.

Moreover, certain critical aspects of any evaluation endeavor are under the stakeholders' control. This book has attempted to show that, although there are numerous ways to communicate and report evaluation findings, whether these methods will lead to learning is highly dependent on individuals', groups', and organizations' readiness to support learning. If key organizational members do not support an infrastructure for learning and evaluation, the potential for an evaluation's impact is significantly limited (Preskill & Torres, 1999). However, if evaluators can determine an organization's readiness for learning through evaluation, they may be able to either better prepare the organization for evaluation or help position the evaluation in a way that increases its success.

To help evaluators establish an organization's readiness for learning from evaluation, two of this book's authors have developed a diagnostic instrument entitled Readiness for Organizational Learning and Evaluation (ROLE) (available from the authors). This 80-item instrument includes questions concerning the organization's culture, leadership, systems and structures, communication practices, use of teams, and evaluation. The results often indicate the organization's (or department's) ability and commitment to sharing learning, asking questions, rewarding and recognizing individuals for learning, reflecting on practice, risk taking, working collaboratively, and engaging in evaluation studies. The results can be used to understand the political milieu as well as how an evaluation study may be perceived and supported. Finally, through information about accessibility and information dissemination practices, the findings can inform evaluators about communicating and reporting practices that might be especially beneficial and most likely to be successful.

Parting Thought

Like everything that is involved with teaching and learning, evaluation is a complicated, interdependent, and demanding endeavor. On page 1 we started with Cronbach; he also gives us a fitting conclusion.

> *Teaching begins when the evaluator first sits down with members of the policy-shaping community to elicit their questions. It continues during every contact the evaluator has with program participants or with others in his audience. The end report is only one means for enabling audiences to understand the program and how it impinges on their interests. (Cronbach, 1982, p. 9)*

Appendix A

Key Terms

Audiences: Those who receive information about the evaluation and its findings. Audiences include, but are not limited to stakeholders (e.g., staff from other programs who would benefit from information about a particular program).

Client(s): The individual, group, or organization who commissions or requests the evaluation. Typical evaluation clients are funding agencies, program managers, leaders of organizations, legislators, and/or policymakers. In this text we often refer to clients as primary stakeholders.

Evaluand: The program, project, process, organization, product, issue, or policy that is the subject of the evaluation.

Evaluation: A process of systematic data collection to provide information about some object—program, project, process, organization, product, issue, or policy—in order to assess its quality and/or improve it.

Evaluation use: Any consequence, result, or outcome of an evaluation. Use includes (1) new understandings of or perspectives on a situation, program, or organization (*conceptual use*); (2) action taken as a result of an evaluation (*instrumental use*); and (3) learning that takes place among stakeholders as a result of evaluation processes, such as greater understanding of and/or appreciation of evaluation, learning about evaluation practices, and/or stakeholders' learning about themselves, each other, or the organization (*process use*).

Evaluative inquiry: An ongoing process for investigating and understanding critical organizational issues. It is an approach to learning that is fully integrated with an organization's work practices, and as such, it engenders (1) organization members' interest and ability in exploring critical issues using evaluation logic; (2) organizational members' involvement in evaluation processes; and (3) the personal and professional growth of individuals within the organization.

External evaluation: Evaluation conducted by evaluators who are employed by organizations outside those that house the program being evaluated.

Formative evaluation: Evaluation that provides information about how a program or organization operates and how to improve it. Typical audiences for formative evaluation are program staff and managers.

Internal evaluation: Evaluation conducted by evaluators who are employed by the same organization that supports the programs they evaluate.

Organizational learning: A continuous process of growth and improvement (1) that uses information or feedback about both processes and outcomes (i.e., evaluation findings) to make changes; (2) is integrated with work activities, and with the organization's infrastructure (e.g., its culture, systems and structures, leadership, and communication mechanisms); and (3) invokes the alignment of values, attitudes, and perceptions among organizational members.

Stakeholders: Those individuals, groups, or organizations who may be affected by the planning, activities, and/or findings of the evaluation. For instance, those who request the evaluation and program staff are stakeholders. Stakeholders also might include groups such as parents of students in a particular school program. They do not directly participate in a program but do have a vested interest in it.

Summative evaluation: Evaluation that provides information about the overall effectiveness, impact, and/or outcomes of a program. Typical audiences for summative evaluation are funders, sponsors, and/or organizational leaders.

Appendix B

Summary of Chapter 3 Implementation Tips, Guidelines, and Cautions

_____ **Design and Layout**

Implementation Tips

- Plan for the resources you will need to create your evaluation communications and reports.
- When creating evaluation documents, use design principles that maximize readability.
- Break up long stretches of text with lists, boxed text, tables, and graphics.
- Choose a typeface consistent with the length and formality of the evaluation document.
- Design reports in easily understood and engaging formats to enhance their readability.
- Use columns to make text more inviting.
- Use signposts, headers, and/or footers to help readers find their way around, especially in longer reports.
- Use clip art or other graphic images to improve the overall look of evaluation documents, convey meaning, and/or reduce complexity.
- Avoid overdesign.
- Use a consistent page layout and format for various evaluation documents seen by the same audience.

_____ **Tables and Figures**

Implementation Tips

- Think about the essence of the message and the type of presentation that will describe it most accurately and effectively.

- Compile all available summarized data.
- Keep your tables and figures simple.
- Include headings and titles for all tables and figures.
- If including tables and figures in the text, describe the information to be found in each.
- Construct the tables and figures first, then write the text.
- Make tables and figures accessible within a report.
- Do not overuse color.
- Allow sufficient time for developing tables and figures.
- Always present tables and figures to outside audiences with a verbal or written explanation.

Guidelines for Constructing Tables

- Assign each table an Arabic numeral if you are using several tables.
- Present tables sequentially within the text.
- Always place the title immediately above the table.
- Make each quantitative table self-explanatory by providing titles, keys, labels, and footnotes so that readers can accurately understand and interpret them without reference to the text.
- When a table must be divided so it can be continued on another page, repeat the row and column headings and give the table number at the top/bottom of each new page.

Guidelines for Constructing Pie Charts

- Use six or fewer slices to illustrate information.
- Arrange the slices with the largest or the most important data starting at the 12 o'clock position, with the remaining slices positioned in a clockwise fashion.
- Increase the readability of pie charts by using bright, contrasting colors to emphasize a certain piece of data or by moving a slice out from the circle. (Most computer graphing programs allow you to do this.)
- Label the pie slices on the slices themselves or right next to them.
- If you use three-dimensional pie charts, be aware that distortions of the data are possible because the slices that seem closest to the viewer will be deemed the most important ones.

Guidelines for Constructing Bar Charts

- Use as few bars as possible. Six is typically considered the maximum unless you are showing data over a 12-month period.
- Emphasize one aspect of the data by changing a bar's color or texture.

- To make the data in the chart easier to comprehend, (1) place the numbers showing each bar's value at the top of the bar or inside it in a contrasting color, or (2) draw horizontal lines across the chart, beginning at each interval of the vertical axis.
- Use patterns of icons or blocks of color to make the image more attractive to the eye. For example, use apples or figures for students to show an increase in student achievement. Most programs allow you to modify the size and shape of the selected images to fit the size of the chart.

Guidelines for Constructing Line Graphs

- Label the lines rather than using a legend.
- Three lines are the recommended maximum, and each should be a different color if possible, with the most important line being the brightest color.
- If printing in black and white, each line should be a different shape or texture.
- Always title the graph clearly and concisely at the center of the page, above or below the graph.

Guidelines for Creating Illustrations

- Keep the illustration as simple as possible—if it needs a lot of explanation, it is probably too complicated.
- Be careful not to over-illustrate within any one communication. Save the use of illustrations for instances where they make a significant contribution to communicating your message.
- Include a key that identifies or defines all the symbols used.
- Depending on its dimensions, present the illustration in a horizontal position for easy reading.
- Provide enough white space around and within the illustration.
- Make sure that the illustration's meaning is clearly described in the text.

Writing

Implementation Tips

- Avoid jargon and technical terms that your audience may not understand.
- Adopt a direct, conversational style.
- Check the clarity of long sentences.
- Limit the use of the passive voice.
- Use word-processing tools for spelling, grammar, and writing style.

- To improve your writing, write and rewrite.
- Use collaborative writing to stimulate creativity and reduce individual workloads.
- Allow sufficient time for writing several drafts, getting feedback, and proofreading.

Guidelines for Writing in Active Voice

- Place the subject matter of the sentence at the beginning of the sentence.
- Place the verb close to the subject.
- Avoid making the subject matter the object of some action.
- Avoid "-ion" words (Scott, 1989; Williams, 1989).

Memos and E-mail

Implementation Tips

- Before deciding to use e-mail, determine stakeholders' and clients' e-mail access.
- Determine whether to send a memo within the text of an e-mail, as an e-mail attachment, or on hard copy.
- Beware of how easy it is to use e-mail.
- To the extent possible, follow up on memos and e-mail you send.
- Consider including a disclaimer at the bottom of all e-mail messages.

Guidelines for Using E-mail

- Make sure you have recipients' current e-mail addresses. Consider setting up a group contact list, and keep it updated.
- Try to keep what you say to one computer screen page—approximately 25 lines of text. Consider sending lengthier documents as attachments.
- Use fairly terse prose—but don't be too blunt. Use constructive and respectful language and avoid any semblance of blaming or hostility.
- Review your e-mails before sending them. Read the e-mail from the perspective of the recipient.
- If you want to emphasize certain words or phrases, use HTML formatting (color, bold, italics, etc.), or use various forms of punctuation with regular type. Use capital letters sparingly, as they connote that you are shouting.
- Add a subject line that pertains to the e-mail body to get people in the right frame of mind to open and read your message.
- Carefully consider which stakeholders should be copied on the e-mail message.

- Keep a log of the e-mails you send to remind you of what communication has taken place.
- If the message is particularly urgent or is time-sensitive, consider labeling it as a "high priority" (if that option is available with your e-mail software). Be careful not to overuse this feature, though.
- Request a return receipt to be notified when the recipient has received your message. (Note that recipients' software must support this feature and the recipient has to have enabled it.)
- Consider including a disclaimer at the bottom of all e-mail messages to provide some protection against misuse of your e-mails.
- Install and frequently update the latest virus protection software on your computer.

Postcards

Implementation Tips

- Use postcards to maintain contact with stakeholders and build interest in the evaluation.
- Use postcards to invite stakeholders to evaluation meetings or events, and/or to remind them of data collection or other upcoming activities.
- Use postcards to solicit reactions to preliminary findings.

Interim Reports

Implementation Tips

- Begin planning for interim reports at the outset of the evaluation to meet early reporting deadlines.
- Consider an informal presentation of findings rather than a formal interim report.
- Use a style and format for the interim report that makes its contents easy to assimilate.
- Emphasize the provisional nature of interim findings to stakeholders and other audiences.
- Provide drafts of formal interim reports for review by stakeholders and other audiences.

Caution

- Despite your best efforts, information in interim reports can be interpreted inappropriately.

Final Reports

Implementation Tips

- Carefully consider the need for a formal, comprehensive final report with stakeholders at the time the evaluation is being designed. Budget adequate time and funds to produce a final report.
- Recognize that developing the final report plays a key role in the analysis and integration of findings.
- Involve clients/stakeholders in the preparation and review of final reports.
- Select an organizing framework for the findings that maximizes the report's relevance and use for evaluation audiences.
- Consider alternative sequencing for the arrangement of report sections.

Executive Summaries

Implementation Tips

- Tailor the content of the executive summary to audience information needs and dissemination plans.
- Format the executive summary for easy assimilation of its contents.
- Use a summary process to ensure coherent, consistent content.
- Allow sufficient time for creating summaries.
- Once the final report has been developed, if possible, create and disseminate an executive summary while the full report is in final production.
- Include the executive summary at the front of the final report, to reach those evaluation audiences who might not read the entire report.

Guidelines for Writing a Summary

- *Read the original document from beginning to end.* It is important to fully understand all aspects of the original document before attempting to summarize it.
- *Reread and underline all key ideas, significant statements, and vital recommendations.* Focus on the main ideas and major supporting statements.
- *Edit the underlined information.* Eliminate all but key phrases; you will rework these into sentences later.
- *Rewrite the underlined information.* Do not worry about conciseness; you will edit later.

- *Edit the rewritten version.* Eliminate needless/repetitive words and phrases and combine related ideas.
- *Check the edited version against the original document.* Focus on verifying that you have captured the essential information/message of the original. Check to see if you have altered the meaning of any statements or added unrelated information; if so, delete.
- *Rewrite your edited work.* This final version should be written for clarity and conciseness, focusing on smooth transitions and clear connections of ideas.

Caution

- Summaries can be misused or misinterpreted by audiences who have limited contact with the program and/or evaluation.

Newsletters, Bulletins, Briefs, and Brochures

Implementation Tips

- Determine the type of publication best suited for your purpose and audience(s).
- Maximize your use of space, while providing sufficient detail to support the publication's purpose.
- Determine the resources required and frequency of publication.
- Develop a project management plan to ensure timely and efficient production.
- Consider posting newsletters, bulletins, and briefs on the Web.

Guidelines for Creating Newsletters and Brochures

- Select the data, graphics, and other information to be presented, keeping in mind that your goal is to make the content interesting for the intended audience(s) with attractive formatting and well-organized information.
- Collect brochures and newsletters from other organizations. Decide what you like or dislike about the formatting of these. Diagram a sample layout for your own newsletter or brochure.
- Make sure that each section, while concise, has a clear beginning, middle, and end.
- Use no more than two or three typefaces.
- Verify that all facts listed are accurate.

- Keep records that document the sources of all evaluation findings presented.
- Use colors, background, and text that are clear and easy to read.
- Make sure graphics are used consistently, contribute to the overall flow of information, and do not clutter or confuse the reader.
- Proofread the material carefully before going to press. (It is always best to have someone other than the author of the material proofread.)
- Select paper color that is not too bright or too dark. Matte finish reduces glare for the reader.
- Include contact information.
- Reference other published evaluation documents, including URLs if appropriate.
- If reprinting material from other publications, be sure to clear permissions from the sources.

Particular to Newsletters

- Decide on a name (or masthead), format, and frequency of distribution for your newsletter; retain the same format for each publication.
- Decide on an optimum size for the newsletter and word count per article. Brevity and clarity are always a winning combination.
- Make article titles descriptive of content; there should be a headline for every article.
- Be creative with your use of boldface, capitalization, and underlining with any text, particularly for time-sensitive information.
- Include a table of contents to help your readers find the information they need quickly.

Particular to Brochures

- Think about your primary audience(s) and design the front cover to grab their attention and get them to want to open the brochure.
- Consider spreading copy across all three inside panels rather than sticking to the three-column format.
- Avoid being too wordy; leave some white space. Use short sentences, short paragraphs, and clear visuals.
- Limit your use of boldface, capitalization, and underlining.

Cautions

- Once evaluation findings have become available, organizations may make decisions about including them in short publications without consulting the evaluator.
- Audiences may overlook newsletters, bulletins, briefs, and brochures.

News Media Communications

Implementation Tips

- Involve primary stakeholders in the media strategy as much as possible, especially if they are taking action on the findings.
- Contact the media only after primary stakeholders have had a chance to read and reflect on the evaluation findings.
- Enlist the aid of a journalist or someone who has a media communications background.
- Be available to the media. Cooperation will improve media access and fair treatment in the future.
- Have a good summary of the evaluation study prepared to provide to reporters.
- Be selective in choosing reports to send to the media.
- Learn the language of the media and what it means to be "on" or "off the record."
- Deal in facts, and avoid any temptation to lie to a reporter.
- Avoid reporters who appear to have a single agenda and may fail to represent the evaluation's findings accurately.

Guidelines for Press Releases

- Use clear language the general public will understand—avoid jargon.
- Begin the press release with a statement that sparks the interest of reporters. This is called a "lead" and is intended to grab the reader's attention.
- Use the active voice.
- Use short paragraphs.
- Use quotations to make the content more interesting.
- Print it on letterhead or on a "news release" form.
- Indicate the date on which the press is free to use the information with the words, "FOR RELEASE." If the contents' use is not date specific, use the statement, "FOR IMMEDIATE RELEASE."
- Provide the name, institutional affiliation, and phone number of a contact person (typically the evaluator or the organization's public relations officer).
- Use "# # #" or "-30-" to indicate the end of the news release text.
- Target smaller newspapers, since they are more likely to print "community" news.
- Send the release to a particular person at the news agency so that it doesn't get lost in the organization.

Cautions

- The news media may not be an appropriate medium for communicating formative evaluation findings.
- Reports via news media usually must be kept short.
- The news media is a one-way communication system.
- The news media tend to focus on the negative or on failures, especially concerning government or other public agencies and organizations.

Web Site Communications

Implementation Tips

- Determine your audiences' Internet access and practices prior to establishing it as a mainstay for communicating and reporting.
- Before developing a Web site to facilitate evaluation communicating and reporting, determine if one already exists where a section could be used or created for your purposes.
- If building a Web site specifically for the evaluation, determine if you will develop it yourself or seek outside expertise.
- Consider making your Web site and postings accessible to people with disabilities.
- Provide various options for accessing and downloading large evaluation documents.
- Consider securing your posted documents so that they cannot be modified, and/or require password access.
- As with any means of dissemination, make sure that evaluation documents, photographs, videos, and presentations posted on the Web have been fully vetted with your evaluation team, clients, and stakeholders.
- Write summaries of evaluation information/findings for inclusion on Web pages, and post full versions of documents to be downloaded.
- Consider including a mechanism for evaluation audiences to ask questions, request further information, and/or provide feedback.

Guidelines for Developing a Web Site and Creating Web Pages

- Establish the purpose of your Web site, and assemble all of the information you wish to provide.
- Develop a logical flow between introductory information and the content of subsequent pages.

- Review existing Web sites for ideas about design and organization.
- Create the Web pages to fit the width of the lowest monitor resolution the majority of your audience is likely to use.
- Maintain the same basic design across all Web pages on your site.
- Use high contrast between background color and type.
- Choose typeface to maximize readability: Make sure text is not too small. Avoid using all caps, which slows reading time.
- Make sure you use commonly available text fonts (e.g., Arial, New York Times, Helvetica, or Times New Roman). Text fonts not supported by readers' computer systems will be translated into something similar, which could be visually unappealing.
- Position headings close to the related text.
- Choose graphics wisely: Make sure they are related to your topic and will be meaningful for readers. Do not allow too many different graphics to clutter the page. Avoid graphics that require a long download time.
- Make sure your page functions (links, downloads, etc.) properly.
- Test your Web site with different browsers to make sure it appears as you intend and functions properly.

Caution

- Web site communications and reports are highly visible.

Appendix C

Summary of Chapter 4 Implementation Tips, Guidelines, and Cautions

Verbal Presentations

Implementation Tips

- Take the audience's perspective when planning your presentation.
- Focus the presentation on a few selected topics.
- Organize your presentation for yourself and for your audience.
- Plan ways to involve the audience.
- Use handouts to support your presentation.
- Practice your presentation and use effective presentation techniques.
- Consider the room arrangement for your presentation.
- Evaluate your presentations so that you continuously improve your communication of evaluation information.
- Use visuals in your presentation.

Guidelines for Audience Involvement

- Use humor and stories.
- At the beginning of the presentation, solicit expectations and questions about the presentation topic.
- Use worksheets that solicit information from audience members and then ask them to share their ideas.
- Adjust your presentation according to audience reaction and nonverbal cues.
- Use variety in your body language and the pace of your speech to engage and retain the audience's attention.

- Allocate time at the end of the presentation for questions, answers, and discussion.
- Get audience members' reactions to the presentation and ask about additional information needs they have.

Guidelines for Giving a Verbal Presentation

- Direct the audience's attention appropriately throughout the presentation (e.g., turn off the overhead during discussions, use overlays to build an overhead illustration).
- Assume a relaxed, natural posture.
- Move about to enhance your involvement with the audience.
- If you are using visuals, focus on one idea per visual.
- Do not read every word on the visual—they are there to support what you have to say. Make short notes in large print to cue you about what you want to say. This approach helps establish a more personal, conversational style.
- If you want to point to certain words or phrases on a visual, either use a laser pointer directed to the screen or flip chart, or use a small stick or pen on the transparency itself.
- If you are using overhead transparencies, keep track of key slides that you are likely to refer to more than once. Set them aside so that you do not have to hunt for them among the other slides.
- Maintain eye contact with the audience.
- Maintain your attention on the audience, not on the visuals. Remember to face the group when discussing a visual; don't turn your back and read from the visual.
- If you are distributing handouts during the presentation, do so quickly. Alternatively, you can have them available at audience members' seats or to be picked up as they arrive.

PowerPoint Presentations and Transparencies   _____

Implementation Tips

- Design PowerPoint slides and transparencies prudently.
- Budget adequate time for creating your PowerPoint slides or transparencies.
- Gauge the number of slides or transparencies you use according to the time available.
- Be prepared to handle the mechanics of your presentation.

Design Principles for PowerPoint Slides and Overhead Transparencies

Format

- As you develop each slide, make sure that your font style and size, formatting, and grammar are the same for every slide.
- Choose a template (a design) that supports your message—you don't want the design to detract from your message. Use this same design for all your slides.
- Follow the "6 × 6" rule: no more than six lines of text and no more than six words per line per slide. If you start with writing sentences, fine, but go back through and edit down to some key words. Try to present the information in "bullets."
- Number your slides.
- When using PowerPoint animation, it is easier to read text when it drops down from above, or comes from the left. Don't change the direction of entering text for each slide—consistency is key. Don't overdo the special effects.

Color

- Make sure that the font color contrasts with the background color so that the text shows up well.
- Be careful how you use red—the eye goes there first, and some suggest that red is a difficult color for males to see.
- Use no more than five colors on charts and graphs.
- Highlight key points with a bold font or color.

Fonts

- Font size should be no smaller than 20-point (minimum ¼-inch high letters).
- Avoid ornate font styles that could be difficult to read.
- Vary the size of the font to illustrate the relative importance of information, but don't use more than two font styles in your presentation.
- Use upper- and lowercase letters (don't use only uppercase).

Content

- If using photographs, cartoons, or other art in the presentation, consider your audience and how they might react to certain clip art or other visuals embedded in the slides.

- Don't rely on spell check alone. Go through each slide and double-check for typos and misspelled words. Even better, ask someone else to proof-read the slides.

Guidelines for Handling the Mechanics of Projecting Visuals

PowerPoint Presentations

- Make sure that you have your presentation backed up on a disk, in case your computer fails and another one has to be brought in.
- Arrive at the room with plenty of time to set up the projection system, connect it to your computer, set up the screen, and make sure everything is in working order.
- Locate outlets and determine if an extension cord is needed. It is a good idea to bring one with you just in case.
- Bring an extra cable that attaches your computer to the projection system in case the one that is provided does not work.

Transparencies and Overhead Projector

- Before the presentation, make sure that there are two usable bulbs in the projector so that if one burns out, there will be another one easily accessible. It's also a good idea to bring an extra extension cord.
- Make sure that the projector is not blocking anyone's view of the screen. (Corners are considered to be the best place for a screen and projector.)
- Focus the projector before you start your presentation.
- Position the transparency on the projector before turning it on so the bright light does not bother participants.
- Be careful not to stand in front of the screen.
- Position the transparency as high on the projector's screen as possible.
- Turn the projector off after the last slide.
- Since transparencies are prone to slide off the projector, use transparency frames to keep them in place. This will also keep them in better shape if they are to be used again.

Flip Charts

Implementation Tips

- Prepare attractive and legible flip charts.
- Gauge the number of flip charts you will need.
- Determine how you will transport flip charts.
- Use flip charts to record participants' comments and questions during a presentation.

Guidelines for Creating Flip Charts to Present Information

- If possible, prepare flip charts ahead of time and store them carefully so that they do not get folded or torn.
- Write out the content on regular-sized paper before writing it on the flip chart paper.
- Use the largest size paper available to maximize visibility.
- Use markers that do not bleed through the paper, and that have a wide tip, so that the writing can be visible to participants who are farthest away.
- Avoid writing on the bottom quarter of the paper, since this part of the page is often blocked from view.
- Print or write legibly and in a large, bold style.
- Use multiple colored markers to heighten interest and aid retention. Avoid pale colors and red (except as a highlighter). Do not use more than three colors on a page.
- If you have multiple flip chart pages, consider attaching different colored tabs to cue you into where the presentation's topics shift or change.
- If you make an error on a prepared flip chart page, instead of starting all over, cover it with a paper patch and invisible tape.
- Whenever possible, use flip chart paper that has gridlines, allowing the writer to print on the lines.
- Consider lightly writing the content in pencil on the flip chart paper before you write it using the markers.
- Follow the "7 × 7" rule: No more than seven lines of text and no more than seven words per line on a flip chart page.
- Consider writing some notes in pencil on the flip chart page to remind yourself of key points you want to make.
- Consider having a blank sheet of paper between each flip chart page of information. This will prevent the written material from other sheets showing through.
- If you do not have access to an easel, put the flip chart paper up on a wall where the participants can see it.

Guidelines for Using Flip Charts to Record Information

- Be sure that you are capturing the words of the participants as much as possible. If you are unsure, repeat what you have heard to verify the participants' comments.
- If some participants' responses are too lengthy or difficult to paraphrase, consider writing keywords or short phrases, emphasizing with multiple colors, arrows, circles, and underlining. Another approach would be to use check marks next to ideas that have already been offered.

- Consider having someone else mark the flip chart while you facilitate the discussion.
- Consider using two or more flip charts so that you can easily refer back to comments that have been made and charted.
- If you wish to hang the flip chart sheets on the wall, make sure that you have enough wall space on which to do this. Choose a room that can accommodate the activity. Tear off pieces of tape before the meeting so that they are handy and will not slow down the pace of the conversation.
- If you are facilitating the presentation and writing on the flip chart, try to do both at the same time.
- Stand to the side of the flip chart as you write so that your writing is visible to the majority of participants.

Video Presentations

Implementation Tips

- Carefully design the video's purpose and script.
- Establish the criteria for the selection of program events and activities to be included on the video.
- Determine if you will produce the video yourself or engage the services of a videographer.
- Anticipate the need for using video, and budget adequate time and financial resources.
- Obtain permission from program participants prior to filming.
- Make sure videos intended as stand-alone pieces contain sufficient background information about the program and its evaluation.
- Carefully consider the intended audience(s) when determining the length of the video.

Caution

- Low credibility is sometimes associated with video.

Posters and Poster Sessions

Implementation Tips

- Determine how you will produce posters.
- Keep the format of posters simple and easy to read from a distance.
- Include visuals and color to help get your message across.

- Create a storyboard to provide an impression of the program or organization that was evaluated.
- Avoid the use of posters alone to support decision making.

Working Sessions

Implementation Tips

- Assess and refine your skills for facilitating working sessions.
- Build support for participation in working sessions.
- Specifically tailor each working session for your participants, and carefully plan it to achieve clear objectives.
- Do your best to get key stakeholders at the table.
- Determine what information or documents participants should receive ahead of time.
- Consider conducting working sessions as part of other regularly scheduled meetings.
- Provide sufficient background information at the beginning of the working session, and close the session with a clear outline of what is to follow.
- Spend time at the outset of the working session to reach common understandings on basic issues/information about the evaluand.
- Use worksheets to organize the activities of a working session.
- Develop ground rules about the confidentiality of the working session.
- Consider expending evaluation resources on conducting action-planning sessions rather than on producing a final report.
- Follow up with the stakeholders who may not have been able to attend a working session.

Guidelines for Facilitating Working Sessions

- Know your own values, beliefs, and assumptions on the topic at hand, and then check them at the door.
- Explain your role as the facilitator—to guide the process, not the content of the work.
- Help group members get to know each other with introductory exercises (e.g., have participants introduce themselves and explain their role and most satisfying experience to date with the evaluand).
- Review or ask the group to establish norms for how all of you will work together as a team (e.g., everyone participates, speakers are allowed to finish without interruption, etc.).
- Considering the topic, your objectives, and your knowledge of the group, choose the most appropriate process techniques to engage the group productively (e.g., individual recording of responses to a question/issue followed by round-robin sharing out; group categorization of brainstormed

items into themes or patterns; tossing of an object or passing of a "talking stick" to identify who will speak next and thus facilitate full participation).

- Encourage diverse viewpoints and perspectives to surface.
- Call attention to the group process as needed:
  - Watch the time and remind the group where they are on the agenda.
  - When the discussion has evolved away from the objectives at hand, call the group's attention to this and invite them to refocus.

- Note who in the group is participating; invite responses from others as needed.
- Convey both interest and respect in your responses to individuals' input.
- Acknowledge and address the feelings and needs of the group as they emerge.
- Be sensitive to the possibility of underlying agendas or conflicts among participants; diplomatically raise questions to surface and resolve them.
- Be willing to refocus or change the agenda as might be needed.
- Encourage participants to take responsibility for ideas, actions, and statements they make.
- Paraphrase comments; synthesize and integrate emerging ideas and developments for the group.
- Build consensus.
- Balance dialogue with decision making.
- Plan and articulate next steps.
- Ask for feedback about individuals' experiences with the group's process.
- Incorporate what you learn about both group process and substantive content into your next opportunity to work with each group.

Caution

- Working sessions can bring together groups/individuals who are in conflict.

Synchronous Electronic Communications _____

Guidelines for Synchronous Electronic Communications: Chat Rooms, Teleconferences, Videoconferences, Web Conferences

Before

- For first-time use, try out the technology with a trial run. Glitches in getting all participants connected can delay or completely derail the meeting.
- Consider making the first use of synchronous electronic communications deliberately short and relatively simple.
- Identify a person or persons responsible for designing and facilitating the meeting.

- Establish clear outcomes for the meeting and an agenda to reach them, including the processes that will be used (i.e., asking the participants for examples, opinions, ideas, or responses to specific pieces of information; to brainstorm; to reach consensus, vote, or make a specific decision).
- Distribute the agenda, a list of participants, the date and time of the meeting, technical instructions for accessing the meeting, and any supporting documents ahead of time. (Note that documents presented during a Web conference may or may not be distributed ahead.)
- If any preparation is necessary, provide clear instructions about what participants are to do prior to the meeting.

During

- Begin and end the meeting on time.
- If needed, start the meeting with some type of roll call to determine who is participating.
- The facilitator should introduce the meeting by reviewing its objectives and starting with the first agenda item. Check that all participants understand what is to be accomplished during the meeting.
- Throughout the meeting, the facilitator keeps the meeting focused, helping to make sure that one topic is discussed at a time, and that all participants have a chance to be heard.
- At the close of the meeting, summarize outcomes, unresolved issues, and next steps.

After

- Either at the end of or following the meeting, ask participants to provide feedback about both the logistics and content of the meeting.
- Follow up with a written summary that includes information on any questions/issues not answered during the meeting. Also be sure to thank participants.

Chat Rooms

Implementation Tips

- Keep the text that you write clear, concise, and focused.
- When using chat rooms with a variety of stakeholders over a period of time, establish and disseminate specific guidelines and conventions to help chat room dialogue function smoothly.
- Avoid repeated use of chat rooms, without opportunities for communication via telephone and face-to-face meetings.

Cautions

- Chat rooms are not good choices for individuals who have visual impairments, or are not comfortable with written forms of expression.
- Chat rooms provide little opportunity for receiving social cues and, like e-mail communications, can result in misunderstandings.
- Some individuals may feel inhibited in their responses, knowing that their words are being captured in a computer file.

Teleconferences

Implementation Tips

- Limit the teleconference call to no more than 90 minutes to avoid participant distraction and/or fatigue.
- When people speak, ask them to say their names before speaking so that others know who is talking.
- Depending on the format of the call, agree upon the amount of time to speak before asking others to engage in the conversation.
- To assure full participation, call on each participant in turn to respond to specific questions or issues raised.
- Take notes during the call.

Cautions

- Listeners may be distracted by office interruptions, by e-mails, or by other noises.
- It's not always clear who is paying attention during the call—some people might even leave the call without your knowing it.
- Speaker phones vary in quality and do not always capture participants' voices well enough to allow for a fluid, multidirectional conversation.

Videoconferences

Implementation Tips

- Plan and budget for videoconferencing at the outset of your evaluation work. Determine what technical and financial resources you have to support videoconferencing, and choose the optimal method accordingly.
- Establish an overall facilitator and a facilitator at each site.

- Schedule the videoconference well in advance, especially when you will have numerous sites participating.
- When choosing your clothing, avoid plaids, stripes, and prints. Pastel clothing is better than white, which may glare as a result of the lighting in the room. If you do wear white, keep a jacket or sweater on to give contrast.

Immediately Before the Videoconference

- Arrive 15–30 minutes before the videoconference is scheduled to start to make sure that all locations are ready.
- Make sure you have the confirmation or reservation with call instructions readily available.
- Position the camera before the meeting begins.
- Review the agenda for the videoconference.

During the Videoconference

- Be courteous and allow people time to finish sentences. Always address the group as a whole by speaking toward the microphones and facing the camera.
- There is a delay when using video. Give each person plenty of time to respond to questions or comments, and be sure they have finished before you speak.
- Keep slides to a minimum during a presentation, and keep each one on camera for only a short time to maintain interest. Allow questions at the end of the presentation.
- Be aware of your posture; if you need a stretch, then the other participants will probably need one, too.
- In large groups, ask people to raise their hand to signal the camera operator that they would like to speak.
- Remember, all locations see the speaker; the speaker only sees the last site from which a person spoke.
- Mute the microphone when not speaking.
- Look into the camera when you speak. Doing this gives participants at the other site(s) the impression that you are making eye contact with them.
- Pause occasionally so others may make comments.
- Identify yourself as necessary.
- Keep others informed by announcing your actions. For instance, let others know when you are going to display a graphic so they don't try to transmit an image at the same time.
- Minimize extraneous noise. For example, avoid coughing into the microphone, shuffling papers, and engaging in side conversations.

- Be cognizant of which camera you are using. If you use the document camera to show a graphic, remember to switch back to the main camera when the discussion moves on to another topic.
- Reposition the camera periodically.
- If your videoconference is longer than one hour, include a break.
- Allow five to ten minutes at the end of your meeting to give participants the time to say goodbye and to arrange for any follow-up activities.

Cautions

- The most reliable videoconferencing technology can be costly to use, and may not be supported by your evaluation budget.
- Without the technical expertise of a videoconference service provider or IT professionals, you may run into technical difficulties that can derail the conference.
- Videoconferencing is the most invasive of all synchronous electronic communications. As the conference proceeds, it can be easy to forget that you are visually in the presence of others. Not all people are comfortable with this level of interaction.

Web Conferences

Implementation Tips

- Plan and budget for Web conferencing at the outset of your evaluation work. Determine what technical and financial resources you have to support it, and choose the optimal method accordingly.
- Plan each Web conference, deciding what features you will use based on the purpose of the meeting and the number of participants who will be involved.
- Determine whether participants have the necessary hardware and software to participate in the Web conference. Set up a trial run to make sure everyone can get connected successfully.
- Schedule Web conferences for significant aspects of the evaluation work in advance.
- Make sure that each participant has received information about how to access the Web conference.
- For stakeholder groups that you work with regularly, consider using Web conferencing for ad hoc meetings.

Immediately Before the Web Conference

- If using one, position your Web camera before the meeting begins.
- Review the agenda for the Web conference.

During the Web Conference

- Keep slides to a minimum during a presentation. Consider inviting participants to ask questions about slides using the "chat" feature, and responding to them via audio to all participants at the end of the presentation.
- If you are using a Web camera, look into it when you speak. As with a videoconference, doing this gives participants the impression that you are making eye contact with them.
- Pause occasionally so others may make comments.
- Identify yourself as necessary.
- Keep others informed by announcing your actions.
- Be aware of what other participants are seeing. It can be frustrating if you, as the facilitator, are changing images on your screen too quickly.
- If your Web conference is longer than one hour, include a break.
- Allow five to ten minutes at the end of your meeting to give participants the time to say goodbye and to arrange for any follow-up activities.

Caution

- Without the technical expertise of a Web conference service provider or IT professionals, you may run into technical difficulties that can derail the conference.

Personal Discussions

Implementation Tips

- Plan ahead for how you will handle both prearranged and impromptu one-on-one conversations.
- Be aware of the political context of the evaluation.
- During the evaluation, provide the least amount of information that addresses the concerns of an inquiring stakeholder but still maintains an effective working relationship.
- Make efforts to make the content of one-on-one conversations known to other stakeholders.

- Beware of the frequency of and participants in the one-on-one conversations you have throughout the course of the evaluation.
- Be prepared to conduct one-on-one conversations with clients and key stakeholders during or following a site visit.
- Supplement written evaluation reports with planned one-on-one conversations with stakeholders.
- Keep records of one-on-one conversations to ensure the accuracy of further communication about what has been discussed.

Cautions

- The contents of personal communications are frequently based upon selective recall.
- Informally communicated information is less likely to be recommunicated accurately.
- It will not always be possible to document or follow up to reconfirm the contents of (and/or decisions made during) one-on-one conversations.

Appendix D

Summary of Chapter 5 Implementation Tips and Cautions

Photographs

Implementation Tips

- Consider the appropriateness of photography for your evaluation participants.
- Plan your use of photography for data collecting and reporting.
- Support photography with other forms of data collection.
- Consider using photographs primarily as a reporting method—to facilitate audience understanding of the program, its participants, and/or context.
- Negotiate permission to photograph.
- Use several photographers to get multiple perspectives.
- Be aware of participant reactivity.
- Determine how you will analyze the photographs.
- Solicit stakeholder feedback.
- Provide details about your sampling and analysis methods.
- Prepare photographs for discussion with and feedback from program participants.

Cartoons

Implementation Tips

- Determine how you will select topics or findings for illustration with cartoons.
- Determine how you will create your cartoons.

- Write simple call-outs and captions for your cartoons.
- Solicit participant feedback.
- Use cartoons in combination with other communicating and reporting formats.

Poetry

Implementation Tips

- Consider the appropriateness of poetry for you evaluation stakeholders.
- Determine how you will construct poems to represent key findings, themes, or issues in the evaluation data.
- Share poems with a sample of evaluation participants for feedback prior to dissemination or publication.
- If poems are being presented in a working session or verbal presentation, consider asking stakeholders to read the poems aloud.
- Facilitate discussion about the poetry by asking for participant reactions.
- Use poetry in combination with other communicating and reporting formats.

Drama

Implementation Tips

- Consider the appropriateness of drama for your evaluation stakeholders.
- Consider your options for creating the script for the theater performance.
- Select those who will perform the theatrical piece and make sure they are thoroughly familiar with the evaluation study.
- Set the context for the performance.
- Create a physical space for the theater performance that maximizes audience and actor interaction.
- Use dramatic performances in combination with other communicating and reporting formats.
- Consider using technology-based formats that can be used to increase audience access to dramatic performances.

Creative Forms of Communicating and Reporting

Caution

- Creative forms of communicating and reporting can be time and resource intensive.

Appendix E

Summary of Chapter 6 Implementation Tips and Cautions

Communicating and Reporting With Diverse Audiences

Implementation Tips

- Use a fully participatory approach with diverse evaluation stakeholders.
- Form teams of evaluators to include those from multiple cultural contexts.
- Identify the dominant language(s) among evaluation stakeholders and provide all communications and reports in this language or languages.
- Use language appropriate for diverse participants and reflective of their voices.
- Avoid relying primarily on written communications.
- Select photographs and video footage that are representative of stakeholders' race/ethnicity, socioeconomic status, age, and gender.
- With heterogeneity among evaluation stakeholders, allow additional time for communicating and reporting activities.

Caution

- Despite your best efforts in any given instance, your communicating and reporting efforts may still not be as respectful and sensitive to diverse audiences as they could be.

Communicating Negative Findings

Implementation Tips

- From the outset, position the evaluation within a learning context.
- Involve stakeholders and program participants in the evaluation's design, data collection, and analysis activities.
- Communicate as much as possible with stakeholders throughout the evaluation.
- Keep stakeholders' perspectives in mind.
- Assist stakeholders in processing negative findings.
- If possible, stay engaged beyond the immediate evaluation effort to work with stakeholders on using evaluation findings.
- Present positive findings first.
- Avoid using the words "positive" and "negative."

Caution

- Ultimately, there is no way to control the reaction of clients and stakeholders to unfavorable evaluation findings.

tegrating Quantitative d Qualitative Methods

Implementation Tips

- Form teams of evaluators to provide expertise in both qualitative and quantitative data collection, analysis, and reporting.
- Develop a framework that can guide the integration of qualitative and quantitative findings, and focus the report.
- Determine the primary audiences' preference for different types of data when deciding if one type should take center stage over another.
- Consider which communicating formats are most conducive to reporting qualitative and/or quantitative data.

utions

Evaluations that combine both qualitative and quantitative approaches can be resource intensive and time consuming, especially the analysis and reporting.

Despite your conviction that a combined approach is best, some clients nd stakeholders may still prefer one approach to the other.

Developing Recommendations

Implementation Tips

- Make sure there is a clear linkage between recommendations and the evaluation findings.
- If recommendations are initially developed by you, submit them to stakeholders for review, discussion, and modification.
- Increase stakeholders' ownership of recommendations by developing them collaboratively.
- Consider grouping recommendations into categories.
- Work with the stakeholders to develop action plans for implementing various recommendations.
- In multiyear evaluations, review the fate of recommendations previously made.
- Allow time for work on developing recommendations and plans for acting on the recommendations.

Caution

- Occasionally, clients and stakeholders may insist that you provide recommendations that you alone develop.

Multisite Evaluations

Implementation Tips

- Help clients and stakeholders develop common goals and/or outcomes across sites.
- Assess the political and organizational contexts of each site.
- Hold periodic meetings with staff from each site.
- Create site-specific reports as well as a comprehensive final report.
- Enlist stakeholders at each site to help in the communication and reporting process.
- Use combinations of various communication formats.

Caution

- Different sites are likely to have unique communicating and reporting needs.

References

Abma, T. A. (1998). Text in an evaluative context: Writing for dialogue. *Evaluation, 4*(4), 434–454.

Algarin, M., & Holman, B. (Eds.). (1994). *Aloud: Voices from the Nuyorican Poets Cafe.* New York: Henry Holt.

Alkin, M. C. (1985). *A guidebook for evaluation decision-makers.* Beverly Hills, CA: Sage.

Alkin, M. C. (1990). *Debates on evaluation.* Newbury Park, CA: Sage.

Alkin, M. C. (Ed.). (2004). *Evaluation roots: Tracing theorists' views and influences.* Thousand Oaks, CA: Sage.

Altheide, D. L., & Johnson, J. M. (1994). Criteria for assessing interpretive validity in qualitative research. In N. R. Denzin and Y. S. Lincoln (Eds.), *Handbook of qualitative research,* pp. 485–499. Thousand Oaks, CA: Sage.

American Psychological Association (2001). *Publication manual (5th edition).* Washington, DC: Author.

Anderson, P. V. (1991). *Technical writing: A reader-centered approach.* Chicago: Harcourt Brace Jovanovich.

Austa, S. (2003, June 27). Cartoonists: They say it all. *The Tribune.* Retrieved April 10, 2004, from http://www.tribuneindia.com/2003/20030627/career.htm.

Barley, Z. A., & Dodson, S. (2000). *A study of a consortium model to support school district systemic reform.* Paper presented at the annual meeting of the American Educational Research Association, New Orleans.

Barley, Z. A., & Jenness, M. (1993). Cluster evaluation: A method to strengthen evaluation in smaller programs with similar purposes. *Evaluation Practice, 14*(2), 141–147.

Beardsley, R. M., & Miller, M. H. (2002). Revisioning the process: A case study in feminist program evaluation. In D. Seigart & S. Brisolara (Eds.), Feminist evaluation: Explorations and experiences. *New Directions for Program Evaluation, 96,* 57–70.

Beatty, P. (1994). *Joker, joker, deuce.* New York: Penguin Group.

Beauvais, F., & Trimble, J. E. (1992.) The role of the researcher in evaluating American Indian alcohol and other drug abuse prevention programs. In *Office of Substance Abuse Prevention, Cultural competence for evaluators: A guide for alcohol and other drug abuse prevention practitioners working with ethnic/racial communities,* pp. 173–201. Rockville, MD: U.S. Department of Health and Human Services.

Becker, H. S. (1979). Do photographs tell the truth? In T. D. Cook & C. S. Reischardt (Eds.), *Qualitative and quantitative methods in evaluation research* (pp. 99–117). Beverly Hills, CA: Sage.

Berger, A. A. (1993). *Improving writing skills: Memos, letters, reports, and proposals.* Newbury Park, CA: Sage.

Blitz, B. (2001). *The big book of cartooning.* Philadelphia: Running Press.

Blum, J., Holman, R. (Producers), & Pellington, M. (Director) (1996). *The United States of poetry.* San Francisco: Independent Television Service.

Boal, A. (1992). *Games for actors and non-actors.* New York: Routledge.

Boal, A. (1998). *Legislative theatre*. New York: Routledge.

Bonnet, D. (1997). Packing it in with horizontal bars. In G. T. Henry (Ed.), Creating effective graphs: Solutions for a variety of evaluation data. *New Directions for Program Evaluation, 73,* 9–16.

Brady, I. (2000). Anthropological poetics. In N. R. Denzin & Y. S. Lincoln (Eds.), *Handbook of qualitative research,* pp. 949–979. Thousand Oaks, CA: Sage.

Braskamp, L. A. (1982). A definition of use. *Studies in Educational Evaluation, 8,* 169–174.

Braskamp, L. A., & Brown, R. D. (Eds.). (1980) Utilization of evaluative information. *New Directions for Program Evaluation, 5.*

Brookfield, S. (1991). The development of critical reflection in adulthood. *New Education, 13*(1), 39–48.

Brooks, J. G., & Brooks, M. G. (1993). *In search of understanding: The case for constructivist classrooms.* Alexandria, VA: Association for Supervision and Curriculum Development.

Brown, H., Marks, K., & Straw, M. (1997). Use of graphics to illustrate responses to multi-part survey items. In G. T. Henry, Creating effective graphs: Solutions for a variety of evaluation data, *New Directions for Evaluation, 73,* 17–24.

Bruner, J. (1986). *Actual minds, possible words.* Cambridge, MA: Harvard University Press.

Bruner, J. (1990). *Acts of meaning.* Cambridge, MA: Harvard University Press.

Campbell, D. (2000). *The socially constructed organization.* London: H. Karnac.

Caracelli, V. J., & Greene, J. C. (1997). Crafting mixed-method evaluation designs. In J. C. Greene & V. J. Caracelli (Eds.), Advances in mixed-method evaluation. *New Directions for Evaluation, 74,* 19–32.

Center for Research on Learning and Teaching, (2002). *CRLT Players at the University of Michigan* [Brochure]. Ann Arbor, MI: Author.

Checkoway, B., & Richards-Schuster, K. (2003). Youth participation in community evaluation research. *American Journal of Evaluation, 24*(1), 21–33.

Chen, H. (1997). Applying mixed methods under the framework of theory-driven evaluations. In J. C. Greene & V. J. Caracelli (Eds.), Advances in mixed-method evaluation. *New Directions for Evaluation, 74,* 61–72.

Chin, M. C. (2002). *Evaluation of the Flare Elementary School SRA Reading Program.* Report for the 2001–2002 School Year.

Chin, M. C. (2003). An investigation into the impact of using poetry and cartoons as alternative representational forms in evaluation reporting. Unpublished doctoral dissertation, Florida State University.

Chin, M. C. (2005). Cartooning. In S. Mathison (Ed.), *Encyclopedia of Evaluation* (p. 42–43). Thousand Oaks, CA: Sage.

Collier, J. (1967). *Visual anthropology: Photography as a research method.* New York: Holt, Rinehart & Winston.

Conner, R. F. (2004). Developing and implementing culturally competent evaluation: A discussion of multicultural validity in two HIV prevention programs for Latinos. In M. Thompson-Robinson, R. Hopson, & S. SenGupta (Eds.), In search of cultural competence in evaluation: Towards principles and practices. *New Directions for Program Evaluation, 102.*

Cook, J. A., Carey, M. A., Razzano, L. A., Burke, J., & Blyler, C. R. (2002). The pioneer: The employment intervention demonstration program. *New Directions for Evaluation, 94,* 31–44.

Cousins, J. B. (2003). Utilization effects of participatory evaluation. In T. Kellaghan & D. L. Stufflebeam (Eds.), *International handbook of educational evaluation.* Norwell, MA: Kluwer.

Cousins, J. B., & Earl, L. M. (1992). *Designing evaluations of educational and social programs.* San Francisco: Jossey-Bass.

Cousins, J. B., & Whitmore, E. (1998). Framing participatory evaluation. *New Directions for Evaluation, 80,* 5–23.

Cranton, P. (1994). *Understanding and promoting transformative learning.* San Francisco: Jossey-Bass.

Cronbach, L. J. (1980). *Toward reform of program evaluation.* San Francisco: Jossey-Bass.

Cronbach, L. J. (1982). The case for participatory evaluation. *Educational Evaluation and Policy Analysis, 14*(4), 397–418.

Dahler-Larsen, P. (2003). *Using forum theatre to explore the effects of evaluation.* Paper presented at the annual meeting of the American Evaluation Association, Reno, NV.

Datta, L. (1994). Paradigm wars: A basis for peaceful coexistence and beyond. *New Directions for Program Evaluation, 61,* 53–70.

Datta, L. (1997). A pragmatic basis for mixed-method designs. In J. C. Greene & V. J. Caracelli (Eds.), Advances in mixed-method evaluation. *New Directions for Evaluation, 74,* 33–46.

Denzin, N. (1994). The art and politics of interpretation. In N. R. Denzin & Y. S. Lincoln (Eds.), *Handbook of qualitative research,* pp. 500–515. Thousand Oaks, CA: Sage.

Denzin, N. (2000). The practice and politics of interpretation. In N. R. Denzin & Y. S. Lincoln (Eds.), *Handbook of qualitative research,* pp. 897–922. Thousand Oaks, CA: Sage.

Dirkx, J. M. (1998, March). *Knowing the self through fantasy and imagination: Implications for adult learning in the context of work.* Paper presented at the Academy of Human Resource Development Conference, Chicago, IL.

Dixon, N. (1994). *The organizational learning cycle.* London: McGraw-Hill.

Drezek, S. (1982). Designing useful evaluations. *Evaluation News, 3*(4), 63–64.

Dunn, R., & Dunn, K. (1993). *Teaching secondary students through their individual learning styles: Practical approaches for grades 7–12.* Boston: Allyn & Bacon.

Eisner, E. W. (1990). The meaning of alternative paradigms for practice. In E. Guba (Ed.), *The paradigm dialog,* pp. 88–102. Newbury Park, CA: Sage.

Endo, T., & Joh, C. (2003). *Shifting our thinking: Moving toward multicultural evaluation.* Woodland Hills, CA: The California Endowment.

English, F. W. (1988). The utility of the camera in qualitative inquiry. *Educational Researcher, 17*(4), 8–15.

Farley, J. (1991). Sociotechnical theory: An alternative framework for evaluation. In C. L. Larson & H. Preskill (Eds.), *Organizations in transition: Opportunities and challenges for evaluation,* pp. 51–62. San Francisco: Jossey-Bass.

Fetterman, D. F. (1997). Videoconferencing over the Internet. *Qualitative Health Journal, 7*(1), 154–163.

Fetterman, D. M. (1989, October). *From qualitative to quantitative and back again: Philosophical and methodological transitions.* Paper presented at the annual meeting of the American Evaluation Association, San Francisco.

Fetterman, D. M. (1998). *Ethnography: Step by step* (2nd ed.). Thousand Oaks, CA: Sage.

Fetterman, D. M. (2001). *Foundations of empowerment evaluation.* Thousand Oaks, CA: Sage.

Fetterman, D. M. (2002). Web surveys to digital movies: Technological tools of the trade. *Educational Researcher, 31*(6), 29–37.

Fielding, N. G., & Fielding, J. L. (1986). *Linking data* (Qualitative Research Methods, No. 4). Beverly Hills, CA: Sage.

Fitzpatrick, J. L. (1994). Alternative models for structuring of professional preparation programs. *New Directions for Program Evaluation, 62,* 41–50.

Fitzpatrick, J. L., Sanders, J. R., & Worthen, B. R. (2003). *Program evaluation: Alternative approaches and practical guidelines* (3rd ed.). Englewood Cliffs, NJ: Pearson, Allyn & Bacon.

Gardner, H. (1983). *Frames of mind: The theory of multiple intelligences.* New York: Basic Books.

Gartner Group, Inc. (2000, October 17). *Top emerging technologies announced during Gartner Symposium/ITxpo 2000* [Press release]. Lake Buena Vista, FL: Author.

Glesne, C. (1997). That rare feeling: Re-presenting research through poetic transcription. *Qualitative Inquiry, 3,* 202–221.

Glesne, C. (1999). *Becoming a qualitative researcher.* New York: Addison Wesley Longman.

Goodyear, L. (1997). *"A circle that it's time to open": Using performance as representation of a participatory evaluation.* Unpublished masters thesis, Department of Policy Analysis and Management, Cornell University, Ithaca, NY.

Goodyear, L. (2001). *Representational form and audience understanding in evaluation: Advancing use and engaging postmodern pluralism.* Unpublished dissertation, Department of Policy Analysis and Management, Cornell University, Ithaca, NY.

Grassroots Educare Trust. (1993). *Annual report 1993.* Gatesville, South Africa: Author (ED369507).

Greene, J. C. (2001). Evaluation extrapolations. *The American Journal of Evaluation, 22(3),* 397–402.

Greene, J. C. (1988). Stakeholder participation and utilization in program evaluation. *Evaluation Review, 12*(3), 91–116.

Greene, J. C., & Caracelli, V. J. (1997). Defining and describing the paradigm issue in mixed-method evaluation. *New Directions for Evaluation, 74,* 5–17.

Greene, J. C. Chandler, M., Costantino, T., & Walker, K. (2003). *Performance and evaluation: An illustration.* Plenary presentation at the annual meeting of the American Evaluation Association, Reno, NV.

Greene, J. C., Lincoln, Y. S., Mathison, S., Mertens, D. M., & Ryan, K. (1998). Advantages and challenges of using inclusive approaches in evaluation practice. *American Journal of Evaluation, 19*(1), 101–122.

Guba, E., & Lincoln, Y. (1982). *Effective evaluation.* San Francisco: Jossey-Bass.

Harmon, M. (1995). The changing role of assessment in evaluating science education reform. In R. O'Sullivan (Ed.), Emerging roles of evaluation in science education reform. *New Directions for Program Evaluation, 65,* 31–51.

Harper, D. (2000). Reimaging visual methods. In N. R. Denzin & Y. S. Lincoln (Eds.), *Handbook of qualitative research,* 717–732. Thousand Oaks, CA: Sage.

Harrison, R. (1981). *The cartoon: Communication to the quick.* Thousand Oaks, CA: Sage.

Hart, C. (2000). *Cartooning for the beginner.* New York: Watson-Guptill.

Hathaway, W. E. (1982). Graphic display procedures. In N. L. Smith (Ed.), *Communication strategies in evaluation.* Newbury Park, CA: Sage.

Hedrick, S. C., Sullivan, J. H., Ehreth, J. L., Rothman, M. L., Connis, R. T., & Erdly, W. W. (1991). Centralized versus decentralized coordination in the adult day health care evaluation study. In R. S. Turpin & J. M. Sinacore (Eds.), Multisite evaluations. *New Directions for Program Evaluation, 50,* 19–31.

Hedrick, T. E. (1994). The quantitative-qualitative debate: Possibilities for integration. *New Directions for Program Evaluation, 61,* 45–52.

Hendricks, M., & Handley, E. A. (1990). Improving the recommendations from evaluation studies. *Evaluation and Program Planning, 13,* 109–117.

Hendricks, M., & Papagiannis, M. (1990). Do's and don't's for offering effective recommendations. *Evaluation Practice, 11*(2), 121–125.

Hopson, R. (Ed.) (2000). How and why language matters in evaluation. New Directions for Program Evaluation, *86.*

Hopson, R. (2001). Global and local conversations on culture, diversity and social justice in evaluation: Issues to consider in a 9/11 era. *American Journal of Evaluation, 22*(3), 375–380.

Hopson, R. (2003). *Overview of multicultural and culturally competent program evaluation: Issues, challenges & opportunities.* Woodland Hills, CA: The California Endowment.

House, E. R. (1986). Drawing evaluative conclusions. *Evaluation Practice, 7*(3), 35–39.

House, E. R. (1994). Integrating quantitative and qualitative. *New Directions for Program Evaluation, 61,* 13–22.

House, E. R. (2001). Unfinished business: Causes and values. *American Journal of Evaluation, 22*(3), 309–315.

Hunter, D., Taylor, W., & Bailey, A. (1995). *Art of facilitation: How to create group synergy.* Cambridge, MA: Perseus.

Indian Health Service (2002). *Indian Health Service Indian health manual.* Albquerque, NM: Department of Health and Human Services, Diabetes Control Program.

Ingle, H. T. (1984). Microcomputers in schools: The video case study as an evaluation tool. In J. Johnston (Ed.), Evaluating the new information technologies. *New Directions for Program Evaluation, 23,* 43–51.

Iriti, J. E., Bickel, W. E., & Nelson, C. A. (2003, November). *Using recommendations in evaluation: A decision-making framework for evaluators.* Paper presented at the annual meeting of the American Evaluation Association, Reno, NV.

Jarvis, P. (1992). *Paradoxes of learning.* San Francisco: Jossey-Bass.

Jenness, M., & Barley, Z. A. (1995). Using cluster evaluation in the context of science education reform. *New Directions for Program Evaluation, 65,* 53–69.

Joint Committee on Standards for Educational Evaluation. (1994). *The program evaluation standards* (2nd ed.). Thousand Oaks, CA: Sage.

Kardia, D., Miller, A. T., & Steiger, J. (2004). Interactive theatre as a multicultural change agent in faculty development. In Matthew Ouellett (Ed.), *Teaching inclusively.* Centreville, MA: New Forums Press.

King, J. A. (1998). Making sense of participatory evaluation practice. *New Directions for Program Evaluation, 80,* 57–67.

King, J. A. (2004). Takkun Olan: The roots of participatory evaluation. In M. C. Alkin (Ed.), *Evaluation roots: Tracing theorists' views and influences.* Thousand Oaks, CA: Sage.

Kingsbury, N., & Hedrick, T. E. (1994). Evaluator training in a government setting. *New Directions for Program Evaluation, 62,* 61–70.

Kinlaw, D. C. (1996). *Facilitation skills: The ASTD trainer's sourcebook.* New York: McGraw-Hill.

Kistler, S. (2004, March). Personal communication.

Kolb, D. (1984). *Experiential learning: Experience as the source of learning and development.* Englewood Cliffs, NJ: Prentice Hall.

Kontzer, T. (2003, May 26). Web conferencing embraced. *Information Week.* Retrieved March 14, 2004, from http.//www.informationweek.com/story/showArticle.jhtml?articleID 10100075.

Krueger, R. (2000). *Focus groups: A practical guide for applied research* (3rd ed.). Thousand Oaks, CA: Sage.

Kushner, S. (2000). *Personalizing evaluation.* Thousand Oaks, CA: Sage.

Lannon, J. M. (1991). *Technical writing* (5th ed.). New York: HarperCollins.

Lawrenz, F., & Huffman, D. (2003). How can multi-site evaluation be participatory? *American Journal of Evaluation, 24*(4), 471–482.

Leff, H. S., & Mulkern, V. (2002). Lessons learned about science and participation from multisite evaluations. *New Directions for Evaluation, 94,* 89–100.

Lin, C. (2003). Literacy instruction through communicative and visual arts. *Digest No. 186.* Washington, DC: The Clearinghouse on Reading, English, and Communication (EDO-CS-03-07).

Lincoln, Y. S. (1990). The making of a constructivist: A remembrance of transformations past. In E. Guba (Ed.), *The paradigm dialog* (pp. 67–87). Newbury Park, CA: Sage.

Lincoln, Y. S. (1994). Tracks toward a post-modern politics of evaluation. *Evaluation Practice, 15*(3), 299–310.

MacNeil, C. (2000). The prose and cons of poetic representation in evaluation reporting. *American Journal of Evaluation, 21*(3), 359–367.

Macy, D. J. (1982). Research briefs. In N. L. Smith (Ed.), *Communication strategies in evaluation* (pp. 179–189). Beverly Hills, CA: Sage.

Madison, A. M. (2000). Language in defining social problems and in evaluating social programs. *New Directions for Evaluation, 86,* 17–28.

Manson, S. (1989). *Journal of the National Center* (entire edition), 2(3), 7–90.

Mark, M. M. (2001). Evaluation's Future: Furor, futile, or fertile. *American Journal of Evaluation, 22*(3), 457–479.

Mark, M. M., Feller, I., & Button, S. B. (1997). Integrating qualitative methods in a predominantly quantitative evaluation: A case study and some reflections. *New Directions for Evaluation, 74,* 47–59.

Marquardt, M. J. (1996). *The learning organization.* New York: McGraw-Hill.

Mathison, S. (1994). Rethinking the evaluator role: Partnerships between organizations and evaluators. *Evalation and Program Planning, 17*(3), 299–304.

Mayer, A. M., Brown, T., & Kelly, J. (1998). Of Maktuk and men. *Diabetes Spectrum, 11,* 141–143.

McCall, M. M. (2000). Performance ethnography: A brief history and some advice. In N. R. Denzin and Y. S. Lincoln (Eds.), *Handbook of qualitative research* (pp. 421–433). Thousand Oaks, CA: Sage.

McColskey, W., Parke, H. M., Harman, P., & Elliott, R. M. (1995). Evaluators as collaborators in science education reform. *New Directions for Program Evaluation, 65,* 71–91.

McElroy, A., & Jezewski, M. A. (2000). Cultural variation in the experience of health and illness. In G. L. Albrecht, R. Fitzpatrick, & S. C. Scrimshaw (Eds.), *The handbook of social studies in health and medicine* (pp. 191–209). Thousand Oaks, CA: Sage.

Meilach, D. Z. (1994). Even the odds with visual presentations. *Presentations, 8(11, Suppl.),* 1–10.

Mertens, D. M. (1994). Training evaluators: Unique skills and knowledge. *New Directions for Program Evaluation, 62,* 17–27.

Mertens, D. M., (2004). *Research and evaluation in education and psychology: Integrating diversity with quantitative, qualitative, and mixed methods* (2nd ed.). Thousand Oaks, CA: Sage.

Mezirow, J. (1991). *Transformative dimensions of adult learning.* San Francisco: Jossey-Bass.

Microsoft Corporation (1997, April). Deere & Company case study. *Business Review.* Retrieved April 26, 2004, from http://www.microsoft.com/Windows/NetMeeting/InAction/deere. ASP.

Morabito, S. M. (2002). Evaluator roles and strategies for expanding evaluation process influence. *American Journal of Evaluation, 23*(3), 321–330.

Morris, L. L., Fitzgibbon, C. T., & Freeman, M. E. (1987). *How to communicate evaluation findings.* Newbury Park, CA: Sage.

Nee, D., & Mojica, M. I. (1999). Ethical challenges in evaluation with communities: A manager's perspective. *New Directions for Evaluation, 82,* 35–45.

Noblit, G. W., & Eaker, D. J. (1987, April). *Evaluation designs as political strategies.* Paper presented at the annual meeting of the American Educational Research Association, Washington, DC.

Office of Inspector General (2004). *Inspectors General Auditor Training Institute: FY 2004 Course Catalog.* Arlington, VA: Author.

Office of Substance Abuse Prevention (1992). *Cultural competence for evaluators: A guide for alcohol and other drug abuse prevention practitioners working with ethnic/racial communities.* Rockville, MD: U.S. Department of Health and Human Services.

Office of Vocational and Adult Education (1994). *Materials for serving homeless adult learners: A resource guide.* Washington, DC: Division of Adult Education and Literacy.

O'Sullivan, R. G. (2004). *Practicing evaluation: A collaborative approach.* Thousand Oaks, CA: Sage.

Owen, J. M., Day, N. A., & Joyce, C. (1991). *Informing decisions about jobs and courses.* Parkville, Australia: Centre for Program Evaluation, The University of Melbourne.

Owen, J. M., & Lambert, F. C. (1998). Evaluation and the information needs of organizational leaders. *American Journal of Evaluation, 19*(3), 355–365.

Parker, L. (1992). Collecting data the e-mail way. *Training & Development, 46*(7), 52–54.

Patton, M. Q. (1986). *Utilization-focused evaluation* (2nd ed.). Beverly Hills, CA: Sage.

Patton, M. Q. (1997). *Utilization-focused evaluation: The new century text* (3rd ed.). Thousand Oaks, CA: Sage.

Patton, M. Q. (2002). Feminist, yes, but is it evaluation? *New Directions for Evaluation, 96,* 97–108.

Pettersson, R. (1989). *Visuals for information: Research & practice.* Englewood Cliffs, NJ: Educational Technology Publications.

Piontek, M. (1994). *An exploratory study of sentient evaluators: Communication, ethics, and relationships in the evaluation process.* Unpublished doctoral dissertation, Western Michigan University, Kalamazoo.

Posavac, E. J., & Carey, R. G. (2003). *Program evaluation: Methods and case studies,* 6th ed. Upper Saddle River, NJ: Prentice Hall.

Preskill, H. (1994a, April). *Building the potential for systematic change: Evaluator as facilitator of organizational learning.* Paper presented at the annual meeting of the American Educational Research Association, New Orleans.

Preskill, H. (1994b). Evaluation's role in enhancing organizational learning. A model for practice. *Evaluation and Program Planning, 17*(4), 291–297.

Preskill, H., & Caracelli, V. (1997). Current and developing conceptions of use: Evaluation use TIG survey results. *Evaluation Practice, 18*(3), 209–225.

Preskill, H., King, D. T., & Hopkins, J. M. (1994). Rings around Saturn. *The Executive Educator, 16*(5), 43–46.

Preskill, H., & Russ-Eft, D. (2005). *Building evaluation capacity: 72 activities for teaching and training.* Thousand Oaks, CA: Sage.

Preskill, H., & Torres, R. T. (1999). *Evaluative inquiry for learning in organizations.* Thousand Oaks, CA: Sage.

Preskill, H., & Torres, R. T. (1999). *Evaluative Inquiry for Learning in Organizations.* Thousand Oaks, CA: Sage.

Preskill, H., Zuckerman, B., & Matthews, B. (2003). An exploratory study of the factors that influence process use. *American Journal of Evaluation, 24*(4), 423–442.

Preskill, S. (2004). Personal communication.

Puchta, C., & Potter, J. (2004). *Focus group practice.* Thousand Oaks, CA: Sage.

Reichardt, C. S. & Rallis, S. F. (1994a). Qualitative and quantitative inquiries are not incompatible: A call for a new partnership. *New Directions for Program Evaluation, 61*, 85–91.

Reichardt, C. S., & Rallis, S. F. (1994b). The relationship between the qualitative and quantitative research traditions. *New Directions for Program Evaluation, 61*, 5–11.

Richardson, L. (1994). Writing: A method of inquiry. In N. R. Denzin & Y. S. Lincoln (Eds.), *Handbook of qualitative research* (pp. 516–529). Thousand Oaks, CA: Sage.

Richardson, L. (2000). Writing: A method of inquiry. In N. R. Denzin & Y. S. Lincoln (Eds.), *Handbook of qualitative research* (pp. 923–948). Thousand Oaks, CA: Sage.

Rosenstein, B. (1997). A reflective approach to program evaluation. In Hans E. Klein (Ed.), *Interactive teaching and learning: Case method and other techniques*. Edinburgh, Scotland: WACRA.

Rossi, P. H. (1994). The war between the quals and the quants: Is a lasting peace possible? *New Directions for Program Evaluation, 61*, 23–36.

Rossi, P. H., Lipsey, M. W., & Freeman, H. E. (2004). *Evaluation: A systematic approach* (7th ed.). Thousand Oaks, CA: Sage.

Rossman, G. B., & Rallis, S. F. (2003). *Learning in the field: An introduction to qualitative research*, 2nd ed. Thousand Oaks, CA: Sage.

Running Wolf, P., Soler, R., Manteuffel, B., Sondheimer, D., Santiago, R. L., & Erickson, J. S. (2002, April). *A brief history of and future considerations for research in American Indian and Alaska Native communities*. Paper presented at the Symposium on Research and Evaluation Methodology: Lifespan Issues Related to American Indians/Alaska Natives With Disabilities, Washington, DC.

Russ-Eft, D., & Preskill, H. (2001). *Evaluation in organizations*. Cambridge, MA: Perseus.

Russell, C. K., Gregory, D. M., & Gates, M. (1996). Aesthetics and substance in qualitative research posters. *Qualitative Health Research, 6*, 544–554.

Russon, C. (2004). A decade of international trends in evaluation. *The Evaluation Exchange, 9*(4), 12–19.

Sabo, K. (Ed.) (2003). Youth participatory evaluation: A field in the making. *New Directions in Program Evaluation, 98*.

Satterfield, D.W., Burd, C., Valdez, L., Hosey, G., & Eagle Shield, J. (2001). The "In-between" people: Participation of community health representatives in diabetes prevention and care in American Indian and Alaska Native Communities. *Health Promotion Practice. 3*(2), 166–175.

Schwartz, R. (2002). *The skilled facilitator: A comprehensive resource for consultants, facilitators, managers, trainers, and coaches* (3rd ed.). New York: Wiley.

Scott, D. H. (1989). *Secrets of successful writing*. San Francisco: Reference Software International.

Sinacore, J. M., & Turpin, R. S. (1991). Multiple sites in evaluation research: A survey of organizational and methodological issues. In R. S. Turpin & J. M. Sinacore (Eds.), Multisite evaluations. *New Directions for Program Evaluation, 50*, 5–18.

Smith, J. K., & Heshusius, L. (1986). Closing down the conversation: The end of the quantitative-qualitative debate among educational inquirers. *Educational Researcher, 15*, 4–12.

Smith, M. L. (1986). The whole is greater: Combining qualitative and quantitative approaches in evaluation studies. In D. D. Williams (Ed.), *Naturalistic evaluation* (pp. 37–54). San Francisco: Jossey-Bass.

Smith, M. L. (1994). Qualitative plus/versus quantitative: The last word. *New Directions for Program Evaluation, 61*, 37–44.

Smith, M. L. (1997). Mixing and matching: Methods and models. *New Directions for Evaluation, 74*, 73–85.

Smith, N. L. (Ed.) (1982). *Communication strategies in evaluation*. Beverly Hills, CA: Sage.

Sonnichsen, R. C. (2000). *High impact internal evaluation*. Thousand Oaks, CA: Sage.

Sontag, S. (1977). *On photography*. New York: Noonday Press.

Spicer, E. (1976). Beyond analysis and explanation. *Human Organization, 35*(4), 335–343.

Stake, R. E. (1985). An evolutionary view of educational improvement. In E. House (Ed.), *New directions in educational evaluation* (pp. 89–102). London: Falmer.

Stake, R. E. (2004). *Standards-based and responsive evaluation*. Thousand Oaks, CA: Sage.

Stallworth, Y., & Roberts-Gray, C. (1987). Reporting to the busy decision maker. *Evaluation Practice, 8*(2), 31–35.

Straw, R. B., & Herrell, J. M. (2002). A framework for understanding and improving multi-site evaluations. *New Directions for Evaluation, 94*, 5–15.

Sue, D. W. & Sue, D. (2003). *Counseling the culturally diverse: Theory and practice* (4th ed.). New York: John Wiley & Sons, Inc.

Symonette, H. (2004). Walking pathways towards becoming a culturally competent evaluator: Boundaries, borderlands and border-crossings. In M. Thompson-Robinson, R. Hopson, & S. SenGupta (Eds.). In search of cultural competence in evaluation: Towards principles and practices. *New Directions for Program Evaluation, 102*.

Tatchell, J. (1990). *How to draw cartoons and caricatures*. Allentown, PA: Usborne.

Templin, P. (1981). *Handbook in evaluating with photography*. Portland, OR: Northwest Regional Educational Laboratory.

Templin, P. (1982). Still photography in evaluation. In N. L. Smith (Ed.), *Communication strategies in evaluation*. Beverly Hills, CA: Sage.

The California Endowment (2003). *Voices from the field: Health and evaluation leaders on multicultural evaluation*. Woodland Hills, CA: Author.

The World Bank (2003). *Assisting Russia's transition: An unprecedented challenge*. Washington, DC: Author.

Thibault, M., & Walbert, D. (2003, September). Reading images: An introduction to visual literacy. *Learn North Carolina*. Retrieved April 10, 2004, from http.//www.learnnc.org/ Index.nsf.

Thompson-Robinson, M., Hopson, R., & SenGupta, S. (Eds.) (2004). In search of cultural competence in evaluation: Towards principles and practices. *New Directions for Program Evaluation, 102*. San Francisco: Jossey-Bass.

Torres, R. T. (1991). Improving the quality of internal evaluation: The evaluator as consultant-mediator. *Evaluation and Program Planning, 14*(3), 189–198.

Torres, R. T. (1994a). Concluding remarks: Evaluation and learning organizations: Where do we go from here? *Evaluation and Program Planning, 17*(3), 339–340.

Torres, R. T. (1994b). Linking individual and organizational learning: The internalization and externalization of evaluation. *Evaluation and Program Planning, 17*(4), 327–337.

Torres, R. T. (2001). Communicating and reporting evaluation activities and findings. In D. Russ-Eft & H. Preskill, *Evaluation in organizations: A systematic approach to enhancing learning, performance, and change*. Boston: Perseus.

Torres, R. T. (2002). What is a learning approach to evaluation? *The Evaluation Exchange, 8*(2), 4.

Torres, R. T. (2005). Theory in action. In S. Mathison (Ed.), *Encyclopedia of Evaluation* (p. 420). Thousand Oaks, CA: Sage.

Torres, R. T., & Preskill, H. (2001). Evaluation and organizational learning: Past, present, and future. *American Journal of Evaluation, 22*(3), 387–395.

Torres, R. T., Preskill, H., & Piontek, M. (1997). Communicating and reporting: Practices and concerns of internal and external evaluators. *Evaluation Practice, 18*(2), 105–125.

Vygotsky, L. S. (1978). *Mind in Society: The development of higher psychological processes*. Cambridge, MA: Harvard University Press.

W. K. Kellogg Foundation (1989). *Program evaluation manual.* Battle Creek, MI: Author.

Wagner, J. (1979). *Images of information: Still photography in the social sciences.* Beverly Hills, CA: Sage.

Webber, C. F. (1987). *Program evaluation: A review and synthesis.* (ERIC Document Reproduction Service No. ED 291 771).

Webne-Behrman, H. (1998). *The practice of facilitation: Managing group process and solving problems.* Westport, CT: Greenwood.

Williams, J. M. (1989). *Style: Ten lessons in clarity and grace* (3rd ed.). Glenview, IL: Scott, Foresman.

Wholey, J. S. (2001). Managing for results: Roles for evaluators in a new management era. *American Journal of Evaluation, 22*(3), 343–347.

Williams, R. (2004). *The non-designer's design book* (2nd ed.). Berkeley, CA: Peachpit Press.

Wolcott, H. F. (2001). *Writing up qualitative research* (2nd ed.). Thousand Oaks, CA: Sage.

Wooldridge, S. G. (1996). *Poemcrazy: Freeing your life with words.* New York: Three Rivers Press.

Worthen, B., Sanders, J., & Fitzpatrick, J. (1997). *Program evaluation* (2nd ed.). New York: Longman.

Wynne, E. A. (1993). *A year in the life of an excellent elementary school.* Lancaster, PA: Technomic.

Youth in Focus (2003). *Youth REP step by step: An introduction to youth-led research and evaluation.* Oakland, CA: Youth in Focus.

Index

About the Authors

Rosalie T. Torres, Ph.D. is president of Torres Consulting Group, an evaluation and management consulting firm specializing in the feedback-based development of programs and organizations. Formerly, she was the Director of Research, Evaluation, and Organizational Learning at the Developmental Studies Center (DSC), an educational nonprofit based in Oakland, California. She earned her Ph.D. in research and evaluation in 1989 from the University of Illinois. Over the past 27 years, she has conducted more than 60 evaluations in education, business, healthcare, and nonprofit organizations, serving in both internal and external evaluator roles. She has authored or coauthored numerous books and articles articulating practice-based theories of evaluation use; the relationship between evaluation and individual, team, and organizational learning; and communicating and reporting evaluation findings. Among them are *Evaluative Inquiry for Learning in Organizations* (Preskill & Torres, 1999) and *Evaluation Strategies for Communicating and Reporting: Enhancing Learning in Organizations* (Torres, Preskill, & Piontek, 1996). She is a recent past board member of the American Evaluation Association, and served as the staff director for the 1994 revision of the Joint Committee's *Program Evaluation Standards.* She has taught graduate-level research and evaluation courses at Western Michigan University and the University of Colorado (Denver and Colorado Springs campuses), and routinely conducts workshops on various topics related to evaluation practice.

Hallie Preskill, Ph.D., is Professor of Organizational Learning and Instructional Technologies at the University of New Mexico, Albuquerque. She teaches graduate-level courses in program evaluation (introductory and advanced), organizational learning, consulting, and training and organization development. She is coauthor of *Building Evaluation Capacity: 72 Activities for Teaching and Training* (Preskill & Russ-Eft, 2005); coeditor of *Using Appreciative Inquiry in Evaluation* (Preskill & Coghlan, *New Directions for Evaluation #100,* 2003); coauthor of *Evaluation in Organizations: A Systematic Approach to Enhancing Learning, Performance & Change* (Russ-Eft & Preskill, 2001); coauthor of *Evaluative Inquiry for Learning in Organizations* (Preskill & Torres, 1999); and coeditor of *Human Resource Development Review* (Russ-Eft, Preskill, & Sleezer, 1997). She has served on the Board of Directors of the American Evaluation Association and the Academy of Human Resource Development, and is the section editor of the Teaching Evaluation column in the *American Journal of Evaluation*. She received the American Evaluation Association's Alva and Gunnar Myrdal Award for Outstanding Professional Practice in 2002, and the University of Illinois Distinguished Alumni Award in 2004. For over 20 years, she has provided workshops and consulting services in the areas of program evaluation, training, and organization development. She has also written numerous articles and book chapters on evaluation methods and processes, and has conducted program evaluations in schools, healthcare, nonprofit, human services, and corporate organizations.

Mary E. Piontek, Ph.D. is an assistant research scientist at the University of Michigan, Ann Arbor, where she works with individual faculty, departments/units, and schools/colleges that need assistance designing program evaluation and assessing the effectiveness of initiatives to improve teaching and learning. She has considerable experience doing evaluation research in educational settings and has consulted with foundations, schools and districts, institutions of higher education, and private organizations on program evaluation and educational research issues. Her research and evaluation techniques capture the local context of an organization or program through individual and focus group interviews, in-depth participant observation, document and archival analysis, survey research, and qualitative/quantitative mixed designs. Her research interests include the changing roles of evaluators and their client/stakeholder relationships. She holds a B.A. and M.A. in English Literature and a Ph.D. in Measurement, Research, and Evaluation.